CHINA'S STRATEGIC ARSENAL

CHINA'S STRATEGIC ARSENAL

Worldview, Doctrine, and Systems

JAMES M. SMITH AND PAUL J. BOLT, EDITORS

GEORGETOWN UNIVERSITY PRESS / WASHINGTON, DC

The publisher is not responsible for third-party websites or their content. URL links were active at time of publication.

Library of Congress Cataloging-in-Publication Data

Names: Smith, James M., 1948– editor. | Bolt, Paul J., 1964– editor.
Title: China's strategic arsenal : worldview, doctrine, and systems / James M. Smith, Paul J. Bolt, editors
Description: Washington, DC : Georgetown University Press, 2021. | Includes index.
Identifiers: LCCN 2020029093 | ISBN 9781647120788 (hardcover) |
    ISBN 9781647120795 (paperback) | ISBN 9781647120801 (ebook)
Subjects: LCSH: Nuclear weapons—China. | China—Strategic aspects. | China—
    Military policy. | China—Foreign relations—United States. | United States—Foreign
    relations—China.
Classification: LCC U264.5.C6 C637 2021 | DDC 355.8/251190951—dc23
LC record available at https://lccn.loc.gov/2020029093

22 21   9 8 7 6 5 4 3 2 First printing

Printed in the United States of America

Cover design by Erin Kirk
Interior design by BookComp

*We dedicate this book to all of our students
in the hope that they may serve well
and successfully move forward
into the future.*

CONTENTS

ILLUSTRATIONS

TABLES

FIGURES

Introduction

China's strategic capabilities and doctrine have historically differed from the United States' and Russia's. China has maintained a smaller nuclear arsenal than either's, as well as a policy of no first use (NFU). Nevertheless, China has continued to modernize and expand its nuclear arsenal even while Russia and the United States have decreased their deployed weapons stocks. Moreover, the global strategic environment is changing. China's economic influence, military power, and diplomatic clout are advancing at a rapid pace, accompanied by deepening authoritarianism, assertive claims to neighboring seas, and fierce competition with the United States over the development of new technologies. The US-Chinese relationship at the time of this writing has been further fractured by disputes over coronavirus and the status of Hong Kong, to the point where the two states may have descended into a new Cold War. In this context many analysts and policymakers are calling for a fundamental rethinking of the West's policies toward China because the current world order is increasingly being challenged. In the past two years several senior US military and government officials have publicly stated that they see China as the primary military threat to the United States before midcentury.[1] The newest US Nuclear Posture Review (NPR) gives increasing emphasis to American strategic capabilities, partly in response to China's strategic modernization and expansion.[2]

In this context it is imperative to better understand China's strategic weapons systems, the doctrines guiding their use, and Chinese perceptions of what makes for a stable environment. This understanding is central to America's security and will enable us to strive for a stable strategic future with China and prevent misunderstandings over strategic weapons. Such misunderstandings could further strain the Sino-US relationship and perhaps lead to tragic results.

This volume analyzes China as a strategic power, not just a nuclear power. While nuclear weapons are the backbone of strategic power, various security concepts, force structures, and weapons platforms can have strategic military effects. Broader strategies and structures, even those extending beyond the traditional military dimension, can also extend and amplify strategic effects. This book provides an overview of China's strategic world, including China's own interpretation of the political context, its strategic weapons capabilities, its doctrines, and its perception of requirements for stability.

BOOK OVERVIEW

The authors in this volume were selected from among the leading thinkers in their fields; they were asked to relate recent developments, current statuses, and anticipated future directions in their focus areas. They also were asked to provide analysis from a Chinese perspective. These authors are not Chinese—they hail from the United States, Japan, and Australia—but they study Chinese behaviors and developments; many travel regularly in China; some speak, read, and research in Chinese; and several participate regularly in semiofficial dialogues with Chinese counterparts. They do not represent any one political or ideological perspective and sometimes an issue is interpreted differently. No attempt was made to normalize positions or present a uniform interpretation. This is a pivotal time in Sino-US relations and honest, expert analysis is what is most needed. Readers should note that these chapters were drafted one year into the 2017–21 Donald Trump administration, and only minor updates have been possible since that early drafting. However, the underlying context and analytical foundations presented here remain valid.

Chapter 1 provides historical context for understanding the changing nature of the Sino-US relationship and crucial background information for understanding strategic developments in China.

In chapter 2 Andrew Scobell provides essential context for examining China's geopolitical worldview, giving an overview of its resulting grand strategy and introducing key fundamentals of China's strategic doctrine. Scobell establishes the supremacy of the inner sanctuary of China and the roles of the concentric rings of security surrounding it, as well as Chinese views of how the United States challenges Chinese security in each of the nested rings. He suggests how nuclear weapons are viewed within this construct and summarizes a grand strategy of "national rejuvenation," including the country's major economic and military objectives and how challenges from the United States are being addressed. This approach to grand strategy is consistent with a holistic strategic doctrine—diplomatic, economic, political, and military—that today also includes a "local war" dimension. Within that doctrinal focus, deterrence, which was once seen as a negative concept of nuclear coercion by the nuclear superpowers, is now accepted as a core element that has both global and regional components. Finally, Scobell introduces the key concept of active defense, as it raises questions about the role of preemption and the Chinese definition of NFU, two issues dealt with in subsequent chapters.

With the stage set within the context of China's strategic self-image of its place in the region and the world, in chapter 3 Christopher Twomey turns to examine China's nuclear doctrine and deterrence concepts within its evolving strategic environment. Twomey's analysis establishes China's longstanding strategic thought and its current expression: from the tradition of limited deterrence via reliance on a small number of countervalue retaliatory strikes to the broader doctrine of nuclear weapons that suggests changes in Chinese thinking. In so doing Twomey examines important issues of doctrine and policy that are today being reexamined in light of changes in perceived threats and emerging Chinese capabilities: NFU, local/regional/integrated war, and escalation-management imperatives. These and other issues hold critical importance for US policy and strategy.

The United States has several allies and partners in the Indo-Pacific region and chapter 4 presents one perspective of the evolving Chinese strategic challenge from Japan. Sugio Takahashi addresses the region in terms of the changing concept of strategic stability in this evolving environment. He analyzes the stability-instability paradox in light of China's rapidly developing conventional and nuclear capabilities, adding the specific context of regional stability as it affects overall stability and regional allies. The emerging regional escalation ladder, which is very different from the environment of the Cold War, and the critical element of escalation stability are now key analytical constructs for understanding China, its neighbors, and the United States. Takahashi makes the case that extended deterrence cannot be taken for granted and is a primary US imperative in this theater.

Several authors touch on the developing Chinese weapons capabilities. In chapter 5 Hans Kristensen analyzes the entirety of the Chinese strategic nuclear modernization effort and the resulting nuclear posture. Kristensen chronicles the current fourth phase of Chinese nuclear modernization, the resulting stockpile of arms, and future projections. In the numbers and capabilities he reports he includes weapons and launch vehicles as well as an analysis of doctrinal options and implications. Kristensen surveys China's land-based missiles, both the conventional and nuclear-capable versions, including dual-use systems. His examination addresses the majority medium- and intermediate-range systems and resulting regional warfare capabilities as well as intercontinental-range systems for strategic warfare, road mobile options, and multiple warhead possibilities. The assessment extends to sea-based ballistic missiles and long-range bomber options, both of which are under current development, with a view to their long-term potential impacts. His review concludes with coverage of strategic defensive capabilities found in China's early warning systems.

In today's strategic environment the major powers have combined nuclear and nonnuclear systems at the regional and global levels and have devised nonnuclear systems capable of delivering strategic effects. Chapter 6, by Phillip Saunders and David Logan, provides an analysis of Chinese developments in these nonstrategic nuclear capabilities and strategic nonnuclear systems. Their analysis covers nonstrategic nuclear system development/nondevelopment decisions; bomber-delivered and submarine-delivered systems; strategic conventional capabilities, including counter-land and counter-ship conventional ballistic missiles; hypersonic options; counterspace systems; artificial intelligence (AI); and offensive cyber capabilities. A particularly significant portion of their discussion addresses integrated strategic deterrence concepts and active defense, including joint-fire strike campaigns and the resulting conventional nuclear entanglements. All of these systems and concepts pose important issues for the United States and for Sino-US strategic relations.

Another dimension of China's strategic future is the organization of its military forces and resulting operational and command-and-control relationships. Chapter 7 presents Bates Gill's analysis of China's military reorganization begun in late 2015. This ongoing reorganization is designed to enable China's military to attain an integrated strategic deterrence posture within a flattened organizational structure under the Central Military Commission (CMC). It has resulted in a shift from seven military regions to five theaters, with clarification of strategic command coming directly from the CMC, operational control coming from the theaters, and force development being decided by the individual services. The reorganization has also created two new services in addition to the PLA Army, the PLA Navy, and the PLA Air Force: the Rocket Force (the former Second Artillery) and the Strategic Support Force (including space, cyber-, and electronic warfare). Much of Gill's analysis is devoted to the two new services, particularly issues of organizational entanglement and the remaining challenges as the reorganization continues apace.

As Thomas Schelling asserts, even in conflict relationships there is a cooperative dimension.[3] Moving beyond strategic weapons systems, strategy, and doctrine, in chapter 8 Nancy Gallagher presents a detailed analysis of China's approach to arms control, nonproliferation, and strategic stability. Gallagher argues that because China's perspectives and assumptions about strategic security and deterrence differ from the US perspectives and assumptions, its approach to arms control differs as well. Gallagher surveys those different perspectives; she tracks continuity and change in China's approach to nonproliferation, confidence-building measures, and the Comprehensive Test Ban Treaty through and beyond the Cold War; and she examines how the policies of the George W. Bush and Barack Obama administrations influenced Chinese policies. Gallagher also examines the influence of space, cyber, and nonnuclear strategic advances on security cooperation and plots some possible ways forward, given the early policy directives of the Trump administration.

Finally, in chapter 9 Brad Roberts ties together many of the threads developed across the chapters by suggesting a few key predictions, analyzing important uncertainties, and examining several central drivers behind China's path forward. Roberts predicts that China will develop more military and technical capabilities, that its enhanced capabilities will provide the potential for greater integration and even further development, and that as a result it will be more confident and more willing to accept military risk. Associated uncertainties include whether a more capable China will in fact become more assertive militarily and politically, whether enhanced strategic capabilities will result in a gain in influence and a more favorable strategic balance with the United States, and whether enhanced capabilities will result in changes to longstanding strategic policies and doctrines. Roberts asks what approach China will take to competition in space and cyberspace and what China's course will be after the 2049 centennial of the Chinese Communist Party. Key drivers include structural factors (technological change, recent military experience, the role of Russia, and China's internal political context), China's vision of the evolving security environment and its role therein, and China's assessment of the United States. Roberts's analysis ends with a discussion of US choices, reminding us again of Washington's critical role in China's strategic calculus. Roberts's chapter, like the chapters preceding it, stands as a snapshot in time, tracing trends and laying out alternatives as a departure point for continuing examination of China's strategic development and continuous shaping of US approaches to an emerging strategic China.

NOTES

1. For example, in testimony to the Senate Armed Services Committee on September 26, 2017, the chairman of the Joint Chiefs of Staff, Gen. Joseph F. Dunford Jr., stated: "I think China probably poses the greatest threat to our Nation by about 2025." See testimony transcript at https://www.armed-services.senate.gov/imo/media/doc/17-80_09-26-17.pdf.
2. Office of the Secretary of Defense, *Nuclear Posture Review* (Washington, DC: US Department of Defense, February 2018).
3. See, for example, Thomas C. Schelling, *The Strategy of Conflict* (Cambridge, MA: Harvard University Press, 1960).

ONE

The US-Chinese Relationship and China as a Twenty-First-Century Strategic Power

James M. Smith and Paul J. Bolt

The chapters in this book are fundamentally about China—its strategic world-view, its doctrines, and its systems. In prelude to and as context for that detailed analysis, our chapter provides a broad yet brief overview of Sino-US relations across the second half of the twentieth century and into the first two decades of the twenty-first century. We do so largely from a US perspective, since the context for the Chinese perspective is the focus of the remainder of the book. The Cold War relationship, characterized by a path from conflict to limited cooperation, is outlined first, followed by the mixed cooperation and competition of the post–Cold War era and then today's renewed great-power competition.

THE COLD WAR SINO-US STRATEGIC RELATIONSHIP

The Sino-US relationship during the Cold War can be divided into two phases. The first phase began with the entry of China into the Korean War in 1950 and lasted until Richard Nixon's visit to China in 1972; the second phase extended from Nixon's visit until 1989. The first phase was characterized by war, threats of war, and nuclear tensions. The second witnessed rapprochement and hope for a productive relationship, but disagreements, disappointments, and misunderstandings persisted, especially over Taiwan. The second phase concluded when the People's Liberation Army (PLA) crushed the student-led demonstrations in Beijing in 1989.

After World War II American security strategy in the Asia-Pacific evolved rapidly due to shifting strategic realities. In late 1945 the US government envisioned a future defined by a neutral Japan, a stable China, and collective security for the region based on principles defined at Yalta in 1945. However, as it became

7

clear that communist forces led by Mao Zedong were winning the Chinese civil war, American policymakers were forced to adapt. In 1948 George Kennan, director of policy planning at the State Department, presented a new strategy for the Pacific that focused on offshore maritime control. Two years later the United States was fighting on the Korean Peninsula and then drawn into an unantici-pated land war against Chinese troops on the Asian mainland. The war poisoned US relations with the People's Republic of China (PRC) for two decades and led the United States to develop a series of alliances in Asia to contain communism and China, the so-called hub-and-spokes system.[1]

The first phase of the Cold War relationship between the United States and China was defined by mutual hostility. Patrick Tyler describes the period as "a barely arrested state of war" between the two countries.[2] Harry Harding asserts that the United States considered the PRC government to be "dangerously rad-ical and irresponsible," while China saw the United States as the world's leading capitalist power and supporter of the Kuomintang (KMT), the ruling party of the Republic of China (ROC) and confined to Taiwan.[3] Chinese historian Dong Wang asserts that "the defining character of American-Chinese relations in the 1950s and 1960s was the American-led crusade against Communism which attempted to set the ground rules for the governance of China and other parts of the world."[4]

Two related issues that divided the United States and China in the first phase of the Cold War were ideology (with a strategic component) and the status of Taiwan. Washington's containment policy was designed to resist the spread of communism. Thus while China sought to create international space for itself and promote its ideology internationally, particularly in the developing world, the United States endeavored to isolate Beijing.[5] China's alliance with the Soviet Union deepened American antagonism. After 1949 American policymakers worried that China, backed by Soviet nuclear weapons, might dominate Asia.[6]

Following the Korean War armistice, Taiwan figured most prominently as the physical locus of Chinese-American tensions. The American decision to send the Seventh Fleet to guard the Taiwan Strait after the onset of the Korean War ensured that Beijing's forces would be unable to drive the KMT out of Taiwan and unable to unify the mainland and Taiwan under the rule of the PRC. While Beijing considered the subject of Taiwan to be an internal affair and unfinished business left over from the Chinese civil war, the United States diplomatically recognized only the ROC. The Mutual Defense Treaty between the United States and the ROC, signed in 1954, committed the United States to the defense of Taiwan and the Pescadores Islands (although the treaty excluded Kinmen and Matsu).

During this early Cold War period the United States threatened to use nuclear weapons against China on multiple occasions. For example, in pressuring China to reach an armistice at the end of the Korean War, the Dwight Eisenhower administration warned that the United States would be willing to use its nuclear weapons. During the First Taiwan Strait Crisis of 1954–55, Eisenhower suggested at a news conference that American tactical nuclear weapons might be used in Asia (a signal to the Chinese). In the Second Taiwan Strait Crisis in 1958 Eisenhower told the Joint Chiefs to be ready to use nuclear weapons, and B-47s armed with nuclear bombs were deployed to Guam. Furthermore, the United States based its Matador nuclear missiles in Taiwan during the Cold War.[7] Nevertheless, John Pomfret suggests Eisenhower was mainly bluffing.[8]

Mao had famously stated in the 1940s that nuclear weapons were "paper tigers." Although much was made of his comment outside China, the statement indicates that Mao believed nuclear weapons had military and political limitations. However, Mao also knew that having nuclear weapons was a crucial deterrent in itself. Thus in the 1950s China began a nuclear program in response to American nuclear deployments in Asia and US threats to use nuclear weapons against China. Mao and Zhou Enlai asserted that China's nuclear program was defensive and designed to prevent blackmail.[9] A Chinese statement in 1963, by which time China was striving to break the nuclear monopolies of both the United States and the Soviet Union, insisted that "nuclear weapons in the possession of a socialist country are always a means of defense against nuclear blackmail and nuclear war."[10] Although the Soviets had promised nuclear aid to China, they failed to provide an expected prototype of an atomic bomb and relations between the two socialist states deteriorated in the late 1950s.[11]

As China approached its first atomic test on October 16, 1964, American intelligence officials assessed the likely timing of the event. While the CIA expected a test after 1964, State Department analyst Allen Whiting's best estimate was October 1.[12] American government analysts debated how detrimental this test would be to the security of the United States. In a State Department report from April 1964 Robert Johnson downplayed the risks of a Chinese nuclear test. Johnson asserted that the benefits of a test for China would be largely political rather than military. The great preponderance of American nuclear power made it highly unlikely that China would engage in a first strike in any context that didn't threaten the survival of the PRC regime, and Chinese weapons would not deter the United States from assisting its Asian allies anyway. As a result, the United States did not need to consider any major policy changes.[13]

On the other side of the debate, the document "China as a Nuclear Power," issued by the Office of International Security Affairs at the Department of Defense less than two weeks before China's test, presented a bleak view of the future, with China emerging as a nuclear power. The report suggested China could soon be producing thirty to fifty weapons per year, with intercontinental capability to destroy San Francisco, Chicago, New York, and Washington by

1975. Moreover, Chinese nuclear weapons could greatly limit American freedom of action in Asia and elsewhere. Possession of nuclear weapons would not make China more cautious, but rather would be a tool in China's efforts to dominate Asia.[14]

Both the John F. Kennedy and Lyndon B. Johnson administrations considered taking military action against Chinese nuclear facilities. However, the Soviets rebuffed American efforts to gain their support for an attack.[15] An example of one American government report considering military action was produced by the US Arms Control and Disarmament Agency in December 1964, two months after China's first test. The report evaluates four potential options that were raised in a prior (and still publicly unavailable) American government report: US nonnuclear air attacks against Chinese nuclear facilities, an air attack by the ROC, covert attacks launched by agents in China, and the insertion by air of ROC sabotage teams into China to destroy nuclear facilities. The report criticizes the conclusions of State Department analyst Johnson, suggesting that he underestimated the dangers of Chinese nuclear capabilities to American interests.[16]

After China's test of an atomic bomb, both the United States and China issued statements. President Johnson, at a press conference on October 16, 1964, stated that the United States was not surprised at China's test but reassured the public that the United States would remain more powerful than China and Chinese nuclear weapons would not deter the United States from assisting its allies.[17] The written Chinese statement issued on October 16 asserted that the atomic test was an achievement in the Chinese people's "struggle to strengthen their national defence and oppose the US imperialist policy of nuclear blackmail and nuclear threats."[18] The document goes on to say that "in developing nuclear weapons, China's aim is to break the nuclear monopoly of the nuclear powers and to eliminate nuclear weapons." The statement promised that China will never use nuclear weapons first, and called for an international conference on the prohibition and destruction of nuclear weapons. Critics of American policy toward China charge that Washington never took Beijing's statement seriously or understood that China's development of nuclear weapons was a response to American threats.[19]

During the remainder of the Cold War, China's development of nuclear weapons followed a very different path from that of the United States and Soviet Union. China did not try to match either superpower in numbers of weapons and it appeared to have consciously avoided a nuclear arms race. Instead, Beijing maintained a policy of NFU, adopted a small but varied and reliable nuclear force with minimum retaliatory capabilities, shunned the development of tactical nuclear weapons, and held a countervalue strategy aimed at cities.[20]

Until the 1980s China also was deeply suspicious of any agreements that limited nuclear weapons or halted their proliferation. For example, China strongly objected to the Treaty Banning Nuclear Weapon Tests in the Atmosphere, in Outer Space and Under Water, also known as the Partial Test Ban Treaty or Limited Test Ban Treaty, which entered into force in 1963. The Chinese Communist Party (CCP) called it a "US nuclear fraud" that would "manacle the socialist countries" and saw it as an effort to prevent China from obtaining nuclear weapons.[21] On the contrary, from 1961 until 1964 China held a doctrine of "socialist proliferation," arguing that socialist and nonaligned countries should develop nuclear weapons to deter nuclear war and pressure other nuclear powers to agree to complete nuclear disarmament. China was also deeply suspicious of the 1968 Nonproliferation Treaty (NPT) and the 1972 SALT I agreement, holding that these were attempts to cement a US-Soviet nuclear monopoly.[22]

While the Vietnam War was another source of Sino-US tension, by the late 1960s both sides were beginning to reconsider their relationship. China was moved to change its policies following the Soviet invasion of Czechoslovakia in August 1968, the release of the Brezhnev Doctrine later that year (which asserted the right of the Soviet Union to intervene in the affairs of socialist states), and the Soviet military buildup on the Chinese border that led to the 1969 Sino-Soviet border conflict. This drove the United States to improve ties with China: Nixon worked to extract the United States from the Vietnam War, seeing the need for leverage against the Soviet Union in the Cold War and believing that the long-term interests of the United States required a better relationship with an emerging China. Communications between American and Chinese diplomatic personnel began in Warsaw in 1969 and took place in Pakistan as well. A long series of events culminated in Nixon's historic trip to Beijing in 1972 and the Shanghai Communique that ushered in Sino-American rapprochement.[23]

Nixon's visit to Beijing did not eliminate all tensions between China and the United States, however. Harry Harding characterizes the relationship between the two countries from 1972 to 1992 as "an oscillating pattern of progress and stagnation, crisis and consolidation."[24] In particular, Taiwan continued to be a source of tension over the latter half of the Cold War, as it had been during the drafting of the Shanghai Communique. The status of the ROC almost derailed normalization between the United States and China in 1979 and played a controversial role in Ronald Reagan's relations with China as well. On August 17, 1982, Washington and Beijing issued the US-Chinese Joint Communiqué on United States Arms Sales to Taiwan, in which the United States promised to gradually reduce arms sales to Taiwan conditional on peaceful PRC policies toward the island. However, the agreement was vague enough to ensure continued disputes. During the George H. W. Bush administration, China and the United States struggled to deal with the fallout of the PLA's killing of Chinese citizens in 1989.

Nevertheless, after Nixon's visit to China war between the United States and China was off the table for the rest of the Cold War, as relations were normalized. Chinese nuclear weapons developments were not a major issue between Washington and Beijing, although proliferation did present an obstacle to relations. During the Reagan administration a civilian nuclear cooperation agreement between the two sides never went into effect, due to concerns in Congress regarding Chinese proliferation. Beijing was unhappy about perceived US interference in China's internal affairs, stemming from required adherence to the conditions of the US Nuclear Non-Proliferation Act of 1978 and in 1991, following Chinese aid in the construction of an Algerian nuclear reactor, the issue became important as Congress debated China's most favored nation status.[25] However, by the 1980s China was beginning to support the principle and institutions of nonproliferation.

Important elements of the late Cold War relationship between the United States and China are seen from the first four US national security strategies.[26] The 1987 and 1988 documents emphasize the US objective to have closer ties with China and recognize that there are differences in political systems but also strong common interests. The 1990 and 1991 documents focus on the necessity of maintaining ties with China despite the events of June 1989 and continued Chinese political repression. None of the four documents comment on Chinese military threats to Asia nor on Chinese nuclear weapons. The relationship between China and the United States was very different from the first half of the Cold War. However, it was to evolve again during the post–Cold War period.

THE SINO-US STRATEGIC RELATIONSHIP AFTER THE COLD WAR

The Cold War Sino-US strategic relationship has been characterized by first, a period of conflict extending from China's entry into the Korean War until the Nixon visit in 1972, and second, a period of relative rapprochement from the Nixon visit until Tiananmen Square in 1989. Following through the post–Cold War period and using the same template, the post-Tiananmen period can be broadly characterized from a US perspective as one with elements of both cooperation and competition—even with occasional situational conflict. The United States' hope for an internal political transition in China to accompany continuing economic moderation, which was dashed at Tiananmen, remained in the background of increasing and often optimistic developments in the economic sphere, but with recurring issues in trade intervening as well. Security disputes have arisen, although none to the directly strategic level, and the overall relationship has kept on a slow path toward real progress. In the end the US characterization today is of a return to great power competition—with China seen fully as one of those great power competitors—and with added caution at the strategic level.

The transition of the Soviet Union and the fall of the Communist Party did not have a parallel in Asia, so it had no direct strategic effect on the region. For example, at the strategic nuclear level "in the Cold War, China was largely a footnote to U.S. nuclear policy, which dealt with a bipolar world order and intense military standoff in Europe."[27] Thus there were no dramatic changes in the bilateral relationship or in US policy toward China as the wall came down in Germany.

Our review of post–Cold War US strategic policy toward China begins with the last National Security Strategy (NSS) report released by the George H. W. Bush administration in 1993, just before Bill Clinton's inauguration. Noting again that this was after Tiananmen Square, it is still interesting that the outgoing president—the president who knew China best after having served as ambassador to Beijing, as director of the CIA, and as vice president during the formative years of the modern Sino-US relationship—left office on a note of caution. In addition to the aspirational direction to "encourage democratic reform" and "advocate positive change," the NSS stated a primary agenda item: "We must carefully watch the emergence of China onto the world stage and support, contain, or balance this emergence as necessary to protect U.S. interests."[28] President Bush expressed caution toward China but, based on strategic relations with post-Communist Russia, he withdrew all nuclear weapons from East Asia and from naval surface warships.[29] Russia and Europe still dictated global strategic nuclear decisions.

President Clinton also took a cautious approach to China's continued development. Listing it with Russia as the "other great powers," his initial NSS stated "China maintains a repressive regime even as that country assumes a more important economic and political role in global affairs."[30] His administration sought "a broader engagement with the People's Republic of China that will encompass both our economic and strategic interests." This engagement included democratic reform, but noted that "each nation must find its own form of democracy" to allow for Chinese adaptations rather than seeking to dictate a Western political system.[31]

This flexible approach was consistent with the "Engagement and Enlargement" theme of the 1994 NSS and with the 1994 Quadrennial Defense Review that looked beyond Russia and Europe to other "major theater wars" and addressed the increasingly complex international environment. 1994 also saw the completion of the first NPR that centered on a "lead but hedge" strategy: lead in cuts to late–Cold War weapons and in arms control initiatives but hedge against the reversal of Russia to a hostile status and any proliferation that creates an additional hostile regional nuclear power.[32] Addressing the dangers of nuclear proliferation and adapting deterrence to new targets and relation-ships were central to the challenges of the *second nuclear age*.[33] These revisions required tailoring of policies and strategies to individual regions and specific powers, each having its own requirements, cultures, and challenges.

The Clinton team also put major emphasis on nonproliferation, includ-ing extending the NPT indefinitely and signing the Comprehensive Test Ban Treaty (CTBT). China also signed the NPT and the CTBT (although neither the United States nor China has ratified the CTBT as of this writing). Despite some parallel tracks regarding nonproliferation and arms control, China and the United States also were forced to address some serious challenges during Clinton's two terms.

As a serious independence sentiment found a formal home within the ROC political system on Taiwan, Beijing sent a message by conducting missile tests nearby. Washington responded by sailing two carrier battle groups toward Tai-wan, a move that China took seriously as a signal of US willingness to risk war over Taiwan. The Chinese response also initiated rapid military modernization and restructuring (discussed in other chapters in this book). This Taiwan crisis of 1995–96 increased Chinese caution toward the United States, which was reinforced in the Chinese mind when US aircraft accidentally bombed the Chi-nese embassy in Belgrade during the Serbia conflict in 1999.[34] China has con-tinued to question whether this strike was accidental or was a signal to Beijing.

Later the Clinton administration published a summary NSS (1999), stating:

> A stable, open, prosperous People's Republic of China (PRC) that respects international norms and assumes its responsibilities for building a more peaceful world is clearly and profoundly in our interests. The prospects for peace and prosperity in Asia depend heavily on China's role as a respon-sible member of the international community. Our policy toward China is both principled and pragmatic, expanding our areas of cooperation while dealing forthrightly with our differences. Despite strains in the relationship resulting from the tragic accidental bombing of the PRC embassy in Bel-grade, we have continued to engage China on these issues.[35]

The NSS goes on to outline cooperative efforts in government-to-government discussions, arms control and nonproliferation, regional security (with emphasis on Taiwan), trade and the market-based economic system, and human rights.

George W. Bush came to office seeking a "new strategic framework" founded on a now-positive Russia-US relationship, though he saw China as a potential adversary and sought to improve that relationship. This less-optimistic view of China was also reportedly repeated in the 2001 Bush NPR. That NPR was never publicly released, but leaks to the press reported that China was cited as a target. China saw these developments, coupled with the US decision to withdraw from the Anti-Ballistic Missile Treaty while pursuing both national and theater ballistic missile defenses, as threatening.[36] China's continuing strategic modernization during this period is discussed in later chapters.

Perhaps these messages might have been softened had the context provided by the NSS preceded them, but the events of September 11, 2001, forced a delay in the NSS. The 2002 NSS highlighted that the United States sought to avoid a renewal of great-power competition involving transitioning powers, especially Russia, India, and China. It noted encouraging recent developments, and continued that "the relationship with China is an important part of our strategy to promote a stable, peaceful, and prosperous Asia-Pacific region." It was believed this strategy would be enhanced through more progress on political reform and avoidance of the development of advanced military capabilities that are taken as threatening by regional neighbors. In seeking a "constructive relationship with a changing China," the strategy seeks greater transparency, sociopolitical moderation, and responsible trade development through "consultation, quiet argument, sober analysis, and common action."[37] The 2006 Bush NSS continues these themes, emphasizing that China's political-economic transition is incomplete and encouraging moderating reforms while also hedging against a more confrontational course.[38]

The slow pace of progress in Sino-US relations during this period was dictated largely by US preoccupation with the events of 9/11, but also by Chinese reluctance to proceed based on broader events and perceptions. In 2001 a Chinese fighter plane was involved in a midair collision with a US reconnaissance aircraft. The US aircraft made an emergency landing on China's Hainan Island and the crew was detained for eleven days. In 2002 the Bush NPR was leaked, with China identified as a nuclear target according to the leak. Add also the Bush abrogation of the ABM Treaty, which China saw as opening the door to enhanced US defenses against its assured retaliation capability, and China saw itself militarily threatened by the United States. China was also concerned with the combination of continuing US demands for its political transformation against the context of the US emphasis on preemption and forced regime change in Afghanistan and particularly in Iraq. Strategic understanding and a degree of trust had to be established, and without regular official and high-level communication between the two countries it was a very slow process, with several setbacks and even reversals.[39]

Taking the NSS and the implementing National Defense Strategy as top-level statements of US interests, objectives, and concerns, it is noteworthy that the unclassified summary of the Bush administration's 2008 National Defense Strategy (NDS) first openly raised China to the top tier of US strategic security concerns. Issued by Secretary of Defense Robert Gates in June 2008, the NDS highlights the challenge of renewed great-power competition, naming China over Russia as the state for which the United States must prioritize its hedging strategy.[40] Welcoming the "peaceful and prosperous" development of China, the NDS expressed a cautionary note over China's continuing military developments and called for increased transparency and the "establishment and pursuit of continuous strategic dialogue with China to build understanding, improve communication, and to reduce the risk of miscalculation."[41]

Barack Obama came to office with a background of interest and involvement as a senator in the Nunn-Lugar cooperative threat reduction programs in Russia and other former Soviet republics. This foundation in nonproliferation, disarmament, and arms control shaped his Prague agenda and strategic policy. That agenda is most commonly associated with its long-term goal: "So today, I state clearly and with conviction America's commitment to seek the peace and security of a world without nuclear weapons." But the Obama administration also sought to implement the follow-on corollary: "As long as these weapons exist, the United States will maintain a safe, secure and effective arsenal to deter any adversary, and guarantee that defense to our allies."[42] The Prague agenda addressed nuclear weapons reductions through arms control, reduced weapons roles, increased limitations on testing and fissile material availability, increased civil nuclear security cooperation, and nuclear materials security. It was an ambitious arms reductions and nonproliferation agenda.

The 2010 NPR provided the rationale and strategic foundations for the cuts that were formalized in the New START Treaty signed by Russia and the United States. The NPR placed major deterrence emphasis on regional nuclear challenges—specifically North Korea and Iran—with a concurrent focus on extended deterrence and especially assurance of regional allies and partners. At the same time the NPR sought to shift the foundation of the United States' strategic relationships with Russia and China into one of strategic stability and expanded dialogue.[43] In China's case, Beijing opted for unofficial dialogue and further study of what such a relationship would imply. Sino-US strategic dialogue remained informal.

In broader policy terms, China was not a prominent focus of the early Obama administration. For example, the 2015 NSS addressed China primarily as a regional "center of influence" along with other states such as Russia and India. It expressed hope for China to assume a positive regional leadership role but also expressed caution toward Chinese military modernization programs.[44]

By the time the 2015 NSS was issued the administration had announced a "rebalance" to Asia and the Pacific in order to pursue and secure economic developments in the region: "India's potential, China's rise, and Russia's aggression all significantly impact the future of major power relations."[45] Also by 2015 China and key US allies had confronted each other in the East China and South China Seas and around the disputed islands, and the United States had adopted an AirSea Doctrine to ensure access against Chinese denial strategies. Freedom of navigation and overflight was a central element of the US strategy; in one case the United States purposely violated what it considered an illegal Chinese imposition of an Air Defense Identification Zone with a B-52 flyover.

China was given special attention within the NSS:

> The United States welcomes the rise of a stable, peaceful, and prosperous China. We seek to develop a constructive relationship with China. . . . We seek cooperation on shared regional and global challenges. . . . While there will be competition, we reject the inevitability of confrontation. At the same time, we will manage competition from a position of strength while insisting China uphold international rules and norms. . . . We will closely monitor China's military modernization and expanding presence in Asia, while seeking ways to reduce the risk of misunderstanding or miscalculation.[46]

The Donald Trump administration picked up on this recognition of competition and raised it to a new level. The 2017 NSS states: "China and Russia challenge American power, influence, and interests, attempting to erode American security and prosperity."[47] Regarding China specifically, the NSS goes on to note that "China has mounted a rapid military modernization campaign designed to limit U.S. access to the region and provide China a freer hand there."[48]

The 2018 NDS expands on this competition theme of the 2017 NSS:

> China is leveraging military modernization, influence operations, and predatory economics to coerce neighboring countries to reorder the Indo-Pacific region to their advantage. As China continues its economic and military ascendance, asserting power through an all-of-nation long-term strategy, it will continue to pursue a military modernization program that seeks Indo-Pacific regional hegemony in the near-term and displacement of the United States to achieve global preeminence in the future.[49]

The 2018 NDS is the clearest open US statement to date calling out China as a current regional and potential future global threat. The 2018 NPR adds a nuclear dimension: "China's military modernization has resulted in an expanded nuclear force, with little or no transparency into its intentions."[50] The NPR also highlights Chinese aggressive activities in space and cyberspace, and it outlines a tailored, flexible US strategy to prevent any Chinese nuclear use. Finally, the NPR calls for the development of low-yield, sea-based nuclear options for the US military. While the NPR discussion and most of the public rationale for these weapons centers on Russia's "escalate to deescalate/escalate to win" doctrine, particularly in the shadow of the US withdrawal from the INF treaty, the Chinese take these moves as aimed at ensuring US regional access and countering any Chinese advantages in their home region.

For the post–Cold War Sino-US relationship, Brad Roberts perhaps puts it best:

> In sum, over the last twenty-five years, both the United States and China have tried to strengthen areas of cooperation while trying to manage the sources of competition and conflict between them. Unlike the U.S.-Russia relationship, there has been no regular cycle of rising expectations followed by disappointment and reset. Instead, there has been a steady process of work in both capitals to move the relationship in directions each deems positive while managing the sources of competition and conflict amid dynamic economic and political factors. . . . There is, however, a rising debate in the United States (as elsewhere) about whether China's external relations are at a fundamental turning point.[51]

Trump administration policy documents clearly reflect the cautionary side of this debate.

This book presents an analysis of strategic China—where it is coming from, where it stands, and where it might be going—toward better shaping the US-Chinese relationship into the future. The hope is to limit the adversarial dimensions of that relationship, to manage the competition within peaceful bounds, and to better understand China's strategic worldview, military doctrine, and systems to the extent that China must be confronted.

NOTES

The views in this chapter are the authors' alone and in no way represent the opinions, standards, or policy of the United States Air Force Academy or the United States government.
   1. Michael J. Green, *By More than Providence: Grand Strategy and American Power in the Asia Pacific since 1783* (New York: Columbia University Press, 2017), 245–84.
   2. Patrick Tyler, *A Great Wall* (New York: Century Foundation, 1999), 39.
   3. Harry Harding, *A Fragile Relationship: The United States and China since 1972* (Washington, DC: Brookings Institution, 1992), 25.
   4. Dong Wang, *The United States and China* (Lanham, MD: Rowman & Littlefield, 2013), 210.
   5. See Harding, *Fragile Relationship*, 26–31.
   6. Michael Schaller, *The United States and China*, 3rd ed. (New York: Oxford University Press, 2002), 122.

7. See Robert G. Sutter, *US-Chinese Relations*, 2nd ed. (Lanham, MD: Rowman & Littlefield, 2013), 57; John Wilson Lewis and Xue Litai, *China Builds the Bomb* (Stanford, CA: Stanford University Press, 1988), 40; John Pomfret, *The Beautiful Country and the Middle Kingdom* (New York: Henry Holt, 2016), 409, 421–22; Green, *By More than Providence*, 295; and Tyler, *Great Wall*, 39. Even as late as the Vietnam War, American generals were seriously considering the use of nuclear weapons in Asia. See, for instance, David E. Sanger, "U.S. General Considered Nuclear Response in Vietnam War, Cables Show," *New York Times*, October 6, 2018, https://www.nytimes.com/2018/10/06/world/asia/vietnam-war-nuclear-weapons.html.

8. Pomfret, *Beautiful Country*, 405.

9. Sun Xiangli, "The Development of Nuclear Weapons in China," in *Understanding Chinese Nuclear Thinking*, ed. Li Bin and Tong Zhao, 79–101 (Washington, DC: Carnegie Endowment for International Peace, 2016), 82; Nicola Horsburgh, *China and Global Nuclear Order: From Estrangement to Active Engagement* (Oxford: Oxford University Press, 2015), 40–42; and Yao Yunzhu, "Chinese Nuclear Policy and the Future of Minimum Deterrence," in *Perspectives on Sino-American Strategic Nuclear Issues*, ed. Christopher P. Twomey, 111–24 (New York: Palgrave Macmillan, 2008), 114.

10. Lewis and Xue, *China Builds the Bomb*, 36. Lewis and Xue provide a detailed story of how China developed atomic weapons.

11. Zhihua Shen and Danhui Li, *After Leaning to One Side: China and Its Allies in the Cold War* (Washington, DC: Woodrow Wilson Center Press and Stanford University Press, 2011), 132; and Lorenz M. Lüthi, *The Sino-Soviet Split* (Princeton: Princeton University Press, 2008), 137–38.

12. See Special National Intelligence Estimate, "The Chances of an Imminent Communist Chinese Nuclear Explosion," August 26, 1964, https://nsarchive2.gwu.edu/NSAEBB/NSAEBB1/docs/doc02.pdf; and William Burr, ed., "The United States, China, and the Bomb," National Security Archive Electronic Briefing Book no. 1, https://nsarchive2.gwu.edu/NSAEBB/NSAEBB1/. Burr summarizes the documents cited in this chapter, all of which have been declassified.

13. Robert H. Johnson, "Implications of a Chinese Communist Nuclear Capability," with forwarding memorandum to President Johnson by Policy Planning Council director Walt W. Rostow, US State Department Policy Planning Staff, April 17, 1964, https://nsarchive2.gwu.edu/NSAEBB/NSAEBB1/docs/doc01.pdf.

14. "China as a Nuclear Power (Some Thoughts Prior to a Chinese Test)," October 7, 1964, https://nsarchive2.gwu.edu/NSAEBB/NSAEBB1/docs/doc04.pdf.

15. Horsburgh, *China and Global Nuclear Order*, 53–55.

16. G. W. Rathjens, "Destruction of Chinese Nuclear Weapons Capabilities," US Arms Control and Disarmament Agency, December 14, 1964, https://nsarchive2.gwu.edu/NSAEBB/NSAEBB1/docs/doc06.pdf.

17. Gregory Kulacki, "Nuclear Weapons in US-China Relations," in *Understanding Chinese Nuclear Thinking*, ed. Li Bin and Tong Zhao, 251–65 (Washington, DC: Carnegie Endowment for International Peace, 2016), 251.

18. The Chinese government document is found as an appendix in Lewis and Xue, *China Builds the Bomb*, 241–43.

19. See Kulacki, "Nuclear Weapons," 251–65.

20. Litai Xue, "Evolution of China's Nuclear Strategy," in *Strategic Views from the Second Tier*, ed. John C. Hopkins and Weixing Hu, 167–89 (New Brunswick,

NJ: Transaction, 1995), 172–73; and Sun, "Development of Nuclear Weapons," 79–101.

21. Lüthi, *The Sino-Soviet Split*, 266, 269–72.

22. Horsburgh, *China and Global Nuclear Order*, 2, 48–53, 67–69.

23. Harding, *Fragile Relationship*, 35–37; Tyler, *Great Wall*, 44–179; and Green, *By More than Providence*, 323–62.

24. Harding, *Fragile Relationship*, 5.

25. Harding, 183–86, 275–77.

26. These can be found in the National Security Strategy Archive at http://nss archive.us/.

27. Michael Nacht, Sarah Laderman, and Julie Beeston, *Strategic Competition in China-US Relations*, Livermore Papers on Global Security no. 5 (October 2018): 103.

28. George H. W. Bush, *National Security Strategy of the United States* (Washington, DC: The White House, January 1993), 1, 19, and 7.

29. Nacht, Laderman, and Beeston, *Strategic Competition*, 103.

30. William Clinton, *A National Security Strategy of Engagement and Enlargement* (Washington, DC: The White House, July 1994), 1.

31. Clinton, *National Security Strategy* (1994), 24.

32. Brad Roberts, *The Case for U.S. Nuclear Weapons in the 21st Century* (Stanford, CA: Stanford University Press, 2016), 16–18.

33. See Roberts, *Case for U.S. Nuclear Weapons*, 20–21, for a summary discussion of the amended proliferation and deterrence concepts that this captures.

34. Nacht, Laderman, and Beeston, *Strategic Competition*, 100.

35. William Clinton, *A National Security Strategy for a New Century* (Washington, DC: The White House, December 1999), 36.

36. Roberts, *Case for U.S. Nuclear Weapons*, 22–23; Nacht, Laderman, and Beeston, *Strategic Competition*, 103–4.

37. George W. Bush, *The National Security Strategy for the United States of America* (Washington, DC: The White House, September 2002), 26–28.

38. George W. Bush, *The National Security Strategy of the United States of America* (Washington, DC: The White House, March 2006), 41–42.

39. See, for example, Michael O. Wheeler, *Track 1.5/2 Security Dialogues with China: Nuclear Lessons Learned*, Institute for Defense Analyses Paper P-5135, September 2014. Online at IDA.org/research-and-publications.

40. Robert M. Gates, *National Defense Strategy* (Washington, DC: US Department of Defense, June 2008), 3.

41. Gates, *National Defense Strategy* (2008), 10.

42. Barack Obama, "Remarks by President Barack Obama, Hradcany Square, Prague, Czech Republic," April 5, 2009, www.whitehouse.gov, 3.

43. Office of the Secretary of Defense, *Nuclear Posture Review Report* (Washington, DC: US Department of Defense, April 2010).

44. Barack Obama, *National Security Strategy* (Washington, DC: The White House, May 2010).

45. Barack Obama, *National Security Strategy* (Washington, DC: The White House, February 2015), 4.

46. Obama, *National Security Strategy* (2015), 24.

47. Donald Trump, *National Security Strategy of the United States of America* (Washington, DC: The White House, December 2017), 2.

48. Trump, *National Security Strategy* (2017), 46.
49. James Mattis, *Summary of the 2018 National Defense Strategy of the United States of America* (Washington, DC: Department of Defense, 2018), 2.
50. Office of the Secretary of Defense, *Nuclear Posture Review* (Washington, DC: US Department of Defense, February 2018), 2.
51. Roberts, *Case for U.S. Nuclear Weapons*, 146.

TWO

China's "Nested" Worldview

Andrew Scobell

To fully appreciate the People's Republic of China (PRC) as a twenty-first-century strategic power is to grasp Beijing's contemporary worldview, its grand strategy, and its fundamental strategic principles. This chapter illuminates how the PRC envisions the resumption of its rightful place on the global stage, how it intends to get there, and the role of strategic weapons in that future. What is China's strategic worldview? What roles does China see for itself in the Asia-Pacific and the world? What are the PRC's internal and external priorities and what are the primary challenges to achieving them? What is China's grand strategy, and what are the PRC's fundamental strategic principles?

This chapter examines the PRC's worldview, sketches out the contours of its grand strategy, and identifies the fundamentals of Chinese military doctrine. A major theme is that China possesses a "nested" conception of its place in the world and its national security posture. In other words, the PRC seeks to create a protected inner sanctuary for the leadership in Beijing by constructing and then maintaining a set of nested rings of security. While the intent is for each ring to fit snugly inside the other to derive enhanced security at the core, because of their deeply rooted insecurities the PRC rulers exist in a perpetual state of insecurity. Central to this continued semblance of nested security is the ability to maintain credible nuclear deterrence.

A full appreciation of the importance of strategic weaponry to China in the twenty-first century requires a thumbnail sketch of the earliest years of the PRC and the origins of its nuclear program. When the PRC was formally established in October 1949, the nascent state was militarily and economically weak and diplomatically isolated. Following decades of political and military struggle, the indigenous Communist movement that had emerged victorious from the Chinese civil war felt extremely vulnerable and friendless. The Chinese Communist Party (CCP) led by Mao Zedong perceived the United States as hostile to the new regime, whose capital was in Beijing. The PRC was fearful of the

United States and its regional and global network of allies and partners. Perhaps the clearest indicator in Mao's mind about the adversarial US disposition was its continued backing of the CCP's major rival in the war: the Guomindang (GMD), or Nationalist Party, led by Jiang Jieshi (Chiang Kai-shek). Although the CCP had militarily defeated the armed forces of the GMD and expelled them from mainland China, Jiang and hundreds of thousands of soldiers and supporters had retreated to the island of Taiwan, where the GMD continued to claim that its Republic of China (ROC) was the sole legitimate government of all China. The perception of American hostility was reinforced by the US response to North Korea's invasion of South Korea in June 1950: President Harry Truman ordered ground and air forces to come to the defense of South Korea and naval forces to protect the ROC soldiers and supporters on Taiwan.

Though Mao had in 1946 famously dismissed nuclear weapons as a "paper tiger," he was painfully aware of the "nuclear blackmail and nuclear threats" that the United States employed against China in the Taiwan Strait during two crises—in 1954–55 and then again in 1958. The first of these two crises prompted Mao to make the final decision to develop China's own nuclear weapons program a top priority.[1]

Mao, in consultation with other senior CCP leaders, made the "strategic decision" that China would build its own nuclear program in January 1955—in the midst of the Taiwan Strait Crisis.[2] Six months later preparations ramped up when the Politburo established a three-person leadership group to oversee the development of the program: Nie Rongzhen, a veteran military commander (who three years later took over sole responsibility for the nuclear program); Chen Yun, an economist and expert on industrial policy; and Bo Yibo, a skilled planner and manager. While the Soviet Union said it was prepared to provide the PRC with assistance in building its nuclear program, Moscow in the end refused to deliver the goods to Beijing.[3] This episode produced great consternation in Beijing and contributed to the breakup of the Sino-Soviet alliance in 1960.

FROM THE INSIDE OUT: CHINA'S WORLDVIEW

While the PRC is often described as a "party-state," the term is not entirely accurate because the depiction omits mention of a third bureaucratic entity: the People's Liberation Army (PLA). A more accurate label is "party-military-state," since the armed forces are a distinct, large institution separate from but intertwined with the regime's two civilian institutions: the party and the state.[4] It is worth outlining the sequence in which these institutions were established: first came the CCP, founded in 1921; second came the PLA, founded in 1927; and third came the PRC, established in 1949. While official regime rhetoric refers to the celebration of "two centenaries"—the foundings of the CCP and the PRC—the PLA's centenary, which will occur in 2027, will also be a major cause for commemoration. Thus it is most appropriate to refer to the regime as a double-hyphenated construct: the CCP-PLA-PRC. Nevertheless, in the interest of brevity, hereafter the tripartite regime will be identified simply as "the PRC," "China," "Beijing," or "China's leaders."

The regime is preoccupied with safeguarding its own rule, with a resultant all-consuming focus on domestic security and national security being conflated with regime security. Consequently, Beijing allocates vast resources to ensuring internal security. According to the PRC's own annual budget figures, it is costlier to maintain domestic stability than it is to fund the official defense budget.[5] Essentially this preoccupation acts as a "domestic drag," making it impossible for Beijing to focus fully upon addressing external threats.[6]

The foremost security goal of China's rulers routinely is misleadingly characterized as "regime survival." The use of the word "survival" implies a sense of desperation and a day-to-day struggle for the regime's very existence. This is far from the reality. China's leaders are not worried about collapse or overthrow tomorrow, next week, next month, or even next year. They are confident about the short term. It is the medium to long term—five years, ten years, twenty years, thirty years from now—that worries them most. Thus, a more appropriate descriptor would be "regime perpetuation."[7] The consuming focus of China's leaders is perpetuating the regime through constant vigilance and extensive central planning. I describe Chinese leaders as "ambitious alarmists." Though deeply insecure, they are nevertheless extremely ambitious, they think big, and they plan for the long term. Indeed, a leitmotif of the PRC throughout its existence has been launching mass movements and executing mega projects. In the Mao era (1949–76), these ideology-inspired mass mobilization efforts included the Great Leap Forward of the 1950s and the Great Proletarian Cultural Revolution of the 1960s. In the reform era (since 1979), examples of massive prestige-focused regime-sponsored projects include the construction of the domestic Three Gorges Dam (1992–2006) and the overseas Belt and Road Initiative (BRI) that was officially launched by President Xi Jinping in 2013.[8]

Prime examples of highly ambitious projects that spanned both eras are the nuclear weapon and the ballistic missile programs. These defense projects are the logical manifestations of a highly determined Leninist regime possessing "an extreme sense of insecurity."[9] The origin of the nuclear program was described earlier; the missile program involves a similar tale of concentrating resources and scientific expertise in pursuit of a top regime priority.[10] The PRC's strategic rocket force was officially established in July 1966.[11] It was formally named the Second Artillery Corps (*dier paobing*, now known as the Rocket Force) reportedly to differentiate it from the PLA's regular artillery forces. The decision to develop guided missiles was made by the Politburo in 1956 and the

PRC's first guided missile technology research institute was formed by October of that year.[12]

Chinese leaders embrace a geostrategic outlook from their vantage point in Beijing. When members of the ruling CCP Politburo look out from their leadership compound at Zhongnanhai, they nervously perceive their security environment composed of four concentric circles.[13] The first ring begins in the street outside their office windows and encompasses all the territory within the borders of the PRC that Beijing controls or claims. The second ring of security comprises the PRC's immediate periphery—a zone that includes fourteen neighbors, five of which China has fought wars against within the last seventy-five years. The third ring encircles the entire Asia-Pacific neighborhood; the fourth and outermost ring extends to the world beyond.

Chinese leaders believe that enemies and threats lurk everywhere—both inside and outside the borders of the PRC—but their worst fear is that adversaries at home and abroad will link up or coordinate. From the vantage point of Beijing, the regime identifies only one other country in the world that can seriously challenge China in all four rings: the United States. Moreover, Washington poses multidimensional threats to the regime. These include the threat from US soft power—namely, subversive ideas about democracy, freedom, and human rights that threaten to undermine regime legitimacy.[14] America's threat also includes hard-power dimensions, namely economic clout and military might. The economic threat was made very concrete in 2018 with the imposition of tariffs on China by the United States—a move that has been labeled a "trade war."[15] A very visible component of American hard power long perceived as threatening by Chinese leaders is the US military, which has both a significant forward-basing presence in the Asia-Pacific and air and naval platforms routinely operating around China's periphery, especially in the East China Sea and the South China Sea.[16]

America's military threat is not only conventional, it is also nuclear. As noted earlier, the PRC sees itself as long being victimized by nuclear powers, that is, the target of nuclear threats and nuclear blackmail. In the 1950s and 1960s China was concerned about the possibility of a US nuclear strike; in the 1960s and 1970s China was primarily concerned about the threat of nuclear attack from the Soviet Union. This sustained Cold War nuclear menace from one or both of the superpowers not only propelled forward Beijing's own quest to acquire nuclear weapons, it also consumed PRC defense planning and prompted countrywide preparations to survive a massive nuclear strike. Chinese citizens were exhorted to "dig tunnels deep" to be ready to "fight an early, major, nuclear war [*zaoda, dada, da hezhanzheng*]."[17]

While the strategic landscape of the post–Cold War era has become more complicated over time, China's foremost adversary continues to be the United

States. Thus, despite the emergence of new nuclear powers—including three countries contiguous to China—it is the US nuclear posture that absorbs Beijing's primary attention.[18]

PRC thinking about nuclear weapons and nuclear proliferation have evolved significantly over the decades. During the Cold War Beijing perceived nuclear weapons as being monopolized by the two superpowers and a handful of Western European powers intent upon preserving their privileged positions and using nuclear weapons to blackmail nonnuclear powers. Once the PRC had acquired its own nuclear weapons it was willing to share its nuclear weapons technology at least with a select group of countries—the most noteworthy being Pakistan.

Global Landscape

In these early years of the twenty-first century Chinese leaders see a unipolar world in which the actual distribution of power is concentrated in one superpower: the United States. Beijing is best described as being "dissatisfied" with the global status quo rather than as a "revisionist power."[19] Certainly, the regime desires a more Sinocentric world, but precisely what this ought to look like is unclear. Although PRC leaders have repeatedly spoken of their desire for a more "democratic" or "multipolar" world, their words should not be accepted as a definitive or even authoritative statement of China's blueprint of its desired future world order for several reasons. First, Beijing has yet to articulate a cogent and detailed vision of what kind of world it would like to see. While it is possible that PRC leaders have produced a blueprint but are keeping it secret, the more likely explanation is that Beijing does not know what kind of future world it wants. Second, a truly multipolar world would only serve to dilute China's global power and influence. Indeed, there are indications that Chinese leaders recognize this. For example, continued discourse about a "G-2" or "Group of 2" comprised of China and the United States suggests much about the desires of some Chinese to have a Sino-American condominium for the foreseeable future. Nevertheless, this power configuration is implausible and unworkable, even though it does offer insights into Chinese wishful thinking.[20]

Despite these conditions, PRC leaders are extremely pragmatic and have recognized that the formation of a G-2 with the United States is improbable. Moreover, Beijing has assessed that US strategy toward China has been hardening since the 1990s. Recognizing that China remains weak relative to the United States (although the gap is shrinking), in an effort to balance against the preponderance of US power, Beijing has identified states with significant heft who are not allies or friends of Washington. The list of such powers is a short one since most great powers and middle powers are already allies or partners of the United States. One of the few that fits the bill is Russia: Moscow is the only other Permanent Five member of the United Nations Security Council that is not an ally of Washington. Moreover, Russia has sizeable conventional armed forces and a significant strategic arsenal. Beijing no longer perceives Moscow as a significant threat to China; on the contrary, Russia is now considered a key strategic partner, with the two states officially sharing a "comprehensive strategic partnership of cooperation" to counter US power as well as working together in expanding energy resources and military technology.[21]

Other blocs/states with "heft" include the European Union (EU), Brazil, South Africa, Iran, Japan, and India. The countries of the EU are all staunch US allies but China does not see Europe as threatening. Brazil and South Africa are nonaligned and members—along with China, Russia, and India—of BRICS (Brazil, Russia, India, China, and South Africa). While Brazil and South Africa both have global stature, each is primarily a regional player with limited power and influence beyond Latin America and Africa, respectively. Meanwhile, Iran is a major regional power and a long-standing Chinese partner with which Beijing has had extended security cooperation and significant economic interaction.[22] Moreover, Tehran is the Middle East capital with the most contentious and consistently adversarial relationship with Washington since its 1979 revolution.

Regional Landscape

Chinese leaders perceive the current distribution of power in the Asia-Pacific as multipolar (with multiple regional powers mostly weaker than China but China is not permitted to dominate). China aspires to establish a sphere of influence across the entire region and in which Beijing completely dominates. But regional powers, notably Japan and India, have been unwilling to yield and the PRC is especially focused on these two as primary states of strategic concern. Beijing perceives Tokyo as being an enduring strategic rival that poses a serious threat to China.[23] This perception is fueled not only by a history of hostility but also by persistent maritime territorial disputes as well as Japan's status as a committed US military ally.

India is of growing interest and concern to China for multiple reasons. First, India is very large, it is positioned within China's immediate neighborhood with unresolved territorial disputes, and it is a nuclear power. For Beijing, New Delhi is a proximate geostrategic rival on continental Asia.[24] China views with alarm any greater security cooperation or closer alignment between India and the United States, including multilateral efforts such as the Quadrilateral Security Dialogue (aka "the Quad"), which brings together New Delhi and Washington with Tokyo and Canberra.[25]

During the Cold War, Beijing provided critical assistance to Islamabad's nuclear weapons program between 1974 and 1996.[26] Motivating this case of nuclear proliferation is the awareness that India—Pakistan's nemesis and China's rival since the early 1960s—was also actively developing a nuclear weapons program. Noteworthy is that India and Pakistan both declared their nuclear status through tests that came only weeks apart, in May 1998. Interviews with PRC security specialists in the immediate aftermath of New Delhi's and Islamabad's tests evinced no signs of great alarm beyond acknowledgment that the detonations had caught Beijing by surprise. China's relationship with Pakistan is arguably the closest thing Beijing has to an alliance in the early twenty-first century—indeed, a great power would likely share this very sensitive technology only with a close friend or ally.[27]

By the dawn of the twenty-first century the PRC had reconsidered its stance on proliferation and appears to have concluded that expanding the club of countries with nuclear weapons was not in the country's best interests. Moreover, this shift in policy would help ensure that Beijing enjoyed better relations with Washington. Indeed, sustained engagement between the community of US arms control scholars and its counterpart scholars in China appears to have contributed to this policy change.[28]

It seems the PRC has refrained from exporting nuclear material and technology (although China has demonstrated far less restraint on the export of ballistic missiles). Moreover, China has been public about opposing nuclear proliferation and active in its efforts to cooperate with the United States and other countries to halt the acquisition of or encourage the elimination of nuclear weapons by various states. For example, the PRC was a key player in the Joint Comprehensive Plan of Action (JCPOA) signed with Iran in 2015.[29]

However, the highest-profile effort by China on the nuclear front was Beijing's unprecedented initiative to organize and host multiple rounds of the so-called Six Party Talks between 2003 and 2009. The diplomatic offensive to bring together North Korea along with four other states—the United States, South Korea, Japan, and Russia—proved an extremely complex multilateral and multiyear endeavor. The effort was ultimately in vain, as North Korea detonated its first nuclear device in October 2006 and proceeded to build up an arsenal.

Following Pyongyang's acquisition of nuclear devices, China staked a consistent position favoring the denuclearization of North Korea along with maintaining peace and stability on the Korean Peninsula: *bu zhan, bu luan, wu he* (translated as "no war, no chaos, denuclearization"). However, until at least 2011 Beijing quite clearly gave a far higher priority to avoiding war and chaos in Korea than working to eliminate Pyongyang's nuclear weapons program. Yet, by 2015 there appeared to be a realization that without denuclearization, the potential for lasting peace and stability in Korea was not possible.[30] Nevertheless, since 2017 the prospects for peaceful denuclearization remain highly uncertain: first, because rising tensions on the peninsula and the prospect of war seemed to increase by the end of 2017, and then, in 2018, because of a charm offensive by Pyongyang that dramatically defused tensions. But the remarkable improvement in inter-Korean relations, US-North Korean relations, and Sino-North Korean relations does not necessarily make full denuclearization more likely or more imminent. North Korean leader Kim Jong-un has masterfully played a weak hand by engaging in multiple bouts of summitry with his counterparts in Seoul, Beijing, and Washington. Kim's commitment to his country's denuclearization has yet to be put to the test. Moreover, PRC president Xi, ROK president Moon Jae-in, and Russian president Vladimir Putin do not seem to have made denuclearization their top priority in the same way that the Trump administration has.[31]

China also opposes the nuclearization of other states in the Asia-Pacific. China's attitude toward Japan is particularly noteworthy. Beijing has long accused Tokyo of "remilitarizing" and refusing to atone for its World War II atrocities in China. Although there remains a strong taboo sentiment as well as significant political and constitutional impediments in Japan to the country becoming a nuclear power, the move is technically relatively straightforward.[32] Yet, so long as the United States provides Japan with extended deterrence defense, this eventuality seems unlikely. But it is also possible that South Korea could acquire nuclear weapons, most conceivably through unification with North Korea. While Seoul could also seek to develop its own nuclear program were tensions to reemerge with Pyongyang, it is far less likely, especially if the United States continues to provide its Korean ally with a nuclear umbrella.

The PRC will never tolerate Taiwan acquiring is own nuclear weapons and there is currently little incentive for Taipei to attempt it because doing so would be clearly seen as crossing a Beijing "red line." Such a move would only invite disaster. It should be noted that Taiwan did attempt to secretly develop a nuclear program in the 1960s, but the effort was decisively quashed by the United States in 1977. Washington also terminated a second attempt by Taipei to develop a nuclear weapons program in 1988.[33]

China views the East China Sea, the Yellow Sea, the Taiwan Strait, and the South China Sea together as the maritime component of its second ring of security. These "near seas" are intended to form a kind of buffer zone, where US air and naval assets operate only at significant risk. During the past decade the PRC has launched a concerted effort to build up its maritime capabilities, not just naval but also coastguard. In 2013 Beijing consolidated multiple maritime security forces into a single agency, which became the most sizeable and substantial coastguard in Asia. It includes vessels that are much larger and far better armed than the navies of many of China's neighbors.[34]

The South China Sea may be of special significance in PRC thinking about its strategic arsenal. The PLA Navy established the Yulin Naval Base on the south side of Hainan Island, where submarines can come and go without surfacing in plain view. Beijing's territorial claims in the South China Sea have been strengthened since 2014 through a massive coordinated effort to construct artificial islands in the water. The aim appears to be to establish new "facts in the water," with the goal of essentially turning the South China Sea into a de facto PRC lake where PLA surface and subsurface naval platforms can operate unfettered.[35] In such an environment the semiclosed sea could logically function as an "SSBN [ballistic missile submarine] bastion."[36]

DREAMING OF NATIONAL REJUVENATION: CHINA'S GRAND STRATEGY

China's grand strategy is best summed up as "national rejuvenation," or what could be dubbed "making China great again." Chinese leaders have a powerful sense of a national destiny, in large part because of past glories and the impressive accomplishments of Chinese civilization. Certain ideas transcend national boundaries and cultural divides. Just as the articulation of a vision of restoring national eminence resonated strongly with many US voters during the 2016 US presidential campaign, so the idea of returning China to its rightful place in the world reverberates powerfully among many PRC citizens.

Although some scholars question whether China actually possesses a grand strategy, if a grand strategy is defined as "the process by which a state relates long-term ends to means under the rubric of an overarching and enduring vision to advance the national interest," then the PRC can be said to have one.[37] Indeed, as noted earlier, contemporary Chinese rulers are highly ambitious and prone to extensive central planning, they have identified ambitious goals, and they have articulated a path forward with vision.

As for the specified goals, the most important are economic. Under President Xi the PRC has identified specific goals to be achieved by 2021 and 2049. PRC economic strategy is aimed at securing a modern economy that can provide its ruling party legitimacy and create a "moderately prosperous society" for its 1.4 billion citizens. This goal has been reiterated by two consecutive PRC leaders in various policy documents, and the Thirteenth Five Year Plan has re-enshrined this goal in time for the CCP's centennial celebration coming in 2021.[38] By 2049 the goal is for China to have become "a socialist modernized society." Although Beijing recognizes the importance of a continued role for markets and unleashing the innovative energies of the Chinese people, the impulse to retain the central planning mechanisms and concomitant control hamper the PRC's ability to the achieve such ambitious goals.

Beijing also has articulated explicit military goals. These twenty-first-century goals build upon a vision attributed to Adm. Liu Huaqing (1916–2011) for phased naval expansion, first articulated in the early 1980s.[39] It stated that by 2000 the PLA Navy would extend its routine operations out to the so-called First Island Chain: the Kurils, Japan, the Ryukyus, Taiwan, the Philippines, Borneo, and Natuna Besar; by 2020 it would be able to project operations out to the so-called Second Island Chain: the Bonins, the Marianas, and the Carolines. By 2050 the PRC was to become a global sea power with the PLA Navy operating across the Pacific and around the world. China appears to be moving smartly along this maritime trajectory on or at least close to schedule.

Building a strong military is part and parcel of building China's dream of national rejuvenation. The thoroughgoing reorganization of the PLA launched by Xi Jinping in 2014 is motivated by the CCP's "goal of building a strong military, respond[ing] to the state's core security needs, aiming at building an informationized military and winning informationized wars."[40] The organizational reforms were thus intended "to build [the PLA] into a people's military that follows the [CCP's] commands, can fight and win, and boasts a fine style of work."[41] This reorganization means centralizing command and control under the Central Military Commission and reorienting the PLA toward being better able to project power beyond the PRC's borders.[42] China's overseas interests continue to expand, especially as long as the BRI initiative continues to be a high priority. Along with these infrastructure projects come more Chinese citizens living and working abroad, as well as expanding PRC investments, both of which become security concerns.[43] There are a variety of ways to protect China's overseas interests, including establishing military bases.[44] The PLA established its first overseas military base in Djibouti in 2017 and there are likely more bases to be established in the future.

Great powers, particularly rising powers, are driven to counter all perceived threats. Indeed, executing a grand strategy often tends to become a matter of responding to a state's greatest existential threat. For Beijing the greatest enduring security challenge emanates from Washington. Indeed, the PRC is consumed with countering the multifaceted threat it perceives from the United States. This includes dealing with the US challenge in each of the four rings of security. In the first ring (within China itself), where Beijing's priority goal is continued regime rule, the threat is subversion—inspired or orchestrated by Washington—and the primary strategy for achieving the goal is maintaining "control." In the second ring (the near geographic neighborhood) the priority PRC objective is to use a "buffer strategy" to substantially "restrict the United States" from having a presence in or operating within this area. In the third ring (the Asia-Pacific region) the main PRC goal is to significantly "limit access to the United States" via a primary strategy of maintaining a Chinese "sphere of influence." In the fourth ring (the rest of the world) the PRC's goal is to "balance against the United States," with a primary strategy of being a soft competitor with Washington.[45]

ENDURING STRATEGIC CONCEPTS AND CONTEMPORARY DOCTRINAL PRINCIPLES

While the most elegant way to understand how another country conceives of its national security and defense is through a realist lens, such a framework provides an insufficient appreciation of that state's strategic outlook, grand strategy, and military posture. Geography, history, and culture should not be ignored and the ideational drivers of national security should not be overlooked. Scholars such as Iain Johnston have demonstrated that the construct of "strategic culture" can be useful in interpreting and understanding China's strategic behavior.[46] Strategic culture can simply be defined as the impact of culture upon strategy. A more precise definition would be "the set of fundamental and enduring assumptions about the role of collective violence in human affairs and the efficacy of applying force [as] interpreted by a country's political and military elites."[47] Indeed, Chinese strategists and scholars strongly believe that culture exerts an important influence on Chinese society, politics, and approach to security and military matters; certainly, strategic culture is routinely included in most authoritative PLA textbooks. Moreover, many scholars of China insist that culture is an essential dimension in any analysis of that country.[48]

Research of ancient and modern China has discerned a Chinese strategic culture with multiple strands. One key finding is that China possesses a dominant realpolitik strand of strategic culture, though scholars often disagree on the impact of other strands and how multiple schools of strategic thought interact with each other. I contend that in contemporary China real existing strategic culture blends a legalist/parabellum (hard realpolitik) strand with a Confucian/Mencian (idealist) strand.[49]

The concept of strategic culture was originally formulated by Jack Snyder in the late 1970s to interpret and explain a puzzle presented by Soviet nuclear doctrine.[50] It is appropriate, then, to turn to fundamental doctrinal principles to understand the PLA's conventional and strategic deterrence and warfighting. Two dominant strategic concepts—China's holistic approach to security and the PRC's evolving understanding of deterrence—and one fundamental doctrinal principle—the enduring principle of active defense—are explored.

The Overall Situation

First, the PRC takes a holistic approach to security—looking at the overall situation or big picture instead of focusing solely on the military balance or operational environment.

Since the 1980s Beijing has emphasized repeatedly that the key trends of the times are "peace and development," in contrast to the Maoist era assessment that the key trends were "war and revolution." The clear implication is that the PRC can allow itself to focus on economic modernization since a world conflagration is not anticipated. However, this does not mean that wars will not occur. Indeed, there is every expectation that small wars will occur around the world as well as in China's own neighborhood. Officially, documents refer to *"jubu zhanzheng"* which in translation means "partial war" or anything short of a global conflict, and in English is often translated as "local war."[51] Hence China should be prepared to engage in such conflicts to defend its interests.

Xi Jinping is credited with emphasizing a "comprehensive" approach to the PRC's security. This may be so, but the big picture conception of China's security situation and holistic strategic framework is not new. Moreover, Beijing believes that "traditional and non-traditional security threats are interwoven."[52] This means that Beijing tends to adopt a broad approach instead of one solely focused on military matters.

The PRC experience underscores both the importance of sound economic development as a firm foundation and the value of a vibrant science and technology sector. Beijing does not take its economy for granted. China has suffered from economic backwardness which has taken decades to surmount. Moreover, one of the important lessons Chinese leaders took from the collapse of the Soviet Union is that Moscow got sucked into an arms race with the United States and did not pay enough attention to economic development.[53] Furthermore, the PRC also suffered from technological backwardness during the Maoist era and has made improving the quality of its scientists and technical personnel a top priority in the reform era. Deng Xiaoping championed the so-called Four Modernizations during the late 1970s and 1980s. The four modernizations were: agriculture, industry, science and technology, and defense. Initially the military was the lowest priority because Deng and other reformists realized that China's most pressing needs were economic modernization and the need to rebuild its education system to produce competent scientists and technical personnel.[54] More recently Beijing has been consumed with the question of how best to foster innovation in science and technology. In the twenty-first century the PRC emphasizes how technological innovation can benefit both the commercial and defense spheres through approaches such as "civil-military integration" and "fusion."[55]

Evolving Thinking about Deterrence

Second, the concept of deterrence has long been integral to Chinese military thought but rarely expressed in the same manner as in the West. The idea of avoiding war has long been present in Chinese strategic thinking, including in the writings of Sunzi (Sun-tzu). One way of avoiding actual military conflict is to overawe your adversary by stressing the futility of resisting because of either the inevitability of defeat or the extremely high cost of conflict. This was how deterrence seemed to work when China was strong. In the contemporary era, however, when China tended to be militarily weaker than many of its major adversaries—especially where strategic weaponry was concerned—deterrence took on a very different meaning and significance.

The Era of War and Revolution

For more than three decades "deterrence" had extremely negative connotations for leaders of the CCP. Since the establishment of the PRC in 1949, CCP leaders have believed that their country has been constantly threatened and terrorized by more powerful states. The insistence that these states were simply trying to "deter" China from acts of aggression did not resonate in Beijing. In fact, the Chinese word for deterrence, *weixie*, literally translates as "terrorize."[56] While the word "deter" comes from the Latin word "frighten" or "generate fear," the Romance language root of the English word fails to pack the punch of the Chinese characters. Moreover, the many US analysts and scholars who think and write about deterrence do so in abstract and antiseptic terms. The tendency is to overintellectualize the concept and in the process overlook the visceral roots of the word and a feeling of being defenseless against nuclear Armageddon.[57]

For Mao Zedong and other first-generation CCP leaders the term deterrence was virtually synonymous with "blackmail" or "coercion."[58] Deterrence is conceived of as something a strong state does to bully a weaker state. For most of the Cold War Beijing believed that both superpowers—the United States and the Soviet Union—used their superior conventional military might and nuclear arsenals to intimidate China. Moreover, the legacy of this mindset still endures in China today.[59] Not until the 1980s did Chinese thinking about deterrence begin to shift, as PRC strategists and leaders started to use the term themselves.

China's key concern in the 1960s was how to deter a Soviet attack. Beijing assumed that such an attack would consist of a massive conventional invasion and nuclear strike. The PRC's deterrent effort emphasized bravado and shock. In 1969 PLA troops on Zhenbao Island in the middle of the Ussuri River, which separates China from the Soviet Union, conducted a well-planned ambush of a Red Army detachment.[60] The operation was reportedly executed under the personal direction of Mao. While the Soviets were irate and the Red Army did retaliate, the provocation achieved its intended goal of shocking Moscow. The act served to underscore China's low-tech but massive conventional land forces combined with vast nonmilitary capabilities: population, resources, and geographic size. The greatest deterrent to a Soviet attack and invasion of China was the likelihood of a protracted conflict and quagmire that would threaten to bog down Soviet forces in a war without end. Moreover, the Chinese-initiated clash served to highlight Beijing's dogged determination—its willingness to fight a long, drawn-out epic struggle in order to outlast any invader. The Chinese calculation was that Soviet leaders did not relish such a scenario and hence were extremely reluctant to escalate the event beyond a minor albeit bloody border clash.

Mao Zedong was a master of the measured threat and calculated provocation. His bombastic rhetoric was intended to signal to the Soviet Union that China was prepared for a major war and thereby deter Beijing's more powerful adversary and aimed at raising the morale of the Chinese people. The PRC was on a highly publicized quasi-war footing for much of the 1960s and early 1970s.[61]

The Era of Peace and Development

The term deterrence was reportedly first used by PRC leaders in August 1978 in reference to China's own national defense, when Deng Xiaoping and senior military officials were listening to a report being delivered by Song Renqiong of the Seventh Machine Building Ministry. The report discussed Chinese ballistic missiles as a "deterrence force."[62]

A seminal event in China's evolving deterrent calculus was the 1995–96 Taiwan Strait Crisis.[63] Beijing's goal in the crisis was to deter Taipei from moving down the road to independence. President Lee Teng-hui's June 1995 visit to the United States was ostensibly unofficial and low-key: to attend a reunion event at Cornell University in upstate New York. But the event was anything but low profile as Lee sought to hype his Taiwan nationalist credentials during a rare trip to the United States. He gave a triumphal speech lauding the accomplishments of the Republic of China on Taiwan, which appeared to enrage PRC leaders. This was in addition to the fact that from Beijing's perspective, Washington had reneged on a promise not to issue a visa to the Taiwan leader. As a result, the PRC felt it necessary to launch missiles near Taiwan and conduct military exercises in the area in the time period between Lee's speech at Cornell and the presidential election in Taiwan. The effort to deter Taiwan from continuing down the road toward independence consisted of hawkish rhetoric, especially salvos fired by PLA leaders, and provocative acts, including missile tests and military exercises.

Although the PRC declared victory in the aftermath of the election, Lee won the popular vote and remained in office. Moreover, Chinese leaders appeared to be surprised by the dispatch of not one but two US Navy carrier strike groups near the island. The act highlighted Beijing's need to pay more attention to deterring the United States from intervening in any future Taiwan scenario. The episode appears to have been a turning point in Chinese thinking about deterrence. China's first biannual defense white paper, issued in late

1998, used the term deterrence, as did its first white paper on arms control released three years earlier.[64] However, the references in both documents were negative and the label was applied to what the two superpowers had done to weaker countries like China.

By the start of the twenty-first century China had embraced the idea of deterrence and it became a key concept in Chinese strategic thought. The authoritative *Science of Military Strategy* (*Zhanlue xue*), published by the Academy of Military Sciences in 2001 and translated into English four years later, identified deterrence as a key function of the PLA, second only to actual warfighting.[65] According to this doctrinal text, there are three components to strategic deterrence: adequate strength, determination, and effective communication. Of these, "determination is the soul of deterrence." To signal China's determination, the PLA articulates harsh public statements and threats as "part and parcel of a latter-day calculus of deterrence, a pattern of rhetoric and behavior first identified decades ago."[66]

By the late 2000s Beijing was no longer only focusing on preparing for a Taiwan scenario. A realization of wider interests and expanding ambitions resulted in a broadening out of thinking about the use of force beyond Taiwan to other locations on China's periphery.[67] A key dimension of this change was clarifying how to deter the United States from projecting military power so close to China, particularly inside the First Island Chain, the maritime region that Beijing refers to as the "near seas"—comprising the East China Sea, the Yellow Sea, the Taiwan Strait, and the South China Sea. Chinese efforts at deterrence have been labeled by the United States as a strategy of anti-access/area denial (or A2/AD). Chinese leaders refer to it as a "counterintervention" strategy that amounts to a concerted effort to deter the United States from operating its air and naval forces inside the First Island Chain.[68] Beijing does this by emphasizing the threats China poses to the United States in multiple domains.

The PLA believes that the US military is heavily reliant on technology for command, control, communications, computers, intelligence, surveillance, and reconnaissance (C4ISR), and has sought to demonstrate that it has the capability to sabotage or at least disrupt internet communications and satellite transmissions. Chinese cyber operations since at least 1999 have intended to send this message, based upon the assumption that the United States possesses a cyber strategy that is offensive.[69] Moreover, since at least the late 2000s, with the anti-satellite test of January 2007, China has signaled its ability to put US military satellites at risk. Indeed, one strategist has labeled this demonstration as an act of deterrence.[70] In addition, the PLA's growing arsenal of anti-ship cruise missiles and the improved accuracy of these missiles mean that the US Navy confronts serious threats from ballistic and cruise missiles in the Near Seas.[71]

The Absolute Flexibility of Active Defense

The PLA's most important doctrinal principle is "active defense." This principle, which dates to the early days of the CCP-PLA struggle in rural China, was first raised to draw a clear distinction between a dynamic defense and a static form of defense when insurgent forces in rural areas confronted more powerful conventional forces. Mao rejected the idea that weaker armed groups would completely avoid combat and not engage in offensive operations. He noted that though the PLA would adopt a strategically defensive stance, its doing so did not preclude offensive operational actions when conditions were appropriate. This principle has been repeatedly stressed by individual Chinese military leaders as well as in key documents, including successive PRC defense white papers.[72]

Perhaps the most essential element of China's active defense strategy is the idea that communist forces should seize and maintain the initiative. To this day PLA doctrine emphasizes that the PRC should never surrender the initiative to an adversary.[73] While the reality has often tended to be different—and China has frequently found itself in reactive mode in a crisis or conflict—this way of thinking continues to be influential.

In the peace and development era, active defense takes on additional significance at the strategic level, along with the prospect of greater Chinese unpredictability. Whereas in the era of war and revolution active defense was focused at the operational level while China sought to postpone its strategic counteroffensive until it had accumulated greater strength, in the present era the concept of protracted war—along with its three phases, from strategic defense through to strategic offense—has little if any relevance.[74] Hence, as Taylor Fravel observes, since the 1990s a central question confronting the PLA has been "how to carry out 'active defense' under these [new] conditions."[75] Military conflicts in the peace and development era are expected to be of short duration, which places added pressure on China to seize the initiative at the strategic level from the outset. Nan Li notes that active defense has taken on "new meaning," with ominous implications for any future Chinese adversaries as the PLA acquires more potent offensive capabilities and adheres to accelerated operational tempos with shorter time lines.[76] This sets the stage for crisis situations of increased strategic volatility.

Indeed, active defense is a fluid and ambiguous doctrinal principle and a manifestation of the "absolute flexibility" concept highlighted by Iain Johnston.[77] The ambiguity exists because of a significant blurring of the difference between what are defensive operations and what are offensive. According to one scholar, "Active defense strategy does not acknowledge the difference between defense and offense."[78] Chinese strategists appear to interpret any military action the PRC undertakes as "defensive," even if China strikes first.[79]

Thus, all instances of the PRC's use of military force are described as "self-defense counter-attacks," which suggests that the principle of active defense does not preclude a preemptive strike.[80] In the context of strategic weapons, it is unclear what this fluid interpretation of active defense means for the PRC's long-standing public no first use (NFU) pledge. Would China be allowed to launch a nuclear weapon first if Beijing determined that another country was preparing to launch a nuclear attack against it? Would the NFU stance apply if China believed that a nuclear base was the target of a conventional attack?

CONCLUSION

The PRC possesses a nested worldview that reflects the outlook of Beijing's profoundly insecure leaders. Consequently, regime leaders look to buffer themselves in the center by surrounding themselves with multiple rings of security. The PRC has adopted a grand strategy of national rejuvenation in which the regime is building a powerful and prosperous China through the execution of a series of ambitious national strategies. Chinese security concepts emphasize a holistic approach to national security that includes not just ambitious military initiatives but also political, economic, and diplomatic components. In recent decades the PLA has increasingly emphasized the importance of deterrence as a military mission that is distinct from warfighting. The concept of deterrence has become especially important where China's strategic weaponry is concerned. It is unclear what the long-cherished doctrinal principle of active defense means for the future of China's nuclear posture.

NOTES

1. John W. Lewis and Xue Litai, *China Builds the Bomb* (Stanford, CA: Stanford University Press, 1988), chap 3. The quote is from appendix A, 241, which contains the text of the PRC's public statement issued on October 16, 1964, that announced its first nuclear test. Mao was very much aware of the implicit nuclear threat from Washington in these cases—as well as threats from Korea in 1953. Nevertheless, it is important to note that no explicit nuclear threat was received by Mao from the administration of Dwight Eisenhower despite Eisenhower's firm belief that Washington had signaled such threats to Beijing. See Richard K. Betts, *Nuclear Blackmail and Nuclear Balance* (Washington, DC: Brookings Institution Press, 1987), 37–47 (regarding 1953 Korea); 54–62 (regarding 1954–55 Taiwan Strait); and 66–79 (regarding 1958 Taiwan Strait).
2. M. Taylor Fravel, *Active Defense: China's Military Strategy Since 1949* (Princeton, NJ: Princeton University Press, 2019), 250. See also Lewis and Xue, *China Builds the Bomb*, 47. Fravel's research indicates that Chinese leaders began thinking seriously about acquiring nuclear weapons in mid-1952. He notes that in late 1954

Mao asked Nikita Khrushchev for Soviet help in developing a Chinese nuclear program (Fravel, *Active Defense,* 248–49); and highlights the importance of the discovery of uranium in southern China in late 1954 and Beijing's driving desire to acquire a strategic deterrent in the lead-up to the 1955 decision (237).

3. Lewis and Xue, *China Builds the Bomb,* 61–65.
4. Andrew J. Nathan and Andrew Scobell, *China's Search for Security* (New York: Columbia University Press, 2012), 38. This configuration is a central feature of a Leninist regime. See Andrew Scobell, "Making Sense of North Korea: Pyongyang and Comparative Communism," *Asian Security* 1, no. 3 (December 2005): 250–51.
5. Adrian Zenz, "China's Domestic Security Spending: An Analysis of Available Data," *China Brief* 18, no. 4 (March 12, 2018).
6. Andrew Scobell and Andrew J. Nathan, "China's Overstretched Military," *Washington Quarterly* 34, no. 4 (Fall 2012): 135–48.
7. Andrew Scobell, "China Engages the World, Warily," *Political Science Quarterly* 132, no. 2 (Summer 2017): 343–44.
8. Construction of the Three Gorges Dam began in the early 1990s and was essentially completed in 2006 (although additional work was required). The idea for the dam itself dates back at least one hundred years, with the first ROC leader, Sun Yat-sen, usually being credited with suggesting the project. On the Belt and Road Initiative, see Nadege Rolland, *China's Eurasian Century: The Political and Strategic Implications of the Belt and Road Initiative* (Seattle: National Bureau of Asian Research, 2017).
9. Scobell, "Making Sense of North Korea," 352.
10. For an engaging account of the origins of China's ballistic missile program that highlights the role of one scientist, see Iris Chang, *Thread of the Silkworm* (New York: Basic, 1995).
11. Bates Gill, James Mulvenon, and Mark Stokes, "The Chinese Second Artillery Corps: Transition to Credible Deterrence," in *The People's Liberation Army as Organization: Reference Volume v.1.0,* ed. James C. Mulvenon and Andrew N. D. Yang, 510–86 (Santa Monica, CA: RAND Corporation, 2002), 517.
12. Gill, Mulvenon, and Stokes, "The Chinese Second Artillery Corps," 518.
13. Nathan and Scobell, *China's Search for Security,* 3–7.
14. Nathan and Scobell, 97–99, and chap. 12.
15. Jane Perlez, "China Is Confronting New U.S. Hostility, But Is It Ready for the Fight?," *New York Times,* September 23, 2018, https://www.nytimes.com/2018/09/23/world /asia/china-us-trade-war.html.
16. Nathan and Scobell, *China's Search for Security,* 93–96.
17. Lewis and Xue, *China Builds the Bomb,* 211.
18. See, for example, David M. Lampton, *Following the Leader: Ruling China from Deng Xiaoping to Xi Jinping* (Berkeley: University of California Press, 2014), 134.
19. Nathan and Scobell, *China's Search for Security,* chap. 13. See also Michael J. Mazarr, Timothy R. Heath, and Astrid Struth Cevallos, *China and the International Order* (Santa Monica, CA: RAND Corporation, 2018); and Alastair Iain Johnston, "Is China a Status Quo Power?," *International Security* 27, no. 4 (Spring 2003): 5–56.
20. Elizabeth C. Economy and Adam Segal, "The G-2 Mirage: Why the U.S. and China are not Ready to Upgrade Ties," *Foreign Affairs* 88, no. 3 (May–June 2009): 14–23.

21. Richard J. Ellings and Robert G. Sutter, eds., *Axis of Authoritarianism: Implications of China-Russia Cooperation* (Seattle: National Bureau of Asian Research, 2018); see also Paul J. Bolt and Sharyl N. Cross, *China, Russia, and Twenty-First Century Global Geopolitics* (Oxford: Oxford University Press, 2018).

22. John W. Garver, *China and Iran: Ancient Partners in a Post-Imperial World* (Seattle: University of Washington Press, 2006).

23. Sheila Smith, *Intimate Rivals: Japanese Domestic Politics and a Rising China* (New York: Columbia University Press, 2015).

24. T. V. Paul, ed., *The China-India Rivalry in the Globalization Era* (Washington, DC: Georgetown University Press, 2018).

25. Sumit Ganguly and Andrew Scobell, "The Himalayan Impasse: Sino-Indian Rivalry in the Wake of Doklam," *Washington Quarterly* 41, no. 3 (Fall 2018): 185.

26. Henrik Stålhane Hiim, *China and International Nuclear Weapons Proliferation* (New York: Routledge, 2019), chap. 3.

27. Andrew Small, *The China-Pakistan Axis: Asia's New Geopolitics* (New York: Oxford University Press, 2015).

28. Evan S. Medeiros, *Reluctant Restraint: The Evolution of China's Nonproliferation Policies and Practices, 1980–2004* (Stanford, CA: Stanford University Press, 2007).

29. John W. Garver, "China and the Iran Nuclear Negotiations: Beijing's Mediation Effort," in *The Red Star and the Crescent: China and the Middle East*, ed. James Reardon-Anderson, 123–48 (New York: Oxford University Press, 2018).

30. Andrew Scobell, *China and North Korea: Bolstering a Buffer or Hunkering Down in Northeast Asia?* (Washington, DC: RAND Corporation, 2017), 2–3.

31. Lee Jeong-ho, "China, Russia, North Korea Call for Adjusted Sanctions Ahead of Denuclearization," *South China Morning Post*, October 10, 2018, https://www.politico.com/story/2018/10/10/china-russia-north-korea-sanctions-891640.

32. Peter J. Katzenstein, *Cultural Norms and National Security: Police and Military in Post-War Japan* (Ithaca, NY: Cornell University Press, 1996). See also Richard C. Bush, *The Perils of Proximity: China-Japan Security Relations* (Washington, DC: Brookings Institution Press, 2010), 288.

33. David Albright and Corey Gay, "Nuclear Nightmare Averted," *Bulletin of Atomic Scientists* 54 (January–February 1998): 54–60.

34. Lyle J. Morris, "Blunt Defenders of Sovereignty: The Rise of Coast Guards in East and Southeast Asia," *Naval War College Review* 70, no. 2 (Spring 2017): 75–112.

35. Andrew Scobell, "The South China Sea and U.S.-China Rivalry," *Political Science Quarterly* 133, no. 2 (Summer 2018): 201.

36. Christopher Twomey, "The Military-Security Relationship," in *Tangled Titans: The United States and China*, ed. David Shambaugh, 235–62 (New York: Rowman & Littlefield, 2013), 243.

37. See, for example, Wang Jisi, "China's Search for a Grand Strategy: A Rising Power Finds Its Way," *Foreign Affairs* 90, no. 2 (March–April 2011): 68–79. See the definition at Andrew Scobell et al., *China's Grand Strategy: Trends, Trajectories, and Long-Term Competition* (Santa Monica, CA: RAND Corporation, 2020), 5.

38. Compilation and Translation Bureau of the Central Committee of the Chinese Communist Party, "Thirteenth Five Year Plan," Beijing, December 2016, 6.

39. Bernard D. Cole, *The Great Wall at Sea: China's Navy in the Twenty-First Century* (Annapolis, MD: Naval Institute Press, 2010), 174–77.

40. State Council Information Office, *China's Military Strategy* (Beijing: People's Republic of China, May 2015), "Section IV: Building and Development of China's Armed Forces," http://english.www.gov.cn/archive/white_paper/2015/05/27/content_2814 75115610833.htm.

41. State Council Information Office, *China's Military Strategy* (Beijing: People's Republic of China, May 2015), "Section II: Missions and Strategic Task of China's Armed Forces," http://english.www.gov.cn/archive/white_paper/2015/05/27/content_281475115610833.htm.

42. Phillip C. Saunders and Joel Wuthnow, "China's Goldwater-Nichols?: Assessing PLA Organizational Reforms," *Joint Force Quarterly* 82 (July 2016): 68–75.

43. Jonas Parello-Plesner and Mathieu Duchâtel, *China's Strong Arm: Protecting Citizens and Assets Abroad* (London: International Institute for Strategic Studies, 2015).

44. Andrew Scobell and Nathan Beauchamp-Mustafaga, "The Flag Lags but Follows: The PLA and China's Great Leap Outward," in *Chairman Xi Remakes the PLA: Assessing Chinese Military Reforms*, ed. Phillip C. Saunders et al., 171–99 (Washington, DC: National Defense University Press, 2019).

45. Andrew Scobell et al., *At the Dawn of Belt and Road: China in the Developing Road* (Santa Monica, CA: RAND Corporation, 2018), 26.

46. See, for example, Alastair I. Johnston, "Cultural Realism and Grand Strategy in Maoist China," in *The Culture of National Security: Norms and Identity in World Politics*, ed. Peter J. Katzenstein, 216–68 (New York: Columbia University Press, 1996).

47. Andrew Scobell, "China's Real Strategic Culture: A Great Wall of the Imagination," *Contemporary Security Policy* 35, no. 2 (August 2014): 213.

48. Andrew Scobell, *China and Strategic Culture* (Carlisle Barracks, PA: US Army War College Strategic Studies Institute, 2002), 1ff.

49. Andrew Scobell, *China's Use of Military Force: Beyond the Great Wall and the Long March* (New York: Cambridge University Press, 2003), chap. 2; Scobell, "China's Real Strategic Culture," 211–26. Iain Johnston contends that only the parabellum strand is operative and the Confucian/Mencian is just for symbolic discourse. See Alastair I. Johnston, *Cultural Realism: Strategic Culture and Grand Strategy in Chinese History* (Princeton, NJ: Princeton University Press, 1995).

50. Jack Snyder, *The Soviet Strategic Culture: Implications for Nuclear Options* (Santa Monica, CA: RAND Corporation, 1977).

51. State Council Information Office, *China's Military Strategy* (Beijing: People's Republic of China, May 2015), "Section I: National Security Situation," http://english.www .gov.cn/archive/white_paper/2015/05/27/content_281475115610833.htm.

52. State Council Information Office, "I: National Security Situation."

53. David Shambaugh, *China's Communist Party: Atrophy and Adaptation* (Berkeley: University of California Press, 2008).

54. For a recent assessment, see Denis Fred Simon and Cong Cao, *China's Emerging Technological Edge: Assessing the Role of High-End Talent* (New York: Cambridge University Press, 2009).

55. State Council Information Office, *China's Military Strategy* (Beijing: People's Republic of China, May 2015), "Section IV: Building and Development of China's Armed Forces," http://english.www.gov.cn/archive/white_paper/2015/05/27/content_2814 75115610833.htm.

56. See also the discussion in Betts, *Nuclear Blackmail and Nuclear Balance*, 3–5.

57. Austin Long, in his review of six decades of RAND research on the topic, observes that, fundamentally, "deterrence is the generation of fear." See Long, *Deterrence: From Cold War to Long War* (Santa Monica, CA: RAND Corporation, 2008), 7.

58. Jeffrey Lewis, *Paper Tigers: China's Nuclear Posture* (London: International Institute for Strategic Studies, 2014), 29–30.

59. See, for example, Xu Weidi, "Embracing the Moon in the Sky or Fishing the Moon in the Water?: Some Thoughts on Military Deterrence," *Air & Space Power Journal* 26, no. 4 (July–August 2012): 13.

60. For an authoritative account of the clash, see Thomas W. Robinson, "The Sino-Soviet Border Conflicts in 1969: New Evidence Three Decades Later," in *Chinese Warfighting: The PLA Experience Since 1949*, ed. Mark Ryan, David M. Finkelstein, and Michael A. McDevitt, 198–216 (Armonk, NY: M. E. Sharpe, 2003).

61. See, for example, John Wilson Lewis and Xue Litai, *Imagined Enemies: China Prepares for Uncertain War* (Stanford, CA: Stanford University Press, 2006), chap. 3.

62. Wang Niaozhong, "Zhongguo heweixie sixiangde lishi yanjiu" (The development of nuclear deterrence theory in China), *Junshi sixiangshi yanjiu* 5 (2012): 10.

63. See, for example, Andrew Scobell, "Show of Force: Chinese Soldiers, Statesmen, and the 1995–1996 Taiwan Strait Crisis," *Political Science Quarterly* 115, no. 2 (Summer 2000): 227–56; and Robert S. Ross, "Navigating the Taiwan Strait: Deterrence, Escalation Dominance, and U.S.-China Relations," *International Security* 27, no. 2 (Fall 2002): 48–85.

64. The official English-language texts of these two documents are available at http://eng.mod.gov.cn/Database/WhitePapers/.

65. Peng Guangqian and Yao Youzhi, eds., *The Science of Military Strategy* (Beijing: Military Science Publishing House, 2005), 213–15.

66. Andrew Scobell, "Is There a Civil-Military Gap in China's Peaceful Rise?," *Parameters* 29, no. 2 (Summer 2009): 11.

67. See, for example, Roy Kamphausen, David Lai, and Andrew Scobell, eds., *Beyond the Strait: PLA Missions Other Than Taiwan* (Carlisle, PA: US Army War College Strategic Studies Institute, 2009).

68. While analysts may disagree on how to label China's strategy, they generally agree on its substance. See M. Taylor Fravel and Christopher P. Twomey, "Projecting Strategy: The Myth of Counter-Intervention," *Washington Quarterly* 37, no. 4 (Winter 2015): 171–87; and Timothy Heath and Andrew S. Erickson, "Is China Pursuing Counter Intervention?," *Washington Quarterly* 38, no. 3 (Fall 2015): 143–56.

69. See Joe McReynolds, "Chinese Thinking on Deterrence and Compellence in the Network Domain," paper presented to CAPS/RAND/NDU Conference in Taipei, Taiwan, November 14–15, 2013.

70. Bao Shixiu, "Deterrence Revisited: Outer Space," *China Security*, no. 5 (Winter 2007): 2–11.

71. "Zhongguo fanchuan dandao daodan yiju jichen soumeiduo hangmu nengli" (China's anti-ship cruise missiles already have the capability to strike and sink many US aircraft carriers), *Huanqiu shibao*, November 2, 2013, http://mil.huanqiu.com/mlitaryvision/2013–11/2714897.html.

72. For more quotations, discussion, and analysis, see Scobell, *China's Use of Military Force*, 34–35.

73. See, for example, Paul H. B. Godwin, "Change and Continuity in Chinese Military Doctrine, 1949–1999," in *Chinese Warfighting: The PLA Experience Since 1949*, ed. Mark Ryan, David M. Finkelstein, and Michael A. McDevitt, 23–55 (Armonk, NY: M. E. Sharpe, 2003), 50.

74. Scobell, *China's Use of Military Force*, 47–50. See also Mao Zedong, "On Protracted War (May 1938)," in *Selected Works of Mao Tse-tung* (Peking: Foreign Languages Press, 1967), 187–267.

75. M. Taylor Fravel, "Shifts in Warfare and Party Unity: Explaining China's Changes in Military Strategy," *International Security* 42, no. 3 (Winter 2017–18): 78.

76. Nan Li, "The PLA's Evolving Warfighting Doctrine, Strategy, and Tactics, 1985–1995: A Chinese Perspective," *China Quarterly* 146 (June 1996): 452.

77. Scobell, *China's Use of Military Force*, 35. See also Johnston, *Cultural Realism*, 148–52.

78. Bi Jianxiang, "The PRC's Active Defense Strategy: New Wars, Old Concepts," *Issues and Studies* 31 (November 1995): 94.

79. Lewis and Xue, *Imagined Enemies*, 11–12, 40–42, 253–56.

80. Scobell, *China's Use of Military Force*, 32.

THREE

China's Nuclear Doctrine and Deterrence Concept

Christopher P. Twomey

Although China has long been a nuclear power, its strategic forces have played a relatively muted role in the country's security policy. This is particularly the case relative to the United States and the Soviet Union/Russia, although that comparison could be extended to other countries as well. Nevertheless, as China's rise has reshaped geopolitics in myriad areas, so too have strategic nuclear affairs been affected. While the quantitative buildup in China's force still leaves it well behind the top two players, Beijing now commands a much more capable set of forces and is starting to probe new areas of strategic thinking.

The developments surrounding China's nuclear capabilities suggest this area warrants considerable study. First, in proportional terms China's arsenal size has grown more over the past decade than any of the other established five nuclear powers. Second, China's set of delivery systems has diversified. Although this follows the practice of the other established powers, it does create new challenges for China's management of its force and potential for escalatory dynamics. Finally, China inhabits a particularly challenging nuclear environment, with four nuclear powers on its borders, and it faces the United States in extended (and direct) deterrent relations. Together these are likely to pressure Beijing to continue evolving its policy.

Fundamentally, China's nuclear policy serves its broader security policy objectives. As discussed by Andrew Scobell in his chapter in this volume, China has a range of important security interests that at least tangentially rely on both nuclear deterrence and statecraft to achieve. First and foremost among these is the goal to eventually reunify Taiwan into the People's Republic of China. Central to this is a need to (at the least) preclude full-scale US intervention in any potential conflict over the island. This is the primary circumstance that plausibly could involve nuclear weapons.[1] But in the long term the rivalry with India or potential competition with Russia pose distinct challenges for the Chinese nuclear force. Additionally, while predicting the future trajectory of the North Korean nuclear program is a highly speculative endeavor, China's interest in ensuring a buffer state between US allies and its own territory will guarantee Chinese involvement in any military conflict on the Korean Peninsula. Given the extant status of the North Korean arsenal today, this automatically engages nuclear statecraft in any crisis involving North Korea and the United States. Finally, a range of secondary concerns (e.g., territorial disputes over the South China and East China Seas) are likely to be settled at much lower levels of competition. Nevertheless, the balance of nuclear arms casts a long shadow in general and would be likely to play some, albeit perhaps distant, role in these areas.

Frustratingly, the study of China's strategic policy faces a major challenge due to the pervasive opacity of the Chinese system. Certainly there is a proliferation of writings, many of them "authoritative," now available in China.[2] Nevertheless, as discussed later, these provide only a superficial understanding of Chinese thinking and much must be inferred rather than definitively concluded. The prohibition against publication of anything that appears to challenge long-standing political Chinese strictures on nuclear policy (in particular regarding the "no first use" [NFU] policy articulated by Mao Zedong) forces analysts to carefully scrutinize the margins of such publications to assess the details and changes of Chinese policy. Comparing such statements with (declassified) assessments from Western governments further supplements our understanding of this area.

Cognizant of these challenges, this chapter evaluates China's nuclear doctrine and deterrence concepts in its evolving security environment. It begins by briefly surveying the historical background of China's nuclear policy. As noted, China's historical legacy plays an important constraining role on contemporary Chinese strategic thought. The current declaratory policy is described, as are the emerging hints at evolving thinking and the drivers of such. The focus then turns to a detailed description of the security challenges China is preparing to address and the nature of its planned response. These responses are predominantly conventional in traditional terms, but they blur into the strategic arena through the involvement of information and cyber capabilities along with a reliance on conventional missile capabilities. The linkage between conventional and strategic capabilities is described, highlighting the challenges they pose. All of these are complicated by the aforementioned external strategic challenges that China faces. The strategic stability of East Asia in the twentieth century will not thrive through the remainder of the twenty-first.

TRADITIONAL CHINESE STRATEGIC THOUGHT

Chinese strategic thought remained relatively constant from 1964 to perhaps the early 2000s. Mao's declaration of the NFU policy in 1964 remained as sacrosanct as the picture of him hanging in Tiananmen Square. Mao also had dismissed nuclear weapons as "paper tigers" early in the Cold War.[3] Although his views on this certainly evolved over time, Mao's statements laid something of a foundation for Chinese thinking on nuclear weapons that downplayed their utility.[4] This baseline has curtailed the development of strategic thought on nuclear arms in China until very recently. That is, since China's policy as laid out by Mao was nearly untouchable, there was limited value in thinking through alternative conceptions of a nuclear posture.

China faced a number of instances of attempted nuclear coercion during the Cold War. Toward the end of the Korean War, Washington threatened attacks to expedite treaty negotiations.[5] Taiwan Straits crises later in the 1950s also prompted US threats of nuclear escalation.[6] In a period of significant domestic chaos and facing the animosity of both the United States and the Soviet Union, China also had to face down Soviet nuclear signaling during the 1969 Sino-Soviet border war.[7] This has created an enduring Chinese concern with avoiding facing coercive threats by nuclear-armed adversaries that Beijing cannot address with its own deterrence capabilities. This lesson continues to have resonance today.

Given the limitations in Chinese nuclear forces and related support elements during the late Cold War, and because of that restrictive declaratory policy of NFU, China has generally had a fairly existential or limited deterrent approach to nuclear affairs. Traditionally this meant merely maintaining the ability to strike a modest number of any potential adversary's cities at a time of Beijing's choosing. Such "countervalue" strikes would be undertaken with relatively large (and not particularly accurate) warheads. There is a markedly reduced sense of urgency in this kind of retaliation scenario, at least relative to US and Soviet practices of prompt, or even preemptive, response.

Chinese force posture, as described by Hans Kristensen elsewhere in this volume, was traditionally quite low-key as well. The functional separation of warheads from delivery systems in peacetime ensured robust positive control and was particularly important given the absence of automated systems to limit the ability of a rogue commander to launch a strike independently (such as "permissive action links").[8] Not inconsequentially from Beijing's perspective, this element of the deployment posture also served to display concrete evidence of Beijing's public relations campaign as a responsible nuclear power.

Many of these elements continue to exert some constraints on China today. Certainly the NFU declaratory policy remains central to external Chinese messaging. Further, the strategic imperative to avoid nuclear coercion remains strong.[9] The next section outlines the continuities and changes in the Chinese approach to nuclear affairs in the twenty-first century.

EVOLVING THREATS AND SECURITY DOCTRINE

China's security situation has shifted rather dramatically since the end of the Cold War, and particularly during the twenty-first century. Changes in the global strategic environment and in China's relative capabilities have opened up new options, and these have created new dynamics in the strategic arena. China's nuclear doctrine is evolving, no matter the consistency in the declaratory policy of NFU.

Two major trend lines are worth highlighting; both have distinct impacts on the strategic situation of China. First, the dramatic collapse of the Soviet Union removed the leading threat that had driven Chinese thinking about its security in the 1970s and 1980s. This greatly increased China's security across the board. (Recall that by the late Cold War the Soviet Union had deployed over twenty divisions of army forces along the border with China, in the Soviet Far East.[10]) This occurred just as the Chinese were creating a robust and survivable nuclear arsenal. China's first deployment of an intermediate range ballistic missile (IRBM) was in 1971 and an intercontinental ballistic missile (ICBM) in 1984. This shift in the threat reduced the need to deploy a large arsenal.[11]

The second, subsequent change is ongoing: the massive increase in Chinese conventional military capabilities. As Kristensen notes, Chinese nuclear forces have increased in quantity and quality. But the massive increase in real defense spending since the mid-1990s has greatly expanded China's ability to secure long-dormant aspirational interests, such as the control of Taiwan and various smaller maritime features in the South China and East China Seas. While China's ability to address these interests has increased substantially, China's radically changed interaction with the global economy following its "reform and opening" policy (begun in 1978) has created a new interest for Beijing: ensuring continued secure involvement in the trade and investment patterns that have facilitated its growth. The coincidence of these two factors has engendered within China an interest in avoiding major provocations and thus has incentivized a range of "hybrid" challenges and "gray zone" provocations by China.[12] Central to such challenges to the established order is a desire for Beijing to avoid the potential for any escalation, either toward intense conventional war or nuclear conflict. Indeed, it emphasizes a need to carefully manage the prospects for escalation; at the same time, increasing China's own strategic capabilities leads others to think twice about escalation.

At a broader level China's emphasis on conventional missiles as part of its military modernization has created a third element to consider. To some extent this is simply a reflection of the nature of military technology today. Missiles provide cost-effective options for many countries, particularly those with local maritime interests to defend.[13] But for several reasons China would likely depend heavily on such capabilities in most relevant situations.[14] Compared to either Taiwan or particularly Japan, China would be facing adversaries with advanced air defenses and capable fighter aircraft. Missiles are believed to provide an ability to achieve political gains without defeating or disabling those opposing forces.[15] Further, in an extended campaign against either actor, China would need to use a missile force to directly attack airfields and surface-to-air missile sites to facilitate follow-on attacks with its own air force. These conventional missiles presumably would operate separately from nuclear forces. Nevertheless, they would provide the ability for some "strategic" direct attacks and blur the line between conventional and nuclear attacks, as they rely on the same delivery mechanism and achieve their effects without first destroying enemy defenses.[16]

CHINESE CONCEPTS OF MODERN WARFARE INTEGRATION

In the context of these strategic and technological environment changes, Chinese writings have undergone a number of major shifts. From the increasing role of information technology and aspirations for enhanced joint operations, as implemented in major organizational changes, these shifts have been massive in scale for an institution that deeply influences global affairs. It is interesting to note that essentially none of this centers on nuclear weapons issues. That is to say, while the Chinese military has put tremendous effort into adjusting to the contemporary security and technology environment, its changes are not seen to fundamentally alter much in the strategic nuclear realm. Nevertheless, nuclear weapons possess secondary, and worrisome, implications for the evolution of Chinese thinking about the role of nuclear weapons.

These are highlighted at the broadest level through the evolution of Chinese Military Strategic Guidelines (*junshe zhanlüe fangzhen*), which serve as the "core and collected embodiment of military strategy," according to the Chinese Academy of Military Science, which promulgates its thinking.[17] Major substantive developments have been documented in the guidelines over time, from early strategies for defending the homeland by luring a superior enemy into Chinese territory and then wearing it down, to a variety of more proactive strategies that hold Chinese adversaries at bay through "active defense." The current guidelines focus on "winning informationalized local wars."[18] They represent the culmination of steady increases in the role of informationaliza-tion—which is best thought of as the broad role of information technology in enhancing all elements of C4ISR over time. The evolution began in the 1980s and the evolution can be charted in this way:

- "Dealing with local wars and military conflicts" (in 1988);
- "Winning local wars under high technology conditions" (in 1993);
- "Winning local wars under informationalized conditions" (in 2004); and
- "Winning informationalized local wars" (in 2016).[19]

One can clearly see the steady increase in and importance of the role of infor-mation technology's contribution to Chinese military operations.

These shifts have indirect implications for Chinese nuclear thinking. Cold War–era military strategic guidelines focused on deterring the United States and the Soviet Union from conducting major offensives against the territorial heartland of China. There the contribution and benefit of a Chinese nuclear force is clear and credible. However, finding ways for the Second Artillery and Rocket Forces to contribute to newer strategic goals requires new thinking. Additionally, the emphasis on technology and informationalization applies to the nuclear force as well. Enhancing command-and-control capabilities could include merely developing a resilience to interference (jamming, cyber intrusion, etc.). Informationalization is clearly a manifestation of these shifts in China. However, the guidelines also express an effort to make command-and-control nimbler, even if cast in defensive terms: "Make a decision on a course of action, deploy forces, and deal with emergencies and change."[20] This inherently creates operational flexibility for the nuclear force that is only useful for counterforce or integrated nuclear and conventional plans. Traditional "city busting" countervalue deterrence concepts do not require such flexibility.

Similarly, an emphasis on increased situational awareness (the ISR side of the acronym, referring to intelligence, surveillance, and reconnaissance) also has implications for a nuclear force's role. Some elements might focus on increased survivability: understanding when you are under attack increases one's prospect for survival but it also increases a force's ability to track moving and time-sensitive targets.

Concurrent with this evolution has been a steady increase in China's development of joint operations across all services. The current guidelines focus on "integrated joint operations" as the "main form of operations" (a key category characterized in each of the successive guidelines). "China's inter-pretation of [integrated joint operations] focuses on the development of joint command organizations with integrated command networks to enable rapid combat decision and execution."[21]

In 2016 Chinese military newspapers began to increasingly report on cross-theater joint exercises, chronicling progress in this area. Nevertheless, it is important to recognize that there continue to be challenges in implementing reforms.[22] For instance, there has been greater attention to the so called "five cannot do's": "Commanders will not correctly judge the situations, will not understand their commander's intent, will not instill a fighting mentality, will not correctly deploy, and will not adjust to unexpected situations."[23] Other writings warn of the "two gaps in [China's] military modernization . . . [and] the problem of two insufficient capabilities."[24] Thus it is important to not overstate the progress in the nuclear arena. Nevertheless, the incorporation of the Rocket Forces in integrated exercises certainly shows an increased role for these forces at all stages of conflict, or at least aspirations for such.

Finally, in terms of large organizational changes in the PLA, the move to theater commands (TCs) has facilitated an integration of the military branches and services. Each has a component commander assigned to each theater within a joint command structure. The PLA Rocket Forces thus have representatives in each of the TCs, having "assigned approximately 100 officers to the five new TCs to support planning and training."[25] Although the level of integration of the People's Liberation Army Rocket Force (PLARF) into the new TCs is apparently somewhat lower than that of the other traditional services, nevertheless it represents integration in war-fighting (rather than strategic escalation-controlling) commands.

CONTEMPORARY STRATEGIC DOCTRINE

At one level the broad Chinese doctrine of NFU, sacrosanct since Mao's original pronouncement of it in 1964 at the dawn of China's nuclear age, remains unchanged. The core of Chinese nuclear thinking continues to be focused on the deterrence of others' use of nuclear weapons against China. While Chinese interlocutors admit there were some debates on the merit of perhaps adjusting this thinking sometime around 2010–12, they characterize those misgivings as having been definitively quashed by the political leadership.[26] The most recent Chinese white paper, "China's National Defense in the New Era," gives a fairly comprehensive restatement of it being put to rest:

> China is always committed to a nuclear policy of no first use of nuclear weapons at any time and under any circumstances, and not using or threatening to use nuclear weapons against non-nuclear-weapon states or

nuclear-weapon-free zones unconditionally. China advocates the ultimate complete prohibition and thorough destruction of nuclear weapons. China does not engage in any nuclear arms race with any other country and keeps its nuclear capabilities at the minimum level required for national security. China pursues a nuclear strategy of self-defense, the goal of which is to maintain national strategic security by deterring other countries from using or threatening to use nuclear weapons against China.[27]

None of this is to say that China's NFU would necessarily be abided by in a conflict, should strategic imperatives warrant. The question often posed is "Should one believe China's NFU?" This question is too broad to be useful. China has in many ways sized and structured its force such that it can implement an NFU declaratory policy to the detriment of other approaches to strategic nuclear affairs. Arguments for force structure aimed at achieving credibility of alternative nuclear doctrines would be viewed as illegitimate within internal Chinese decision-making circles. Nevertheless, that is starting to change. Some of these changes highlight questions about the wide range of nuclear doctrines that are compatible with NFU. (For example, what does it mean to "use" a nuclear weapon? Is a nuclear threat in some sense "use"?) Beyond such internal questioning, nothing that China (or any other country, for that matter) says in peacetime need necessarily constrain its actions during an intense conflict. Or, put another way, while the NFU approach has exerted an influence on the force structure that China will bring into a crisis, it should not be assumed to play a highly constraining role within a crisis when other important Chinese goals are at stake. To argue otherwise ignores the paramount and overriding objectives of all states: to ensure security goals.[28]

More concrete, however, are the number of training regimens, emerging doctrinal and definitional discussions, and potential force posture developments, which raise questions about important shifts in China's doctrinal approach. Evidence for these changes shows up in official reports about military exercises, in military training manuals, and within military newspaper stories. The main areas of focus are: how to address conventional strikes against nuclear targets, the demand for early warning, how to train for rapid implementation of a nuclear attack, discussions of launch-on-warning postures, the potential for nuclear weapons to deter conventional war, a discussion of transwar deterrence, and the need for some degree of warfighting within a nuclear war. None of these has been codified in a declared nuclear policy, and the evidence is not overwhelming in any individual case. However, in the aggregate these distinct changes suggest that a significant rethinking of the role of nuclear weapons is occurring within China. Each area is discussed in turn.

NFU, with an Asterisk (or Two)

It has become crystal clear that a major caveat must be acknowledged regarding the NFU stance in the face of conventional strikes on Chinese nuclear forces. As US capabilities to strike distant targets with a high degree of accuracy have increased, the security—indeed, the very survivability—of the Chinese silo-based ICBMs has been called into question. Increasingly, in Track 1.5 meetings Chinese semiofficial and even official interlocutors have signaled that such attacks would constitute a crossing of the nuclear threshold.[29] Although this perception is to some extent understandable, it is a sign that the apparently straightforward NFU comes with some uncertainty at its margins.

Other ways that the boundaries of the NFU's applicability have been blurred are also apparent. For instance, some evidence suggests that China might consider moving to a launch-on-warning or launch-on-threat posture. This raises some important questions: How would such warning be assessed? What capabilities do the Chinese have to differentiate between a nuclear and a nonnuclear attack? Both of these are challenging for many states. China's signal of flexibility in this regard serves to enhance its ability to deter conventional attacks that might be mistaken for nuclear strikes (such as conventionally armed, submarine-launched Trident missiles).

Indeed, such a scenario highlights a broader issue: What constitutes "use"? While at some level it could be considered a trivial (and pedantic) issue, the question does require some examination. Certainly, the destruction of nuclear weapons (through, perhaps, the use of conventional munitions or a cyber attack) affects their future usability. So, would that cross the threshold that would allow China to use other nuclear weapons? Similarly, would the simple launching of nuclear weapons (that is, prior to detonation) cross the threshold of use? Even without engaging in a sophisticated ontological discussion about use, it should be clear that different actors will have different perspectives about precise definitions.

Broader Political Utility

A number of Chinese sources suggest an increased perception in the value of nuclear weapons beyond mere deterrence of their use against China. For instance, the *Liberation Army Daily* reported that "Xi Jinping stressed that the rocket force is a core force of our country's strategic deterrence, is a strategic support of our country's major power status, and is a major foundation stone for safeguarding national security."[30] The view that nuclear weapons somehow enhance China's major power status is new and suggests a perception that they broadly contribute to China's security, well beyond mere deterrence of an adversary's nuclear attack. Similarly, an authored opinion article in the *Rocket Forces News* asserts other sweeping contributions:

The development of the Rocket Force's weaponry and equipment, the enhancement of its actual combat capabilities, and its determination and will of being capable and resolved to fight have been shown to the world in a timely way, shaping strategic deterrence to a noticeable extent and *posing strong strategic pressure on the main opponents and potential adversaries, deterring them from infringing upon our nation's core interests, from staging aggression* or even launching a nuclear war against our nation, and thus achieving the purpose of "subduing the enemy without fighting."[31]

Gen. Wang Jiasheng, the political commissar of the PLARF, also emphasized the broad role for nuclear weapons at an annual "symposium on strategic subjects" convened by the PLARF: "The use of strategic power for deterrence is a strategic measure for molding the structure and seizing the initiative."[32] None of the comments from the above passages "support[ing] . . . major power status," "deterring infringement on core interests," or "seizing the initiative" has any clear-cut connection to NFU deterrence. But they are all signs that Chinese military and political leaders are seeking some additional value from their strategic force.

Although we have very little evidence about how the Chinese Navy views its nuclear weapons, one interesting signed commentary published in a recent issue of the *People's Navy Times* addresses the contribution of nuclear weapons in general: "Strategic nuclear weapons not only remain the foundation of deterrence and constraint, they are the ultimate guarantors of the limited nature of war. Tactical nuclear weapons, with their greater hit precision and smaller yield, might be used in actual war, and they would be effective in lowering the cost of war."[33] The author, Li Dapeng, is a senior captain (roughly equivalent to a US one-star admiral) with a technical background, including nuclear engineering. Li's quote ties nuclear forces to "limiting" conflict. So while his first comment could be viewed as limiting conflict to conventional use (by deterring nuclear use), the next sentence is clearly describing the utility of actually *using* tactical nuclear weapons.

Finally, there are some minor pieces of evidence that China might consider using nuclear weapons in a situation in which national (or regime?) survival is called into question. Again, while not surprising in a broad sense, this does go beyond the narrow confines of strict adherence to NFU. While not explicitly saying this, the statement within the Chinese 2019 white paper highlights the broad importance of nuclear weapons for the survival of the nation: "Nuclear capability is the strategic cornerstone to safeguarding national sovereignty and security."[34] Similarly, a recent PLARF article notes: "The Rocket Force's deterring and fighting capability is the [foundation] and the strategic backup for defending our nation's sovereignty security and territorial integrity and guarding our nation's strategic rear from direct strikes."[35] Both of these statements are far broader than statements that merely assert the PLARF force's goal to deter nuclear use (i.e., the narrow goals of NFU). "Threats to sovereignty security" is a much more expansive concept.

Transwar Deterrence, Limiting War, and Warfighting

There is clearly increased Chinese thinking about and discussion of the ways nuclear weapons limit war. At the extreme the change could be entirely consistent with a basic articulation of a modern NFU policy that views nuclear weapons as having only the circumscribed utility to limit wars from "going nuclear." But the contemporary Chinese discussions go further.

China has traditionally displayed a relaxed view of the timeliness of any possible nuclear retaliation.[36] If nuclear weapons are intended only to deter nuclear use against China, there is a logic to this approach. As long as the retaliation is inevitable, there is limited urgency for doing it. However, if there is a need to signal to an adversary its willingness to escalate in the early stages of an escalating nuclear exchange, then speed of nuclear attack is important.

Some signs indicate that China's relaxed view is starting to change and that China is looking for ways to ensure timely retaliation (or attack). At a broad strategic level the changing emphasis on the speed of response is clear: "The Rocket Force acts by the core standards and requirements of 'able to fight at any time, able to launch on time, [and] able to inflict casualties and destruction effectively.'"[37] More narrowly, though, some military newspaper articles describe the Rocket Forces as having an emphasis on rapid response in exercises. For instance, one article boasts about a unit's successes in efficiency: the "transfer time was shortened by two thirds compared to the previous transfer time"; it notes that the unit set "new records for brigade rapid launch in the dark of night."[38] As a result, "the time to get ready for combat has been reduced by four fifths and their quick reaction capability has been improved significantly as well."[39] Another article proclaims improvements in the use of automation to speed preparations for launch.[40] All of this suggests a growing sense that Chinese nuclear forces need to be more responsive and flexible to achieve the country's strategic goals.

Even more interesting is the emerging evidence of Chinese thinking about transwar deterrence that raises a number of questions. For instance, one of the most authoritative (if increasingly outdated) sources, the *Science of Second Artillery Campaigns*, explicitly addresses the subject of controlling nuclear escalation: "During nuclear counterstrike operations, dividing nuclear counterstrike forces between the first strike group, the follow-on strike group, and support group and reserve units is beneficial to utilizing reserve strike forces as an important weight in containing an escalation in nuclear warfare."[41] Reserving a portion of a nuclear arsenal suggests that the actor at least thinks there is a chance of nuclear warfare being controlled and limited.

Other authoritative sources focus on making deliberate choices about the scale of the nuclear response. Fiona Cunningham and M. Taylor Fravel cite one textbook published by the PLA on strategy: "It is necessary to . . . control the scope of the nuclear counterattack, do not conduct equivalent nuclear strikes to an adversary, do not let oneself be led by the nose by an adversary, but play to one's strengths."[42] Sun Xiangli, an analyst at the Center for Strategic Studies within the Chinese Academy of Engineering Physics, wrote a comprehensive book on China's nuclear thinking in 2014. It included substantial discussion about the differences between limited nuclear deterrence and warfighting as well as a broader discussion regarding escalation control.[43]

Similar views pervade a recent PLARF newspaper article's statements about the nature of nuclear affairs in general, and make a broad point: "Nuclear weapons . . . play an important role in stopping large-scale aggression, stalling war escalation, and preventing the outbreak of full-scale nuclear warfare." And far more detailed statements make clear that this thinking applies to Chinese forces: "The development of the Rocket Force's weaponry . . . posing strong strategic pressure on the main opponents and potential adversaries, *deterring them from infringing upon our nation's core interests, from staging aggression* or even launching a nuclear war against our nation, and thus achieving the purpose of 'subduing the enemy without fighting.'"[44] The same source describes the PLARF as "the strategic backup for defending our nation's sovereignty, security, and territorial integrity; and guarding our nation's strategic rears from direct strikes; and is also an important means and a supportive force for advancing our efforts to drive cooperation-based security, to cope with international crises and conflicts, to establish relatively stable relations with other great powers, to shape a favorable strategic posture, and to safeguard a peaceful and stable security environment."[45] Other sources also discuss the way that nuclear forces aid in managing escalation within a nuclear war. Thus, in a published interview one political commissar of a PLARF strategic nuclear brigade said, "It is our mission to maintain nuclear deterrence, deliver nuclear counterattack, prevent escalation of war, and instill shock and awe against our strong enemy."[46]

Another aspect of China's force development is the increasing accuracy of Chinese ballistic (and cruise) missiles. Chinese media reports on the PLARF strategic forces also note this trend: "At the turn of the century, among China's strategic missile units, a new elite force was quietly founded to carry out the special mission of 'delivering precision strikes on high-valued targets.'"[47] This raises additional questions about the potential for missile technology to contribute to some degree of warfighting in a nuclear conflict. Accuracy is not needed to hold the adversary's cities at risk; it is, however, important to be able to either reduce the other side's nuclear forces (particularly fixed silo-based missiles) or attack key logistics nodes vital to supplying conventional forces.

Thus, as China starts to discuss the need for (and incorporate) accuracy into its strategic force, these sorts of doctrinal changes may be on the horizon.

Finally, the shift in the organizational structure of the PLA has worrisome implications for the issue of nuclear use during conventional conflict. (See the earlier discussion here, as well as Bates Gill's chapter elsewhere in this volume.) It is clear that the move toward joint force integration in the TCs is a major undertaking. Yet there remain serious questions about the nature of the changes that are entailed. In Track 2 engagements Chinese interlocutors emphasize that the nuclear elements of the Rocket Forces remain in the direct control of the central leadership (through the body of the Central Military Commission). Further exhaustive studies of the reforms in the West suggest that it appears the Rocket Forces remain at least slightly outside this discussion about increased emphasis on integrated services: "It is clear that the Rocket Force is emphasizing efforts to enhance coordination with the theater commands and other services and is undertaking steps to deepen that coordination. . . . It is not yet clear how far the PLA will integrate Rocket Force units into the joint operations command and control over the theater commands or why that integration has proceeded more slowly than the integration of units from the other services."[48] Nevertheless, there are at least some signs that that integration is continuing. For instance, one article that repeatedly focused on strategic systems also included a discussion of exactly such integration: "The [PLARF] base has been connected into the Theater Command's joint operations command information system" and "We [PLARF] forces shall take part in multiple joint exercises conducted by the Theater Command."[49]

LOOKING TO THE FUTURE

Unfortunately, changes in Chinese thinking on the role and posture of their nuclear forces are likely to evolve. Such changes are likely to both exacerbate emerging Sino-US security dilemmas and greatly complicate the strategic environment in East Asia. China is facing strategic imperatives and internal politics that will almost certainly impel a further evolution in China's approach. As noted above, China has found ways for change at the margin of its approach to nuclear affairs already. This should be expected to continue.

Externally China faces an increasingly complex strategic environment. Paramount among these challenges is the nuclear proliferation taking place in Asia. India's arsenal is growing and its adherence to its own NFU has been called into question.[50] North Korea has now achieved a degree of acceptance as an established nuclear power.[51] While relations with Russia are currently stable, China is well aware of the innovation in Russia's nuclear arsenal.[52] China's concerns about the shifts in the US nuclear posture only add to the unsettled environment. The world has not previously faced a situation of multipolar nuclear competition.[53] China will be substantially pressured by it.

Beyond mere nuclear affairs, the new diversity in strategically relevant systems in Asia will also put pressure on China's approach to nuclear weapons (see the discussion in the chapter by Phillip Saunders and David Logan for some results in this area). Proliferating missile defense systems throughout Asia have only increased the challenges for China's conventional missile capabilities (central to A2/AD strategies) but also to its ability to ensure even a reliable second strike against India or to hold at risk key US allies in a war that threatened to cross the nuclear threshold. Missile defense systems aimed to protect the continental United States would certainly be used in any Sino-US conflict, and so must also be taken into consideration by Chinese planners.[54] The integration of new technologies such as cyber and space systems only complicates the situation further. This, too, will push the Chinese to think about how to develop their nuclear capabilities. Finally, the United States' withdrawal from the treaty on intermediate-range nuclear forces (INF) will almost certainly lead to the stationing of additional US conventional missiles in the region. Even if this is the full extent of the change for the US posture, it will complicate the strategic environment in many cases.[55] If the United States goes further and also deploys nuclear forces with INF systems, the potential for further competition would be increased dramatically.

Domestic imperatives are also likely to serve as a further impetus for development of strategic thought. It is clear that a wide variety of domestic imperatives have shaped Chinese approaches to nuclear weapons in the past. Elsewhere I have argued that long-term trends in China's governing system "open the door to relatively greater influence by bureaucratic actors in nuclear decision-making than was the case under the first two generations of Chinese leadership."[56] It is clear from recent research that the career paths of Chinese PLARF officers cross between the nuclear and conventional sides of the force. This will provide an additional bureaucratic source of doctrinal innovation.[57]

China's doctrinal change to date has been modest. Among the many global and regional sources of strategic instability, Beijing's contribution is modest. Nevertheless, it is both apparent and likely to worsen. Given the scale of China's power, any change has major international implications. There is little ground for optimism about the future.

NOTES

The author recognizes the Naval Research Program at the Naval Postgraduate School for its support for this research. Notwithstanding this support, this chapter represents the author's views and not those of the US Department of Defense nor any other government entity.

1. Regarding the nuclear escalatory potential, see Caitlin Talmadge, "Would China Go Nuclear?: Assessing the Risk of Chinese Nuclear Escalation in a Conventional War with the United States," *International Security* 41, no. 4 (May 2017): 50–92. Regarding the role of deterring the United States in this context, see M. Taylor Fravel and Christopher P. Twomey, "Projecting Strategy: The Myth of Chinese Counter-Intervention," *Washington Quarterly* 37, no. 4 (January 2015): 171–87.

2. Several categories of Chinese publications are useful when researching China's nuclear program. Official documents from the Ministry of National Defense (MND) such as the regular defense white paper generally include a few paragraphs on nuclear issues. Similarly, official spokespersons at the MND and the Ministry of Foreign Affairs occasionally provide comments. But other publications are far more informative. Military manuals published by the Academy of Military Science or the PLA Rocket Force Command College can be valuable as they are used to teach the Chinese military. Inferring some elements of policy from those is likely to be a fairly accurate undertaking. Military newspapers such as the *PLA Daily* or the *Rocket Forces Daily* can supplement this information. Though sometimes they are used as vehicles for strategic deception, much of their focus is on promoting the Chinese military's capabilities to a Chinese audience. Again, these can be a useful source from which to make cautious inference. Materials that have been declassified and released by the US Department of Defense and other members of the intelligence community can be used to cross-check these contents in some cases. For more on this issue of "authoritative sources" see commentary from Alice Miller (who had a career watching China for the Central Intelligence Agency) in Michael Swaine, "Chinese Leadership and Elite Responses to the U.S. Pacific Pivot," *China Leadership Monitor* 38, no. 5 (Summer 2012): note 2.

3. Christopher P. Twomey, *The Military Lens: Doctrinal Differences and Deterrence Failure in Sino-American Relations* (Ithaca, NY: Cornell University Press, 2010).

4. This is not to overstate the point. Even relatively early in China's possession of nuclear weapons during the Cold War, Beijing practiced nuclear diplomacy. See John Wilson Lewis and Xue Litai, *China Builds the Bomb* (Palo Alto, CA: Stanford University Press, 1988); Lyle J. Goldstein, "Do Nascent WMD Arsenals Deter?: The Sino-Soviet Crisis of 1969," *Political Science Quarterly* 118, no. 1 (2003): 53–80, https://doi.org/10.2307/30035822; and Michael S. Gerson, *The Sino-Soviet Border Conflict: Deterrence, Escalation, and the Threat of Nuclear War in 1969* (Alexandria, VA: Center for Naval Analyses, 2010).

5. Roger Dingman, "Atomic Diplomacy during the Korean War," *International Security* 13, no. 3 (Winter 1988/89): 43; and Mark A. Ryan, *Chinese Attitudes toward Nuclear Weapons: China and the United States during the Korean War* (Armonk, NY: M. E. Sharpe, 1989).

6. Dingman, "Atomic Diplomacy"; Ryan, *Chinese Attitudes*; and Twomey, *Military Lens*.

7. Goldstein, "Do Nascent WMD Arsenals Deter?"

8. Although the details of most nations' permissive action links are highly classified, no credible public information that China has recently gained these exists. But there would be no reason to hide it; indeed, there would be grounds for China to publicly note this if it were true (as it has in media reports of other aspects of its force) to reassure other nations of China's identity as a responsible nuclear power.

9. Although I am not a proponent of the "strategic culture" argument, the "organizational culture" existing within many militaries is a particularly strong vehicle for

furthering such predispositions. In this case the PLA views on avoiding coercion are strong and continue to endure. See Christopher P. Twomey, "Lacunae in the Study of Culture in International Security," *Contemporary Security Policy*, no. 2 (2008): 338–57; and Twomey, *Military Lens*.

10. Chen Jian, *Mao's China and the Cold War* (Chapel Hill, NC: University of North Carolina Press, 2001).

11. Lewis and Xue, *China Builds the Bomb*.

12. Michael Green et al., *Countering Coercion in Maritime Asia: The Theory and Practice of Gray Zone Deterrence* (Lanham, MD: Rowman & Littlefield, 2017); Van Jackson, "Tactics of Strategic Competition: Gray Zones, Redlines, and Conflicts before War," *Naval War College Review* 70, no. 3 (Summer 2017): 39–61.

13. Wayne P. Hughes and Robert Girrier, *Fleet Tactics and Naval Operations* (Annapolis, MD: Naval Institute Press, 2018).

14. Christopher P. Twomey, "The People's Liberation Army's Selective Learning: Lessons of the Iran-Iraq 'War of the Cities' Missile Duels and Uses of Missiles in Other Conflicts," in *Chinese Lessons from Other Peoples' Wars*, ed. Andrew Scobell, David Lai, and Roy Kamphausen, 115–52 (Carlisle, PA: Strategic Studies Institute, 2011).

15. Lt. Gen. Zhao Xijun, *She zhan: daodan weishe zongheng tan* (Coercive warfare: A comprehensive discussion on missile deterrence) (Beijing: NDU Press, 2003).

16. Not counting missile defense capabilities, of course. Such forces are likely to face saturation attacks (as well as cyber and special operations attacks) and be overwhelmed. On the broader issue, see Thomas C. Schelling, *The Strategy of Conflict* (Cambridge, MA: Harvard University Press, 1960).

17. M. Taylor Fravel, "Shifts in Warfare and Party Unity: Explaining China's Changes in Military Strategy," *International Security* 42, no. 3 (January 2018): 37–83.

18. The Chinese phrase *xinxihua* is not as cumbersome as its English translation, "informationalized."

19. See Fravel, "Shifts in Warfare," for a detailed discussion of this evolution.

20. On both these points, see, for instance, Cai Ruijin, Yang Yonggang, and Wang Weidong, "Rainbow-Like Trajectories Traced in the Vast Sky: Rocket Force Solidly Grasps the Building of Strategic Capabilities," *PLA Daily (Jiefangjun bao)*, January 13, 2019, translated by Open Source Center.

21. See the reference to the October 4, 2010, Academy of Military Science journal, *China's Military Science (Zhongguo junshi kexue)*, in Cortez Cooper III, "PLA Military Modernization: Drivers, Force Restructuring, and Implications," testimony presented before the US-China Economic and Security Review Commission, February 15, 2018.

22. For a discussion on these and related Chinese concerns, see Dennis Blasko, "The Chinese Military Speaks to Itself, Revealing Doubts," War on the Rocks website, February 18, 2019, https://warontherocks.com/2019/02/the-chinese-military -speaks-to-itself-revealing-doubts/.

23. Yu Qifeng, "Pojie 'wu ge bu hui' nanti yao cong yuantou rushou" (Comprehensively address the 'five cannot do' problem), *Jiefangjun bao*, October 13, 2015.

24. "Xuexi Xi Jinping zong shuji guanyu qiang jun mubiao de zhongyao lunshu" (Studying General Secretary Xi Jinping's important discussion on aiming to strengthen the army), *Guangming ribao*, July 22, 2013.

25. Kevin McCauley, "China's Western Theater Command," *China Brief* 17, no. 1 (January 13, 2017); and author's conversations with PLA officers in 2018.

26. See, for instance, annual reports for "U.S.-China Strategic Dialogue," a Track II meeting on strategic nuclear affairs attended by US and Chinese military officers, government officials, scholars, and think tank analysts, funded by the US DoD's Defense Threat Reduction Agency; specifically note Christopher Twomey, Michael Glosny, and Diana Wueger, "U.S.-China Strategic Dialogue," Phase XI, *PASCC Report 2018-001*, December 2016.

27. State Council Information Office of the People's Republic of China, "China's National Defense in the New Era," July 2019, 9.

28. John J. Mearsheimer, *The Tragedy of Great Power Politics* (New York: W. W. Norton, 2001).

29. "Track 1.5" are meetings attended by both scholars/analysts and current sitting government and military officials. Track 1 refers to official diplomatic or military-to-military exchanges; Track 2 traditionally refers to exchanges attended by scholars/analysts and retired government officials.

30. "Solidly Improve Our Strategic Capabilities—Earnestly Study and Implement the Important Speech Given by Chairman Xi Jinping During His Inspection of the Headquarters of the PLA Rocket Force," *Liberation Army Daily (Jiefangjun bao)*, September 27, 2016, 1, translated by Open Source Center.

31. Wan Huilan and Lu Xuejuan, "Firmly Bear in Mind the Sacred Missions, Forge the Nation's Potent Force," *Rocket Forces Newspaper (Huojianbing bao)*, September 23, 2017, translated by Open Source Center (italics added).

32. Zhang Changwei, He Tianjin, and Ge Song, "The Rocket Force Convenes the Fourth Changying Forum in Beijing, Deeply Studying the Issue of Building the Rocket Force's Strategic Deterrence and Actual Fighting," *Rocket Forces Newspaper (Huojianbing bao)*, September 26, 2017, translated by Open Source Center. General Wang is a full general and the second ranking official within the PLARF.

33. Sr. Capt. Li Dapeng, "What Will Future War Be Like?," *People's Navy Times*, July 3, 2017.

34. State Council Information Office, "China's National Defense," 13.

35. Wan and Lu, "Firmly Bear in Mind."

36. See, for instance, the discussion of food stores kept in PLARF tunnels, in CCTV–Xinwen *Live News*, July 21, 2017, transcribed by Open Source Center (ID 4542/3B2T7).

37. A similar emphasis on timely response is found in Cai, Yang, and Wang, "Rainbow-Like Trajectories."

38. Zhang Qiang and Song Wei, "The Nuclear Missile Section of the Parade: An Array of 'Trump Card' National Treasures," *Science and Technology Newspaper Online*, August 9, 2017, translated by Open Source Center from *Keji ribao*.

39. Transcript of CCTV–Xinwen *Live News* (Profile of Intercontinental Strategic Missile Brigade of Chinese Rocket Force), July 21, 2017.

40. Wang Qin, Wang Weidong, and Cai Ruijin, "Busy Engaging in Scientific Research and Problem Solving, Actively Accelerating Strong Army Pace," *PLA Daily (Jiefangjun bao)*, October 15, 2017, translated by Open Source Center.

41. Yu Jixun and Li Tilin, *Di erpao huobing zhanyixue* (Science of Second Artillery campaigns) (Beijing: *Jiefangjun chubanshi*, 2004), 145. Fiona Cunningham and M. Taylor Fravel interpret this passage slightly differently in their excellent work "Dangerous Confidence?: Chinese Views of Nuclear Escalation," *International Security* 44, no. 2 (Fall 2019): 61–109.

42. Zhou Xinsheng, ed., *Junzhong zhanlue jiaocheng* (Study guide to military service strategy) (Beijing: Junshi kexueyuan chubanshe, 2013), 206, as quoted in Cunningham and Fravel, "Dangerous Confidence?," 86.

43. Sun Xiangli, *Heshidai de zhalue xuanze: Zhongguo hezhanlue wenti yanjiu* (Strategic choices in the nuclear age: Research on China's nuclear strategic issues) (Beijing: Chinese Academy of Engineering Physics Research Center, 2013), chaps. 5 and 3, respectively.

44. Wan and Lu, "Firmly Bear in Mind." Italics added to highlight non-NFU like elements.

45. Wan and Lu, "Firmly Bear in Mind." Most elements in this quote would seem to go beyond NFU/deterrent roles.

46. CCTV–Xinwen *Live News*, July 21, 2017.

47. Li Bingfeng, Fan Yongqiang, and Song Haijun, "Cruise Missiles Manifest Power—Profile of a New-Type Missile Brigade of the Rocket Force Being Reviewed in the Military Parade," *Xinhua Newswire Online (Xinhua Wang)*, August 4, 2017, translated by Open Source Center.

48. David C. Logan, "Making Sense of China's Missile Forces," in *Chairman Xi Remakes the PLA: Assessing Chinese Military Reforms*, ed. Phillip C. Saunders et al., 393–436 (Washington, DC: National Defense University Press, 2019), 415.

49. Wang Weidong and Song Haijun, "Concentrate on Sword Sharpening, Toughen the Strategic Iron Fist," *Liberation Army Daily (Jiefangjun bao)*, February 6, 2018, translated by Open Source Center.

50. Christopher Clary and Vipin Narang, "India's Counterforce Temptations: Strategic Dilemmas, Doctrine, and Capabilities," *International Security* 43, no. 3 (February 2019): 7–52.

51. Even if North Korea's capabilities do not threaten China in the short term, the change increases the role of nuclear weapons in regional affairs.

52. It is striking that these developments were discussed explicitly in China's most recent defense white paper, "China's National Defense in the New Era" (2019).

53. Aaron L. Friedberg et al., "North Korea and Asia's Evolving Nuclear Landscape: Challenges to Regional Stability," *NBR Special Report* 67 (Seattle: National Bureau of Asian Research, 2017).

54. The United States has made explicit its intention to use its capabilities in such a contingency in the latest US Department of Defense's *Nuclear Posture Review* (Washington, DC: Office of the Secretary of Defense, 2018).

55. The change would be modest if the United States focused on anti-ship missiles of INF ranges only.

56. Eric Heginbotham, Jacob L. Heim, and Christopher P. Twomey, "Of Bombs and Bureaucrats: Internal Drivers of Nuclear Force Building in China and the United States," *Journal of Contemporary China* 28, no. 118 (July 2019): 538–57.

57. David C. Logan, "Career Paths in the PLA Rocket Force: What They Tell Us," *Asian Security* 15, no. 2 (May 2019): 103–21.

FOUR

Strategic Stability and the Impact of China's Modernizing Strategic Strike Forces

Sugio Takahashi

The rise of China has been a vibrant topic of contemporary strategic studies, with particular attention being paid to China's "gray zone" security challenges, peacetime challenges to change the status quo without kinetic utilization of military forces, and conventional anti-access area denial (A2/AD) threats.[1] China's modernization of its nuclear forces, with the goal of achieving an invulnerable second-strike capability, has also been an important issue. However, China's nuclear modernization and the resulting changes to strategic stability between the United States and China tend to be discussed separately from conventional and gray zone challenges. This is unfortunate. The nuclear component of a country's strategic strike capability should not be treated as a distinct topic because it casts a "nuclear shadow" over regional strategic issues, affecting the strategic calculations of regional states that face conventional military and paramilitary pressure on potential flashpoints. While the trans-Pacific strategic community has primarily paid attention to Beijing's efforts to develop an invulnerable second-strike capability China's emerging nuclear force that includes nuclear counterforce capabilities and theater nuclear forces that should not be overlooked. It is time to start treating China's nuclear and conventional strategic components in a holistic way. The interaction among the conventional and nuclear components of Chinese and US forces will have serious strategic implications on regional crisis stability and escalation control.

The United States and its allies in the Asia-Pacific have long enjoyed conventional superiority over potential adversaries. This was true even during the Cold War era, in contrast to the European theater. In the Asia-Pacific maritime environment, air and naval forces are key assets shaping the strategic balance and the air and naval balance in this region until now has greatly favored the United States and its allies.

However, due to China's development of a conventional A2/AD capability, the United States and its allies can no longer take conventional superiority for granted. China's success at combining A2/AD threats with modernized theater and strategic nuclear forces may have changed the strategic game in the region. This chapter analyzes the implications of China's emerging nuclear capability, beginning with two clarifications to the concept of strategic stability.

First, "strategic stability" must be understood as operating at two levels: the strategic nuclear level and the regional level. Traditionally strategic stability has been discussed in the context of the strategic interaction of US and Soviet nuclear arsenals; only later, since the end of the Cold War, has it been applied to the relationship between the United States and China. But when the concept of strategic stability is applied to the relationship between the United States and China, strategic stability at the regional level (as distinct from strategic nuclear forces) should be considered, for two reasons. First, considering the maritime geographic characteristics of East Asia, regional-level conflict might start without a ground invasion. In a sense the difference between the strategic nuclear level and the regional level is only weapon range and the invulnerability of a second-strike capability would be an important variable feeding into crisis stability at the regional level. Second, stability at the strategic nuclear level may cause a "stability-instability paradox." But if strategic stability can be formulated at the regional level, the stability-instability paradox can be mitigated; the paradox would be intensified if strategic stability at the regional level is fragile. Thus strategic stability at the strategic nuclear level and regional level can affect each other. Setting regional strategic stability as an analytical concept deepens observers' understanding of regional strategic dynamics.

A second concept to be discussed is "escalation stability," a subcategory of strategic stability that extends crisis stability to an escalated situation. Traditionally strategic stability includes three subcategories: crisis stability, arms race stability, and first-strike stability (though first-strike stability is often considered a variation of crisis stability).[2] "Crisis stability" refers to strategic stability at a crisis moment, while first-strike stability refers to a nuclear first strike when conflict breaks out. Escalation stability is intended to shed light on intrawar deterrence by extending the essence of crisis stability beyond a crisis (preconflict) situation, and first-strike stability to situations other than nuclear first strike.

Using the framework of these two conceptual developments, this chapter analyzes the strategic implications of China's emerging nuclear capability in addition to its invulnerable second-strike capability. China's emerging precision intercontinental ballistic missiles (ICBMs) combined with multiple independent reentry vehicles (MIRVs) creates a counterforce option for Beijing, while its dual-capable modernized theater ballistic missile force reinforces the current favorable balance in regional strike by neutralizing the American low-yield nuclear option. But because the trans-Pacific strategic community has focused only on China's invulnerable second-strike capability, the strategic implications of these capabilities have been overlooked. This chapter will conduct a thought experiment to discover the impact of these emerging capabilities.

CHINA'S EMERGING NUCLEAR CAPABILITY

With the end of the Cold War and the rise of China, China has been considered a strategic focus point. China is a legitimate nuclear weapon state, and one big variable in the strategic equation for the United States and its allies is its nuclear force. At the same time, unlike the Soviet Union, China has not rushed to expand its nuclear arsenal and has seemingly focused on developing a minimum deterrence/retaliation posture. For a long time, outside observers of Chinese military affairs have paid attention to China's effort to develop robust invulnerable second-strike forces, and how to formulate "strategic stability" between the United States and China has been a significant agenda for the trans-Pacific strategic community.

In the near future, however, a different agenda will emerge. In addition to invulnerable second-strike capabilities, China's investment in modernization of its nuclear arsenal is going to produce a counterforce capability, given its precision strike potential. This emerging counterforce capability of China will have significant implications on the strategic environment in the Asia-Pacific.

The Development of China's Nuclear Force and Strategy

Since the 1960s, when China tested its first atomic bomb and began to develop its nuclear force, China's nuclear strategy has been characterized by minimum deterrence and its self-declared no first use (NFU) policy. M. Taylor Fravel and Evan Medeiros point out that China's nuclear strategic doctrine was underdeveloped in the early days of the nuclear force's existence because of China's Cultural Revolution and its engineer-led nuclear force development.[3] With the gradual quantitative growth in nuclear warheads, Alastair Ian Johnston suggests, China's nuclear strategy would transform from minimum deterrence to limited deterrence and the embrace of a limited nuclear option.[4] However, China's effort to develop its nuclear force has been moderate, at least in terms of quantity, compared to its efforts to modernize and expand conventional A2/AD capabilities that include ballistic missiles and maritime forces.

Section 1202 of the US National Defense Authorization Act of 2000 requires the secretary of defense to make an annual report to Congress assessing the current and future military power of China, taking into consideration advances in the country's military technologies. Since then the Department of Defense's annual assessments have provided important clues for open source analysis of China's military forces. The first report, published in 2002, stated that China's strategic deterrent consisted of 20 DF-5 ICBMs, which were replaced by DF-5As (with an extended range) as well as around 10 of the shorter-range DF-4s (silo-based liquid fuel missiles).[5] The 2005 version of the report noted that China had 10 to 14 silos for the DF-4 and 20 to 24 missiles, with about 20 missiles and silos for the DF-5. These quantitative estimates were carried forward into the 2006 and 2007 assessments. The 2010 edition of the report carried a new estimate that about 30 DF-31 and DF-31A (an extended-range version of the DF-31) road-mobile solid fuel ICBMs were deployed, in addition to 20 DF-5s and DF-4s each. In the 2011 edition the way of expressing such quantities changed: it gave totals slightly below previous estimates and the projected total of 55 to 60 DF-4s, DF-5s, DF–31s, and DF-31As combined. The 2012 edition of the report showed figures slightly higher than the previous year's estimate, reaching 50 to 75 total.

In the 2015 edition of the Department of Defense (DoD) report, the DF-4, DF-5A, DF-31, and DF-31A estimates were revised somewhat downward, to a total of 50 to 60. The 2015 estimates included the DF-5B, which is regarded as a MIRV with three warheads. In the 2016 edition observers will find a significant upward revision of the number of missiles, nearly double the estimate of the previous year: it assumes that the total DF-4, DF-5A, MIRV DF-5B, DF-31, and DF-31A missiles had reached 75 to 100. This estimate is carried forward to the 2018 edition, but the 2019 edition indicates a more specific number of 90 total.[6]

As these estimates demonstrate, China's efforts at nuclear missile expansion are restrained, considering its rapid economic growth and abundant resource availability that enable Beijing to mobilize more resources for its nuclear forces. And in contrast to Johnston's previously noted prediction in the early 1990s, the shift to a limited nuclear option—which implies a shift from minimum deterrence to a nuclear utilization orientation—has not been observed, at least in declaratory policies or observed force structures. Medeiros and Fravel argue that the main focus of China's nuclear force continues to be retaliation but entails more than "minimum deterrence," calling China's current nuclear deterrence strategy "minimum retaliation." Considering its relatively moderate quantity, much smaller than US and Russian arsenals, adding "minimum" as a prefix to "retaliation" or "deterrence" is a reasonable way to describe China's nuclear strategy. As a result, debate on the strategic implications of China's growing capability has focused on China's invulnerable second-strike capability and strategic stability between the United States and China.

Strategic Stability between the United States and China

In its nuclear modernization China has prioritized the construction of an invulnerable second-strike capability through the development of road-mobile ICBMs and submarine-launched ballistic missiles (SLBMs). With deployment of these delivery means, potential adversaries will not have a viable first-strike option. In terms of strategic stability, dealing with China's second-strike capability or, more specifically, whether the United States should accept mutual vulnerability with China, became an important agenda item for the American nuclear strategy community in the 2000s.

Mutual vulnerability is a key concept for crisis stability. No party would have a *first*-strike incentive if all parties are vulnerable to a rival's *second* strike. To hold other parties at risk all parties must have an invulnerable second-strike capability. If country A's strategic strike capability is vulnerable to a first strike, country B might have an incentive to launch a first strike to disarm country A. But if country A's strategic strike capability is invulnerable to country B's first strike, country A can retaliate after country B's strike, eliminating the first-strike advantage for country B. This is a classic example of crisis stability based on mutual vulnerability.

Some have argued that because China has a degree of nuclear retaliation capability against the United States, and the United States cannot realistically hope to develop damage-limitation capabilities to neutralize a Chinese second strike, the United States should therefore recognize mutual vulnerability with China as "a fact of life."[7] On the other hand, some note that retaliation-based deterrence has often failed and the development of damage-limitation capabilities through missile defense is important. Others point out that because of the growth of capabilities to detect and track mobile targets, counterforce strikes against road-mobile missiles could appear in the near future.[8]

In parallel with debates in the United States, the Japanese strategic community has discussed this same issue. Since the way in which the United States treats China's invulnerable second-strike capability has serious implications for the credibility of extended deterrence, Japan also has a stake in how this issue is addressed. Regarding the question of whether the United States should accept mutual vulnerability with China, Japanese analysts are somewhat skeptical. Attention in Japan has been particularly directed to the "stability-instability paradox" and there was concern that US acceptance of mutual vulnerability will only intensify this paradox. The stability-instability paradox applies to a situation in which mutual deterrence at the strategic level paradoxically enables a challenger's aggressive behavior at the regional level because the challenger perceives that its counterpart will refrain from responding to avoid escalation.[9] Japanese concern over this paradox can be summarized this way: if the United

States explicitly accepts mutual vulnerability with China, Beijing may take even bolder moves and risk escalation from gray zones to conventional conflicts, based on its assessment that the United States will want to avoid a showdown at the strategic nuclear level due to mutual vulnerability. In this way, crisis stability based on mutual vulnerability at the strategic level could cause instability at the theater level in the Asia-Pacific.[10]

In addition to the stability-instability paradox, the relevance of mutual vulnerability has also been discussed in Japan. This argument emphasizes that China's vulnerability to American nuclear-strike capability and America's vulnerability to China's second-strike capability are asymmetrical and should not be treated on an equal footing.[11] China's second-strike capability is basically only a countervalue capability; it lacks counterforce alternatives and thus the options for China in the event of a nuclear exchange are limited (such as how many American cities should it destroy). On the other hand, even in that scenario the United States would retain a wide range of options, including massive conventional strikes against mainland China, limited and selected nuclear strikes against military targets, limited and selected nuclear countervalue strikes, and an all-out nuclear strike. From the perspective of escalation control, such a significant gap in the effects of nuclear forces would provide advantages for the United States. In other words, the strategic effect of vulnerability is different for each side. Even after China's acquisition of an invulnerable second-strike capability, its capabilities are limited to countervalue options only. Thus China could only make US cities vulnerable. But countervalue strike is the last option for China in an actual contingency because it will trigger all-out nuclear retaliation from the United States. On the other hand, the United States makes not only China's cities but also military facilities vulnerable. Therefore, the United States can retain some options which should be expected not to invite China's full countervalue strikes, such as limited strikes against selected military targets limiting collateral damage, with casting a shadow of a massive nuclear strike. Considering such asymmetrical vulnerability, official American acceptance of mutual vulnerability implies placing both countries' nuclear-strike capabilities on an equal footing and abandoning the American advantage of flexibility of target selection. Thus the Japanese strategic community has shown a negative attitude toward the debate on mutual vulnerability.

In addition, Japan's strategists contemplate arms race stability as well.[12] They emphasize that China's lack of transparency regarding its nuclear arsenal makes the foundation of arms race stability highly fragile. Due to the lack of credible, authoritative sources on nuclear doctrine and force structure, the other countries have incentive to increase their nuclear arsenals.

The US government demonstrated its position on mutual vulnerability through the 2010 Ballistic Missile Defense Review (BMDR) and Nuclear Posture

Review (NPR). The 2010 BMDR concludes that the ballistic missile defense (BMD) system for the US homeland deals only with a limited number of ICBMs (which North Korea and Iran could potentially deploy in the future) and does not address the ICBM threat posed by China's nuclear capabilities. On the other hand, the BMDR indicates that the United States intends to expand the deployment of theater-level BMD. Following the BMDR, the 2010 NPR mentions strategic stability in the context of Russia and China. However, there are differences in the descriptions of the concept of strategic stability between the United States and Russia and between the United States and China, and the specific implications of each are not the same. Regarding the US-Russia relationship, the NPR refers to mutual vulnerability as the basic concept of strategic stability during the Cold War. However, in the case of the US-Chinese relationship, the report mentions strategic stability in the context of dialogue and transparency but lacks nuance indicating mutual vulnerability. This language suggests that the United States is going to seek strategic stability with China by emphasizing arms race stability, where the incentives for an arms race are reduced by improving transparency. In short, the Obama administration's position on this issue was that of not seeking to physically negate mutual vulnerability as a fact while at the same time not publicly recognizing mutual vulnerability. In other words, the 2010 NPR manifested the US position on mutual vulnerability as "neither confirms nor denies." In the same vein, the 2018 NPR released by the Trump administration does not accept mutual vulnerability.[13]

Strategic Implications of China's Emerging Capabilities

The debate about US-Chinese mutual vulnerability sheds light on the strategic implications of China's invulnerable second-strike capability. However, paying attention to its invulnerable second-strike capability does not address all of the strategic implications of China's nuclear force modernization. Exclusive focus on a second-strike capability misses two important aspects of China's nuclear force.

The first missing piece in the debate is China's ongoing development of precision MIRV ICBMs. As the DoD reports suggest, the size of China's strategic nuclear force has been gradually increasing. The latest estimates suggest the number of ICBMs is around 90, with a shift from traditional silo-based missiles to road-mobile missiles. In addition to this change to a mobile deployment mode, the other important points are the development of MIRVs and the potential improvement in accuracy. Regarding MIRVs, China is believed to be developing the DF-41 solid-fuel and road-mobile ICBM with rail-mobile and silo-based modes, a missile that is estimated to be capable of mounting 10 warheads. This is the same number of warheads as the Cold War Soviet SS-18 and the American Peacekeeper. If the DF-41 is deployed, the number of projectable warheads available to China will increase significantly. Considering the accuracy of China's recently deployed conventional theater ballistic missiles, the next generation of ICBMs like the DF-41 can leap ahead of previous generations in accuracy, although the actual circular error probable (CEP) is unknown.

Traditionally debates in both the United States and Japan about China's strategic nuclear force have proceeded based on an assumption of modest size and inaccurate warheads. With limited numbers China's ICBMs cannot inflict significant damage on the US ground-based nuclear force; with limited accuracy its ICBMs cannot hold US ICBM silos at risk. Previously their only possible option has been attacks against US cities. In other words, the debates over this issue have focused on China's second-strike capability against US population centers.

However, if China succeeds in deploying highly accurate MIRVed DF-41 missiles it will have a degree of counterforce capability against the United States (and Russia) in addition to its current countervalue minimum retaliation capability. For example, based on the New START Treaty, the United States deploys 400 active-duty silos for the single-warhead Minuteman III. If China plans a counterforce strike against US ICBMs, that means four hundred targets. Allocating 2 warheads against 1 silo, China needs to deploy 80 DF-41s with 10 fully loaded warheads. While China's warhead production capability is totally unknown, being able to deploy 80 DF-41s is not an unrealistic goal considering China's vast recent defense expenditures. The US strategic nuclear deterrent includes nuclear-capable strategic bombers, but they are stationed at only three bases and would not significantly increase the number of targets for China. If China succeeds in its development of the DF-41, it is possible for it to gain a counterforce strike capability against US ground-based strategic nuclear forces by deploying about 80-plus DF-41s.

This is similar to the "window of vulnerability" problem that was discussed in the late 1970s and 1980s.[14] At that time, US analysts feared the Soviet SS-18 was capable of destroying the majority of US Minuteman III silos in a first strike. In such a scenario, and given the Polaris SLBM's limited accuracy (the lack of a counterforce capability), the only option for the United States would have been to launch SLBM retaliatory strikes against Soviet cities. Because the Soviets would then have launched against American cities, a decision to use SLBMs would have been difficult to make. However, a similar window of vulnerability will not occur for the current US strategic nuclear arsenal. With Trident D5 SLBMs, which are as accurate as ICBMs, even if the Minuteman III forces are eliminated by a nuclear first strike the United States can still retain counterforce options against an adversary. Therefore, while the strategic effects of the DF-41 are similar to those of the SS-18 from the Cold War era, American SLBMs prevent the window of vulnerability problem. But since the DF-41 will create new options for China's decision-makers in the event of a crisis, its strategic implications must be seriously analyzed.

The second often-missing piece in the traditional debate is China's theater nuclear force. China has developed a significant theater ballistic missile force, as opposed to the modest size of its strategic nuclear force. Some of these missiles are estimated to be dual-capable. The DF-26, which was first seen by foreign observers in 2015 at a People's Liberation Army (PLA) military parade, is estimated to have a 4,000-km range and is capable of performing as an anti-ship ballistic missile as well. China declared the DF-26 to be dual-capable, meaning it can launch both conventional and nuclear strikes. In the past, when China's theater ballistic missiles had poor accuracy, nuclear warheads were necessary to achieve certain military effects. However, recent significant improvements in accuracy have made China's ballistic missile force capable of conducting more missions that use conventional warheads, thus creating serious concern in the region.[15]

In terms of expected effects against regional military targets, China no longer necessarily requires theater nuclear forces because its modernized and accurate conventional ballistic and cruise missiles can inflict serious damage to the regional military facilities of the United States and its allies. So why does China retain its theater nuclear force and even deploy new dual-capable missiles? Such a nuclear-capable missile posture suggests that the PLA continues to allocate missions for theater nuclear forces, which has been overlooked by both the United States and Japan.

These two missing pieces, along with China's accurate conventional ballistic missile force, need to be integrated into the strategic calculations of the United States and its allies. Analysts cannot just discuss an invulnerable second strike. The chemistry of these elements should cause a reframing and reevaluation of the strategic balance for China's adversaries. To be sure, the potential counterforce capability of the DF-41 and its theater nuclear strike capability are not consistent with China's traditional strategic doctrine of minimum deterrence and NFU. But with the qualitative and quantitative development of strike capability at both the theater and strategic levels, China may be reviewing its nuclear employment doctrine.

REFRAMING STRATEGIC BALANCE IN EAST ASIA: FINE-TUNING THE CONCEPT OF STRATEGIC STABILITY

The concept of strategic stability is an important product of nuclear deterrence theory that developed during the Cold War and its meaning was heavily affected by that strategic context. If the contemporary strategist wants to apply the concept of strategic stability to the Asia-Pacific of the twenty-first century, the concept must be modified in accordance with current realities. Especially relevant are differences in geography and military posture between twenty-first-century Asia-Pacific and Cold War Europe. Given such differences, the concept of strategic stability must be tuned in two ways: grasping strategic stability in a layered way (i.e., on both a strategic level and a theater level) and creating the notion of "escalation stability."

Emerging Layered Strategic Stability

Strategic stability is an important concept in deterrence theory. It does not imply stable strategic relations among major players. Instead, the meaning is more specific and often includes three subcategories: crisis stability, first-strike stability, and arms race stability.

Crisis stability applies to crisis situations where both countries involved are concerned about escalation to war. Crisis stability is more likely to occur when neither side perceives an advantage in striking first. If force postures, military technology, and geography are not favorable for a first strike, and both sides' militaries are capable of absorbing a first strike without significant reduction in combat power, neither side has an incentive to attack first and crisis management is easier. On the other hand, if a first-strike attacker can gain a clear advantage, both sides will believe that suffering a first strike means defeat and will consider launching a first strike. The incentive to strike first is strong and inevitably makes crisis management difficult.

A situation with a higher degree of crisis stability, first-strike stability is similar to an environment with a minimum "security dilemma." The security dilemma is intensified in an offense-dominant situation, which is determined by military technology, force structure, doctrine, and geography. Here the side that launches the first strike can gain significant advantage and thus both sides have a first-strike incentive.[16] To complicate matters, a mutual nuclear-deterrence situation is considered as a defense-dominant situation because when both sides deploy an invulnerable second-strike capability, neither side has a first-strike incentive.[17] This first-strike stability is a variation of crisis stability. Crisis stability works during a crisis, before war breaks out. First-strike stability exists when neither side feels an incentive to launch a nuclear first strike after a conventional conflict breaks out.[18]

Arms control stability is a concept that expresses relationships in peacetime, meaning a situation where mutual force postures, trends in military technology, and other military-related variables do not intensify an arms race. When sufficiency for national defense is clearly identifiable, arms race stability is more achievable. Invulnerable second-strike capability forms an important component of arms race stability. If both sides deploy an invulnerable second-strike capability, which makes them confident in their deterrence capacity, the incentive for an arms race can be mitigated. This is especially true if such deterrence is based on countervalue capabilities, where force sizing is determined by the number of the other side's countervalue targets (such as cities) rather than the size of the other side's military force. Here force size can be determined independent of the other side's force size and an arms race is unlikely to occur, resulting in a higher degree of arms race stability.

Thus strategic stability can mitigate the possibility of both a first strike and an arms race by tailoring technical elements such as force structure and military technology. It does not depend on improving political relations among stakeholders. In this sense it does not refer to a stable strategic environment in general.

The notion of strategic stability was developed during the Cold War. At that time avoiding a nuclear war, which could have destroyed humanity, was the top priority for the defense intellectual community. Strategic stability was viewed as the means for decreasing the possibility of nuclear war through the tailoring of technical elements, even without political reconciliation between superpowers.

The first front of the Cold War was Europe and it was assumed that conflict there would consist of armored combat on a massive scale. Because the Soviet side enjoyed quantitative conventional superiority, many assumed that the North Atlantic Treaty Association (NATO) would be forced to use nuclear weapons first, resulting in a serious risk of nuclear escalation. Whether the notion of an "escalation ladder" was shared by both the United States and the Soviet Union is unclear, but both sides developed and deployed multiple levels of nuclear weapons: tactical, theater-level, and strategic. Strategic stability, maintained through the terror of invulnerable second-strike capabilities and limiting missile defenses, was expected to lessen the possibility of actual combat in Europe.

Even after the Cold War ended the notion of strategic stability lingered. During the Cold War the sources of confrontation were ideological and strategic competition, and by the end of it these sources of confrontation disappeared. However, the technical elements of strategic stability utilized by the United States and Russia survived, as demonstrated in the debate over US ballistic missile defense at the end of the 1990s and early 2000s.[19] In that debate Russia maintained that the development of an American ballistic missile defense system for the US mainland, then called National Missile Defense, would harm strategic stability.

As observed in the previous section, the notion of strategic stability has been extended to the relations between the United States and China. But the application of a concept like strategic stability, which was developed during the Cold War, to the current world situation requires a rethinking of the concept.

During the Cold War strategic stability was applied only to the strategic nuclear level. In the contemporary environment strategic stability should be analyzed in a layered way, looking at both the strategic and regional levels.

Regional Level Strategic Stability and Escalation Stability

In the contemporary security environment, strategic stability is relevant for the relationship between the United States and Russia and between the United States and China. But strategic stability between the United States and both countries should not be considered at the strategic nuclear level only. Because of the current dynamics of the strategic interaction between China and US allies in the Asia-Pacific, and Russia and US allies in Europe, strategic stability at the regional level should be analyzed as well. The necessity for considering regional-level strategic stability is more evident in the Asia-Pacific, whose geo-strategic characteristics are fundamentally different than Europe's.

As mentioned previously, the notion of strategic stability is a product of the strategic debate regarding Cold War Europe. The strategic condition for NATO was based on inferiority in conventional forces, the need to consider first use of nuclear weapons, and the development of an escalation ladder. Even during the Cold War the Asia-Pacific had different strategic conditions: the United States enjoyed superior conventional air forces and the US Navy maintained control of the sea. Therefore the United States was unlikely to consider using nuclear weapons first and the role of nuclear forces in Asia was mainly to deter first use by the Soviets.[20] As a result, debates about an escalation ladder were not normally applied to Asia.[21] This contrast between Europe and Asia was due also to geographical differences. The European continental environment allowed Soviet ground forces to enjoy superiority and thus be able to apply military pressure. Conversely, in the maritime environment of the Asia-Pacific superior American air and naval forces have long determined the military balance. Because this is no longer true in the current world, the trans-Pacific strategic community needs to develop the notion of layered strategic stability.

In Europe during the Cold War it was presumed that war would entail full-scale armored combat and intrawar deterrence of nuclear conflict would be attempted to minimize the risk of nuclear escalation. Through that process relatively little consideration could be given to civilian collateral damage because it would be difficult to minimize collateral damage by heavy armored units in highly populated areas. Similarly, the targets of air and missile strikes would be determined largely on military considerations only.

But there are no armored divisions at sea. Therefore, in an Asia-Pacific maritime environment, especially after the Cold War, war was presumed to begin with missile strikes, and air and maritime engagements. Ground warfare would only be conducted as the last phase of amphibious warfare, if at all. As a result, war planners would consider the need to minimize civilian collateral damage and the decision about whether missile strikes should be limited to military facilities or expanded to urban areas once war broke out would be very important. Considering strategic stability at the regional level merits deeper analysis because a first-strike incentive would be an important element in determining the timing and targets of missile strikes. In this context crisis stability would be more important than arms race stability.

The geostrategic characteristics of the contemporary Asia-Pacific region result in a different kind of escalation ladder. In Cold War Europe the rungs of the escalation ladder went from conventional forces to tactical, theater, and strategic nuclear forces. In the current Asia-Pacific environment the escalation ladder can be formulated as potential sets of missile strike targets, from military facilities, to military facilities near/in cities, to cities. This can be summarized as regional counterforce and countervalue. The rungs of the Asia-Pacific escalation ladder start with military assets (aircraft and warships). At this stage there is no civilian collateral damage because engagements are limited to between military (and paramilitary) assets at sea and in the air. Escalation moves to attacks against military facilities using high-precision strikes that avoid collateral damage, strikes against military facilities with some civilian collateral damage, and strikes against cities that result in widespread civilian collateral damage. Each rung of this escalation ladder is formulated by the type of target, as opposed to the escalation ladder during Cold War Europe, which was determined by the type of weapon.

If theater strike forces of either side are vulnerable, the other side might have an incentive to attack first in time of crisis. To avoid this each side needs to improve its survivability. In this way crisis stability can work at the regional as well as the strategic nuclear level.

To tease out the dynamics of regional strategic stability it is helpful to extend the notion of strategic stability to an additional existing subcategory: escalation stability. Escalation stability can be interpreted as a variation of crisis stability and first-strike stability. Crisis stability refers to stable deterrence in a crisis situation; it operates before a war breaks out. First-strike stability is concerned with a nuclear first strike after a conventional conflict has broken out. Escalation stability relates to management of intrawar deterrence during both crisis and wartime situations. Escalation stability extends crisis stability to intrawar deterrence, not just during prewar crisis, and extends the concept of first-strike capability to the conventional level, not just the nuclear domain. Once a military conflict breaks out, all-out engagement may start in some cases but both sides may want to control escalation, in some instances by beginning the conflict in a limited way.

As broadly recognized, the process of escalation is uncertain. It is not clear that both sides share the same assessment of the significance of each rung; even notions of escalation itself might not be accepted by both sides in the same manner. The foundational assumption underlying escalation stability is a mutual understanding that the rungs of the escalation ladder exist and both parties assume the conflict might escalate. Based on this assumption, there are two ways in which escalation might occur. The first is a deliberate escalation in which one party recognizes the current situation as being unfavorable to its interests. It judges that it can establish a more advantageous position by initiating escalation and it makes a deliberate decision to do so.

The other type of escalation is inadvertent. There are various ways such escalation might occur, including misunderstanding an opponent's views on the nature of the escalation ladder. For example, the deliberate escalation by one side may be perceived as overescalation by the other side, which in turn escalates even further in its counterattacks. Inadvertent escalation is also likely to occur when the military assets necessary for an escalated rung on either side are vulnerable. If either side sees the situation as "use these military assets or lose them," it may preemptively escalate the situation to avoid the disadvantage that would be incurred were the other side to initiate escalation first.

In this way, even after conflict breaks out the vulnerability of military assets for use on upper rungs of the escalation ladder affects how to manage intrawar deterrence. If both sides are confident that their military assets needed for the next rung are invulnerable and are effective even after the other side escalates first, the incentive for preemptive escalation can be minimized and escalation control will be more stable. On the other hand, if one side believes that the other's forces are vulnerable and it can significantly damage its upper-rung attacks through preemptive escalation, that side would have strong incentive to escalate. If both sides perceive the situation in this way, both have incentive to escalate first and a higher possibility of inadvertent escalation exists.

Insufficient escalation stability can also be created by the simple fact of the deployment mode of weapons. If conventional forces and nuclear forces collocate, similar to the way China deploys ballistic missile forces, inadvertent escalation is likely to occur.[22] In this case there would be some possibility that conventional strikes intended to damage conventional assets might incidentally affect nuclear forces and trigger escalation to a nuclear exchange. This situation lacks escalation stability.

Escalation stability as a concept can address the danger of preemptive and inadvertent escalation. In the Asia-Pacific, where target selection is a key determinant of the escalation ladder, escalation stability can be an important part of regional strategic stability. A conflict is likely to start with engagements between maritime and air assets, with no civilian collateral damage. That level of conflict may escalate to ground strikes against military facilities. This rung can be split into two levels: cautious precision strikes with few civilian casualties and more aggressive strikes with less consideration for collateral damage. In more escalated situations, cities and economic centers could be targets. Escalation stability provides a clue for controlling this kind of escalation process.

Stability at the Strategic Nuclear Level and the Regional Level

The previous section split strategic stability into two levels—the strategic nuclear level and the regional level—and extends the traditional category of strategic stability to escalation stability, which works during a conventional conflict. Utilizing these two concepts, strategic stability can be analyzed in a layered way. One approach is an assessment of the stability-instability paradox. When crisis stability is achieved at the regional level, the stability-instability paradox is mitigated even when mutual vulnerability based strategic stability is formulated at the strategic nuclear level. But if regional-level crisis stability is insufficient, the stability-instability paradox is intensified when strategic stability at the strategic nuclear level is formulated.

There are four patterns of nexus between the two levels of strategic stability. The first pattern is strategic stability, which is achieved at both the strategic nuclear level and regional level. In this case crisis management and escalation control is relatively achievable compared to other patterns, and the negative impact of the stability-instability paradox can be mitigated. The second pattern is when strategic stability is achieved at the strategic nuclear level but not the regional level. The stability-instability paradox is likely to be intensified in this pattern, but the potential for escalation of conflict to the strategic nuclear level can be managed. The third pattern occurs when strategic stability is insufficiently achieved at the strategic nuclear level but achieved at the regional level. In this pattern it is more probable that regional conflict can be avoided, and therefore the lack of stability at the strategic nuclear level is unlikely to become problematic. The fourth pattern, when strategic stability is insufficient at both levels, is extremely unstable, and once a conflict breaks out there is risk of escalation to a nuclear exchange.

In the contemporary security environment, a conflict that involves strategic nuclear arsenals will be a product of escalation from a regional flashpoint. The possibility of an out-of-the-blue nuclear exchange occurring between the United States and China is almost inconceivable. If stakeholders can manage a conflict at the regional level, the role of strategic nuclear arsenals only casts a shadow if they are actually utilized. But if a regional conflict seriously escalates, strategic nuclear forces may be expected to play a kinetic role, just as they did during the Cold War era. In the nexus of strategic stability between the two levels, crisis management and escalation control at the regional level is critically important to avoid escalation to a nuclear conflict. These efforts at the regional level would be more important in the second and fourth patterns, where regional strategic stability is insufficient. In cases where regional conflict breaks out and participants attempt to control escalation, the degree of escalation stability at the regional level determines the difficulty of escalation control. If a high degree of escalation stability exists at the regional level, conflict can be managed without escalation to the strategic nuclear level regardless of crisis stability and escalation stability at the strategic nuclear level. But if the regional level lacks escalation stability, either player in the conflict will have incentives for preemptive escalation and the conflict could be escalated to the strategic nuclear level. Here crisis stability and escalation stability at the strategic nuclear level will determine whether the situation further escalates or not.

IS THE GAME CHANGING?

With China's modernized nuclear and conventional capability, military balance at the theater level is going to shift. China's theater precision missile force provides a first-strike advantage for China and makes escalation stability fragile. And with developing precision and counterforce-capable nuclear forces, the stability-instability paradox will be intensified. The major question for security in the contemporary Asia-Pacific realm is how China's growing capabilities will affect strategic stability at the regional and strategic nuclear levels. This section delves into the question of strategic stability between China, the United States, and US allies.

Overview of the Asia-Pacific Security Environment and Strategic Stability

The Asia-Pacific is currently the most dynamic region in the world, with remarkable region-wide economic development since the mid-1980s. Despite this economic success story, however, the security environment in the region is not necessarily stable. Immediately after the end of the Cold War, even the 1995 version of Japan's National Defense Program Guidelines (NDPG), the capstone document of Japan's defense strategy, described the Asia-Pacific region as "unclear and uncertain."[23] In the twenty-first century this unclear and uncertain situation is getting worse due to China's rapid military modernization and its assertive military and paramilitary activities as well as North Korea's nuclear and missile development programs. These trends in the regional security environment pose significant challenges to regional deterrence.

The major security concerns in the Asia-Pacific are the Taiwan Strait, the East China Sea, the South China Sea, and the Korean Peninsula. (This chapter will not cover strategic stability on the Korean Peninsula because it is largely an issue only between the United States and North Korea.) The origin of the Taiwan Strait issue dates before World War II, when the Chinese Communist Party and the Kuomintang (KMT) that led the Republic of China engaged in a civil war on mainland China. The CCP emerged victorious and established the People's Republic of China in 1949; the KMT fled to Taiwan. Since then the Taiwan Strait has been an ongoing and contentious regional flashpoint. Taiwan is believed to be China's highest-priority long-term political issue, and the PLA's modernization efforts have focused on potential contingencies against Taiwan, with some resources devoted to preparation for a "beyond Taiwan" contingency.[24] The potential for conflict over Taiwan is an existential issue for the CCP, so the full range of military capabilities might be mobilized, including nuclear assets.

The other sources of concern are the East China Sea and South China Sea. Two security challenges exist in the East China Sea: the first relates to the Senkaku Islands and the second is the demarcation of exclusive economic zones (EEZs).[25] Tension regarding the Senkaku Islands is ongoing, and the Japanese Self-Defense Force has emphasized developing the capabilities for island defense in its defense strategies of 2010, 2013, and 2018.[26] At the same time these flashpoints are considered gray zones, where paramilitaries play an important role in securing and challenging the status quo.[27]

Tension in the South China Sea is characterized by a number of participants larger than the number operating in the East China Sea. Multiple territorial disputes exist, mainly over the Paracel Islands and the Spratly Islands. The serious challenge in the South China Sea is China's land reclamation projects at various islets and rocks, including at Johnson South Reef, Woody Island, and Fiery Cross Reef. These projects include building airstrips and port facilities that can be utilized for military purposes. They are perceived as gray zone issues and constitute part of China's efforts to develop an A2/AD capability, which could thwart US military intervention in a regional contingency. Therefore, they are recognized as low-intensity issues compared to Taiwan. In this sense the paramilitary and conventional military balance is important. While nuclear arsenals could cast a shadow over the stakeholders' perceptions and behaviors, and the stability-instability paradox is important in shaping these issues, actual nuclear utilization may not be considered as a realistic option in a gray zone.

Considering the seriousness of the issue, it is necessary to contemplate the possibility of nuclear escalation over Taiwan and its unlikelihood in the East China Sea and the South China Sea. However, once a war starts it will have its own dynamics. Therefore, as long as nuclear threats exist and nuclear deterrence continues to be necessary, the way conflicts might escalate to the nuclear level merits serious analysis. In addition, even without actual warfighting, strategic calculations regarding military balance, including the nuclear component, shape peacetime policy options, just as arguments over strategic balance did in Europe during the Cold War. Such calculations can be a kind of thought experiment to evaluate the strategic balance between related powers. Insights from these thought experiments influence perceptions of possible policy choices for stakeholders. If one player believes the military balance with a potential challenger is unfavorable, that player may take an accommodative policy toward that challenger. Analysis of strategic stability is an important part of such calculations. For example, if one player can know the possibilities inherent in the stability-instability paradox beforehand, it can take countermeasures. Or if a player can recognize some specific possibility of inadvertent escalation, it can reinforce escalation stability to prevent it.

Characteristics of Regional Strategic Stability in the Asia-Pacific

In addition to the geographic characteristics of a maritime environment, strategic stability in the Asia-Pacific is characterized by striking power asymmetry among regional countries. American regional allies have only nominal ground-strike capabilities, and those lack strategic depth. This causes an asymmetry in vulnerability within the region.[28] While China and North Korea have acquired invulnerable theater strike capabilities with road-mobile missiles, Japan, South Korea, and Taiwan lack or only have a small amount of such capabilities. In this sense China and North Korea enjoy one-sided invulnerability at the theater level. This asymmetrical invulnerability is offset only by US theater and strategic strike capabilities, which hold China and North Korea's full range of targets at risk. By "importing" US military assets, regional mutual vulnerability is attained even without regional allies possessing their own strike capabilities. However, it also magnifies the fear of "decoupling" among regional allies and friends.

As discussed previously, if a conflict in the maritime environment of the Asia-Pacific breaks out, it will come from a completely different sequence than the conflict in Europe during the Cold War. In gray zones in the East China Sea and South China Sea a clash would likely begin as a showdown between paramilitary forces. This level is the first rung of the regional escalation ladder. If conflict escalates to the military level, combat might occur on the sea or in the air, away from civilians. This level of conflict would be the second rung of the escalation ladder. If the level of armed conflict is confined to this phase, it would remain limited. But if one side executes attacks against enemy air bases and naval facilities to gain an advantage in the combat arena, the conflict would likely escalate and escalation stability would come into play. If both sides in the conflict consider their own strike assets to be vulnerable to an enemy first strike and believe an escalation to ground strike by either side would inflict significant disadvantages, or if one side considers the other side's strike assets to be vulnerable and therefore considers preemptive escalation (a situation with insufficient escalation stability), the first phase of military-to-military engagements could easily escalate to regional counterforce strikes against ground-based military facilities.

There could be some variation in this regional counterforce phase. For example, an attacker might be cautious in employing precision-guided weapons in order to avoid civilian casualties. But if such cautious attacks are perceived to be insufficient to achieve the goal, then the attacker might launch less discriminating strikes with the possibility of more civilian casualties. Or if the target military facility is located near a population center, the likelihood of causing civilian casualties increases. Once civilian casualties are inflicted on country B by country A, country B would likely escalate its retaliation, resulting in civilian casualties in country A. With repeated exchanges the conflict might escalate to the regional countervalue phase.

To control escalation to the regional countervalue phase and avoid civilian deaths, escalation stability at the regional counterforce phase is important. But at the counterforce phase the United States and its allies are vulnerable and China would have an incentive to escalate if military-to-military combat on the battlefield phase goes badly. If China escalates to a regional counterforce phase, it might gain advantages. And since some bases in the Asia-Pacific are built near population centers, even counterforce strikes may cause civilian casualties, which makes the possibility of escalation to a regional counter-city phase more likely. Considering these factors, escalation stability in this region will be low. The next section analyzes regional strategic stability more deeply.

Changing Military Balance in the Asia-Pacific and Regional Strategic Stability

Along with its rapid economic growth, China has invested significant resources into military modernization. The development of conventional A2/AD capabilities to physically prevent US military intervention are seemingly the highest priority areas. Ironically, but not surprisingly, these Chinese capabilities have been developed to counter US high-tech conventional military capabilities. After the 1991 Gulf War, when the United States clearly demonstrated its dominant information-based precision-strike capability, and the 1995–96 Taiwan Strait Crisis, when the United States sent two aircraft carrier battle groups near Taiwan to send a robust message to China not to intimidate Taiwan's voters in its first presidential election, China established "local war under high-tech conditions" as a key strategic concept. This began with major research and development programs to produce "counter intervention" capabilities to thwart potential US military intervention in the event of another Taiwan contingency.[29]

Within the trans-Pacific intellectual community in the United States these A2/AD threats have been a hot topic. Significant debate has occurred over the "air-sea battle" following the 2010 Quadrennial Defense Review (QDR) and the Center for Strategic and Budgetary Assessment (CSBA) report.[30] In addition, the "Third Offset Strategy," rolled out in the second half of the Obama administration, also aimed to develop US capabilities against A2/AD threats.[31]

China's A2/AD capability has also been a major topic of the annual DoD reports on China's military power. While the term "A2/AD" only came into use in 2006, cautious attention has been paid to China's efforts to develop capabilities to block foreign military intervention in littoral and blue-water areas since the third edition of the Chinese military power report released in 2004.[32] The 2019 report focuses on these A2/AD capabilities: long-range precision strikes, ballistic missile defense, surface and undersea operations, information operations, space and counterspace operations, cyber operations, integrated air defense systems, and air operations.[33]

Especially from a regional strategic stability perspective, Chinese long-range precision strike capabilities could undermine US forces in theater because they make regional fixed military bases, which the United States and its allies rely on, vulnerable. To counter this threat the United States has emphasized the importance of geographical dispersion and operational resiliency since the 2010 QDR, although concrete and discernable steps to significantly improve such resiliency have not been observed.[34] Considering the maritime geographical characteristics of the Asia-Pacific and the combat radius of current and next-generation tactical aircraft, the United States will continue to utilize forward-deployed fixed bases, which lack strategic depth for dispersion. These bases are vulnerable to China's conventional precision ballistic and cruise missiles.

Since American allies lack or possess only nominal ground strike capabilities, if a conflict were to escalate to the regional counterforce phase, only the United States would be able to conduct ground-strike operations. For such operations, US theater strike forces have two components: ground-based aircraft and maritime-based cruise missiles. On the other hand, China's theater strike forces are composed of road-mobile missile systems and aircraft that are operated from dispersed airbases that enjoy the strategic depth of mainland China. Comparing the two sides' ground-strike capabilities, significant gaps exist. In the US capability portfolio, the mission to strike road-mobile missile launchers is expected to be conducted by tactical aircraft. But fixed airbases for such aircraft are highly vulnerable to China's precision-strike missile forces. Sea-launched cruise missiles are an invulnerable strike force, but they cannot hold mobile targets at risk. Therefore China would gain first-strike advantage against US forward-deployed fixed bases, creating a situation in which escalation stability is insufficient.

If serious regional conflict were to break out, it could begin with military-to-military combat between China and local American allies/friends. Even though the military capabilities of US allies are inferior to China's modernized air and naval forces, if the United States joined the fight the military balance would be expected to favor the United States and allies. American assistance, however, is reliant on fixed-ground bases. Therefore, once China escalates to a regional counterforce strike phase by using precision ballistic missiles to neutralize American tactical aircraft, China can gain the military advantage again.

Of course, the United States also has an option to escalate its strike operations to the regional counterforce phase utilizing maritime and air-launched cruise missiles. But after fixed bases are destroyed by China's ballistic missiles, the effective options for the United States would be limited. First, cruise missiles can hardly destroy mobile targets, so China's road-mobile ballistic and cruise missiles can continue to operate even after the United States begins regional counterforce strikes. Second, cruise missiles can be used against China's fixed airbases to damage tactical aircraft. However, China's aircraft can disperse to bases deep inside mainland China. Certainly the destruction of airstrips in and near the theater would make these dispersed aircraft strategically useless because they could no longer operate effectively from distant airbases. However, cruise missiles have limited lethality against hard targets like airstrips. When the United States launched cruise missile strikes against a Syrian airbase in April 2017 with about sixty Tomahawks, the damage prevented further military operations for only a few days. Subsonic terminal velocity limits the lethality of cruise missiles against hard targets. To destroy runways one needs higher terminal velocity weapons such as ballistic missiles or hypersonic projectiles for conventional warheads.

In this situation, escalation to regional counterforce would benefit the Chinese. One possible reaction by the United States to offset Chinese advantage in theater strike forces is to utilize nuclear forces, as some analysts have begun to consider.[35] In this sense, as the 2018 NPR makes clear, developing a low-yield nuclear option like the low-yield Trident D5 and sea-launched cruise missiles (SLCMs) would help restore escalation stability in the region. Such invulnerable theater nuclear forces would equalize the balance of theater-level strike forces and neutralize China's advantage in initiating escalation to regional counterforce strikes. And if China recognizes that escalation to regional counterforce strikes has a risk of escalation to regional nuclear counterforce strikes, China will be cautious in escalating from military-to-military combat at the battlefield phase to the regional counterforce phase. However, China's emerging nuclear capability, such as precision ICBMs and modernized theater nuclear forces, will make the situation more complex. Now is the time to integrate regional and strategic stability, bringing both conventional and nuclear capabilities into a consistent analytical framework to address strategic stability at the strategic nuclear level.

The Impact of China's Emerging New Capabilities on Regional Strategic Stability

China's developing DF-41 will give it counterforce capabilities against the American strategic nuclear arsenal. But even the completion of the DF-41 will not create a "window of vulnerability" situation, due to the US Trident D5. At the same time, however, China's new precision MIRVed ICBM might offset any current US strategic nuclear operational advantages. Under the current balance of strategic nuclear arsenals there is significant asymmetry in what effects can be brought by strategic nuclear forces. While China has seemingly succeeded in being able to deploy an invulnerable second-strike capability against the United States, it can basically only conduct countervalue strikes. Therefore the only decision for China's leaders considering nuclear utilization would be the number of US cities that should be destroyed. On the other hand, since US strategic nuclear forces have accurate guidance systems and high operational readiness, the president has a wider range of choices: massive conventional strikes against mainland China, limited and selective nuclear strikes against military targets, limited and selective nuclear countervalue strikes, and all-out nuclear strikes. While the options for China's decision-makers imply a choice between all-out nuclear exchange or not, the options for the American president include less than all-out nuclear war.

This difference makes the American strategic deterrent more credible. But the gap of credibility will be mitigated by China's development of the DF-41. With the DF-41 China will be able to choose a wider range of targets beyond cities. For example, China may choose selective strikes against ICBM silos located far from urban areas, or it might attack strategic bomber bases, or it might engage in exemplary attacks to signal resolve.

Once China acquires a counterforce capability, the asymmetry of both countries' strategic nuclear forces will affect stability at the strategic nuclear level. Comparing the two countries' legs of the nuclear triad, a clear difference can be easily seen. Regarding ICBMs, the US Minuteman III carries a single warhead and is silo-based, while China's ICBM is road-mobile with MIRVs. Regarding SLBMs, China's weak anti-submarine warfare (ASW) capabilities make American ballistic missile submarines (SSBNs) invulnerable. (China cannot hold SSBNs in the eastern Pacific at risk now or for the foreseeable future. And even though China can develop expeditionary ASW submarine forces in the long term, it is inconceivable that China could hold SSBNs in the Atlantic Ocean at risk.) China's SSBN forces are relatively vulnerable against American and allied ASW forces in the western Pacific. Regarding strategic bombers,

China's fleet cannot hold the US mainland at risk, so it should not be included in strategic nuclear forces.

The challenge for strategic stability at the strategic nuclear level comes from the differences in these legs. First, China's ICBM warheads are stored separately from the missiles that carry them. If China continues this deployment mode, in the event of a crisis the United States may have first-strike incentive before Chinese forces mount the warheads. Once the warheads are mounted, China's road-mobile ICBMs will start to disperse and at that point it becomes impossible to destroy them by missile strike. On the other hand, American stealth bombers can penetrate mainland China, giving them some potential to track and strike road-mobile systems if data links with sensors, including those based in space, are established. Considering this unique capability of the stealth bombers, China may have first-strike incentive against strategic bomber bases. These different first-strike incentives for both sides decrease escalation stability of the strategic counterforce phase at the strategic nuclear level.

The other emerging piece of China's nuclear arsenal, the theater nuclear force, also has important implications for strategic stability, in this case at the regional level. In light of China's precision A2/AD threats, a low-yield nuclear option for the United States could offset disadvantages in conventional strike forces. One possible scenario is that China leads escalation to the regional counterforce phase and gains strategic advantage at that level. The role expected for the low-yield option would be to destroy airbases and command-and-control nodes for road-mobile missile forces. While nuclear utilization is a highly escalatory measure, one effective choice for the United States would be to utilize its nuclear forces' comparative advantage over other nuclear weapon states in its operational readiness and adaptive planning capability.[36] Considering these strengths in nuclear warfighting, the United States would be able to control nuclear escalation by limiting nuclear utilization strictly for regional counterforce strikes against military targets.

With China's deployment of modernized precision theater nuclear forces, however, different strategic calculations are necessary due to China's ability to proportionally respond to American nuclear utilization. Before the appearance of such forces, China's only counterforce strike option against the use of American low-yield nuclear weapons was to use nuclear weapons in a manner that caused large collateral damage, making counterforce strikes no different from countervalue strikes. This response would necessarily invite an American escalated nuclear response. But with modernized precision nuclear forces with a low-yield option, China will be able to conduct selective nuclear counterforce strikes and avoid collateral damage, even if the United States launches nuclear counterforce strikes to offset its conventional disadvantage. Thus the United States will no longer be able to utilize a nuclear option effectively to neutralize China's A2/AD advantage. In other words, China's modernized theater nuclear force would deny American advantages of escalation control between the regional conventional counterforce phase and the regional nuclear counterforce phase. China's modernized theater nuclear force would provide counter escalation control capability with regional nuclear counterforce capabilities. That would work to deter US escalation using the low-yield nuclear option at the regional level to offset China's advantage in the conventional counterforce phase.

This does not mean development of an American low-yield option would be strategically irrelevant. With China's deployment of a modernized theater nuclear force, the United States should also have a similar type of capability that can operate under A2/AD threat. In the current situation the only low-yield American option is the B61 gravity bomb carried by dual-capable aircraft. Given China's conventional A2/AD capability, dual-capable aircraft may not be credible, meaning the United States needs to develop penetrable low-yield options such as a low-yield Trident and/or SLCMs.

Combining the arguments described, eight rungs of the escalation ladder will be created through China's modernization of both conventional and nuclear military forces: (1) gray zone showdown between paramilitaries; (2) military-to-military combat on the battlefield; (3) regional conventional counterforce; (4) regional nuclear counterforce; (5) regional conventional countervalue; (6) regional nuclear countervalue; (7) strategic counterforce; (8) strategic countervalue. Escalation will not necessarily occur in a linear manner and some rungs might be skipped (e.g., moving from regional conventional countervalue to strategic counterforce, skipping the regional nuclear countervalue rung). The important challenge for strategic stability in the Asia-Pacific is that escalation stability might be somewhat fragile at some rungs, such as the level between military-to-military combat on the battlefield and regional conventional counterforce. With China's development of a strategic counterforce capability, escalation stability on strategic counterforce from the regional level might be affected.

Furthermore, China's emerging nuclear capability will make US escalation control more tenuous and provide more options to China's decision-makers beyond just nuclear strikes against cities, which necessarily would invite massive nuclear retaliation. China's modernized theater nuclear force will enable countermeasures against the American low-yield option. Moreover, its emerging strategic counterforce capability creates broader options to strike the United States, such as exemplary strikes against ICBM silos.

These emerging Chinese nuclear capabilities are synonymous with China acquiring a nuclear warfighting capability, which Alastair Johnston predicted in the late 1990s. Paradoxically, such a Chinese nuclear warfighting capability would reinforce the firebreak between conventional and nuclear weapons. At the strategic nuclear level, even though both sides might have a first-strike incentive, each player needs to be cautious because actually launching strikes might trigger mutual counterforce strikes. At the regional level, the US possession of a nuclear option to offset disadvantages in conventional striking power might be deterred by China's modernized theater force. In this sense China's emerging nuclear forces will set a higher bar for American nuclear utilization. As a result, even a lower degree of escalation stability will work to reinforce the nuclear firebreak by making both sides' decision-makers more cautious about escalation.

However, this does not mean that China's nuclear force has a positive influence on regional security. Rather, the opposite is true. Reinforcement of the nuclear firebreak is actually a perfect recipe for intensifying the stability-instability paradox; it will enable China to gain the strategic upper hand over other regional states. In the Asia-Pacific, American allies have only nominal striking power against China. If the United States is restrained from utilizing its forces, the strategic landscape of the Asia-Pacific could be fundamentally refor-mulated and the final consequence for regional security could be disastrous.

There are two ways to prevent such negative strategic consequences. The first is to restore the conventional balance between China and the United States and its allies. Reducing the vulnerability of local allied forces is especially important in order to lessen China's escalation incentive to launch regional counterforce strikes first. The second is to strengthen US damage limitation capabilities at the strategic nuclear level, which would physically deny mutual vulnerability with China. China's emerging counterforce capability gives it selective nuclear strike options, such as limited attacks against ICBM silos and strategic bomber airbases. But if the United States quantitatively and qualitatively improves its homeland BMD capability, limited strikes by China would become difficult because small numbers of warheads may not be able to penetrate BMD. To conduct counterforce strikes against a country with a significant BMD shield an attacker must be able to launch many missiles to overcome defenses. By definition this kind of strike would not be limited and the difference between counterforce and countervalue would be blurred, meaning the United States would be more likely to choose a full-scale counterforce option. Were China to assess the strategic situation in this way, it would realize a limited strike is not an option. If mutual vulnerability is physically denied, the stability-instability paradox caused by China's counterforce capability can be avoided.

CONCLUSION

China's nuclear development has been an important issue for Asian security. So far analysts have focused on China's conventional A2/AD capability and the development of an invulnerable second strike. But these two pieces do not cover all of China's modernized nuclear arsenal. There are other emerging capabilities, such as counterforce potential and modernized theater nuclear forces. Leaders must consider how the strategic landscape will be changed in light of China's development of these new systems, introducing the notions of regional strategic stability and escalation stability. Such a thought experiment does not mean that a nuclear exchange is likely to occur. Similar to the works by Glenn Snyder and Herman Kahn in the 1960s and 1970s, the objectives here are to assess the strategic advantages and disadvantage of each side and develop policy alternatives that reinforce deterrence and avoid actual conflict.[37]

In sum, China's emerging counterforce capability and modernized theater nuclear force suggest it is going to have a nuclear warfighting capability. Paradoxically, this capability will actually reinforce the nuclear firebreak in regional security. A strengthened nuclear firebreak sounds good for regional security, but the actual strategic effect is to set the US nuclear arsenal aside and make the local conventional military balance more essential. Given the characteristics of the Asia-Pacific region, where local allies of the United States rely on US conventional and nuclear strike forces to secure strategic stability, neutralization of the US nuclear capability through China's efforts will sharpen the stability-instability paradox.

To avoid such a heightened stability-instability paradox the United States and its allies need to develop capabilities for damage limitation. At a regional level they need to make efforts to restore a conventional military balance. Resiliency of ground-based aircraft must be prioritized and conventional strike capabilities also need to be strengthened. In this sense the end of the Intermediate-Range Nuclear Forces Treaty will have significant implications. At the strategic nuclear level the United States should accelerate the enhancement of a homeland BMD system that can neutralize China's limited strategic counterforce options. Both measures require significant resources from the United States and its allies, but the cost is more reasonable than the cost of nuclear war. Unfortunately, *si vis pacem, para bellum* is now very true in the Asia-Pacific.

NOTES

1. Regarding gray zone and A2/AD threats, see Jan van Tol et al., "AirSea Battle: A Point-of-Departure Operational Concept," Center for Strategic and Budgetary Assessments, May 18, 2010, https://csbaonline.org/uploads/documents/2010.05.18 -AirSea-Battle.pdf; Sugio Takahashi, "Counter A2/AD in Japan-U.S. Defense Cooperation: Toward 'Allied Air-Sea Battle,'" *Futuregram* 12-003, Project 2049, April 18, 2012, https://project2049.net/2012/04/18/counter-a2-ad-in-japan-u-s-defense -cooperation-toward-allied-air-sea-battle/; T. X. Hammes, "Offshore Control: A Proposed Strategy for an Unlikely Conflict," *Strategic Forum* 278 (June 2012); Robert Martinage, *Toward a New Offset Strategy: Exploiting U.S. Long-Term*

Advantages to Restore U.S. Global Power Projection Capability (Washington, DC: Center for Strategic and Budgetary Assessment, 2014), https://csbaonline.org /uploads/documents/Offset-Strategy-Web.pdf; Evan Braden Montgomery, "Contested Primacy in the Western Pacific: China's Rise and the Future of U.S. Power Projection," *International Security* 38, no. 4 (Spring 2014): 115–49; Michael Mazzar, *Mastering the Gray Zone: Understanding a Changing Era of Conflict* (Carlisle, PA: Strategic Studies Institute, 2015), https://ssi.armywarcollege.edu/pdffiles/PUB1303 .pdf; Stephen Biddle and Ivan Oelrich, "Future Warfare in the Western Pacific: Chinese Antiaccess/Area Denial, U.S. AirSea Battle, and Command of the Commons in East Asia," *International Security* 41, no.1 (Summer 2016): 7–48; and Michael Green et al., "Countering Coercion in Maritime Asia: The Theory and Practice of Gray Zone Deterrence," Center for Strategic and International Studies, 2017, https://csis-prod.s3.amazonaws.com/s3fs-public/publication/170505_GreenM _CounteringCoercionAsia_Web.pdf.

2. Regarding first strike stability, see Glenn A. Kant, Randall J. DeValk, and David E. Thaler, "A Calculus of First-Strike Stability (A Criterion for Evaluating Strategic Forces)," *A RAND Note*, June 1988, https://www.rand.org/content/dam/rand/pubs /notes/2007/N2526.pdf.

3. M. Taylor Fravel and Evan S. Medeiros, "China's Search for Assured Retaliation: The Evolution of Chinese Nuclear Strategy and Force Structure," *International Security* 35, no. 2 (Fall 2000): 48–87, esp. 67–70.

4. Alastair Iain Johnston, "China's New 'Old Thinking': The Concept of Limited Deterrence," *International Security* 20, no. 3 (Winter 1995–96): 5–42.

5. For links to the DoD's reports on the Chinese military, see Andrew S. Erickson, "U.S. Department of Defense Annual Reports to Congress on China's Military Power—2002–2017," June 6, 2017, http://www.andrewerickson.com/2017/06/u-s -department-of-defense-annual-reports-to-congress-on-chinas-military-power -2002-17-download-complete-set-here/.

6. Office of the Secretary of Defense, "Annual Report to Congress: Military and Security Developments Involving the People's Republic of China 2018," May 16, 2018, https://media.defense.gov/2018/Aug/16/2001955282/-1/-1/1/2018-CHINA -MILITARY-POWER-REPORT.PDF; and Office of the Secretary of Defense, "Annual Report to Congress: Military and Security Developments Involving the People's Republic of China 2019," May 2, 2019, https://media.defense.gov/2019 /May/02/2002127082/-1/-1/1/2019_CHINA_MILITARY_POWER_REPORT .PDF.

7. Linton Brooks and Mira Rapp-Hooper, "Extended Deterrence, Assurance, and Reassurance in the Pacific during the Second Nuclear Age," in *Strategic Asia 2013–14: Asia in the Second Nuclear Age*, ed. Ashley J. Tellis, Abraham M. Denmark, and Travis Tanner, Kindle ed. (Washington, DC: National Bureau of Asian Research, 2013); and Charles L. Glaser and Steve Fetter, "Should the United States Reject MAD?: Damage Limitation and U.S. Nuclear Strategy toward China," *International Security* 41, no.1 (Summer 2016): 49–98.

8. Keith B. Payne, *The Great American Gamble: Deterrence Theory and Practice from the Cold War to the Twenty-First Century* (Fairfax, VA: National Institute Press, 2008).

9. Glenn H. Snyder, "The Balance of Power and the Balance of Terror," in *The Balance of Power*, ed. Paul Seabury, 185–216 (San Francisco: Chandler, 1965), 199.

10. Takahashi Sugio, "Kaku Heiki wo Meguru Shomondai to Nihon No Anzen Hosho: NPR–Shin START Taisei, 'Kakuheiki no Nai Sekai,' and Kakudai Yokushi" (Issues of nuclear weapons and Japan's security: NPR–New START regime, "nuclear free world," and extended deterrence), *Kaigai Jijo* 58, no. 7–8 (July–August 2010): 30–51.

11. Takahashi Sugio, "Nichibei Doumei ni okeru Yokushi Taisei: Doteki Yokushi to Senryakukaku Yokushi no Renkansei" (Deterrence posture of the U.S.-Japanese alliance: Linkage between dynamic deterrence and strategic nuclear deterrence), *Kaigai Jijo* 61, no. 5 (May 2013): 74–88.

12. Sugio Takahashi, "Redefining Strategic Stability: A Japanese View," in *A Precarious Triangle: U.S.-China Strategic Stability and Japan*, ed. James L. Schoff and Li Bin (Washington, DC: Carnegie Endowment for International Peace, 2017), http://carnegieendowment.org/2017/11/07/redefining-strategic-stability-japanese-view-pub-74631.

13. Office of the Secretary of Defense, "Nuclear Posture Review Report 2018," February 2018, https://media.defense.gov/2018/Feb/02/2001872886/-1/-1/1/2018-NUCLEAR-POSTURE-REVIEW-FINAL-REPORT.PDF.

14. Paul H. Nitze, "Assuring Strategic Stability in an Era of Détente," *Foreign Affairs* 54, no. 2 (January 1976): 207–32.

15. For example, Eric Heginbotham et al., *"The U.S.-China Military Scorecard: Forces, Geography, and the Evolving Balance of Power, 1996–2017"* (Santa Monica, CA: RAND Corporation, 2015), https://www.rand.org/content/dam/rand/pubs/research_reports/RR300/RR392/RAND_RR392.pdf.

16. Stephen Van Evera, *Cause of War: Power and the Roots of Conflict* (Ithaca, NY: Cornell University Press, 1999).

17. Robert Jervis, *The Meaning of the Nuclear Revolution: Statecraft and the Prospect of Armageddon* (Ithaca, NY: Cornell University Press, 1989).

18. Kant, DeValk, and Thaler, "A Calculus of First-Strike Stability."

19. For example, see Ivo H. Daalder, James M. Goldgeier, and James M. Lindsey, "Deploying NMD: Not Whether, But How," *Survival* 42, no. 1 (Spring 2000): 6–28; Dean A. Wilkening, "Amending the ABM Treaty," *Survival* 42, no. 1 (Spring 2000): 29–45; Philip Gordon, "Bush, Missile Defense, and the Atlantic Alliance," *Survival* 43, no. 1 (Spring 2001): 17–36; and Charles Glaser and Steve Fetter, "National Missile Defense and the Future of U.S. Weapons Policy," *International Security* 26, no. 1 (Summer 2001): 40–92.

20. Ogawa Shin'ichi, "'Kaku no Kasa' no Rironteki Kento" (Theoretical analysis on "nuclear umbrella"), *Kokusai Seiji* 90 (March 1989): 91–102.

21. Desmond Ball, "Nuclear War at Sea," *International Security* 10, no. 3 (Winter 1985–86): 26.

22. Caitlin Talmadge, "Would China Go Nuclear?: Assessing the Risk of Chinese Nuclear Escalation in a Conventional War with the United States," *International Security* 41, no. 4 (Spring 2017): 50–92.

23. Cabinet and National Security Council of Japan, "Heisei 8 Nendo Iko ni Kakaru Bouei Keikaku no Taiko ni Tsuite" (National Defense Program guidelines of FY 1996 and after), Government of Japan, 1995, https://www.kantei.go.jp/jp/singi/ampobouei/sankou/951128taikou.html.

24. For example, see Office of the Secretary of Defense, "Annual Report to Congress: Military and Security Developments Involving the People's Republic of China 2013" (Washington, DC: Office of the Secretary of Defense, 2013), 22.

25. The Government of Japan surveyed the Senkaku Islands multiple times from 1885 to 1895 and, based on the principle of "occupation of terra nullius," it made a cabinet decision on January 14, 1895, to formally incorporate these islands into the territory of Japan. No country challenged this incorporation, including during negotiations of the Treaty of San Francisco in 1955. It was not until the 1970s, when the UN Economic Commission for Asia and the Far East (ECAFE) indicated the possible existence of petroleum resources in the East China Sea, that both Taiwan and China asserted the Senkaku Islands as part of their territories. See Japanese Ministry of Foreign Affairs, "Senkaku Islands Q and A," April 13, 2016, https://www.mofa.go.jp/region/asia-paci/senkaku/qa_1010.html. Under the UN Convention on the Law of the Sea (UNCLOS) a country can extend its EEZ 200 nautical miles beyond its territory. In some cases, however, when the distance between two countries is shorter than 400 nautical miles, the countries need to agree about demarcation to solve issues that arise from overlapping EEZs. In the case of the East China Sea area between Japan and China, the Government of Japan's position is that the "boundary delimitation based on the geographical equidistance line is regarded as an equitable solution in the delimitation of such maritime area." On the other hand, China claims the natural prolongation of its continental shelf to the Okinawa Trough, which gives a vast area EEZ to China, compared to a demarcation line that is based on geographical equidistance. Even though the two countries have not agreed on demarcation, China has built many rigs to drill for natural gas in that area. See Japanese Ministry of Foreign Affairs, "Japan's Legal Position on the Development of Natural Resources in the East China Sea," August 6, 2015, http://www.mofa.go.jp/a_o/c_m1/page3e_000358.html.
26. The document on Japan's defense strategy, the "National Defense Program Guidelines," is released periodically as a full cabinet decision document. In the past decade this document was released in 2010, 2013, and 2018.
27. Sugio Takahashi, "Development of Gray-Zone Deterrence: Concept Building and Lessons from Japan's Experience," *Pacific Review* 31, no. 6 (January 9, 2019): 787–810.
28. Ishikawa Taku, "Hokutou Ajia ni Okeru 'Senryakuteki Anteisei' to Nichibei no Yokushi Taisei" (Strategic stability in northeast Asia and the deterrence posture of the United States and Japan), *Kaigai Jijo* 61, no. 3 (May 2013): 36–48.
29. See Tai Ming Cheung, *Forging China's Military Might: A New Framework for Assessing Innovation* (Baltimore: Johns Hopkins University Press, 2014).
30. US Department of Defense, "Quadrennial Defense Review Report," February 2010, http://archive.defense.gov/qdr/QDR%20as%20of%2029JAN10%201600.pdf; Tol et al., "AirSea Battle"; and Hammes, "Offshore Control."
31. Martinage, *Toward a New Offset Strategy.*
32. Office of the Secretary of Defense, "FY04 Report to Congress on PRC Military Power Pursuant to FY2000 National Defense Authorization Act: Annual Report on the Military Power of the People's Republic of China," 2004, https://www.globalsecurity.org/military/library/report/2004/d20040528prc.pdf.
33. Office of the Secretary of Defense, "Annual Report to Congress, 2018," 59–64.
34. Department of Defense, "Quadrennial Defense Review Report," 33.
35. Elbridge Colby, "Promoting Strategic Stability in the midst of Sino-U.S. Competition," Briefing Series, National Bureau of Asian Research, September 2015, https://s3.amazonaws.com/files.cnas.org/documents/US-China_brief_Colby_Sept2015.pdf?mtime=20160906082555.

36. Regarding adaptive planning, see Paul I. Bernstein, "Post–Cold War U.S. Nuclear Strategy," in *On Limited Nuclear War in the 21st Century*, ed. Jeffrey Larsen and Kerry Kartchner, 80–98 (Stanford, CA: Stanford University Press, 2014).

37. Glenn Snyder, *Defense and Deterrence: Toward a Theory of National Security* (Princeton, NJ: Princeton University Press, 1961); Herman Kahn, *On Escalation: Metaphors and Scenarios* (New York: Frederick A. Praeger, 1965).

FIVE

China's Strategic Systems and Programs

Hans M. Kristensen

China is well under way with a comprehensive nuclear weapons modernization program that is introducing significant enhancements in the capability of its nuclear forces. This is the country's fourth modernization phase. The first phase, in the 1960s and 1970s, introduced bombers and liquid-fuel medium-range ballistic missiles (MRBMs) such as the DF-1, DF-2, and the first version of the DF-3. The second phase, in the 1980s and 1990s, introduced liquid-fuel moveable and silo-based intercontinental ballistic missiles (ICBMs), the first solid-fuel road-mobile MRBM (the DF-21), and an experimental nuclear-powered ballistic missile submarine (SSBN) (Type 092). The third phase, in the 2000s, introduced solid-fuel road-mobile ICBMs (the DF-31 and DF-31A), an upgraded ICBM (the DF-5B) with multiple independently targetable warheads (MIRVs), and a small fleet of improved SSBNs (Type 094). This phase also fielded significant conventional medium-range missiles (the DF-21C/D) to complement Chinese nuclear forces and provide the country's leadership with regional strike options below the nuclear threshold. The fourth phase, currently underway, is fielding improved road-mobile ICBMs (the DF-31AG and DF-41), a dual-capable intermediate-range ballistic missile (IRBM) with improved accuracy (the DF-26), and an improved MRBM (the DF-21E). It also involves the preparation of a more active nuclear role for bombers that may include air-launched ballistic missiles as well as the development of a third-generation SSBN (Type 096) with a longer-range submarine-launched ballistic missile (SLBM) (the JL-3).

As a result, over the past decade the Chinese nuclear weapons stockpile has increased by more than two-thirds. This increase has been caused by the fielding of nearly three dozen DF-31A ICBMs, the addition of MIRVs on half of its DF-5 ICBMs, the deployment of at least 70 dual-capable DF-26 IRBMs (some of which have a nuclear mission), and the fielding of four

Jin-class SSBNs with a total of 48 launchers for the JL-2 SLBM. The Chinese warhead stockpile has exceeded the French arsenal and is currently estimated at around 322 warheads (see table 5.1) and is expected to continue to increase over the next decade.

The Pentagon's Missile Defense Review report from January 2018 states that China "has deployed 75–100 ICBMs, including a new road-mobile system and a new multi-warhead version of its silo-based ICBM. Beijing now possesses four advanced JIN-class ballistic missile submarines (SSBN), each capable of carrying 12 new SLBMs, the CSS-N-14. Consequently, China can now potentially threaten the United States with about 125 nuclear missiles, some capable of employing multiple warheads, and its nuclear forces will increase in the coming years."[1]

Mention of Chinese military developments in the Pentagon's annual report released in May 2019 lists a similar number of "90" ICBMs, with the same number of launchers. (In previous reports the numbers of launchers and missiles were different because one ICBM [the DF-4] has one reload; the new report still includes the DF-4.)[2] The number 90 is probably the upper end of a range-scale; previous DoD reports gave a range of approximately 25 weapons. As a result, it is possible that the actual estimate is 65–90 ICBMs (a medium value is about 78). Conversely, the number 90 might be closer to the medium of 75–100 missiles. As a result, the estimated 125 nuclear missiles capable of threatening the United States appears to include the DF-4, DF-5A/B, the DF-31/A, the DF-31AG, and the JL-2s on the four SSBNs. The term "United States" normally refers to the fifty states but not US territories such as Guam.

How much the stockpile will increase in the future is unclear. The Chinese government does not provide public numbers for its current stockpile or the goal for its future size. The US Defense Intelligence Agency (DIA) expects the stockpile will increase significantly. "Over the next decade," DIA director Robert Ashley recently projected, "China is likely to at least double the size of its nuclear stockpile in the course of implementing the most rapid expansion and diversification of its nuclear arsenal in China's history."[3] Whether that projection materializes remains to be seen. DIA past projections for China's nuclear arsenal have generally been wrong—some significantly so (see figure 5.1).

The actual increase will depend on many factors: how many ballistic missiles will be deployed; how many of the them will be dual-capable; how many will be equipped with MIRVs; how many missiles the next-generation submarine will carry; how many bombers will be fielded; how many weapons the bombers will carry; and whether nuclear cruise missiles will be fielded. All of these are uncertain factors that will affect the size and capability of the future Chinese nuclear arsenal.

TABLE 5.1. Estimated Chinese Nuclear Forces, Early 2020

Type/Chinese designation (US designation)	Launchers	Year fielded	Range (km)	Warheads x yield[1]	Warheads
Land-based missiles					
DF-4 (CSS-3)	10	1980	5,500+	1 x 3.3 mt	10
DF-5A (CSS-4 Mod 2)	10	2015	12,000+	1 x 200–300 kt	10
DF-5B (CSS-4 Mod 3)	10	2015	12,000+	3 x 200–300 kt	30
DF-5C (CSS-4 Mod 4?)	n/a	(2021)	12,000+	MIRV	n/a
DF-17 (HGV)	n/a	(2020)	1,800+	(1 x ? kt)[2]	n/a
DF-21A (CSS-5 Mod 1)	40	1994	2,100+	1 x 200–300 kt	40
DF-21E (CSS-5 Mod 6)	n/a	2016	2,100+	1 x 200–300 kt	n/a[3]
DF-26 (CSS-?)	72	2016	up to 4,000	1 x 200–300 kt	36[4]
DF-31 (CSS-10 Mod 1)	8	2006	7,000+	1 x 200–300 kt	8
DF-31A (CSS-10 Mod 2)	24	2007	11,200+	1 x 200–300 kt	24
DF-31AG (CSS-10 Mod 3)	24[5]	2018	(11,200)[6]	1 x 200–300 kt	24
DF-41 (CSS-X-20)	(16)[7]	(2020)	(12,000+)	3 x 200–300 kt	(48)
Subtotal	**198**				**182**
Sea-based missiles					
JL-2 (CSS-N-14)	4/48	2016	7,000+	1 x 200–300 kt	48
	(2/24)	(2021)	7,000+	1 x 200–300 kt	(24)
Bombers[8]					
H-6 (B-6)	20	1965	3,000+	1 x bomb	20
Total	**266 (306)**				**250 (322)[9]**

1. All listed yields are estimates. There is no official public information available about the yield of Chinese warheads.
2. During the 2019 Beijing parade the DF-17 was presented as a conventional missile. In prepared remarks before the US Senate in February 2020, however, STRATCOM stated that the parade "unveiled new strategic nuclear systems, including the . . . DF-17 medium-range ballistic missile." Gen. Charles Richard, Commander, USSTRATCOM, prepared testimony before Senate Armed Services Committee, February 13, 2020, 4, https://www.armed-services.senate.gov/imo/media/doc/Richard_02-13-20.pdf.
3. It is assumed that the new DF-21E (CSS-5 Mod 6) carries the same missile as the DF-21A but has improved off-road capability; both versions are included in the DF-21A total. Only nonnuclear DF-21 versions (DF-21C and DF-21D) are assumed to have been assigned reload missiles.
4. Since the DF-26 is dual-capable, only half are counted as having nuclear warheads. The launcher appears to have a field reload capability but that is assumed to be only for conventional missions.
5. It is assumed the DF-31AG is replacing the DF-31 and DF-31A.
6. It is assumed the missile carried by the DF-31AG is the same as the one carried by the DF-31A.
7. China displayed sixteen DF-41 TELs at the 2019 parade in Beijing and announced that the units came from two brigades. A total of eighteen TELs were visible during rehearsal and at training sites. It is assumed that each brigade eventually will have twelve TELs.
8. The People's Liberation Army Air Force has recently been reassigned a nuclear mission. The table assumes H-6s have had a semi-dormant nuclear capability since the nuclear bomb testing program in the 1960s and 1970s. The DoD's *Nuclear Matters Handbook* from 2020 lists the H-6 as nuclear and predicts it will be completely fielded within ten years. An air-launched ballistic missile with possible nuclear capability is in development, along with a new long-range nuclear-capable bomber.
9. In addition to the some 250 warheads assigned to deployed land-, sea-, and air-based launchers, another 72 warheads are estimated to have been produced for the DF-41 and two additional SSBNs, for a total stockpile of 322 warheads.

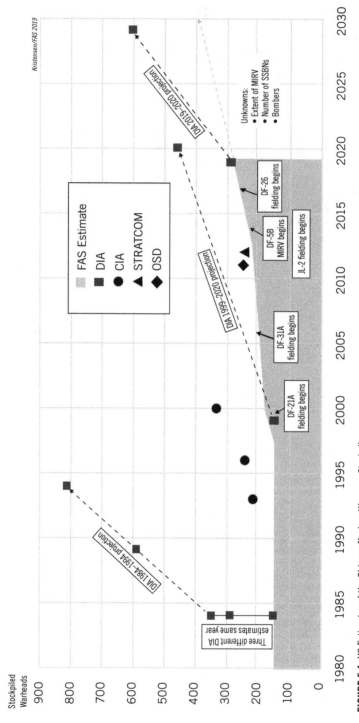

FIGURE 5.1. US Estimates of the Chinese Nuclear Weapons Stockpile

LAND-BASED BALLISTIC MISSILES

The People's Liberation Army Rocket Force (PLARF) operates a total of 660 launchers with 1,340–2,740 missiles, according to the DoD. Of these, 90 launchers are for 270–540 ground-launched cruise missiles (GLCMs). The remaining 570 launchers are for 1,070–2,200 ballistic missiles.[4] The vast majority of launchers—nearly 70 percent—carry conventional missiles. The remaining 30 percent or so (about 180 launchers) are thought to be capable of launching nuclear-armed missiles; many are dual-capable (see table 5.1). Of the 180 nuclear missiles, about 125 (70 percent) can reach some part of the United States and 70 (39 percent) can reach the continental United States. In other words, most of the PLARF's rocket forces (about 90 percent) are intended for regional missions.

A unique and potentially dangerous feature of China's land-based ballistic missile force is that a significant portion of it—about 70 percent—are conventional weapons. The DF-21 MRBM exists in four different versions, half of which are conventional; the new DF-26 IRBM is dual-capable. This mixing of nuclear and conventional capabilities within the missile force—even within individual weapon systems—could potentially create uncertainty and misunderstandings about China's intentions and actions in a crisis were an adversary not able to determine if the PLARF was readying to launch conventional or nuclear missiles. In such a case the adversary may choose to assume the worst and ready its own nuclear forces, which in turn could be misinterpreted by China (if it could detect it) as a preparation for a preemptive nuclear attack. Likewise, if a conventional war has begun, an adversary might mistakenly attack a Chinese nuclear unit that it thought was conventional and unintentionally trigger Chinese nuclear retaliation. Chinese officials are adamant that any attack on China's nuclear forces would be considered a nuclear attack even if carried out using conventional weapons.

The Chinese rocket forces are organized under six base areas, with a total of at least 40 missile brigades (see table 5.2). Of those, approximately half appear to operate nuclear-capable missile launchers. Every brigade is divided into launch units or battalions that are located at smaller bases in the region around the main brigade base; each unit has up to twelve launchers. Many brigade bases have training launchpads that the crews use to practice procedures for readying the launchers for use. Each base also has a variety of technical support units scattered in the area, including nuclear warhead storage and handling units. Most of China's nuclear warheads are kept in the central Base 67 underground storage complex near Baoji in Shaanxi province, but a few weapons are thought to be present at the regional base storage sites. Under normal circumstances the warheads are stored separately from the launchers.[5]

TABLE 5.2. PLARF Missile Force Structure, Early 2020

Base Number (Provinces)	Unit	Location[1]	Weapon Type[2]	Nuclear	Notes
PLARF HQ	HQ	Beijing (40.0352, 116.3197)			
Base 61 (Anhui, Fujian, Guangdong, Jiangxi, Zhejiang)	HQ	Huangshan (29.6957, 118.3025)			
	611 Brigade	Qingyang (30.6903, 117.9011)	DF-21A	Yes	Former DF-3A brigade
	612 Brigade	Leping (28.9797, 117.1205)	DF-21(A)[3]	(Yes)	Nuclear status unclear
	613 Brigade	Shangrao (28.4745, 117.8954)	DF-15B	No	First conventional SRBM unit
	614 Brigade	Yongan (26.0596, 117.3151)	DF-11A	No	First DF-11A brigade
	615 Brigade	Meizhou (24.2828, 115.9708)	DF-11A (DF-17?)	No	Second DF-11A brigade
	616 Brigade	Ganzhou (25.7823, 114.8805)	DF-15	No	Second DF-15 brigade
	617 Brigade	Jinhua (29.1508, 119.6153)	DF-16[4]	No	Second DF-16 brigade
	618 Brigade	?[5]	?	?	Rumored new brigade base
Base 62 (Guangxi, Guangdong, Hainan, Sichuan, Yunnan)	HQ	Kunming (24.9888, 102.8346)			
	621 Brigade	Yibin (28.7607, 104.7914)	DF-21(A)	(Yes)	Former DF-21A brigade
	622 Brigade	Yuxi (24.3601, 102.4942)	DF-31A	Yes	Former DF-21A brigade
	623 Brigade	Liuzhou (24.3856, 109.5726)	DF-10A	No	First DF-10A brigade
	624 Brigade	Danzhou (19.4721, 109.4570)	DF-21C/D	No	New base under construction
	625 Brigade	Jianshui (23.7354, 102.8713)	DF-26	Yes	Possibly third DF-26 brigade
	626 Brigade	Qingyuan (23.6845, 113.1768)	DF-26	Yes	Possible second DF-26 brigade
	627 Brigade	Puning (23.4122, 116.1816)?	? (SRBM, DF-17?)	(No)	Rumored new brigade unit area

Base 63 (Huaihua, Hunan)	HQ	Huaihua (27.5747, 110.0250)		
	631 Brigade	Jingzhou (26.5577, 109.6648)[6]	DF-5B	Yes	HQ base[7]
	632 Brigade	Shaoyang (27.2532, 111.3859)	DF-31AG	Yes	Upgraded from DF-31A
	633 Brigade	Huitong (26.8935, 109.7388)	DF-5A	Yes	HQ base[8]
	634 Brigade	Tongdao (26.1459, 109.7723)?[9]	? (DF-41?)	?	Rumored new brigade base area[10]
	635 Brigade	Yichun (27.8869, 114.3862)	DF-10	No	Second DF-10 brigade
	636 Brigade	Shaoguan (24.7579, 113.6797)	DF-16	No	First DF-16 brigade
Base 64 (Gansu, Inner Mongolia, Ningxia, Qinghai, Shaanxi, Xinjiang)	HQ	Lanzhou (35.9387, 104.0159)		
	641 Brigade	Hancheng (35.4754, 110.4468)	DF-31A	Yes	Second DF-31 brigade
	642 Brigade	Datong (36.9495, 101.6663)	DF-31 (DF-31AG?)	Yes	Possibly upgrading to DF-31AG[11]
	643 Brigade	Tianshui (34.5315, 105.9103)	DF-31AG	Yes	First DF-31AG brigade
	644 Brigade	Hanzhong (33.1321, 106.9361)?	(DF-41)	(Yes)	Rumored DF-41 integration base[12]
	645 Brigade	Yinchuan (38.5938, 106.2269)?	?	?	Rumored new brigade base
	646 Brigade	Korla (41.6946, 86.1734)	DF-21C (DF-26?)	(No)	DF-26s seen in 2019 and 2020[13]
	647 Brigade	Xining (36.6168, 101.7782)?	?	?	Rumored new brigade base area

(Continued)

TABLE 5.2. (Continued)

Base Number (Provinces)	Unit	Location[1]	Weapon Type[2]	Nuclear	Notes
Base 65 (Jilin, Liaoning, Shandong)	HQ	Shenyang (41.8586, 123.4514)			
	651 Brigade	Dengshahe (39.3028, 122.0654)	DF-21A	Yes	DF-26s seen in 2019[14]
	652 Brigade	Tonghua (41.6681, 125.9548)?[15]	DF-21C	No	DF-31As seen training in area
	653 Brigade	Laiwu (36.2332, 117.7154)	DF-21C/D	No	DF-21D seen recently
	654 Brigade	Dengshahe (39.2353, 122.0440)	(DF-26)	(Yes)	Base under construction
	655 Brigade	Tonghua (41.7649, 125.9857)?	?	?	Rumored new brigade base area
	656 Brigade	Laiwu/Taian (36.2164, 117.2069)[16]	(DF-31AG?)	?	Rumored new brigade base area
Base 66 (Henan)	HQ	Luoyang (34.6405, 112.3823)			
	661 Brigade	Lushi (34.0504, 111.0342)[17]	DF-5B	Yes	HQ base[18]
	662 Brigade	Luanchuan (33.7883, 111.5925)[19]	DF-5A/B (DF-4?)	Yes	Potentially upgrading to DF-41
	663 Brigade	Nanyang (33.0117, 112.4145)	DF-31A	Yes	First DF-31A brigade
	664 Brigade	Yiyang (34.5435, 112.1470)?[20]	(DF-31AG?)	Yes	Possibly upgrading to DF-31AG
	665 Brigade	Xinxiang (35.3999, 114.1263)?[21]	?	?	Rumored new brigade base area
	666 Brigade	Xinyang (32.1675, 114.1257)	DF-26	Yes	First DF-26 brigade base
Total:	**40 Brigades**			~21	
Base 67 (Shaanxi)	Central nuclear weapons storage complex. Headquartered in Baoji city. Responsible for storing and handling nuclear warheads at nearby underground storage facility as well as smaller regional storage sites located in each regional base area.				

Sources: Mark Stokes, *PLA Rocket Force Leadership and Unit Reference*, Project 2049 Institute, April 9, 2018; P. W. Singer and Ma Xiu, "China's Missile Force Is Growing at an Unprecedented Rate," *Popular Science*, February 25, 2020; Decker Eveleth, "Mapping the People's Liberation Army Rocket Force," *aboyandthis.blog*, April 20, 2020; research by Ben Reuters, Vinayak Bhat, and others who wish to remain anonymous; and author's observations and estimates. The table is continually updated to reflect new information.

1. Each brigade has several launch battalions (up to six) and support units located in the region. A question mark indicates an unknown or uncertain location. PLARF also operates several training areas not listed, such as at Jilantai and Haixi/DaQaidam; launch units visit these training areas to exercise or integrate new equipment.

2. The type of missile assigned to each base is listed first, followed by other missile type(s) that have been seen at that base (in parentheses). Question mark indicates uncertainty about whether the missile has been integrated. Nuclear DF-21 bases are difficult to determine.

3. Previously with DF-15 SRBMs.

4. In addition to the DF-16, satellite photos occasionally show trucks that resemble the DF-21C and the DF-26, but the trucks appear to be transporters.

5. Some identify this rumored unit (618 Brigade) at the older Xianyou base (25.3165, 118.7119), but it is uncertain.

6. Some put the location of 631 Brigade (at Jingzhou) further north (26.5782, 109.6703).

7. The 631 Brigade HQ base has 4–5 silos and an underground missile storage facility, plus possibly some decoy silos.

8. The 633 Brigade (at Huitong) has 4–5 silos, plus possibly some decoy silos.

9. Location uncertain.

10. A former DF-4 ICBM brigade area. Possibly upgrading to DF-41, potentially with silos.

11. DF-31/A launchers were displayed in June 2011. See Hans M. Kristensen, "Chinese Mobile ICBMs Seen in Central China," *FAS Strategic Security Blog*, March 1, 2012, https://fas.org/blogs/security/2012/03/df-31deployment/. In June 2019 a possible DF-31AG was seen at the 642 Brigade launch unit training site at Haiyan.

12. Decker Eveleth, "China's Mobile ICBM Brigades: The DF-31 and DF-41," *aboyandthis.blog*, July 2, 2020, https://www.aboyandthis.blog/post/china-s-mobile-icbm-brigades-the-df-31-and-df-41

13. Hans M. Kristensen, "China's New DF-26 Missile Shows Up at Base in Eastern China," *FAS Strategic Security Blog*, January 21, 2019, https://fas.org/blogs/security/2020/01/df-26deployment/.

14. Hans M. Kristensen, "China's New DF-26 Missile Shows Up at Base in Eastern China." In 2014 the 651 Brigade base at Dengshahe upgraded its weapons from DF-3A to DF-21A. Hans M. Kristensen, "Chinese Nuclear Missile Upgrade Near Dalian," *FAS Strategic Security Blog*, May 21, 2014, https://fas.org/blogs/security/2014/05/dengshaheupgrade/.

15. Some identify the 652 Brigade as a technical support regiment.

16. Location of 656 Brigade is highly uncertain but rumored to be in Laiwu (to the east), which already has 653 Brigade.

17. Some place 661 Brigade HQ in Lingbao to the north (34.5166, 110.8619); it might be a training unit.

18. The brigade probably has 4–5 silos, plus possibly some decoy silos.

19. Potential silos are located around Shecunzhen to the east.

20. 664 Brigade (at Yiyang) is rumored to be a training complex. In 2019 DF-31As were visible and DF-31AG training was reported.

21. Location uncertain; other potential candidate site is at 35.2604, 114.1090.

In addition to practicing deployments in their respective base areas, missile units often deploy to training areas located hundreds of kilometers from their home bases to practice deployment and launch operations. At one time the northwest training area in Qinghai province was busy with operations that stretched west from the base in Haixi nearly 300 km (170 mi) through Delingha and Da Qaidam to beyond Maihan, but missile activities appear to have decreased in that area in recent years.[6] Instead, the new training area constructed near Jilantai in the southern part of Inner Mongolia has expanded significantly over the past five years and is currently quite active. In January 2019 the Chinese government–sanctioned media reported deployment of the new DF-26 to "northwest China's plateau and desert area," which was later geolocated at the Jilantai training area.[7] In April–May 2019 training operations in the area included the new DF-41, the DF-31AG, the DF-26, and possibly the DF-17 HGV. In addition to performing mobile launcher training, PLARF also appears to be building several missile silos of a new type that could be part of an effort to deploy the DF-41 in silos in the future.[8] It is possible, but unconfirmed, that similar silos are under construction in the 662 Brigade area in Henan province.[9] Other training areas are located in the northeast (near Jingyu in Jilin province), in the southwest (near Guiyang in Guizhou province), and in the west (near Korla in the Xinjiang Uyghur Autonomous Region).[10]

Medium- and Intermediate-Range Ballistic Missiles

China has fielded a wide range of medium- and intermediate-range ballistic missiles to provide the Chinese leadership with nuclear strike options against targets on China's periphery (see figure 5.2). Among the medium-range missiles, two versions of the solid-fuel road-mobile DF-21 are nuclear: DF-21A (CSS-5 Mod 2) and DF-21E (CSS-5 Mod 6). The original nuclear DF-21, which first appeared in the late 1980s, appears to have been replaced with the newer models that have a longer range and improved off-road capability.

The MRBM/IRBM missiles are an interesting category because of the temptation to categorize them as "tactical" nuclear weapons. In US and Russian terminology, anything that is not strategic—meaning "of intercontinental range"—is considered tactical. But China seems to view all of its nuclear weapons as strategic. Regional missiles probably serve a role against India and eastern Russia. But in a war with the United States the regional missiles raise some interesting questions about how China potentially would use nuclear weapons. The shorter range could potentially mean that Chinese strike plans include options other than strategic counterattack on the US mainland, such as against US bases in the western Pacific. In a war situation would the Chinese leadership use all missiles in the same counterattack, or are the regional-range missiles also intended for limited use only, that is, to persuade an aggressor to back down or face Chinese

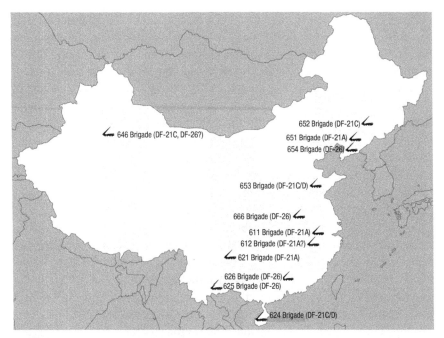

FIGURE 5.2. Estimated Locations of Chinese Medium- and Intermediate-Range Ballistic Missiles. (See table 5.2 for details on specific sites.)

use of long-range strategic weapons? If so, that implies a degree of deescalation thinking. Or the reason for the regional missile could simply be that a single nuclear counterattack would involve strikes against both regional and intercontinental targets.

China does not describe any of its nuclear forces as tactical weapons. In the 1980s, some segments of the US intelligence community believed China had or was developing actual tactical nuclear weapons, including short-range ballistic missiles and nuclear mines.[11] A 1985 US Defense Intelligence Agency estimate of China's nuclear strategy found that "there are indications that the Chinese, having recognized [their lack of tactical and theater options below the strategic level] as a weakness in their strategy, are pursuing a variety of programs aimed at developing shorter-range ballistic missiles and other tactical systems more suited to battlefield use. When they reach fruition in the 1990s, such systems may have a major impact on Chinese strategy, particularly employment plans."[12] Moreover, the CIA believed that some of China's nuclear tests in the early 1990s were related to warheads for short-range ballistic missiles, cruise missiles, and artillery, but such weapons do not seem to have been fielded. Instead, China appears to have mainly chosen to rely on nonnuclear missiles for use in tactical defense scenarios.[13]

Today most of China's nuclear-capable missiles do not have strategic range but only regional range. A DoD fact sheet published with the 2018 Nuclear Posture Review (NPR) report explicitly characterized the DF-21 and DF-26 as nonstrategic weapons: "China is also expanding and modernizing its *nonstrategic nuclear weapons*, including the CSS-5 Mod 6 and DF-26, intended to threaten its neighbors and challenge the U.S.'s ability to conduct regional operations."[14] According to the NPR, US military planners are working on "increasing the range of graduated nuclear response options available to the president" to "strengthen the credibility of our deterrence strategy and improve our capability to respond effectively to Chinese limited nuclear use if deterrence were to fail."[15] So while China may not officially possess tactical nuclear weapons or plan limited attacks, the US military is planning as though it does.

China's first solid-fuel road-mobile MRBM—the DF-21 (SSC-5)—is now in its sixth modification: from the initial nuclear DF-21 (SSC-5 Mod 1) version fielded in the late 1980s (though not deployed in earnest until the early 1990s) to the upgraded DF-21A (SSC-5 Mod 2) in the late 1990s or early 2000s, to the conventional DF-21C (SSC-5 Mod 4) deployed around 2007, to the DF-21D (SSC-5 Mod 5) anti-ship version in 2010, to the latest DF-21E (SSC-5 Mod 6) developed in 2016, which presumably replaces the DF-21As.[16]

The DoD reports that China today has some 150 MRBM launchers for the various versions of the DF-21, with a total of 150–450 missiles.[17] With an estimated range of more than 2,000 km, the DF-21s can target facilities in southeast Russia, Japan, South Korea, the Philippines, and northern India. Each brigade operates several launch battalions; it is estimated there are some 40 nuclear DF-21 launchers of all types, each of which can carry 1 missile with 1 warhead.

In the regional deterrent mission the DF-21 is being supplemented by the new dual-capable DF-26 IRBM, which was first displayed in 2015 and deployed to units in 2016. With a range of approximately 4,000 km, it can target facilities further out from China, that is, as far as Guam. China has had the capability to target Guam with nuclear DF-4 and DF-31 missiles for decades, but the DF-26 adds conventional capability to that mission. The Chinese Ministry of Defense stated in 2015 that the DF-26 "can conduct a fast nuclear counterattack and can carry out conventional medium- and long-range precision strikes."[18] The DoD says PLARF has also fielded an anti-ship ballistic missile (ASBM) variant of the DF-26.

The DoD stated in 2016 that the DF-26, "if it shares the same guidance capabilities [as the conventional version], would give China its first nuclear precision strike capability against theater targets."[19] A similar 2019 report appears to strengthen confidence in that assessment by stating the "DF-26 is capable of conducting conventional and nuclear precision strikes against ground targets."[20] During his confirmation hearing in 2018, INDOPACOM commander Adm. Philip

Davidson stated the DF-26 and the DF-21 missiles "could support a variety of nuclear strike options, tactical-to-strategic and preemptive-to-retaliatory," which other than "preemptive" echoes the Chinese Ministry of Defense's announcement in 2018 that the DF-26 was "capable of firing both nuclear and conventional weapons, [and] is able to conduct rapid nuclear counterattacks."[21] But Davidson added that the increased capabilities "are not-themselves-indicative of any shift in China's no first use policy."[22]

The DF-26 is being fielded in significant numbers. When the DoD first identified the missile in its annual China report in 2016, it listed 16 launchers. That was the same number displayed at the Beijing parade in 2015 and at the PLA's Ninetieth Anniversary Parade in 2017. The Chinese Ministry of Defense announced in April 2018 that the DF-26 had completed trial deployment and operational testing and had officially become operational within the PLARF.[23] The August 2018 DoD report listed 16–20 launchers (with an equal number of missiles), an estimate that increased significantly in the 2019 report, to become 80 launchers with 80–160 missiles (the 160 number implies field reload capability). The 80 number is probably the upper end of a range estimate of 65–80, in which case the actual number might be somewhere between those figures (this article estimates 72 as of early 2020, with many more in production).

The first unit to receive the DF-26 was probably the 666 Brigade stationed on the outskirts of Xinyang in southern Henan province.[24] In April 2018 the Chinese Ministry of Defense reported it had commissioned "a new medium–long range missile system to a newly-established missile brigade" and formally fielded it in the PLARF.[25] Chinese news media carried reports showing DF-26 launchers at an unnamed military facility that was geo-located to what is believed to be the 652 Brigade Base (or Base 65 Technical Support Regiment) in Jinchangzhen, south of Tonghua in southern Jilin province.[26] The area previously was reported to be using the DF-21C/D.[27] All together, satellite images have detected what appear to be DF-26 launchers at four to six bases (see table 5.2), which roughly matches the 65–80 launchers reported by the DoD. Significant DF-26 production appears to be continuing.[28]

There have been widespread reports that the new DF-17 hypersonic glide vehicle also has a nuclear capability.[29] But during the 2019 parade in Beijing the 16 DF-17 launchers were presented by the official announcer as a "conventional missile formation," and the China Global Television Network repeated that the "DF-17 conventional missiles are used for precision strikes against medium-and-close targets."[30] Yet in prepared remarks before the US Senate in February 2020, STRATCOM commander Gen. Charles Richard stated the parade "unveiled new strategic nuclear systems, including the . . . DF-17 medium-range ballistic missile."[31] Whatever its capability, the DF-17 is expected to become operational soon.

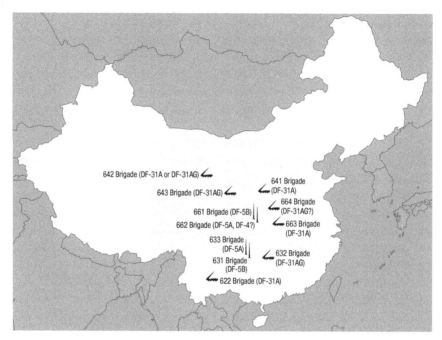

642 Brigade (DF-31A or DF-31AG)
643 Brigade (DF-31AG)
641 Brigade (DF-31A)
661 Brigade (DF-5B)
664 Brigade (DF-31AG?)
662 Brigade (DF-5A, DF-4?)
663 Brigade (DF-31A)
633 Brigade (DF-5A)
631 Brigade (DF-5B)
632 Brigade (DF-31AG)
622 Brigade (DF-31A)

FIGURE 5.3. Estimated Locations of Chinese Intercontinental Ballistic Missiles. (See table 5.2 for details on specific sites.)

Intercontinental Ballistic Missiles

China's ICBM force has undergone significant development over the past fifteen years. The liquid-fuel, limited-range, transportable DF-4, which is now deployed to only a single brigade and may be retired soon, along with the silo-based full-range DF-5 made up the Chinese strategic force for twenty-five years, until the road-mobile DF-31 (SSC-10 Mod 1) and its extended-range variant, the DF-31A (SSC-10 Mod 2) entered the arsenal in 2006 and 2007, respectively. The DF-5 is still being upgraded, most recently with MIRV as the DF-5B version, and after more than twenty years in development, the DF-41 is now being fielded to improve off-road maneuverability and provide MIRV capability to the road-mobile ICBM force for the first time (see figure 5.3).

The DF-5 is now in its third configuration. A fourth version, known as the DF-5C, may be in development. The initial version carried a single multimegaton-yield warhead but in 2005 was replaced with a slightly longer-range version (DF-5A). Ten years later, concern over the effect of the US ballistic missile defense system apparently caused China to modify some of the DF-5As to carry MIRVs. The Chinese military has explicitly stated that the new version, known as the DF-5B or SSC-4 Mod 3, can "carry multiple nuclear warheads and attack several targets,"[32] which suggests that the objective was more than simply overcoming missile defenses. The DF-5B was displayed at both the 2015 and 2019 parades in Beijing and was seen operating in the Jilantai training area in April 2019.[33]

There have been rumors that each DF-5B can carry as many as 8 warheads, but it seems more likely that each can carry 3–5 of the warheads developed for the DF-31. The purpose of MIRVs in China's strategy is not to maximize warhead loading but to ensure that warheads can get through US and Russian missile defense systems, although the quote above hints that targeting may also be a factor. It is estimated that two of four DF-5 brigades have been upgraded to MIRVs, for a total of 40 warheads for 20 missiles. It is possible, but unconfirmed, that all DF-5s will eventually be upgraded to carry MIRVs.

The DF-5 is complemented in the long-range strategic mission by the single-warhead, road-mobile DF-31A that was fielded in 2007. While production of the shorter-range DF-31 appears to have ended after its deployment to only one brigade, the fielding of the DF-31A appears to have peaked at about 32 missiles in four brigades. The DF-31A was not displayed at the 2019 parade in Beijing and is gradually being replaced by the more maneuverable DF-31AG.

The DF-31AG, which is being deployed in greater numbers than the DF-31A, appears to be intended to carry the same missile as the DF-31A but with significantly improved off-road capability. The new launcher has the same number of axles as the DF-31A (eight) but instead of the missile canister being carried aboard a trailer, the new truck looks more like a larger DF-21C. Some private analysts have speculated the DF-31AG missile has improved features and range—some even claim MIRVs—but the 2019 DoD report does not credit it with either. Sixteen DF-31AG transporter erector launchers (TELs) were displayed at the parade in Beijing in October 2019, but 18 TELs could be seen positioned at a base near Yangfang just outside the capital—the same number seen training at Jilantai in April 2019.[34] The first two brigades to receive the DF-31AG were probably the 642 Brigade in Datong and the 643 Brigade in Tianshui (see table 5.2), and more are being added.

China is now fielding the new DF-41 road-mobile ICBM that the DoD says is capable of carrying MIRVs. The weapon has been under development since at least the 1990s. The eight-axle TEL has improved maneuverability—and possibly improved speed—compared with the DF-31A. The DF-41 missile canister extends over the driver cockpit and has a length of 21–22 meters, which is 4–5 meters longer than the 16–17-meter canister on the DF-31A. Sixteen DF-41 TELs were displayed at the 2019 Beijing parade, although 18 were seen at the Yangfang base—the same number seen operating at the Jilantai training area in April 2019.[35] The official parade narrator announced that the 16 DF-41 TELs came from two brigades.[36] At this early stage of development these two brigades are probably engineering brigades that were also involved in fielding the DF-31A.

The 2019 DoD report states that "China appears to be considering additional DF-41 launch options, including rail-mobile and silo basing."[37] A new silo constructed at the Wuzhai test launch complex in northwestern Shanxi province has been widely rumored to be for DF-41 launches, but its features closely resemble those of the older DF-5 test silo located nearby. A more interesting new development is happening at the Jilantai training center 530 km to the west, where it appears that four silos of a new type are under construction. Unlike the silos at Wuzhai, the configuration of the silos at Jilantai more closely resembles Russian ICBM silos.[38] The launch of a solid-fuel DF-41 from a silo could be done considerably quicker than the launch of a liquid-fuel DF-5, which requires extra time to load the fuel. As such, a future force of silo-based DF-41s would be more responsive and could potentially form part of an ICBM alert-posture that is linked to an early warning system, were the Chinese leadership to decide to develop such a posture in the future.

It is unknown how many nuclear ballistic missiles the PLARF plans to deploy in the future. According to data published by the DoD and the National Air and Space Intelligence Center (NASIC), since 2003 the number of ICBM launchers has tripled, from around 30 to nearly 100. The number of warheads available for those ICBMs might now have exceeded 100. The NASIC projected in 2017 that "the number of warheads on Chinese ICBMs capable of threatening the United States is expected to grow to well over 100 in the next 5 years."[39] That projection appears to be coming true, although it is important to remember that the force that can reasonably target all of the continental United States is smaller (the DF-4 and DF-31 don't have the range), that the Chinese ICBM force is less than one-quarter the size of the US ICBM force, and that Chinese ICBMs—unlike those of the United States (and Russia)—are not believed to be loaded with warheads under normal circumstances.

SEA-BASED BALLISTIC MISSILES

After decades of trial and error with its first Xia-class (Type 091) SSBN, a program that produced only a single hull in the early 1980s and that never became fully operational or conducted even one deterrent patrol, China has since built and deployed a small fleet of four Jin-class (Type 094) SSBNs. Two more are being fitted out. Each submarine is equipped to carry up to 12 Julang-2 (JL-2) SLBMs, each capable of delivering 1 nuclear warhead.

All Jin-class SSBNs are homeported with the South Sea Fleet at Longpo Naval Base on Hainan Island (18.2083, 109.6801). The base has been expanded considerably over the past couple of decades to homeport the four SSBNs and other vessels. This includes constructing tunnels into a large underground facility, which is probably capable of housing several submarines and loading weapons outside the reach of foreign spy satellites. The base also includes a unique railway that was covered with a roof a few years ago, presumably to conceal transportation of weapons between the underground facility and what appears to be a missile handling facility. The base also includes what appears to be a demagnetization facility.[40]

The previous SSBN base at Jianggezhuang (Nanyao) near Qingdao in Shandong (36.1108, 120.5767) province on the Yellow Sea is the homeport for the now nonoperational Xia-class SSBN. Jin-class SSBNs occasionally visit the base, which has an underground submarine facility, but the base is mainly used by nuclear attack submarines.[41] A submarine refit and missile flight-test base is located at Xiaopingdao near Dalian in the Liaoning province (38.8199, 121.4915). This is where new SSBNs are fitted out after they are launched from the Huludao shipyard in the Bohai Bay (40.7153, 120.9952) before they are handed over to the People's Liberation Army Navy (PLAN). It is also where SSBNs load flight-test missiles.

In building the Jin-class SSBN fleet China appears to some extent to be trying to mirror the nuclear postures of the United States, Russia, Britain, and France. For the Chinese SSBNs to provide a credible second-strike capability in a tense crisis or war, however, the fleet will have to be capable of deploying safely from port and hiding undetected in the ocean. A sea-based second-strike capability only makes strategic sense if it is *more secure* than PLARF's land-based ICBM force. Its justification must be based on the conclusion that ICBMs are too vulnerable to a first strike and thus a more secure sea-based second-strike force is needed to back it up. But US Naval Intelligence reported a decade ago that the Jin-class SSBN is noisier than the Soviet Delta III-class SSBN built in the 1970s.[42]

If they are too noisy, the Jins could be vulnerable to early detection and attrition, especially if they are deployed to distant patrol areas in order for the missiles to be able to reach important targets. With a range of 7,200–7,400 km (4,470–4,600 mi)—the range estimate given by the US intelligence community for the JL-2 SLBM carried on Jin-class SSBNs—a submarine would need to sail deep into the Pacific Ocean to be able to target the US western coast. To be able to effectively threaten Washington, DC, a Jin SSBN would have to sail even farther away from home.

The Chinese command-and-control system for submarine communications is relatively simple by US standards and largely unproven. A submarine deploying on a deterrent patrol with nuclear weapons onboard would need to be able to maintain contact with the national command authority in order to provide a retaliatory capability. China still seems to have a development gap to close before it can claim to have a credible sea-based second-strike capability.

All of this indicates that the Jin-class SSBN program is a work in progress—a pilot project—and partly intended to develop the technologies, operations, infrastructure, and capabilities needed to create a real sea-based second-strike capability in the future. The next SSBN class, known as Type 096, is expected to be quieter and be equipped with the longer range JL-3. The DoD predicts construction of the Type 096 might begin in the early 2020s but has not yet provided a range estimate for the JL-3. Internet speculations already predict a range of 12,000–14,000 km (7,456–7,700 mi), apparently based on the assumption that the JL-3 will be derived from the DF-41 ICBM, which probably has a range similar to the DF-5 (12,000–13,000 km).[43] However, a range nearly double that of the JL-2 seems unrealistic. Just as the JL-2 was based on the DF-31 (not the extended-range DF-31A), the JL-3 range might similarly be less than the full range of the DF-41 because it must fit inside the length of a submarine missile tube that will be significantly shorter than the 20-meter missile canister of the DF-41. A range up to 10,000 km (6,200 mi) seems more plausible.

But even a significantly longer JL-3 range will still not give Chinese SSBNs the capability to target all of the continental United States from waters near China. A JL-3 that is fired from a Type 096 operating in the South China Sea, for example, would need a range of at least 10,600 km (6,600 mi) to be able to strike Seattle. Holding Washington, DC, at risk would require a range of more than 13,500 km (8,400 mi). If fired from a submarine operating in the shallow Bohai Sea, a JL-3 would need a range of 8,500 km (5,300 mi) to hit Seattle and 11,100 km (6,900 mi) to hit Washington, DC. This suggests that the next-generation SSBN fleet could still be faced with the challenge of operating far from Chinese waters into the Sea of Japan or the northern Pacific Ocean in order to be able to target all of the United States. Even operating inside the First Island Chain could not be considered a safe bastion.

Rather than providing a full strategic retaliatory strike capability, an SSBN fleet equipped with the JL-3 could still serve an important role against US facilities in the US Northwest, Guam, Alaska, and Hawaii—certainly enough to make the point of deterrence. And such SSBNs would be well within range of both India and all of Russia.

The Jin-class SSBN fleet has significantly enhanced the size of the Chinese nuclear arsenal. The four operational boats can carry a combined 48 SLBMs with an equal number of warheads; once the fifth and sixth hulls join the fleet, the sea-based arsenal will increase to 72 JL-2 missiles. Future Type 096–class SSBNs will add further to the arsenal as they become operational in the late 2020s. The number of missiles per submarine is still unknown. Internet speculations have already emerged with claims of about 24 missiles, each with 10 MIRVs per submarine.[44] This is probably an exaggeration; 16 JL-3 missiles per submarine seem more likely. If so, the Chinese SSBN fleet could potentially carry 104 SLBMs with as many warheads by the late 2020s (although only some of those would be operational at any given time). A decision to MIRV the JL-3 would further boost that portion of the fleet.

LONG-RANGE BOMBERS

The nuclear mission of Chinese bombers has varied over the years depending on domestic and international factors. Bombers, including the H-6, were used to deliver at least twelve of the nuclear devices detonated in the Chinese nuclear testing program between 1965 and 1979. The devices demonstrated yields between 10–20 kilotons [kt] to 4 megatons [mt].[45] The DIA estimated in 1984 that China had about 165 nuclear bombs for aircraft, although the agency also said "we are unable to identify associated airfield storage sites."[46] By the late-1980s the estimate had declined to 75 bombs, but the DIA assessed at the time that H-6 and H-5 medium-range bombers and A-5 fighter-bombers were "all capable of delivering nuclear weapons."[47] In 1993 the National Security Council (NSC) informed Congress that China had a "small stockpile of nuclear bombs" but that the nuclear bomber role was limited to a contingency mission only: "The Chinese Air Force has no units whose primary mission is to deliver China's small stockpile of nuclear bombs. Rather, some units may be tasked for nuclear delivery as a contingency mission."[48] Several of those nuclear bomb designs are prominently displayed at Chinese military museums.[49]

This semidormant nuclear bomber mission apparently had the same status as recently as 2017, when the DoD reported that the "PLAAF [People's Liberation Army Air Force] does not currently have a nuclear mission." Yet the DoD also reported that past PLA writings expressing the need to develop a "stealth strategic bomber" suggests "aspirations to field a strategic bomber with a nuclear delivery capability" and that China was developing a strategic bomber that "officials expect to have a nuclear mission."[50] Indeed, in May 2017 DIA director Lt. Gen. Vincent R. Stewart told Congress that China was "upgrading its aircraft . . . with two, new air-launched ballistic missiles [ALBMs], one of which may include a nuclear payload."[51] One year later the DoD reported that the "PLAAF has been re-assigned a nuclear mission" and that the "H-6 and future stealth bomber could both be nuclear capable."[52] The 2019 report explains that at least since 2016 "Chinese media" have been referring to the new H-6K version as a "dual nuclear-conventional bomber."[53] Furthermore, the *Nuclear Matters Handbook* published by the DoD in February 2020 lists the H-6 (probably the K and N versions) as nuclear and expected to be completely fielded within ten years.[54]

The new air-launched ballistic missile reported by the DIA apparently is based on the DF-21 and is known in the US intelligence community as

CH-AS-X-13. The modified H-6 intended to carry the new missile is known as H-6N. The DIA expects the missile could potentially be fielded by the mid-2020s, although the 2020 *Nuclear Matters Handbook* lists the missile as "in research & development within 10 years."[55]

One PLA official disclosed in 2014 that China was designing a new long-range stealth bomber as a replacement for the H-6.[56] This was confirmed by the head of the PLAAF in 2016.[57] The new bomber was referred to as the H-20 by Chinese Central Television in 2018.[58] Although there are rumors of a first flight taking place soon, the bomber will likely not enter the force until the mid to late 2020s.

Reassignment of a nuclear mission to the PLAAF is noteworthy because it indicates Chinese planners might be seeking to broaden the range of nuclear options against regional targets. As described earlier, China already has a significant number of DF-21 medium- and DF-26 intermediate-range ballistic missiles with nuclear capability that can reach such targets, so a nuclear bomber force presumably would be intended to provide more flexible strike options, potentially with long-range cruise missiles in the future.[59]

COMMAND-AND-CONTROL AND STRATEGIC DEFENSE SYSTEMS

China's nuclear forces are controlled by command, control, and communications (NC3) and strategic defense systems that are thought to be highly centralized and less operationally capable than those of the United States and Russia. This is partly a result of China's minimum deterrence nuclear posture as well as its less ambitious military modernization reforms of the past. As such, under normal circumstances its nuclear warheads are thought to be stored separately from launchers but with redundant NC3 systems to ensure that the national leadership can increase alerts during a crisis and transmit launch orders to the PLARF and individual launch units. Efforts are underway to develop a reliable capability to communicate with the emerging SSBN fleet, although a real sea-based deterrent posture would require the Central Military Commission (CMC) to allow deployment of warheads on SSBNs in peacetime if it can't count on being able to flush the SSBNs out to sea during a crisis. In the future bombers will also have to be incorporated into the NC3 system.

China's nuclear forces are under the direct control of the CMC, a body of military and political leaders headed by President Xi Jinping. The NC3 system has undergone several transformations of its computer systems and with an increasingly mobile missile force. Today the system is thought to provide multiple redundant means of communication from the CMC and PLARF headquarters to missile bases and launch units via radio, cables, fiber-optic cables, and satellites.[60]

China's NC3 is uniquely affected by the mixture of nuclear and conventional MRBMs and IRBMs. While nuclear and conventional DF-21 versions appear to be mostly based separately, the separation may not be clear in a crisis and the new DF-26 is dual-capable. The mixing of nuclear and conventional arms raises serious questions about the potential for inaccurate crisis signaling and subsequent misunderstandings and overreactions. Readying of a DF-26 launch unit for a conventional scenario could potentially be misinterpreted as escalation to nuclear alert and cause an adversary to ready its own nuclear force prematurely. And conventional attacks on conventional units could potentially affect nuclear systems as well. The 2019 DoD report expresses considerable anxiety about this possibility:

> China's commingling of some of its conventional and nuclear missile forces, and ambiguities in China's NFU conditions, could complicate deterrence and escalation management during a conflict. Potential adversary attacks against Chinese conventional missile force–associated C2 centers could inadvertently degrade Chinese nuclear C2 and generate nuclear use-or-lose pressures among China's leadership. Once a conflict has begun, China's dispersal of mobile missile systems to hide sites could further complicate the task of distinguishing between nuclear and conventional forces and, thus, increase the potential for inadvertent attacks on the latter. China's leadership calculus for responding to conventional attacks on nuclear forces remains a key unknown.[61]

Modernization of the NC3 systems partly reflects the threat Chinese planners see posed by adversarial offensive forces. To that end, the 2019 DoD report describes how "China is enhancing peacetime readiness levels" for its nuclear forces "to ensure their responsiveness."[62] This does not necessarily imply that China is moving toward a peacetime alert posture of nuclear warheads deployed on the missiles. Rather, the report refers to unidentified "PLA writings" that "express the value of a 'launch on warning' [LOW] nuclear posture, an approach to deterrence that uses heightened readiness, improved surveillance, and streamlined decision-making processes to enable a more rapid response to enemy attack." According to the DoD report, the writings argue that LOW would be consistent with China's NFU policy, "suggesting it may be an aspiration for China's nuclear forces" and adding that "China is working to develop a space-based early warning capability that could support this posture in the future."[63]

While China might want to increase its awareness of potential attacks, this doesn't necessarily mean it is planning to adopt a formal LOW posture for its nuclear forces. Recently, in a keynote address to an international arms control conference in China, the director general of the Arms Control Department of the Chinese Ministry of Foreign Affairs, Fu Cong, stated that a launch on warning posture would be incompatible with China's long-standing promise not to use nuclear weapons first under any circumstances.[64] Similarly, although there has been considerable speculation about possible conditions required for China's NFU policy, the 2019 DoD report concludes: "There has been no indication that national leaders are willing to attach such nuances and caveats to China's existing NFU policy."[65]

China does not yet have a strategic early warning system capable of supporting a strategy to launch its nuclear forces before they can be attacked. Instead China has relied on a system of gradually alerting its forces in a crisis, on concealment of silos, underground storage facilities, and widely dispersed road-mobile launchers to ride out or weaken the effectiveness of a surprise first-strike against its retaliatory nuclear forces. Over the past decade, however, China has constructed a small number of large phased-array radars (LPAR) that appear to form part of an effort to develop an improved ground-based warning system against ballistic missile attacks. There is still uncertainty among the public about the capability of these radars and what official role they serve compared with other radars; some may be related to space tracking or air defense. Ground-based radars would in any case only provide limited strategic warning because of the curvature of the Earth, so China would need to develop a constellation of satellites with infrared sensors capable of detecting missile launches to be able to have a meaningful strategic warning of an attack. It also would need a reliable network of facilities capable of receiving and processing the early warning data and relaying the information to the national command authority. Like other nuclear-armed states, China would have to work its way through years of operational and technical fine tuning—not to mention how to respond to and correct false warnings.

The 2015 white paper, "China's Military Strategy," for the first time publicly emphasized the intention to develop a strategic early warning capability: "China will optimize its nuclear force structure, improve strategic early warning, command and control, missile penetration, rapid reaction, and survivability and protection, and deter other countries from using or threatening to use nuclear weapons against China."[66] The People's Liberation Army Strategic Support Force (PLASSF), established in December 2015, was charged with overseeing China's space, cyber, and electronic warfare (EW) capabilities and effectively integrating them into PLA operations.[67]

Although the precise function of the PLASSF is still uncertain, given its mandate and structure it is possible that it might play a role in managing China's emerging strategic early warning capabilities. During the military's reorganization, the Space Systems Department of the PLASSF subsumed into it the space-related C4ISR units of the former PLA General Staff Department (GSD) and the General Armaments Department (GAD), both of which were then eliminated.[68] The GSD previously commanded the BeiDou Navigation Satellite System—China's effort to establish an alternative to the US-owned Global Positioning System (GPS)—whereas the GAD was in charge of China's satellite development and launches.[69] Based on the units that were incorporated into the PLASSF, it seems evident that the Strategic Support Force is now responsible for all operations involving Chinese satellites and is in command of China's four space launch centers.[70] In early 2016 a website sponsored by the PLA posted remarks from retired Navy Rear Admiral Yin Zhuo, in which he stated: "The PLA Strategic Support Force will play an important role in reconnaissance, warning, communication, commanding, control, navigation," indicating that future developments or operations involving strategic early warning systems will be handled by the PLASSF.[71]

Radar Systems

Since approximately 2009 China has constructed at least four ground-based large phased-array radars (LPARs), which could possibly be used to detect and track incoming strategic missiles.[72] The LPAR at Huanan in Heilongjiang province (46.5279, 130.7552) faces north, meaning it could detect and track missiles on a polar trajectory. ICBMs launched from the US mainland would cross over Canada, the North Pole, and Russia before impacting on Chinese territory, so this radar is likely tasked with tracking this type of strategic threat. It would potentially be tasked with tracking attacks from Russia as well.

The LPAR radar at Yiyuan in Shandong province (36.0255, 118.0916) faces a southeasterly direction, toward Taiwan and the Philippine Sea. When the radar was unveiled at the "Five Years of Enthusiastic Progress" military exhibit in late 2017, Chinese media reported that this "remote warning radar" transmits in P-band frequency (more commonly known as UHF frequency) to a range of approximately 5,000 km, similar to the American PAVE PAWS strategic early warning radar system.[73] The LPAR at Yiyuan appears to have an underground facility associated with it, with an entrance to the southeast.

The LPAR radar north of Longgangzhen in the western part of Zhejiang province (30.2866, 119.1286) also faces southeast, toward Taiwan. The Longgangzhen radar is located next to an older radar facing northwest; a similar older radar is located near Zhuolu in northern Hebei province (40.4478, 115.1171). Given that the missile threat from Taiwan is both minimal and nonnuclear, instead of being used for strategic early warning the Longgangzhen radar might be utilized to bolster Chinese conventional strikes into the East China Sea and the South China Sea, but there is no confirmation of this.[74]

The LPAR at the Korla Missile Test Complex in Xinjiang province (41.6410, 86.2367) looks similar to the other LPAR radars but, unlike the others, it can be turned. Satellite images show the radar in several different orientations but always facing either west, southwest, south, southeast, or east toward the launch facilities—never north. It is therefore likely that the Korla radar is tasked with tracking satellite launches and missile intercept tests, given its proximity to China's hit-to-kill (HTK) launch site and its orientation toward sites from where test missiles and military satellites are launched.[75] Before the creation of the PLASSF, the facility at Korla appeared to be subordinate to the GAD.[76] Given that the space-related elements of the GAD were integrated into the PLASSF during the military reorganization, it seems likely that the LPAR at Korla—and perhaps the other three operational LPARs—are currently operated by the PLASSF.

In addition to giving early warning of ballistic missile attacks, a strategic early warning system would also have to be capable of detecting attacks by long-range bombers and cruise missiles that can also hold missile launchers, and nuclear facilities at risk. China has for many years possessed an extensive air-defense system.[77] This system is undergoing extensive modernization, including integration of the Russian-supplied S-400 air-defense system.

In January 2017 China completed construction of an over-the-horizon (OTH) radar receiver north of Wuchuan in Inner Mongolia (41.4231, 111.07657); construction of its corresponding transmitter is likely to begin soon.[78] This is the second OTH radar system that China has constructed in the past twelve years, with the first coming online around 2007 under the name "Project 2319" in Hubei province.[79] OTH radars are relatively complex systems and operate by reflecting high frequency electromagnetic waves off of the ionosphere, thereby achieving a backscattering effect that allows the operator to detect objects at long distances beyond the horizon. In order to improve the performance of its OTH radars, China has constructed a series of ionospheric measuring stations along its southeastern coastline, some of which are clearly visible through satellite imagery.[80]

China's two new OTH radars are facing in a southeasterly direction and reportedly have a range of approximately 2,500 km. This range would offer coverage of the entire Korean Peninsula, Japan, Taiwan, and a large portion of the western Pacific—nearly reaching Guam. These radars will support Chinese efforts to establish blanket C4ISR coverage over its area of operations.

Satellites

Satellites with infrared sensors are required to be able to track from space the heat signatures of ballistic missiles launched from land or sea. China does not yet have a constellation of such satellites, which would be required to provide space-based early warning. However, following the May 2015 release of the "China's Military Strategy" document, which emphasized improvements to strategic early warning systems, two highly secret Chinese satellite launches in 2015 and 2017 prompted Western and Chinese analysts to speculate that China is developing an early warning satellite constellation similar to the American Space-Based Infrared System (SBIRS) satellites.[81] These geostationary satellites, known as TJS-1 and TJS-2, were officially reported as "communications technology test satellites" by Chinese state media sources;[82] however, the highly secretive nature of the launches and the unusual lack of accompanying technical information may indicate that they serve a military function.[83]

China also maintains a constellation of 31 Yaogan satellite groupings equipped with electronic intelligence (ELINT), synthetic aperture radar (SAR), and optical imaging sensors that offer a C4ISR coverage radius of approximately 3,500 km. These satellites—in conjunction with the new OTH radar systems—give China broad coverage of the Pacific Ocean and will likely play a vital role in targeting enemy surface vessels during a conflict. A May 2016 study by researchers from the Indian National Institute of Advanced Studies found that China's current satellite configuration allows for sixteen precise targeting opportunities of aircraft carrier groups (ACGs) within a twenty-four-hour period using the DF-21D, China's unique anti-ship ballistic missile (ASBM).[84] Therefore China's C4ISR capabilities might offer the PLA an area denial option within its theater of operations. The Yaogan constellation is currently undergoing a modernization program that includes the regular launch of new satellite groupings to replace older units—the most recent of which took place in April 2018.[85]

Implications for China's Nuclear Posture

Chinese nuclear doctrine suggests that as long as a secure second-strike capability is maintained, then there is no need to develop strategic early warning systems because retaliation can be launched hours, days, or even weeks after an attack on Chinese soil. Development of new road-mobile ICBMs with improved mobility can be seen as the latest chapter of this doctrine. Therefore, China's unprecedented emphasis on "rapid response" in its 2015 white paper on military strategy—in addition to its recent advancements in a strategic early warning infrastructure that can detect and track missile launches as well as the construction of what appears to be new silos for solid-fuel ICBMs—could potentially indicate doubt about, or a departure from, its traditional confidence in the survivability of its nuclear arsenal. If so, this would have implications for China's deterrence doctrine and could potentially trigger a gradual shift toward a more launch-ready nuclear missile force.

Rather than trying to ride out an attack on China's nuclear forces, a future alert posture, supported by strategic early warning systems, could potentially indicate an interest in being able to launch a nuclear weapon if the Chinese military detected incoming missiles heading toward Chinese territory. Given that US ICBMs would take roughly 20–30 minutes to reach Chinese targets, and a US SLBM even less time, a Chinese launch-on-warning posture would only allow for a couple of minutes of deliberation before impact. This would dramatically shrink the amount of time available to Chinese leaders to decide on a retaliatory course of action—reducing hours and days to minutes and seconds. It is unclear what the Chinese leadership would gain from such a posture.

Given these challenges, China's continued deployment of improved mobile missile forces, and the fact that the Chinese leadership has shown no indication of abandoning its traditional nuclear policies and doctrines, it seems unlikely—although not out of the question—that the emergence of more capable strategic early warning systems indicate a drift toward a formal nuclear launch-on-warning strategy.

An alternative explanation for the recent emphasis on strategic early warning systems could potentially instead be their utility for supporting ballistic missile defense (BMD) operations. The 2019 DoD report states that "the PLAAF possesses one of the largest forces of advanced long-range SAM systems in the world," currently consisting of the Russian-made S-300 and the indigenously produced HQ-9 but also clearly working toward a long-range BMD capability using HQ-19 and DN-3 midcourse interceptors as well as S-400 regiments purchased from Russia.[86] While the midcourse interceptors can utilize existing advanced Chinese radar systems for detecting and tracking intermediate-range missiles (IRBMs), the systems would be insufficient for detecting and tracking ICBM launches from several thousand kilometers away. Therefore it is plausible that China's recent emphasis on strategic early warning satellites and radar systems is intended to provide the PLA with the ability to intercept ICBMs in the future.

Whether Chinese efforts are intended to support a nuclear launch-on-warning strategy or an ABM capability, Russian president Vladimir Putin recently stated that Russia is "now helping our Chinese partners create a missile attack warning system" that "will drastically increase China's defense capability."[87]

NOTES

Matt Korda provided significant research assistance.

1. US Department of Defense, Office of the Secretary of Defense, *Missile Defense Review*, January 2019, 13, https://media.defense.gov/2019/Jan/17/2002080666/-1/-1/1/2019-MISSILE-DEFENSE-REVIEW.PDF.

2. US Department of Defense, Office of the Secretary of Defense, *Military and Security Developments Involving the People's Republic of China 2019*, May 2019, 44, 66, and 117, https://media.defense.gov/2019/May/02/2002127082/-1/-1/1/2019%20CHINA%20MILITARY%20POWER%20REPORT%20(1).PDF.

3. Lt. Gen. Robert P. Ashley Jr., *Remarks at the Hudson Institute: Russian and Chinese Nuclear Modernization Trends*, May 29, 2019, https://www.dia.mil/News/Speeches-and-Testimonies/Article-View/Article/1859890/russian-and-chinese-nuclear-modernization-trends/.

4. US Department of Defense, *Military and Security Developments 2019*, 117.

5. Mark Stokes, *China's Nuclear Warhead Storage and Handling System*, Project 2049 Institute, March 12, 2010, http://project2049.net/documents/chinas_nuclear_warhead_storage_and_handling_system.pdf.

6. For a description of the Delingha and Da Qaidam training areas, see Hans M. Kristensen, "Extensive Nuclear Deployment Area Discovered in Central China," *FAS Strategic Security Blog*, May 15, 2008, https://fas.org/blogs/security/2008/05/extensive-nuclear-deployment-area-discovered-in-central-china/.

7. See Chen Zhou, "China's Ship-Killer Missile Mobilized to Northwest China Plateau," *Global Times*, January 10, 2019, http://eng.chinamil.com.cn/view/2019–21/10/content_9401149.htm; and Hans M. Kristensen, "Chinese DF-26 Missile Launchers Deploy to New Missile Training Area," *FAS Strategic Security Blog*, January 21, 2019, https://fas.org/blogs/security/2019/01/df-26/.

8. Hans M. Kristensen, "New Missile Silo and DF-41 Launchers Seen in Chinese Nuclear Missile Training Area," *FAS Strategic Security Blog*, September 3, 2019, https://fas.org/blogs/security/2019/09/china-silo-df41/.

9. Scott LaFoy and Decker Eveleth, "Possible ICBM Modernization Underway at Sundian," *Arms Control Wonk*, February 5, 2020, https://www.armscontrolwonk.com/archive/1208828/possible-icbm-modernization-underway-at-sundian/.

10. Mark Stokes, *PLA Rocket Force Leadership and Unit Reference*, Project 2049 Institute, April 9, 2018, 17.

11. US Defense Intelligence Agency, *Nuclear Weapons Systems in China Defense Estimative Brief*, DEB-49-24, April 24, 1984, 4 (obtained under FOIA). The document reconstructed from different FOIA releases is available at http://www.nukestrat.com/china/DIA042484re.pdf.

12. US Defense Intelligence Agency, *Special Defense Intelligence Estimate: China's Evolving Nuclear Strategies*, DDE-2200-221-25, May 1985, 9 (obtained under FOIA).

13. For a description of the CIA's assessment at the time, see Robert S. Norris and Hans M. Kristensen, "Chinese Nuclear Forces, 2008," *Bulletin of the Atomic Scientists*, July 2008, 42–25, https://www.tandfonline.com/doi/pdf/10.1080/00963402.2008.11461157?needAccess=true.

14. US Department of Defense, Office of the Secretary of Defense, *Global Nuclear Capability Modernization: Global Nuclear-Capable Delivery Vehicles*, February 2, 2018 (emphasis added), https://media.defense.gov/2018/Feb/02/2001872878/-1/-1/1/GLOBAL-NUCLEAR-MODERNIZATION.PDF.

15. US Department of Defense, Office of the Secretary of Defense, *Nuclear Posture Review*, February 2018, 32, https://media.defense.gov/2018/Feb/02/2001872886/-1/-1/1/2018-NUCLEAR-POSTURE-REVIEW-FINAL-REPORT.PDF.

16. The DoD's annual report on Chinese military developments has not yet included the DF designation for the latest version of the DF-21, known as SSC-5 Mod 6.

17. US Department of Defense, Office of the Secretary of Defense, *Military and Security Developments Involving the People's Republic of China 2019*, 117, https://media.defense.gov/2019/May/02/2002127082/-1/-1/1/2019%20CHINA%20MILITARY%20POWER%20REPORT%20(1).PDF.

18. Wang Xu, Tianhong Ru, and Tang Shuai, "Rocket Army: 'Dongfeng Family' Continues to Grow and Casts a Shield of Peace," *China Military Network*, March 7, 2016, www.81.cn/bqtd/2016–23/07/content_6945796.htm.

19. US Department of Defense, Office of the Secretary of Defense, *Military and Security Developments Involving the People's Republic of China 2016*, May 2016, 25, https://dod.defense.gov/Portals/1/Documents/pubs/2016%20China%20Military%20Power%20Report.pdf.

20. US Department of Defense, *Military and Security Developments 2019*, 44.

21. See US Congress, Senate Armed Services Committee, *Advance Policy Questions for Admiral Philip Davidson, USN Expected Nominee for Commander, US Pacific Command*, April 17, 2018, 10, https://www.armed-services.senate.gov/imo/media/doc/Davidson_APQs_04-27-28.pdf; and Wang, Ru, and Tang, "Rocket Army."

22. US Congress, *Advance Policy Questions*, 10.

23. Ma Jialong, "Ministry of National Defense: Dongfeng-26 Missiles Installed in the Rocket Army," *China Military Network*, April 26, 2018, http://www.81.cn/bqtd/2018–24/26/content_8017401.htm.

24. Stokes, *PLA Rocket Force Leadership*, 11.

25. Huang Panyue, "China Deploys Dongfeng-26 Ballistic Missile with PLA Rocket Force," *Ministry of National Defense*, April 27, 2018, http://eng.chinamil.com.cn/view/2018–24/27/content_8017502.htm; and Huang Panyue, "China's Rocket Force Embraces New Medium–Long Range Ballistic Missile," *Ministry of National Defense*, April 16, 2018, http://eng.chinamil.com.cn/view/2018–24/16/content_8005761.htm.

26. "He chang jianbei! Huojian jun xin yidai zhong yuancheng dandao daodan jiaru zhandou xulie" (Prepare for both nuclear and conventional ballistic missiles! The PLA rocket force's new generation of medium- and long-range ballistic missiles join the order of battle), *JSTV*, April 16, 2018, http://news.jstv.com/a/20180416/1523843698405.shtml.

27. Stokes, *PLA Rocket Force Leadership*, 10. Note that for training purposes the missile launch units often visit bases that have other missile types. In 2016, for example, a DF-31 ICBM was seen training at a launchpad in the Tonghua area.

28. Hans M. Kristensen, "China's New DF-26 Missile Shows Up at Base in Eastern China," *FAS Strategic Security Blog*, January 21, 2020, https://fas.org/blogs/security/2020/01/df-26deployment/.

29. See, for example, Kristin Huang, "China's Hypersonic DF-17 Missile Threatens Regional Stability, Analysts Warn," *South China Morning Post*, August 23, 2019, https://www.scmp.com/news/china/military/article/3023972/chinas-hypersonic-df-17-missilethreatens-regional-stability; and Ankit Panda, "Introducing the DF-17: China's Newly Tested Ballistic Missile Armed with a Hypersonic Glide Vehicle," *Diplomat*, December 28, 2017, https://thediplomat.com/2017/12/introducing-the-df-17-chinas-newly-tested-ballistic-missile-armed-with-a-hypersonic-glide-vehicle/.

30. "DF 17, DF 100, and DF 41 Make Debuts at National Day Parade," China Global Television Network, October 1, 2019, https://www.youtube.com/watch?v=CMUbpMTfZtE.

31. Gen. Charles Richard, Commander, USSTRATCOM, prepared testimony before Senate Armed Services Committee, February 13, 2020, 4, https://www.armed-services.senate.gov/imo/media/doc/Richard_02-23-20.pdf.

32. Wang, Ru, and Tang, "Rocket Army."

33. Kristensen, "New Missile Silo."

34. Kristensen, "New Missile Silo."
35. Kristensen, "New Missile Silo."
36. "DF 17, DF 100, and DF 41 Make Debuts."
37. US Department of Defense, *Military and Security Developments 2019*, 45.
38. For a description of the silos at Jilantai, see Hans M. Kristensen, "More ICBM Silos Discovered at Chinese Missile Training Area," *FAS Strategic Security Blog*, https:// fas.org/blogs/security/2020/08/jilantai-silos/ (forthcoming); and Kristensen, "New Missile Silo."
39. US Air Force, National Air and Space Intelligence Center, *Ballistic and Cruise Missile Threat*, NASIC-1031-2985-27, June 2017 (corrected version July 2017), 27, http://www.nasic.af.mil/Portals/19/images/Fact%20Sheet%20Images/2017%20 Ballistic%20and%20Cruise%20Missile%20Threat_Final_small.pdf?ver=2017-27 -21-283234-243.
40. For an overview of China's SSBN fleet and fleet facilities, see Hans M. Kristensen, "China's SSBN Fleet Getting Ready—But for What?," *FAS Strategic Security Blog*, April 25, 2014, https://fas.org/blogs/security/2014/04/chinassbnfleet/.
41. Chinese attack submarines (or surface ships) are not thought to have a nuclear weapon capability. But a DoD fact sheet on nuclear modernizations that accompanied the release of the 2018 NPR report lists China as having a nuclear sea-launched cruise missile. See US Department of Defense, Office of the Secretary of Defense, *Global Nuclear Capability Modernization: Global Nuclear-Capable Delivery Vehicles*, February 2, 2018, https://media.defense.gov/2018/Feb/02/2001 872878/-1/-1/1/GLOBAL-NUCLEAR-MODERNIZATION.PDF.
42. US Navy, Office of Naval Intelligence, *The People's Liberation Army Navy: A Modern Navy with Chinese Characteristics*, August 2009, 22, https://fas.org/irp/agency /oni/pla-navy.pdf.
43. Bill Gertz, "China Flight Tests New Submarine-Launched Missile," *Free Beacon*, December 18, 2018, https://freebeacon.com/national-security/china-flight-tests -new-submarine-launched-missile/.
44. Gertz, "China Flight Tests."
45. For a chronology of Chinese nuclear tests, see Thomas C. Reed, "A Tabulation of Chinese Nuclear Device Tests," supplemental material in Thomas C. Reed, "The Chinese Nuclear Tests, 1964–1996," *Physics Today*, September 2008, 47–23, https://physicstoday.scitation.org/doi/pdf/10.1063/1.2982122.
46. US Defense Intelligence Agency, *Nuclear Weapons Systems in China*.
47. US Defense Intelligence Agency, *Chinese Strategic Forces*, n.d. (but possibly 1989), 3, http://www.dia.mil/FOIA/FOIA-Electronic-Reading-Room/FOIA-Reading-Room -China/FileId/39740/.
48. US National Security Council, *Report to Congress on Status of China, India and Pakistan Nuclear and Ballistic Missile Programs*, July 28, 1993, 2 (obtained under FOIA), https://fas.org/irp/threat/930728-wmd.htm.
49. For a unique collection of Chinese museum bomb photos, see "Nuclear Gravity Bombs," GlobalSecurity.org, n.d., https://www.globalsecurity.org/wmd/world/china /nuke-gravity.htm.
50. US Department of Defense, *Military and Security Developments 2017*, 61.
51. Lt. Gen. Vince R. Stewart, *Statement for the Record: Worldwide Threat Assessment*, May 23, 2017, 10, https://www.armed-services.senate.gov/imo/media/doc/Stewart _05–23–27.pdf.

52. US Department of Defense, Office of the Secretary of Defense, *Military and Security Developments Involving the People's Republic of China 2018*, May 16, 2018, 77, https://media.defense.gov/2018/Aug/16/2001955282/-1/-1/1/2018-CHINA-MILITARY-POWER-REPORT.PDF. Note also that a DoD fact sheet on nuclear modernizations that accompanied the release of the 2018 NPR report lists China with a nuclear air-launched cruise missile. See US Department of Defense, Office of the Secretary of Defense, *Global Nuclear Capability Modernization: Global Nuclear-Capable Delivery Vehicles*, February 2, 2018, https://media.defense.gov/2018/Feb/02/2001872878/-1/-1/1/GLOBAL-NUCLEAR-MODERNIZATION.PDF.

53. US Department of Defense, *Military and Security Developments 2019*, 41. For an example of Chinese media referring to the H-6K as nuclear-capable, see Yin Han, "H-6K Bomber Video Showcases PLA Air Force Capability," *Global Times*, April 1, 2018, http://eng.chinamil.com.cn/view/2018–24/01/content_7989853.htm. Note also that a RAND study from 2017 concludes that the H-6K "is not considered nuclear capable." See Derek Grossman et al., *China's Long-Range Bomber Flights: Drivers and Implications*, RAND Corporation, RR-2567-AF, 1, https://www.rand.org/pubs/research_reports/RR2567.html.

54. US Department of Defense, Office of the Deputy Assistant Secretary of Defense for Nuclear Matters, *Nuclear Matters Handbook 2020*, February 2020, 3, https://www.acq.osd.mil/ncbdp/nm/nmhb/docs/NMHB2020.pdf.

55. Ankit Panda, "Revealed: China's Nuclear-Capable Air-Launched Ballistic Missile," *Diplomat*, April 10, 2018, https://thediplomat.com/2018/04/revealed-chinas-nuclear-capable-air-launched-ballistic-missile; Tylor Rogoway, "Is This China's DF-21D Air Launched Anti-Ship Ballistic Missile Toting Bomber?," *The Drive*, August 15, 2017, https://www.thedrive.com/the-war-zone/13511/is-this-chinas-df-21d-air-launched-anti-ship-ballistic-missile-toting-bomber; and US Department of Defense, *Nuclear Matters Handbook 2020*, 3.

56. "China Designing Long-Range Stealth Bomber," WantChinaTimes.com, October 24, 2013, http://www.wantchinatimes.com/news-print-cnt.aspx?id=20131024000030&cid=1101&MainCatID=0.

57. Yao Jianing, "PLA Air Force Commander Confirms New Strategic Bomber," *China Military (China Daily)*, September 3, 2016, http://eng.chinamil.com.cn/view/2016–29/03/content_7241206.htm.

58. Shan Jie, "Trial Flight Soon for New Type of Chinese Stealth Bomber," *Global Times*, October 9, 2018, http://eng.chinamil.com.cn/view/2018–20/10/content_9306574.htm.

59. In addition to strategy considerations, a driver for the nuclear bomber could potentially also be institutional interests in the domestic competition over funding and prestige between the PLAAF, the PLAN, and the PLARF.

60. For an insightful overview of China's nuclear command, control, and communication arrangements, see Fiona S. Cunningham, "Nuclear Command, Control, and Communications Systems of the People's Republic of China," The Nautilus Institute, July 18, 2019, https://nautilus.org/napsnet/napsnet-special-reports/nuclear-command-control-and-communications-systems-of-the-peoples-republic-of-china/.

61. US Department of Defense, *Military and Security Developments 2019*, 66.

62. US Department of Defense, 65.

63. US Department of Defense, 67. For a review of PLA writings on nuclear alert, see Gregory Kulacki, "China's Military Calls for Putting Its Nuclear Forces on

Alert," Union of Concerned Scientists, January 2016, https://www.ucsusa.org/sites /default/files/attach/2016/02/China-Hair-Trigger-full-report.pdf.

64. Gregory Kulacki, "China Rejects Policy of Nuclear Launch on Warning of an Incoming Attack," AllThingsNuclear.org, October 28, 2019, https://allthingsnuclear.org /gkulacki/china-rejects-policy-of-nuclear-launch-on-warning-of-an-incoming -attack.

65. US Department of Defense, *Military and Security Developments 2019*, 66.

66. People's Republic of China, State Council Information Office, "China's Military Strategy" white paper, May 2015, http://news.xinhuanet.com/english/china /2015–25/26/c_134271001_4.htm.

67. Kevin L. Pollpeter, Michael S. Chase, and Eric Heginbotham, "The Creation of the PLA Strategic Support Force and Its Implications for Chinese Military Space Operations," RAND Corporation, 2017, https://www.rand.org/pubs/research_reports /RR2058.html; Yao Jianing, "Expert: PLA Strategic Support Force a Key Force to Win Wars," China Military Online, January 6, 2016, http://english.chinamil.com .cn/news-channels/pla-daily-commentary/2016–21/06/content_6846500.htm.

68. Pollpeter, Chase, and Heginbotham, "Creation of the PLA Strategic Support Force," 1.

69. Kevin Pollpeter, "Space, the New Domain: Space Operations and Chinese Military Reforms," *Journal of Strategic Studies* 39, no. 5-2 (2016): 721, https://www .tandfonline.com/doi/abs/10.1080/01402390.2016.1219946.

70. China Aerospace Studies Institute, *PLA Aerospace Power: A Primer on Trends in China's Military Air, Space, and Missile Forces* (Montgomery, AL: China Aerospace Studies Institute, 2017), 33, https://apps.dtic.mil/dtic/tr/fulltext/u2/1044214.pdf.

71. Yao, "Expert: PLA Strategic Support Force."

72. Andrew Tate, "China Integrates Long-Range Surveillance Capabilities," *IHS Jane's*, 2017, https://www.janes.com/images/assets/477/75477/China_integrates _long-range_surveillance_capabilities.pdf.

73. "Zhongguo zhanlüe he fanji hui zai he shi daxiang zhe bu yuancheng leida jiangcheng guanjian" (When will China's strategic nuclear counterattacks start? This long-range radar will be the key), *Sina Military*, November 7, 2017, http://mil .news.sina.com.cn/jssd/2017–21–27/doc-ifynmvuq9321256.shtml.

74. Tate, "China Integrates Long-Range Surveillance Capabilities."

75. The interceptor test targets are launched from a facility near Jiuquan (41.280468°, 100.304501°). See Catherine Dill, "Tracking Preparations at the Korla Missile Test Base," *Arms Control Wonk*, December 27, 2016, https://www.armscontrolwonk .com/archive/1202634/tracking-preparations-at-the-korla-missile-test-base/.

76. Catherine Dill, "Korla Missile Test Complex Revisited," *Arms Control Wonk*, March 26, 2015, https://www.armscontrolwonk.com/archive/605030/the-korla -missile-test-complex-revisited/.

77. For a US intelligence overview from the late 1980s, see US Defense Intelligence Agency, *China's Early Warning Capability*, n.d. (possibly 1989), http://www.dia .mil/FOIA/FOIA-Electronic-Reading-Room/FOIA-Reading-Room-China/FileId /39726/.

78. Lee Kil-Seong, "China Sets Up More Long-Range Radars," *Chosun Ilbo*, March 14, 2017, http://english.chosun.com/site/data/html_dir/2017/03/14/2017031401319 .html.

79. The Hubei transmitter is located at 32°20'15.01"N, 112°42'30.97"E and the corresponding receiver is located at 31°37'25.93"N, 111°55'17.01"E. See Henri Kenhmann,

"Project 2319: The Chinese OTH-B Radar," *East Pendulum*, August 27, 2016, http://www.eastpendulum.com/projet-2319-radar-oth-b-chinois.

80. The ionospheric measuring station at Xiamen is clearly visible at 24°29'5.50"N, 118° 4'47.76"E.

81. Rui C. Barbosa, "Long March 3B Conducts Another Secretive Launch," *NASA Spaceflight*, September 12, 2015, https://www.nasaspaceflight.com/2015/09/long-march-3b-conducts-another-secretive-launch/; Rui C. Barbosa, "Long March 3B Launches Second TJSW Spacecraft for China," *NASA Spaceflight*, January 5, 2017, https://www.nasaspaceflight.com/2017/01/long-march-3b-with-second-tjsw/.

82. Tongxin Jishu Shiyan-1 and Tongxin Jishu Shiyan-2, which were also reported as TJSW-1, TJSW-2 and as TXJSSY-1 and TXJSSY-2.

83. "China Launches Communication Technology Test," *Xinhua*, September 13, 2015, http://www.xinhuanet.com//english/2015–29/13/c_134619813.htm.

84. S. Chandrashekar and Soma Perumal, "China's Constellation of Yaogan Satellites and the Anti-Ship Ballistic Missile: May 2016 Update," *ISSSP Report* no. 03-2016, National Institute of Advanced Studies, May 2016, http://isssp.in/chinas-constellation-of-yaogan-satellites-the-asbm-may-2016-update/.

85. "Chinese Surprise Launch Lifts Yaogan-31 Electronic Reconnaissance Satellite Trio," Spaceflight101.com, April 11, 2018, http://spaceflight101.com/china-long-march-4c-yaogan-31-21-launch/.

86. US Department of Defense, *Military and Security Developments 2019*, 34–25, 60.

87. President of the Russian Federation, "Valdai Discussion Club Session," October 3, 2019, http://en.kremlin.ru/events/president/news/61719.

SIX

China's Regional Nuclear Capability, Nonnuclear Strategic Systems, and Integration of Concepts and Operations

Phillip C. Saunders and David C. Logan

Most writing on Chinese nuclear capabilities focuses on strategic nuclear weapons and their associated doctrine. China's strategic nuclear deterrent rests on land-based missiles operated by the People's Liberation Army (PLA) Rocket Force and sea-based missiles carried on a nascent fleet of *Jin*-class nuclear-powered ballistic missile–carrying submarines (SSBNs) operated by the PLA Navy. China's nuclear policy is founded upon the principle of "no first use" (NFU) and seeks to maintain a "lean and effective" nuclear deterrent.[1] China's chief concern about its strategic nuclear forces is whether they can survive to mount an effective second strike in the face of an adversary attack and ballistic missile defenses. A related question is whether China's expanding nuclear forces and their operational doctrine contribute to strategic stability with other nuclear powers or raise risks of crisis instability or arms race instability.

Nevertheless, there have also been persistent questions and a small body of literature on the possibility of China possessing and deploying nonstrategic nuclear weapons, also known as tactical nuclear weapons.[2] China's initial efforts at developing and deploying nuclear weapons included a number of air-delivered nuclear weapons that could be considered tactical in nature, given their low yields and the ranges of the aircraft that would deliver them.[3] China has also deployed nuclear-armed DF-21 medium-range ballistic missiles (MRBMs) and DF-26 intermediate-range ballistic missiles (IRBMs) that most countries would consider to be theater rather than strategic assets. China developed and tested a neutron bomb for potential use against a Soviet invasion but appears not to have deployed it.[4]

In addition to its nuclear forces, China has developed a range of conventional capabilities that could potentially have strategic effects. These include accurate conventional ballistic missiles, which provide a precision attack capability; anti-ship ballistic missiles (ASBMs) that can attack aircraft carriers and other surface vessels; an emerging hypersonic weapons capability that can penetrate modern air and ballistic missile defenses; a range of counterspace capabilities that can target satellites and their communications and control systems; offensive cyber attack capabilities; and military applications of artificial intelligence (AI). Chinese analysts and advocates for the development of these systems have highlighted their potential to influence the outcome of a conflict with the United States in China's favor. Moreover, these conventional systems are not constrained by China's nuclear NFU policy and are therefore more likely to be employed in a conflict.

In this chapter we briefly review the evidence for a deployed Chinese tactical nuclear weapons capability and argue that there is no convincing evidence that tactical nuclear weapons are currently deployed. China does deploy medium- and intermediate-range ballistic missiles that give it a regional nuclear capability, but Chinese leaders do not appear to consider these systems tactical in nature. We then explore Chinese conventional systems that may have strategic effects, either by deterring potential adversaries or forcing them to make significant changes in their doctrine, war plans, or force structure. This includes an examination of Chinese efforts to develop and deploy the six types of nonnuclear strategic systems discussed above and an assessment of the PLA's capabilities in each area. We consider how these capabilities might be integrated with other Chinese conventional and nuclear capabilities to enhance operational flexibility and produce strategic effects. The chapter concludes by considering the implications for the United States and China.

NONSTRATEGIC NUCLEAR SYSTEMS

There is no strict definition of what constitutes a nonstrategic nuclear system, though nuclear systems are often classified according to the yield of the warhead or the range of the delivery system. Strategic nuclear forces historically consisted of intercontinental-range systems armed with high-yield warheads. Nonstrategic forces have delivery systems with shorter ranges, warheads with smaller yields, and are intended for use against military targets.

Our analysis focuses on two kinds of nonstrategic nuclear capabilities: tactical nuclear forces and regional nuclear forces. Tactical nuclear forces include very low-yield warheads (a few tens of kilotons [kt]) affixed to short-range (1,000 km or less) ballistic missiles; these are typically used to target conventional military forces on the battlefield. For example, during the Cold War, NATO planners established a rule prohibiting the use of nuclear warheads with yields greater than 10 kt on or above their own territories.[5] Today US nuclear weapons with variable yields of between 5 and 150 kt are sometimes described as tactical.[6] China's regional nuclear force, on the other hand, consists of medium- and intermediate-range ballistic missiles armed with nuclear warheads typically with yields of at least 100 kt. These regional nuclear weapons are believed to be aimed at conventional military forces or at the population centers of the nuclear-armed states bordering China.

There is little evidence that China has deployed tactical nuclear weapons or that it will do so in the near future. By contrast, China appears to have a robust and slowly growing regional nuclear force that could potentially elevate the future role of nonstrategic nuclear weapons within the PLA.

Tactical Nuclear Weapons

While little evidence suggests that China currently has tactical nuclear weapons deployed, it certainly has the industrial base and technical capacity to develop and deploy tactical nuclear weapons if it so desired. However, Chinese thinking on nuclear weapons has historically denied a role to tactical nuclear weapons and the history of China's nuclear weapons program makes it less than ideal to support development of a robust tactical nuclear arsenal.

China's nuclear strategy of assured retaliation does not envision a role for tactical nuclear weapons. The country's political leaders have historically prioritized the development of a strategic deterrent based on ballistic missiles rather than on air-delivered weapons and have consistently emphasized the deterrent and retaliatory functions of nuclear weapons.[7] China has long adopted a relatively restrained nuclear posture, including an NFU pledge and "negative security assurances not to use or threaten to use nuclear weapons against nonnuclear states or nonnuclear zones."[8] China's operational practices have reflected this approach: warheads are unmated and stored separately from their delivery vehicles and units train to survive an adversary first strike and then retaliate by launching their weapons.[9] This suggests an aversion to the use of tactical nuclear weapons, which generally must be deployed at a higher state of readiness and with an implicit willingness to use nuclear weapons first.[10]

There is limited evidence that China has invested in developing or deploying tactical nuclear weapons. The PLA's extensive arsenal of advanced ballistic missiles could provide the necessary delivery vehicles for a tactical nuclear capability but China appears to lack the necessary warheads to arm those missiles. Nearly all of the country's nuclear warhead designs appear unsuitable for a tactical nuclear capability because they would be too heavy to be carried by China's short-range ballistic missiles or too destructive for use in theaters near China's territory.[11]

Although China could eventually develop and field tactical nuclear weapons if it chose to do so, Beijing might face some near-term obstacles in achieving that goal.[12] China's past work on developing a neutron bomb might be relevant to developing some kinds of tactical nuclear weapons but it is unclear how confident China would be in those warhead designs or whether that testing record would support the development of a more diverse tactical nuclear arsenal.[13] US government reports have suggested that China possesses the underlying technical capabilities to produce tactical nuclear weapons. For example, a declassified 1995 Central Intelligence Agency (CIA) report on an upcoming Chinese nuclear test gave this assessment: "This test may include warhead testing for a new ICBM and a cruise missile," which suggests some work on developing a tactical nuclear warhead.[14] Similarly, a declassified 1993 CIA assessment concluded that China had likely developed a nuclear warhead for its short-range DF-15 ballistic missile.[15] However, that same assessment noted possible limitations in China's designs, saying that additional "testing might be needed for final weaponization or for additional warhead options."[16] Ultimately, regardless of whatever past efforts before China stopped nuclear testing in 1996 may be relevant to the development of tactical nuclear weapons, China appears not to have deployed any. Recent editions of the Pentagon's reports on Chinese military power have not included any reference to tactical nuclear weapons, and assessments produced by independent analysts regularly exclude tactical weapons from the Chinese order of battle.[17]

Despite China's historic reluctance to deploy tactical nuclear weapons, some observers have suggested that renewed US and Russian interest in tactical nuclear weapons might trigger similar changes in China. The last US Nuclear Posture Review (NPR) determined that the United States should develop new nonstrategic nuclear weapons in the form of a low-yield warhead for submarine-launched ballistic missiles and a sea-launched cruise missile.[18] Russia is reportedly developing new nuclear-armed air-launched and ground-launched cruise missile systems.[19]

Official Chinese reaction to the latest US NPR was decidedly negative. Shortly after the document's official release, a spokesman for China's Ministry of National Defense said that Beijing strongly opposed it and that "we hope the U.S. side will discard its 'cold-war mentality.'"[20] Much of the attention to the NPR within China focused on the document's proposals for new nonstrategic US nuclear weapons.[21] After an earlier draft version of the NPR was leaked, two researchers from the PLA Academy of Military Science seized upon both reported new language in the draft NPR as well as Russian proposals for new nuclear capabilities to argue that China should strengthen its own nuclear arsenal.[22] Despite these negative reactions, however, it remains to be seen whether or not these developments will significantly alter China's approach to nuclear weapons. One recent US analysis concluded that despite recent discussions in China, "the 2018 NPR is unlikely to dramatically alter the trajectory of China's ongoing nuclear force modernization or result in major changes to its nuclear policy."[23]

Regional Deterrent Capabilities

Though China does not appear to have developed or deployed tactical nuclear weapons, it has been strengthening its regional nuclear capabilities.[24] The core of China's regional nuclear deterrent consists of its land-based DF-21 and DF-26 missiles. With estimated ranges of approximately 1,750 and 4,000 km, respectively, both the DF-21 and DF-26 provide a regional strike capability. China has deployed conventional and nuclear variants of the DF-21 and the DF-26 is capable of carrying either a conventional or nuclear payload.

Considering their ranges and garrison locations, these medium- and intermediate-range ballistic missiles are likely oriented against Russia and India and US forces stationed in the region. Several brigades garrisoned near China's western and southern borders are believed to command either the DF-21 or DF-26. From near China's borders, these systems would be able to strike US bases in Japan, South Korea, and Guam and foreign capitals such as Moscow and New Delhi.

Some analysts suggest that, in addition to its land-based force, China maintains a legacy air-based nuclear capability consisting of an aging fleet of H-6 bombers, though even these assessments suggest that this capability has significantly atrophied.[25] In the early years of its nuclear weapons program, China conducted several airdrop tests of nuclear weapons.[26] However, there is no recent open-source evidence of either air force nuclear weapons training exercises or construction of warhead storage sites associated with air force units. A 2018 Pentagon report indicates that the PLA Air Force has been "*re-assigned* a nuclear mission*,*" suggesting that these legacy air force capabilities are no longer operational.[27]

Recent reports have suggested China is initiating efforts to develop new nuclear-capable systems. Though not definitive, this evidence suggests Chinese interest in new nonstrategic nuclear capabilities, possibly including a new nuclear-armed cruise missile or a new nuclear-capable strategic bomber.

The PLA Air Force has undertaken efforts to build itself into a "strategic air force," which may involve resuming its nuclear deterrent role.[28] In 2016 Gen. Ma Xiaotian, then the PLA Air Force commander, announced: "We are now developing a next generation, long-range strike bomber that you will see sometime in the future."[29] US government reports have attributed a nuclear mission to this bomber.[30] China's next-generation bomber reportedly will have a range of 8,000 km and may have stealth capabilities.[31]

There are also recent reports of work on new nuclear-armed weapons systems to accompany this bomber. In testimony delivered in 2018 to the Senate Armed Services Committee, Director of the Defense Intelligence Agency Lt. Gen. Robert Ashley stated that China has "two new air-launched ballistic missiles, one of which may include a nuclear payload."[32] Subsequent media accounts have claimed that the design of the new missile, which has been tested at least five times, is based on the DF-21 system and that the new air-launched variant is intended to be used with the country's next strategic bomber.[33]

NONNUCLEAR STRATEGIC CAPABILITIES

Understanding China's nonnuclear strategic capabilities rests upon an appreciation for how different weapons can generate effects in the strategic domain. In official publications, the PLA defines strategy as "guidelines and policies for planning and direction of overall war" or "guidelines and policies of overall, high-level, long-term significant issues."[34] For the purposes of this chapter, strategic systems are those with sufficient capability to have strategic effects, whether by deterring potential adversaries, by forcing them to make significant changes in their doctrine, war plans, or force structure, or by producing decisive effects on the battlefield. Due to the enormous destructive capability of nuclear weapons, "strategic" is often used synonymously with "nuclear." Our definition, however, allows a military capability to be considered strategic, regardless of its technical features, so long as it can produce these types of strategic effects. Military systems with shorter-than-intercontinental range or lacking extensive physical destructive capability may still be classified as strategic if they can produce decisive effects.

China has developed a suite of conventional capabilities with potential strategic effects. These include highly accurate conventional ballistic missiles that provide a precision attack capability; anti-ship ballistic missiles (ASBMs) that can attack aircraft carriers; an emerging hypersonic weapons capability that can penetrate modern air and ballistic missile defenses; a range of counterspace capabilities that can target satellites and their communications and control systems; offensive cyber attack capabilities; and military applications of AI. These systems are not constrained by China's nuclear NFU policy and are therefore more likely to be employed in a conflict. Indeed, Chinese military writings often emphasize the need to seize the initiative and the importance of early (and potentially preemptive) use of counterspace and cyber weapons in the event of a conflict.[35] Here, we evaluate the above six current and emerging Chinese nonnuclear capabilities with potential strategic effects.

Conventional Ballistic Missiles

China possesses one of the world's largest and most advanced arsenals of ballistic missiles. This force, which includes short-, medium-, and intermediate-range missiles, is growing increasingly sophisticated in terms of range, accuracy, and responsiveness.[36] Especially when used in combination with conventional strike capabilities from other military services, the ability of these missiles to compel significant changes in US military operations in the region permits China to generate strategic effects with these forces.

The military organization in command of China's land-based missiles, the PLA Rocket Force, began as an exclusively nuclear force and fielded only a few dozen nuclear-armed missiles for the first few decades of its existence.[37] In the 1990s China began to develop and deploy advanced conventionally armed ballistic missiles.[38] Since then, China's conventional ballistic missile arsenal has grown significantly. Today China is believed to deploy over 1,200 advanced conventionally armed ballistic missiles and roughly half of Rocket Force personnel are believed to be assigned to conventionally armed units.[39] There is also some evidence that the Rocket Force may prioritize the conventional mission set over the nuclear one, with officers who have served in the Rocket Force's premier conventional missile base more likely to be promoted than those who have served in bases assigned strategic or regional nuclear mission sets.[40]

Today China's conventionally armed ballistic missile systems include the short-range DF-11, DF-15, and DF-16, with ranges of under 850 km, the medium-range DF-21, with a range of approximately 1,750 km, and the intermediate range DF-26, with a range of 3,000 to 4,000 km. China is believed to have made significant advancements in targeting and guidance systems technology, such that its conventionally armed ballistic missiles may have circular error probables as small as 10 to 50 m.[41] China's latest DF-16 SRBM reportedly features high accuracy, a short launch preparation time, and an improved maneuverable terminal stage.[42] China's medium- and intermediate-range DF-21 and DF-26 systems are believed to incorporate maneuverable reentry vehicle technology, which not only allows for increased accuracy but also potentially provides the ability to strike moving targets such as US surface ships.

The deployment patterns of the short-range DF-11, DF-15, and DF-16 systems suggest that the PLA envisions employing them in a conflict over Taiwan. Most of these conventionally armed short-range missiles are assigned to the Rocket Force's Base 61, headquartered in Anhui province and the brigades operating them are arrayed across China's southeast coast, near the Taiwan Strait.[43] In addition to these short-range conventionally armed missiles, China is believed to have deployed conventional variants of the DF-21 and DF-26 that could be used to target US military forces in the region, including bases on Guam and Okinawa. According to the Pentagon's annual report on Chinese military developments, "PLA writings see logistics and power projection assets as potential vulnerabilities in modern warfare—an assessment that may be driving this growing capability to strike regional air bases, logistics and port facilities, communications, and other ground-based infrastructure."[44]

Chinese writings on its conventional ballistic missile force envision employing them within the context of "active defense," which calls for China to remain on the defensive strategically but to seize the initiative and be proactive at the operational and tactical levels.[45] Chinese writings envision using conventional ballistic missiles in tandem with the precision-strike capabilities of other services in at least three sets of operations: joint firepower strike campaigns, joint blockade campaigns, and joint anti–air raid campaigns.[46]

Anti-Ship Ballistic Missiles

In addition to its traditional conventionally armed ballistic missiles, China is also believed to field two anti-ship ballistic missiles based on the DF-21 and DF-26 systems. Because of their potential to force US surface ships to operate out-of-theater, these systems, by themselves or in coordination with other PLA strike capabilities, may generate strategic effects.

China began to deploy the anti-ship DF-21D in 2010 and today, according to open-source analyses, the PLA Rocket Force might have equipped three launch brigades with the DF-21D.[47] The DF-21D is believed to have a range of 1,500 km, thus providing the PLA the ability to "attack ships, including aircraft carriers, in the Western Pacific."[48] The anti-ship variant of the DF-26 was shown publicly at the September 2015 military parade held in Beijing. Parade commentators identified the system as "a new weapon for strategic deterrence," saying that "it can perform medium- to long-range precision attack on both land and large- to medium-sized maritime targets."[49] These two systems are believed to incorporate maneuverable reentry vehicle technology and media reports suggest that the mobility and ruggedness of the systems allow for faster response times. According to a commentary written by two Academy of Military Science researchers involved in the development of the DF-26, "the missile has advanced mobility and no strict requirements for launch positioning, which is conducive to concealed and wide-ranging movement and contributes to rapid deployment, launch, and transfer of combat units, simultaneously improving the survivability and strike capability of the missile force."[50] The long range of these two systems also permits China to deploy them inland, out of the range of US forces and protected by Chinese air defenses.[51]

Though these systems appear to be technologically advanced, it is unclear how effective they will be in an actual conflict. Observers of China's anti-ship missile developments pose three questions relating to the systems' effectiveness: first, has the system been sufficiently tested to verify its performance in real-world conditions?; second, will China be able to develop the reconnaissance-strike complex necessary to support its anti-ship missile systems?; and third, will the systems be able to overcome US countermeasures?

First, until recently there were significant questions about whether China's ASBMs had been tested sufficiently to demonstrate that they would perform in an actual conflict. Initial tests were conducted over land inside China or against stationary targets. This raised questions about whether China had mastered the terminal guidance and maneuvering capability necessary to attack a moving aircraft carrier, including developing sensors and warheads that could survive the high speeds and temperatures of atmosphere reentry without adversely affecting seeker and warhead performance.[52] However, in August 2020 the PLA answered some of these questions by testing both the DF-21D and DF-26B ASBMs in the South China Sea, reportedly against a moving ship target.[53]

Second, it is not clear that China has developed all the necessary supporting infrastructure to employ its anti-ship systems. Successfully using ASBMs will require developing a suite of advanced communications, surveillance, and reconnaissance capabilities.[54] The challenge of locating and then targeting a moving ship will increase the farther it is from China's shores. China has reportedly made recent progress in this area by developing new space-based reconnaissance capabilities and improving its over-the-horizon radars.[55] However, these systems are still under development and, even once finalized, may be vulnerable to US attack or disruption.[56]

Third, it is not clear that China's anti-ship ballistic missiles will be able to overcome adversary countermeasures. Countermeasures can take various forms, including active measures (such as shooting down incoming ballistic missiles with interceptors) and passive measures (such as hiding the location of ships or disrupting Chinese targeting efforts).[57] US officials have said that the US military has long been investing in developing these countermeasures, which could neutralize China's ASBM systems.[58]

Hypersonic Weapons

China has also been developing new hypersonic weapons, which could have strategic effects.[59] It is not clear how China envisions employing these weapons, though Beijing's interest in these capabilities appears to be driven by concerns about US ballistic missile defenses and a general fear of falling behind in the development of new technologies.

Weapon systems are typically classified as hypersonic if they can travel at least five times the speed of sound. Hypersonic weapons generally take three forms: terminally guided ballistic missiles, hypersonic cruise missiles, and boost-glide weapons.[60] China has reportedly shown interest in developing all three types of hypersonic weapons systems, which have the advantages of being prompt to target, highly maneuverable and thus difficult to counter, and able to penetrate enemy defenses.

China has invested significantly in developing terminally guided ballistic missiles. Authoritative Chinese sources suggest that China has been conducting research on maneuvering reentry vehicle technology since the early 1990s.[61] This technology has been incorporated into China's arsenal of ballistic missile systems.[62] There are reports of Chinese interest in developing hypersonic cruise missiles, though information on these capabilities is more limited.[63]

China has also demonstrated interest in boost-glide weapons. Boost-glide weapons are typically launched on traditional ballistic missiles. However, while traditional ballistic missiles generally arc high beyond the atmosphere before returning on an unpowered ballistic descent back to earth, boost-glide weapons release maneuverable reentry vehicles that quickly execute a "pull-up" maneuver and remain in the upper atmosphere. This reentry vehicle is designed to generate aerodynamic lift that allows it to skip along the upper atmosphere. The glide capability of the reentry vehicle can significantly increase the system's overall range and maneuverability.[64] Since January 2014, China has conducted at least seven tests of its hypersonic boost-glide system, with the tested range varying between 1,250 and 2,100 km, though the glide portion of the system is likely shorter than the overall flight distance.[65] China displayed the DF-17 missile, reportedly equipped with a conventional warhead and boost-glide vehicle, in a 2019 military parade and may have begun to deploy the system. One US expert has observed that the United States is "ahead of China in developing both hypersonic glide vehicles and scramjet-enabled hypersonic cruise missiles."[66] However, some US officials have expressed concern about the pace of Chinese and Russian development of hypersonic weapons and called for an increase in funding for US weapons development programs.[67]

There are many potential drivers of China's interest in hypersonic weapons systems. It may be developing hypersonic systems chiefly to counter US ballistic missile defense capabilities.[68] According to one recent analysis, "roughly a quarter of the Chinese technical studies on hypersonic glide vehicles remain focused on U.S. missile defenses, rather than any A2AD [anti-access area denial] agenda."[69] China's development of hypersonic boost-glide vehicles may also be "driven by a desire to keep pace with U.S. interest in the technology as well as the potential role these systems could play in warfare if they were successfully deployed."[70] A recent review of Chinese writings on hypersonic technology concludes that Chinese efforts are also motivated by interest in comparable Russian programs.[71]

It remains unclear precisely how China envisions using its future hypersonic capabilities. For example, it is still uncertain whether China envisions arming its boost-glide vehicles with conventional or nuclear payloads. An official from the US National Air and Space Intelligence Center (NASIC) has testified that his organization believes China's boost-glide systems will be associated with the country's nuclear deterrent.[72] The most important appeal of hypersonic weapons is their ability to penetrate US ballistic missile defenses to ensure the credibility of China's strategic nuclear deterrent, but they also have utility in delivering conventional strikes on defended targets.[73]

Counterspace Weapons

Chinese thinking about space has been heavily influenced by the study of US space doctrine and by how the US military has used space assets in modern military conflicts, beginning with the Persian Gulf War in 1991. This has sparked Chinese efforts to develop its own space capabilities to support ongoing military modernization, with space systems being a key element of efforts to "informationize" the PLA in order to improve its combat power and ability to conduct joint operations. At the same time, China has also invested in a range of counterspace capabilities intended to exploit the US military's dependence on space, which China sees as a critical US vulnerability. China's 2015 white paper, "China's Military Strategy," declares: "Outer space has become a commanding height in international strategic competition. Countries concerned are developing their space forces and instruments, and the first signs of weaponization of outer space have appeared."[74]

US officials and other experts have noted increasing Chinese emphasis on the space domain. In 2015 then-DIA director Lt. Gen. Vincent Stewart testified before Congress that "Chinese and Russian military leaders understand the unique information advantages afforded by space systems and are developing capabilities to deny U.S. use of space in the event of a conflict. Chinese military writings specifically highlight the need to interfere with, damage, and destroy reconnaissance, navigation, and communication satellites. China has satellite jamming capabilities and is pursuing other antisatellite systems."[75] China specialist Dean Cheng notes that PLA authors emphasize the importance of offensive operations to deny a superior adversary the ability to use space, and that these efforts are not limited to attacking systems in orbit. Cheng observes that Chinese military writings discuss

> a range of efforts aimed at affecting the range of space-related capabilities, from orbiting satellites, through space-related terrestrial facilities, to the data, communications, and telemetry links that tie all these systems together. . . . Space offensive operations include not only applying hard-kill capabilities against satellites, but also attacking launch bases and tracking, telemetry, and control facilities. They also discuss the use of soft-kill techniques, such as jamming and dazzling, against satellites, in order to minimize the generation of debris, and the attendant physical and diplomatic consequences.[76]

China has developed a wide range of capabilities that can potentially be used to target space assets and support systems. In addition to the direct-ascent anti-satellite (ASAT) system China successfully tested in January 2007 and 2014, a Pentagon report notes that China has "a multi-dimensional program to limit or prevent the use of space-based assets by potential adversaries during times of crisis or conflict." The report adds: "Foreign and indigenous systems give China the capability to jam common satellite communications bands and GPS receivers. In addition to the direct-ascent ASAT program, China is developing other technologies and concepts for kinetic and directed-energy (e.g., lasers, high-powered microwave, and particle beam) weapons for ASAT missions. . . . China is improving its ability to track and identify satellites—a prerequisite for effective, precise counter-space operations."[77]

Although some Chinese military experts advocate preemptive attacks on space assets to take advantage of US dependence on them and the need to seize the initiative in the fight for information dominance, it is not clear that these arguments have been fully accepted by the PLA leadership or endorsed by Chinese civilian leaders.[78] Another strand of Chinese thinking emphasizes the importance of China possessing offensive space capabilities as a deterrent measure, partly to exploit the inherent vulnerability of costly space assets as a means of deterring conflict in the first place. However, some PLA writings appear to envision an escalation ladder that runs from testing space weapons to exercising space forces to reinforcing space capabilities (especially in a crisis) to actually employing space forces. Chinese strategists argue that demonstrating the capability and willingness to attack an adversary's space assets is the most credible form of deterrence.[79]

Other relevant aspects of PLA writings on space security issues highlight a preference for "soft kill" measures (which temporarily or permanently denies use of space assets through jamming, blinding, or cyber attack) over "hard kill" ones (kinetic attacks with the potential to generate significant amounts of space debris that might affect China's own satellites). Soft-kill attacks are seen as being more easily deniable and less diplomatically controversial than hard-kill attacks, which may generate debris or involve kinetic strikes on facilities in surrounding countries. Some writings by PLA authors also stress the importance of centralized authorization of these attacks due to their diplomatic costs and potential for escalation.[80]

The PLA also intends to take full advantage of the contribution that space assets can make to military operations, emulating US efforts to use space as an enabler for warfighting. Although the PLA is currently less dependent on space systems than the US military, its emphasis on fighting and winning informationized wars and its specific operational requirements (such as the need to locate US aircraft carriers) will necessarily increase PLA dependence on vulnerable space assets, especially when operating farther away from mainland China. Recent PLA writings, such as the 2013 edition of *The Science of Military Strategy*, place greater emphasis on the importance of space and the contributions space support can make in the air, maritime, and nuclear domains.[81] PLA space experts write that space dominance will be a critical and contested objective throughout any military conflict, with the PLA seeking both to maintain use of its space assets in the face of an adversary's attack and to deny an adversary's ability to use its own space assets.[82]

PLA authors discuss a range of "space defensive operations" to protect space assets and defend against attacks from space. These include the use of camouflage and stealth measures to disguise a spacecraft's functions, the deployment of small and microsatellite constellations rather than single large satellites, maneuverability, the capability for autonomous operation, and the deployment of false targets and decoys to overload an adversary's tracking systems. They also envision offensive operations using both space-based and terrestrial assets to protect space assets.[83] Deployment of mobile launchers would also help the PLA surge additional space assets into low-earth orbit to either augment capabilities or replace damaged satellites. These tactics might have some value in protecting military space assets but would probably do little to protect civilian satellites.

Several writings highlight the strategic importance of the space domain, including the potential for space support operations to serve as a force multiplier for forces operating in other domains and for counterspace operations to limit the effectiveness of space-enabled operations by adversaries. Together they highlight the potential for conventional operations in space to have strategic effects.[84]

Offensive Cyber Capabilities

Much of the PLA's current writing and thinking about space and cyber issues is couched in the emerging PLA doctrine of informationization and reflected in the PLA's task of "fighting and winning informationized wars."[85] As with its consideration of space, this focus derives from the study of US military doctrinal writings and operations, with the Gulf War being especially influential on PLA thinking. *Informationization* is a broad concept that refers to the increasing importance of information and information networks in both the civilian economy and military operations.[86] The PLA seeks to exploit the opportunities provided by networking, but its doctrinal focus on information warfare and information dominance also seeks to exploit adversary vulnerabilities by attacking information systems. Jiang Zemin endorsed the objective of informationizing weapons as early as 2000, and the concept subsequently has been formally studied, debated, and incorporated into PLA doctrinal materials, textbooks, operations regulations, and training guidance.[87] The 2015 white paper released by China states that, "As cyberspace weighs more in military security, China will expedite the development of a cyber force, and enhance its capabilities of cyberspace situation awareness, cyber defense, support for the country's endeavors in cyberspace and participation in international cyber cooperation, so as to stem major cyber crises, ensure national network and information security, and maintain national security and social stability."[88]

One PLA textbook states that the goal of information warfare is to "cut off the enemy's observation, decision making, and troop command and control capabilities at critical times, while maintaining our own command and control ability, thus allowing us to seize information superiority . . . and to create conditions to win the decisive battle."[89] The textbook adds that "the primary task of modern campaigns has become seizing information superiority and taking away the enemy's capability of acquiring information."[90] Key targets include command systems, information systems (intelligence, surveillance, and reconnaissance [ISR] and computer networks), and logistics systems.[91] More recent analyses highlight information dominance as a prerequisite for dominance in other battlespaces, including the land, sea, air, space, and electromagnetic domains.[92] PLA writings clearly suggest that integrating command, control, communications, computers, intelligence, surveillance, and reconnaissance (C4ISR) systems to take advantage of the significant opportunities provided by informationization drives a military to become more dependent on these systems. The struggle for information dominance also requires an emphasis on offensive operations, especially for a military in an inferior position.[93] PLA computer network operations fit under the broader concept of "integrated network electronic warfare," which combines electronic attacks on sensors and communications links (to disrupt the opponent's acquisition and transmission of information) with network attacks (to disrupt an adversary's processing and use of information).[94]

A Pentagon report from 2010 notes that:

China's CNO [computer network operations] concepts include computer network attack, computer network exploitation, and computer network defense. The PLA has established information warfare units to develop viruses to attack enemy computer systems and networks, and tactics and measures to protect friendly computer systems and networks. These units include elements of the militia, creating a linkage between PLA network operators and China's civilian information technology professionals.[95]

One US cyber expert notes that "interviews and [PLA] classified writings reveal interest in the full spectrum of computer network attack tools, including hacking, viruses, physical attack, insider sabotage, and electromagnetic attack."[96] Among the advantages computer network attacks provide are extended range, low cost, and potential to degrade a sophisticated adversary's most advanced C4ISR capabilities. One Chinese author writes that "computer network attack is one of the most effective means for a weak military to fight a strong one."[97]

An analysis of PLA writings suggests a number of characteristics that might govern PLA employment of computer network attacks in a conflict involving the United States.[98] These characteristics include:

- using computer network attacks in the opening phases of a conflict, potentially even via a preemptive attack;
- targeting key nodes through which critical data passes, especially US command-and-control and logistics networks;
- employing computer network and electronic warfare to temporarily paralyze enemy command-and-control systems, thus creating opportunities for attacks on command-and-control systems and on military forces via conventional precision strikes; and
- identifying military and contractor communications and logistics information that travels over civilian networks as particularly vulnerable to attack; these civilian networks may be vulnerable to relatively simple cyber attacks, such as distributed denial-of-service attacks.

Chinese military writings characterize the cyber domain as offense-dominant. Some Chinese analysts see gains from attacking first in order to obtain information superiority.[99] However, the cyber domain differs from the conventional and nuclear domains in that offensive capabilities do not necessarily provide defensive protection (e.g., counterforce operations via preemptive strikes are not necessarily possible). China's initial interest in exploiting asymmetrical US dependence and vulnerability to achieve decisive strategic effects has morphed into a realization that cyberspace will be a contested domain that involves both offensive operations against an adversary's networks and defensive operations to protect one's own networks.

Artificial Intelligence

AI is "the ability of a computer system to solve problems and to perform tasks that would otherwise require human intelligence."[100] AI is a general technology that has a broad range of commercial and military applications. Current "second-wave" AI systems involve large-scale statistical machine learning that uses large-scale exemplar data sets or simulated interactions as inputs, employs algorithms to identify correlations for how particular inputs map to particular outputs, and then uses the resulting models to identify events, patterns, or anomalies in real-world data. "Deep learning" involves an interactive process of analyzing large data sets with a deep neural network and training the algorithm by adjusting parameters until the algorithm reaches a desired level of performance. This approach has proven effective for image classification, object detection, speech recognition, and natural-language processing.[101]

AI has a variety of potential military applications. At the weapons level, applications include optimizing the performance and accuracy of missiles, improving the ability of weapons platforms and missiles to defeat defenses and countermeasures, and increasing the effectiveness of cyber attacks and cyber defenses. These applications could also significantly improve the effectiveness of individual weapons. A second set of applications involves improvements in sensor and image-recognition technology that could reduce the ability of platforms and systems such as nuclear submarines, mobile missiles, and stealth aircraft to survive undetected. This could potentially erode strategic stability by making deterrent forces vulnerable to a first strike. Another set of applications involves the use of AI in autonomous or unmanned systems, either acting independently in swarms or to augment manned systems. AI can also have strategic effects by being incorporated into command-and-control systems, either to develop and plan alternative courses of action for human commanders or to execute plans without human involvement.

Chinese companies, universities, and the PLA have made significant investments in AI for both commercial and military applications. In 2017 the Chinese government announced an ambitious AI development plan that sought to catch up with leading countries by 2020 and make China "the world's premier artificial intelligence innovation center" by 2030.[102] The government is backing this plan with commitments of public resources and incentives to mobilize commercial resources on behalf of national goals. China's military-civil fusion (MCF) strategy seeks to facilitate the flow of technology between the military and civil sectors and to stimulate joint research between commercial, academic, and military entities. The PLA is currently pursuing a wide range of military applications for AI, and Chinese military theorists speak of a potential shift from today's "informationized" warfare to tomorrow's "intelligentized" warfare.[103] China's potential to make significant breakthroughs in commercial and military applications of AI could have significant implications for the US-Chinese strategic balance in particular areas and for US-Chinese strategic competition more generally.

INTEGRATION OF CONCEPTS AND OPERATIONS

China has developed several concepts for integrating these nuclear, conventional, space, and cyber systems into PLA operations. Here, we assess three of these concepts: integrated strategic deterrence, the joint-fire strike campaign, and conventional-nuclear entanglement.

Integrated Strategic Deterrence

China's emerging concept of "integrated strategic deterrence" involves a multidimensional set of military and nonmilitary capabilities that combine to protect Chinese national security interests. According to RAND analysts Michael Chase and Arthur Chan, "Powerful military capabilities of several types—including nuclear capabilities, conventional capabilities, space capabilities, and cyberwarfare forces—are all essential components of a credible strategic deterrent."[104] Although the concept was initially aspirational, improvements in Chinese nuclear, conventional (air, naval, and missile), space, and cyber capabilities are increasingly allowing China to put integrated strategic deterrence into practice.

The Chinese term usually translated as deterrence, *weishe*, encompasses both deterrence and compellence.[105] This conception suggests that successful deterrence not only dissuades adversary attack but can also compel an adversary into submitting to Chinese political demands.

One operational question related to integrated strategic deterrence is whether the PLA can effectively orchestrate the full range of military and nonmilitary capabilities in order to successfully achieve the desired strategic effects. The military reforms announced at the end of 2015 have improved the PLA's ability to orchestrate conventional air, naval, ground, and conventional missile force operations by establishing joint theater commands with both peacetime and wartime control over the conventional forces within their theater.[106] The PLA also has attempted to improve its ability to coordinate space and cyber operations by establishing a new Strategic Support Force (SSF), which has responsibility for both types of capabilities.[107] However, the fact that the theater commands control the conventional forces and the Central Military Commission has operational responsibility for the Rocket Force's nuclear capabilities and other national-level capabilities may complicate the PLA's ability to employ all these forces in a synergistic manner, especially in a rapidly developing crisis that moves in unexpected (and therefore unplanned) directions.[108] The structure of the PLA today is more conducive to these kinds of integrated operations than in the past, though challenges likely remain.

If integrated strategic deterrence consists of merely adding disparate capabilities to produce cumulative strategic effects, this potential lack of coordination may not matter much, at least for purposes of deterring attacks. There is a sense in which "integrated strategic deterrence" appears to function as an amplifier of military capabilities, allowing even basic conventional forces to assert that they are contributing to national strategic objectives. However, if one thinks of deterrence in terms of its compellent meaning, the potential lack of coordination and inability to achieve synergies that multiply operational impact may be a bigger problem for the PLA.

Joint-Fire Strike Campaign

China may also employ its conventional forces in joint-fire strike campaigns, which can produce strategic effects through the coordinated and sequenced use of military units from across the PLA. The joint-fire strike campaign, as defined in the 2006 edition of *Science of Campaigns*, envisions combining precision air, cruise missile, and ballistic missile attacks in a coordinated manner to maximize strategic effectiveness.[109] For example, precision ballistic missile attacks against an adversary's airfields, air defenses, and command-and-control facilities could produce a permissive environment for follow-on air attacks. The joint-fire strike campaign allows planners to mix and match forces and sequence attacks to increase effectiveness.

However, previous army dominance and the former military region system (which existed primarily to support army operations) had impeded the PLA's ability to plan and execute joint operations and campaigns. The military regions did not possess peacetime control of the air, naval, and missile forces within their areas of responsibility. In a crisis or war, the military regions were expected to turn into war zones (*zhanqu*) and acquire operational control over all air, naval, and conventional missile units. This arrangement inhibited effective joint training and imposed major obstacles to executing joint campaigns.

China has increasingly emphasized the need to conduct joint operations, and the recent wave of military reforms has included several changes aimed at improving jointness across the force.[110] The reforms sought to rebalance the military away from the ground forces and promote more coordination among the various services in order to increase the PLA's ability to plan and execute joint operations. The reforms diminished the traditional role of the Army by cutting three hundred thousand troops and replacing the Army-dominated General Staff Department with a new Joint Staff Department focused on joint operations.[111] The reforms also replaced the seven military regions with five new theater commands. Each theater command (TC) has a joint operations command center that is staffed by personnel from each of the military services and focused on joint operations.[112] The PLA has placed greater emphasis on integrated joint operations, making joint exercises a centerpiece of PLA-wide training.[113]

China's military services possess a wide range of precision strike capabilities with differing accuracies, ranges, and payloads. Chief among these are the advanced conventional missiles controlled by the PLA Rocket Force, which are increasing their range, accuracy, and responsiveness.[114] Some of the PLA Air Force's newer H-6K bombers can reportedly be equipped with anti-ship cruise missiles or land-attack cruise missiles.[115] One PLA Navy bomber, the H-6G, has "systems and four weapons pylons for [anti-ship cruise missiles] to support maritime missions."[116] In recent years, according to the Pentagon's 2017 report on the Chinese military, the PLA Army has reportedly emphasized improving air defense systems and that "advanced long-range artillery systems—both conventional and rocket—as well as supporting target-acquisition systems continued to enter the force, providing tactical- and operational-level units with world-class, long-range strike capabilities."[117]

These capabilities can be used in sequenced and coordinated attacks to generate strategic effects. The PLA appears to be increasingly emphasizing a move away from land warfare and preparing for campaigns that will rely more on contributions from the Rocket Force, the Navy, and the Air Force. The *Science of Military Strategy* describes a notional campaign to achieve air superiority near China's shores: "In terms of striking fire . . . guided and precision-guided missiles are to be used to destroy and suppress the enemy's radar stations, ground air defense weapons and airfields."[118] In these operations, PLA Rocket Force units would be used to crater an adversary's runways and airfields and disable missile and air defense systems.[119] These strikes likely would be executed in coordination with land-attack cruise missiles launched by PLA Air Force and Navy assets.[120]

Despite its recent reforms, challenges remain for the PLA in undertaking effective joint-fire strike campaigns. For example, although the newly established theater commands were intended to help rebalance away from ground force's dominance, nine of the ten highest-ranking inaugural officials appointed to lead the TCs were drawn from the PLA Army.[121] Ground force officers also appear to make up a large portion of participants in joint command training courses.[122] The PLA appears to have been slow in integrating units from the PLA Rocket Force into the theater command joint operations command centers.[123] Although the PLA has undertaken important structural reforms to promote joint operations, many military officers appear to lack the necessary training and experience. For example, a recent review of PLA joint exercises stated that "PLA press reporting highlighted cases in which PLA commanders were not well-versed in the wide range of capabilities at their disposal, failed to coordinate and share information among the units under their command, and demonstrated weak command and organization skills."[124]

Conventional-Nuclear Entanglement

In the last several years scholars have highlighted the possibility that entanglement between China's conventional and nuclear-armed ground-based missile systems could present escalation risks in a future conflict. Scholars have identified evidence of geographic, operational, and technological entanglement between China's conventional and nuclear forces.[125] Geographically, China's nuclear and conventional missiles may operate and be garrisoned in the same locations. China's land-based missile forces are assigned to six missile bases, all of which control both nuclear and either conventional or dual-capable missile brigades. Operationally, conventional and nuclear missiles could be subject to overlapping command-and-control structures. Technologically, China is increasingly deploying missile systems with both conventional and nuclear variants, such as the DF-21, and dual-capable missile systems, such as the DF-26, which may be visually indistinguishable.

Entanglement along these geographic, operational, and technological dimensions may generate escalatory pressures in several ways. First, entanglement could inadvertently increase the vulnerability of China's nuclear forces. US strikes aimed at China's conventional forces might inadvertently destroy China's nuclear systems. Even if the US avoids hitting Chinese nuclear systems, Beijing's nuclear forces could still be degraded if the United States undermines shared command-and-control systems or if the United States targets defensive systems that are used to protect both conventional and nuclear missiles. This could potentially generate "use it or lose it" pressures on Beijing. Second, entanglement could generate dangerous misperceptions through target misidentification. Whether or not China's nuclear forces actually become more vulnerable, China could (mis)perceive some US strikes as targeting China's nuclear forces, potentially exacerbating perceptions of a "use it or lose it" dilemma in Beijing. Third, entanglement could cause the United States to misperceive the nature of Chinese strikes and mistakenly believe that the launch of a Chinese conventionally armed ballistic missile was a nuclear attack.

US observers have suggested that this entanglement, to the degree it exists, may be a deliberate choice by Chinese planners.[126] To the extent that entanglement heightens escalation risks, it may give pause to US leaders in the midst of a crisis or conflict. US leaders may be more reluctant to escalate a conflict or crisis or, in the midst of an ongoing conflict, more averse to striking some of China's conventional missiles for fear of triggering escalation to the nuclear threshold. Chinese decision-makers may be resorting to what Thomas Schelling described as the "manipulation of risk."[127] In this way, entanglement of nonstrategic conventional and nuclear systems could still produce strategic effects by deterring the US military from taking action against China.

However, despite the possibility that conventional-nuclear entanglement may enhance China's strategic deterrence against the United States, there is little evidence that entanglement has been a deliberate choice. Chinese writings are notable for the lack of attention paid to either evidence of entanglement or the ways in which entanglement could generate pressures to escalate, although these issues have been raised in US-Chinese Track 1.5 dialogues.[128]

Chinese thinking reportedly envisions a strong firebreak between the conventional and the nuclear domains.[129] If entanglement were a deliberate policy choice, China's missile forces would probably exhibit a higher degree of entanglement than currently exists.

Entanglement is likely the result of more benign operational considerations and choices. Specifically, Chinese decision-makers appear to have adopted policies that result in entanglement in order to exploit economies of scale and operational flexibility. Though armed with different warheads, conventional and nuclear variants of the same missile system are likely to have the same transportation, maintenance, logistics, and personnel requirements. A professor in the Strategy Department of the PLA National Defense University has explicitly noted the "resource savings" that stem from integrating conventional and nuclear forces.[130] Two researchers from the Academy of Military Science, in explaining the motivation for developing the dual-use DF-26, extolled the flexibility such conventional-nuclear dual-use systems provide in selectively augmenting either the nuclear or conventional deterrent.[131] They note that such flexibility is particularly relevant for China, which "does not engage in arms races."[132] Other commentators have noted that dual-use systems "greatly economize manpower and all manner of maintenance costs."[133]

The fact that entanglement between conventional and nuclear forces in China may be unintentional could actually *increase* the escalation risks in a conflict. If Chinese planners have underestimated the risks of entanglement, they may be more likely to view any degradation of their nuclear capabilities by the United States as intentional. This could increase the escalatory pressures facing Beijing and cause leaders to resort to more aggressive signaling of their own.[134]

These risks could be further exacerbated by the perception among US officials that entanglement is a deliberate choice by China. First, US officials may be more willing to risk targeting some of China's nuclear assets, wrongly believing that Beijing understands the risks and can accurately distinguish between US strikes targeting conventional missile systems (which might inadvertently affect some Chinese nuclear capabilities) and strikes deliberately targeting nuclear missile systems (which would presumably seek to destroy as much of China's nuclear force as possible). Second, US decision-makers may be more likely to misinterpret aggressive Chinese signals. Measures taken by China to increase the survivability of its nuclear deterrent could be misinterpreted as preparations for an actual launch. Authoritative Chinese texts specify that PLA troops should take a number of possibly escalatory steps to demonstrate resolve in a crisis. These include raising the alert status of missile systems, dispersing road-mobile missiles toward preestablished launch sites, and conducting "test launches of medium and long range strategic missiles armed with conventional warheads for focused live fire intimidation."[135] These texts advocate publicly broadcasting evidence that the PLA has taken such steps to provide credible signs of resolve.[136] Rather than seeing these moves as Chinese attempts to ensure the survivability of its nuclear deterrent, US observers may misinterpret them as preparations for an actual nuclear strike.

IMPLICATIONS FOR THE UNITED STATES AND CHINA

We have explored the potential for China to possess and deploy nonstrategic nuclear weapons, arguing that thus far there has been no clear evidence of China's deployment of tactical nuclear weapons and that Chinese theater-range nuclear missiles appear to have a strategic rather than tactical role. We have also examined six types of conventional capabilities with potential strategic effects (conventional ballistic missiles that provide a precision attack capability; anti-ship ballistic missiles; hypersonic weapons; counterspace capabilities; offensive cyber attack capabilities; and military applications of AI), and the integration of these capabilities with other Chinese forces, noting the potential impact of PLA organizational reforms on the operational use of these capabilities. We now consider some implications of these types of conventional capabilities.

Offensive Capabilities Not Necessarily Counterforce

In the nuclear domain, a counterforce attack on an adversary's nuclear forces can potentially reduce one's vulnerability to retaliation. Effective counterforce capabilities thus create incentives for first strikes (to disable an adversary's retaliatory capability) and therefore may lead to crisis instability. This is the case for silo-based ballistic missiles, which are vulnerable to attack by nuclear weapons or with conventional precision-guided munitions. (This helps explain China's shift to mobile missiles, which are harder to find and thus less vulnerable.) However, some conventional capabilities may differ from this paradigm in that first strikes may not reduce an adversary's ability to retaliate. This is arguably the case in offense-dominant domains such as space and cyber, where preemptive attacks may not help protect one's own satellites and networks from retaliation. It may also be the case with ASBMs and hypersonic weapons, which are designed to attack other adversary weapons systems and therefore do not have symmetrical counterforce capabilities.

This suggests that certain conventional weapons with strategic effects may not necessarily contribute to crisis instability by increasing incentives for first strikes. However, this requires China to recognize its own vulnerability and the fact that a preemptive attack will not remove this vulnerability. If Chinese leaders recognize this reality, there is potential to negotiate strategic restraint based on mutual deterrence.[137] Unfortunately, many Chinese and US military writings emphasize the importance (and, implicitly, the potential) of achieving space dominance and cyber dominance, as if such dominance would protect space assets and networks against retaliation. Strategic dynamics may work differently in offensive-dominant domains without the potential for counter-force attacks.

Shift from Asymmetric to Symmetric Vulnerabilities

As Chinese military analysts began to focus on the challenge of defeating a superior US military in the mid-1990s, they highlighted US dependence on space and cyberspace as a critical vulnerability that could be exploited. This logic underpinned Chinese efforts to develop and deploy counterspace weapons and offensive cyber attack capabilities. However, Chinese analysts also recognized that the US military's ability to leverage space-based ISR and communications capabilities and computer networks also produced a quantum leap forward in military effectiveness. This realization eventually evolved into the strategic guidance that the PLA must be prepared to fight and win informationized wars.[138]

However, the PLA's pursuit of informationization has increased its dependence on space support systems and computer networks, creating some of the same vulnerabilities that PLA analysts identified and sought to exploit within the US military. Given that a potential conflict with the United States would likely be fought near China, the PLA has a greater ability to substitute ground-based ISR and communications systems for space assets to reduce its vulnerability to attack. However, China also is less able to protect civilian space assets and networks, which means it may remain vulnerable to US attack. This more symmetrical vulnerability may produce caution and incentives for restraint that help stabilize US-Chinese strategic relations.

Increasing Cross-Domain Challenges

Both the US and Chinese militaries routinely train for cross-domain attacks. Examples of relevant assets include China's ASBM capability, which uses the aerospace domain to attack a maritime asset, and China's doctrine of integrated network electronic warfare, which emphasizes the use of electromagnetic and kinetic attacks to disrupt computer networks. While strategists recognize that some systems depend on access to other domains (and thus are vulnerable to cross-domain attack), there is less agreement on the use of this vulnerability to create cross-domain deterrence.[139]

Chinese analysts tend to treat the nuclear domain as inherently strategic and separate from conventional warfighting in other domains. But nuclear command-and-control systems are potentially vulnerable to a cross-domain kinetic or cyber attack, and factors such as conventional-nuclear entanglement complicate Chinese efforts to segregate nuclear weapons from other combat capabilities. This is one reason the Chinese persist in urging the United States to adopt a nuclear NFU policy and are alarmed at any suggestion that the United States might use the threat of nuclear escalation to reinforce conventional deterrence.

What Is the Potential for Arms Race Dynamics as US-Chinese Strategic Competition Intensifies?

Both US and Chinese strategic documents recognize an acceleration of strategic competition in the nuclear, space, cyber, and maritime domains. Chinese documents such as the 2015 white paper "China's Military Strategy" express this sense of competition in veiled terms, noting that "outer space and cyber space have become new commanding heights in strategic competition among all parties" and speaking generally of "revolutionary changes in military technologies and the form of war" that pose "new and severe challenges to China's military security."[140] US strategic documents such as the 2017 National Security Strategy and the 2018 unclassified summary of the National Defense Strategy are more direct in labeling China as a strategic competitor and calling for the United States to adjust its defense policies to compete more effectively.[141]

This sense of heightened competition for regional influence in the Asia-Pacific theater and for military dominance in the maritime, space, and cyber domains has the potential to tilt the balance of competition and cooperation in US-China relations and lead to unrestrained strategic rivalry. The fact that US and Chinese analysts both view the space and cyber domains as critical to success in modern warfare increases the stakes of strategic competition, as does the AI wild card. Unrestrained US-Chinese rivalry would have negative effects for countries in the Asia-Pacific region, which likely would be pressured to choose sides, and worldwide, where US-Chinese rivalry is likely to reduce the effectiveness of global governance institutions and limit their ability to deal with global and regional challenges. While some creative ideas for avoiding worst-case outcomes have been proposed, intensified Sino-US strategic rivalry is likely to aggravate regional and global security challenges.[142]

CONCLUSION

This chapter has documented the salience of conventional military capabilities with strategic effects: they are an important aspect of the Sino-US military balance and an important arena for US-Chinese strategic competition. Neither country is prepared to accept a position subordinate to the other. Even if the United States and China are eventually able to attain a stable nuclear relationship—no easy feat, given each side's nuclear modernization efforts and technological innovations in ballistic missile defenses and hypersonic weapons—arms races in the space, cyber, and maritime domains have the potential to turn bilateral relations into a strategic rivalry with negative consequences for the two countries, for the Asia-Pacific region, and for the world. Finding a way to manage more competitive US-Chinese military relations is likely to be the principal strategic challenge of the twenty-first century.

NOTES

The views expressed are those of the authors and do not necessarily reflect the views of the National Defense University, the Department of Defense, or the US government.

1. M. Taylor Fravel and Evan S. Medeiros, "China's Search for Assured Retaliation: The Evolution of Chinese Nuclear Strategy and Force Structure," *International Security* 35, no. 2 (Fall 2010): 48–87.

2. Charles D. Ferguson, Evan S. Medeiros, and Phillip C. Saunders, "Chinese Tactical Nuclear Weapons," in *Tactical Nuclear Weapons: Emergent Threats in an Evolving Security Environment*, ed. Brian Alexander and Alistair Millar, 110–26 (London: Brassey's, 2003); Fravel and Medeiros, "China's Search for Assured Retaliation"; Fiona S. Cunningham and M. Taylor Fravel, "Assuring Assured Retaliation: China's Nuclear Posture and U.S.-China Strategic Stability," *International Security* 40, no. 2 (Fall 2015): 37–38; Jeffrey Lewis, *Paper Tigers: China's Nuclear Posture* (London: Institute for International and Strategic Studies, 2014); Hans M. Kristensen and Robert S. Norris, "Chinese Nuclear Forces, 2016," *Bulletin of the Atomic Scientists* 72, no. 4 (2016): 205–11; and David C. Logan, "Hard Constraints on a Chinese Nuclear Breakout," *Nonproliferation Review* 24, no. 1–2 (2017): 13–30.

3. These include the short-range A-5 fighter-bomber and the H-6 bomber, the latter of which had a longer range but was incapable of penetrating modern air defenses.

4. Jonathan Ray, *Red China's "Capitalist Bomb": Inside the Chinese Neutron Bomb Program* (Washington, DC: National Defense University Press, 2015).

5. Paul Schulte, "Tactical Nuclear Weapons in NATO and Beyond: A Historical and Thematic Examination," in *Tactical Nuclear Weapons and NATO*, ed. Tom Nichols, Douglas Stuart, and Jeffrey D. McCausland, 13–74 (Carlisle Barracks, PA: Army Strategic Studies Institute, 2012).

6. William C. Potter et al., "Tactical Nuclear Weapons: Options for Control," United Nations Institute for Disarmament Research, UNIDIR/2000/20 (2000), 57, https://unidir.org/publication/tactical-nuclear-weapons-options-control.

7. M. Taylor Fravel, *Active Defense: China's Military Strategy since 1949* (Princeton, NJ: Princeton University Press, 2019), 236–69.

8. Cunningham and Fravel, "Assuring Assured Retaliation," 12.

9. Mark A. Stokes, "China's Nuclear Warhead Storage and Handling System," Project 2049 Institute, March 12, 2010; and Li Bin, "China and Nuclear Transparency," in *Transparency in Nuclear Warheads and Materials: The Political and Technical Dimensions*, ed. Nicholas Zarimpas, 50–57 (New York: Oxford University Press, 2003).

10. Li Bin, "Differences Between Chinese and U.S. Nuclear Thinking and Their Origins," in *Understanding Chinese Nuclear Thinking*, ed. Li Bin and Tong Zhao, 3–18 (Washington, DC: Carnegie Endowment for International Peace, 2016), 6.

11. See the discussion in Logan, "Hard Constraints," 17–23. For information on China's history of nuclear tests, see Lewis, *Paper Tigers*, chap. 2.

12. For an early overview of evidence related to Chinese tactical nuclear weapons, including the argument that China could field such weapons but has chosen not to, see Ferguson, Medeiros, and Saunders, "Chinese Tactical Nuclear Weapons." For a review of some of these "hard" constraints, see Logan, "Hard Constraints."

13. Ray, *Red China's "Capitalist Bomb."*

14. Central Intelligence Agency, "China Nuclear Test [Redacted]," *National Intelligence Daily*, CPAS NID 95-053CX, March 7, 1995, 11, declassified version available at https://nsarchive2.gwu.edu/NSAEBB/NSAEBB200/19950307.pdf.

15. Central Intelligence Agency, "China's Nuclear Weapons Testing: Facing Prospects for a Comprehensive Test Ban," *Intelligence Memorandum 93-20044C M*, September 30, 1993, 5, declassified version available at https://www.cia.gov/library/readingroom/docs/DOC_0000996367.pdf.

16. Central Intelligence Agency, "China's Nuclear Weapons Testing," 5.

17. US Department of Defense, *Military and Security Developments Involving the People's Republic of China, 2017* (Washington, DC: Office of the Secretary of Defense, 2017). On the opinions of analysts, see, for example, Kristensen and Norris, "Chinese Nuclear Forces, 2016."

18. *Nuclear Posture Review* (Washington, DC: Office of the Secretary of Defense, 2018), 54.

19. Robert Ashley, "Statement for the Record: Worldwide Threat Assessment," testimony before the Senate Armed Services Committee, March 6, 2018, https://www.armed-services.senate.gov/imo/media/doc/Ashley_03-06-18.pdf.

20. "China Firmly Opposes U.S. Nuclear Posture Review: Spokesman," *Xinhua*, February 5, 2018, http://en.people.cn/n3/2018/0205/c90000-9423510.html.

21. Michael S. Chase, "Chinese Views of the 2018 Nuclear Posture Review, and Their Implications," *China Brief* 18, no. 4 (2018): 11–14, https://jamestown.org/program/chinese-views-on-2018-npr/.

22. Li Xianrong and Yang Min, "Mei e deng he daguo qianghua he weishe you naxie zhuyao jucuo" (What are the major elements of US, Russian, and other major nuclear states' emphasis on nuclear deterrence?), *Jiefangjun bao*, January 30, 2018, http://www.81.cn/2017xsdqjzxk/2018–01/30/content_7925448.htm.

23. Chase, "Chinese Views of the 2018 Nuclear Posture Review."

24. Though these systems have technical characteristics that are consistent with theater capabilities, they are sometimes treated as strategic systems because they can generate strategic effects.

25. Kristensen and Norris, "Chinese Nuclear Forces, 2016."

26. Michael S. Chase and Cristina L. Garafola, "China's Search for a 'Strategic Air Force,'" *Journal of Strategic Studies* 39, no. 1 (2016): 24; and Kristensen and Norris, "Chinese Nuclear Forces, 2016," 209.

27. US Department of Defense, *Military and Security Developments Involving the People's Republic of China, 2018* (Washington, DC: Office of the Secretary of Defense, 2018), 77 (emphasis added).

28. Chase and Garafola, "China's Search for a 'Strategic Air Force,'" 4–28.

29. Zhao Lei, "PLA Air Force Commander Confirms New Strategic Bomber," *China Daily*, September 2, 2016, http://www.chinadaily.com.cn/china/2016–09/02/content_26683883.htm.

30. US Department of Defense, *Military and Security Developments, 2017*, 61.

31. US-China Economic Review Commission, *2017 Report to Congress* (Washington, DC: Government Printing Office, 2017), 209.

32. US Senate Armed Services Committee, "Ashley Statement for the Record," 8, https://www.armed-services.senate.gov/imo/media/doc/Ashley_03-06-18.pdf.

33. Ankit Panda, "Revealed: China's Nuclear-Capable Air-Launched Ballistic Missile," *The Diplomat*, April 10, 2018, https://thediplomat.com/2018/04/revealed-chinas-nuclear-capable-air-launched-ballistic-missile/.

34. Definition given for "Zhanlüe" (strategy) in *Zhongguo renmin jiefangjun junyu* (PLA Military Terms) (Beijing: Military Science Publishing [Junshi kexue chubanshe], 2011).

35. Dean Cheng, "Chinese Views on Deterrence," *Joint Force Quarterly* 60 (First Quarter, 2011): 92–94; Dean Cheng, "Evolving Chinese Thinking about Deterrence: What the United States Must Understand about China and Space," *Heritage Foundation Backgrounder*, March 29, 2018.

36. National Air and Space Intelligence Center, "Ballistic and Cruise Missile Threat 2017," accessed June 2017, http://www.nasic.af.mil/About-Us/Fact-Sheets/Article/1235024/2017-ballistic-and-cruise-missile-threat-report/; Michael S. Chase, "PLA Rocket Force Modernization and China's Military Reforms," testimony before the US-China Economic and Security Review Commission, Washington, DC, February 15, 2018, 8, https://www.rand.org/pubs/testimonies/CT489.html.

37. As part of the recent wave of military reforms the Rocket Force was established at the end of 2015 to replace the former Second Artillery. For a discussion of the impact of the reforms on China's missiles forces, see David C. Logan, "PLA Reforms and China's Nuclear Forces," *Joint Force Quarterly* 83 (Fourth Quarter 2016): 57–62.

38. Michael S. Chase and Andrew S. Erickson, "The Conventional Missile Capabilities of China's Second Artillery Force: Cornerstone of Deterrence and Warfighting," *Asian Security* 8, no. 2 (2012): 115–37.

39. Jeffrey Lewis, "China's Belated Embrace of MIRVs," in *The Lure and Pitfalls of MIRVs: From the First to the Second Nuclear Age*, ed. Michael Krepon, Travis Wheeler, and Shane Mason, 104–5 (Washington, DC: Stimson Center, 2016).

40. David C. Logan, "Career Paths in the PLA Rocket Force: What They Tell Us," *Asian Security* 24, no. 1–2 (2017): 103–21, https://doi.org/10.1080/14799855.2017.1422089.

41. Akira Marusaki, "Developments in China's Conventional Precision Strike Capabilities," Project 2049 Institute, November 23, 2015, 1–2, https://project2049.net/2015/11/23/developments-in-chinas-conventional-precision-strike-capabilities/.

42. US Department of Defense, *Military and Security Developments, 2018*, 36.

43. For a national Rocket Force order of battle based on information gleaned from open sources, see Mark Stokes, "PLA Rocket Force Leadership and Unit Reference," Project 2049 Institute, April 9, 2018.

44. US Department of Defense, *Military and Security Developments, 2017*, 49.

45. Chase and Erickson, "Conventional Missile Capabilities," 121.

46. Chase and Erickson, 121–22.

47. Stokes, "PLA Rocket Force Leadership."

48. US Department of Defense, *Military and Security Developments Involving the People's Republic of China, 2016* (Washington, DC: Office of the Secretary of Defense, 2016), 25.

49. As quoted in Andrew S. Erickson, "Chinese Anti-Ship Ballistic Missile Development and Counter-Intervention Efforts," testimony before the US-China Economic and Security Review Commission, Washington, DC, February 23, 2017, 2–3, https://www.uscc.gov/sites/default/files/Erickson_Testimony.pdf.

50. Wang Zhangqin and Fang Guangming, "Women weisheme yao fazhan dongfeng-26 dandao daodan" (Why we had to develop the Dongfeng-26 ballistic missile), *Zhongguo qingnian bao*, November 23, 2015, http://zqb.cyol.com/html/2015–11/23/nw.D110000zgqnb_20151123_1–09.htm (hereafter "Why We Had to Develop").

51. Kevin Pollpeter, "The U.S.-China Reconnaissance-Strike Competition: Anti-Ship Missiles, Space, and Counterspace," *Study of Innovation and Technology in China* 9 (January 2017): 4.

52. Dennis M. Gormley, "China's Offensive Missile Forces," testimony before the US-China Economic and Security Review Commission, Washington, DC, April 1, 2015, 8, https:// www .uscc .gov /sites /default /files /Gormley %20USCC %20Testi mony %201%20April %202015 0 .pdf.

53. Kristin Huang, "China's 'Aircraft-Carrier Killer' Missiles Successfully Hit Target Ship in South China Sea, PLA Insider Reveals," *South China Morning Post*, November 14, 2020, https://www.scmp.com/news/china/military/article/3109809/chinas-aircraft-carrier-killer-missiles-successfully-hit-target.

54. Erickson, "Chinese Anti-Ship Ballistic Missile Development," 4–7.

55. Erickson, 4–7; and Gormley, "China's Offensive Missile Forces," 8–9.

56. Gormley, "China's Offensive Missile Forces," 8.

57. Ronald O'Rourke, "China Naval Modernization: Implications for U.S. Capabilities—Background and Issues for Congress" (Washington, DC: Congressional Research Service, April 25, 2018), 82–85.

58. Andrew S. Erickson, *Chinese Anti-Ship Ballistic Missile (ASBM) Development: Drivers, Trajectories and Strategic Implications* (Washington, DC: Jamestown Foundation, 2013), 126–131.

59. US Department of Defense, *Military and Security Developments, 2017*, 68.

60. James M. Acton, "China's Advanced Weapons," testimony before the US-China Economic and Security Review Commission, Washington, DC, February 23, 2017, 1, https://carnegieendowment.org/2017/02/23/china-s-advanced-weapons-pub-68095.

61. Mark Stokes, "China's Advanced Weapons," testimony before the US-China Economic and Security Review Commission, Washington, DC, February 23, 2017, 38, https://www.uscc.gov/sites/default/files/transcripts/China's%20Advanced%20 Weapons.pdf.

62. Stokes, 38–39.

63. Acton, "China's Advanced Weapons," 1–2.

64. For a discussion of the technical aspects of boost-glide weapons, see James M. Acton, "Hypersonic Boost-Glide Weapons," *Science & Global Security* 23, no. 3 (2015): 191–219.

65. Acton, "China's Advanced Weapons," 2–3.

66. Gormley, "China's Offensive Missile Forces," 9.

67. Sharon Weinberger, "Pentagon Official Says U.S. Hypersonic Weapons Research Underfunded," *Foreign Policy*, March 1, 2018, http://foreignpolicy.com/2018/03/01/pentagon-official-says-u-s-hypersonic-weapons-research-underfunded/.

68. Stokes, "China's Advanced Weapons," 40.

69. Lora Saalman, "China's Calculus on Hypersonic Glide," SIPRI, August 15, 2017, https://www.sipri.org/commentary/topical-backgrounder/2017/chinas-calculus-hypersonic-glide.

70. Gormley, "China's Offensive Missile Forces," 9.

71. Saalman, "China's Calculus on Hypersonic Glide."

72. Donald L. Fuell, "Broad Trends in Chinese Air Force and Missile Modernization," testimony before the US-China Economic and Security Review Commission, Washington, DC, January 30, 2014, 37, https://www.uscc.gov/sites/default/files/Lee%20Fuell_Testimony1.30.14.pdf.

73. See Joshua H. Pollack, "Boost-Glide Weapons and U.S.-China Strategic Stability," *Nonproliferation Review* 22, no. 2 (2015): 155–64.

74. People's Republic of China, State Council Information Office, "China's Military Strategy" white paper (Beijing: State Council Information Office, May 2015).

75. US House of Representatives, "Lt. Gen. Vincent R. Stewart Statement for the Record: Worldwide Threat Assessment," Armed Services Committee, February 3, 2015, https://www.dia.mil/News/Speeches-and-Testimonies/Article-View/Article/567087/worldwide-threat-assessment/.

76. Dean Cheng, "China's Space Program," written testimony submitted to the US-China Economic and Security Review Commission, May 11, 2011, https://www.uscc.gov/sites/default/files/transcripts/05.11.11HearingTranscript.pdf.

77. US Department of Defense, *Military and Security Developments Involving the People's Republic of China, 2010* (Washington, DC: Office of the Secretary of Defense, 2010), 36. An earlier study by this author on Chinese interest in ASAT technologies accurately noted that as of 2002 China lacked some capabilities necessary for an operational ASAT system. See Phillip C. Saunders et al., "China's Space Capabilities and the Strategic Logic of Anti-Satellite Weapons," Center for Nonproliferation Studies Research Story of the Week, Monterey, California, July 2002.

78. See Kevin Pollpeter, "The Chinese View of Military Space Operations," in *China's Revolution in Doctrinal Affairs: Emerging Threats in the Operational Art of the Chinese People's Liberation Army*, ed. James Mulvenon and David Finkelstein, 355–62 (Alexandria, VA: CNA, 2005).

79. Dean Cheng, "Prospects for China's Military Space Efforts," in *Beyond the Strait: PLA Missions Other than Taiwan*, ed. Roy Kamphausen, David Lai, and Andrew Scobell, 234–40 (Carlisle, PA: US Army War College, Strategic Studies Institute, April 2009); also see Cheng, "Evolving Chinese Thinking About Deterrence."

80. Pollpeter, "The Chinese View of Military Space Operations"; Kevin Pollpeter and Jonathan Ray, "The Conceptual Evolution of China's Military Space Operations and Strategy," in *China's Evolving Military Strategy*, ed. Joe McReynolds, 265–307 (Washington, DC: Jamestown Foundation, 2016).

81. Academy of Military Science, *Science of Military Strategy* (Beijing: Military Science Press, 2013), 258.

82. Pollpeter, "The Chinese View of Military Space Operations"; Cheng, "Prospects for China's Military Space Efforts."

83. Cheng, "Prospects for China's Military Space Efforts," 231–34.

84. Pollpeter and Ray, "Conceptual Evolutions."

85. "China's Military Strategy."

86. See Dean Cheng, *Cyber Dragon: Inside China's Information Warfare and Cyber Operations* (New York: Praeger, 2016).

87. See Maryanne Kivlehan-Wise and Frederic Vellucci, with Daniel M. Hartnett, "Preparing for Informationized Wars: China's Evolving Concept of Military Informationization," paper presented at China Maritime Studies Institute Conference

"China's Strategy for the Near Seas," US Naval War College, Newport, Rhode Island, May 10–11, 2011.

88. "China's Military Strategy."

89. Academy of Military Science, *Zhanyi xue* (Science of Campaigns) (Beijing: Junshi kexue chubanshe, 2006), 169 (hereafter *Science of Campaigns*).

90. *Science of Campaigns*, 170.

91. *Science of Campaigns*, 95–96.

92. People's Liberation Army Military Informationization Editors Committee, *Dictionary of Military Informationization* (Beijing: PLA Press, 2008), 592.

93. Kivlehan-Wise and Vellucci, "Preparing for Informationized Wars."

94. Dai Qingmin, "On Integrating Network Warfare and Electronic Warfare," *China Military Science* (*Zhongguo junshi kexue*), February 2002, 112–17; and analysis of Dai's writings in James Mulvenon, "PLA Computer Network Operations: Scenarios, Doctrine, Organizations, and Capability," in *Beyond the Strait: PLA Missions other than Taiwan*, ed. Roy Kamphausen, David Lai, and Andrew Scobell, 260–61 (Carlisle, PA: US Army War College Strategic Studies Institute, 2009).

95. US Department of Defense, *Military and Security Developments 2010*, 37.

96. Mulvenon, "PLA Computer Network Operations," 277.

97. Cited in Mulvenon, "PLA Computer Network Operations," 257n3.

98. This paragraph draws on Mulvenon, "PLA Computer Network Operations," 253–86; and Bryan Krekel, "Capability of the People's Republic of China to Conduct Cyber Warfare and Computer Network Exploitation," report prepared by Northrup Grumman for the US-China Economic and Security Review Commission, October 2009.

99. Joe McReynolds, "China's Military Strategy for Network Warfare," in *China's Evolving Military Strategy*, ed. Joe McReynolds, 214–65 (Washington, DC: Jamestown Foundation, 2016), 229.

100. National Security Commission on Artificial Intelligence, *Interim Report* (Washington, DC: National Security Commission on Artificial Intelligence, 2019), 7.

101. National Security Commission on Artificial Intelligence, *Interim Report*, 53–55.

102. Paul Mozur, "Beijing Wants A.I. to Be Made in China by 2030," *New York Times*, July 20, 2017.

103. For an overview of PLA thinking and research lines of effort, see Elsa B. Kania, "Chinese Military Innovation in Artificial Intelligence," testimony before the US-China Economic and Security Review Commission Hearing on Trade, Technology, and Military-Civil Fusion, Washington, DC, June 7, 2019, https://www.uscc .gov/sites/default/files/June%207%20Hearing_Panel%201_Elsa%20Kania_Chinese %20Military%20Innovation%20in%20Artificial%20Intelligence_0.pdf.

104. Michael S. Chase and Arthur Chan, *China's Evolving Approach to "Integrated Strategic Deterrence"* (Santa Monica, CA: RAND, 2016).

105. Cheng, "Chinese Views on Deterrence," 92–94.

106. Joel Wuthnow and Phillip C. Saunders, *Chinese Military Reforms in the Age of Xi Jinping: Drivers, Challenges, and Implications* (Washington, DC: National Defense University Press, 2017). Also see Phillip C. Saunders et al., eds., *Chairman Xi Remakes the PLA: Assessing Chinese Military Reforms* (Washington, DC: National Defense University Press, 2019).

107. See John Costello and Joe McReynolds, *China's Strategic Support Force: A Force for a New Era* (Washington, DC: National Defense University Press, 2018).

108. See Mark A. Stokes, "Employment of National-Level PLA Assets in a Contingency: A Cross-Strait Conflict as Case Study," in *The People's Liberation Army and Contingency Planning in China*, ed. Andrew Scobell et al., 135–55 (Washington, DC: National Defense University Press, 2015); and Phillip C. Saunders, "Beyond Borders: PLA Command and Control of Overseas Operations," *INSS Strategic Forum* 306 (Washington, DC: National Defense University Press, 2020).

109. *Science of Campaigns.*

110. For an overview of the reforms and their implications, see Wuthnow and Saunders, *Chinese Military Reforms.*

111. For more on the PLA's downsizing, see John Chen, "Downsizing the PLA, Part 1: Military Discharge and Resettlement Policy, Past and Present," *China Brief* 16, no. 16 (2016): 20–26, https://jamestown.org/program/downsizing-pla-part-1 -military-discharge-resettlement-policy-past-present/.

112. Joel Wuthnow, "A Brave New World for Chinese Joint Operations," *Journal of Strategic Studies* 40, no. 1–2 (2017): 179–84.

113. Mark R. Cozad, "PLA Joint Training and Implications for Future Expeditionary Capabilities," testimony before the US-China Economic and Security Review Commission, Washington, DC, January 21, 2016, https://www.rand.org/content /dam/rand/pubs/testimonies/CT400/CT451/RAND_CT451.pdf.

114. Chase and Erickson, "Conventional Missile Capabilities," 115–37.

115. US Department of Defense, *Military and Security Developments, 2017*, 28; and Zhao Lei, "Air Force Now Able to Launch Long-Range Precision Strikes," *China Daily*, October 14, 2014, http://www.chinadaily.com.cn/china/2015–10/14/content _22178512.htm.

116. US Department of Defense, *Military and Security Developments, 2017*, 28; and Zhao Lei, "Anti-Ship Cruise Missile Wins Award," *China Daily*, January 10, 2018, http://usa.chinadaily.com.cn/a/201801/10/WS5a556a83a3102e5b17371c1d.html.

117. US Department of Defense, *Military and Security Developments, 2017*, 22.

118. Quoted in translation in Oriana Skylar Mastro and Ian Easton, "Risk and Resiliency: China's Emerging Air Base Strike Threat," Project 2049 Institute, November 8, 2017, 3, https://project2049.net/2017/11/08/risk-and-resiliency-chinas-emerging-air -base-strike-threat/.

119. Mastro and Easton, 3.

120. Mastro and Easton, 7.

121. Phillip C. Saunders and John Chen, "Is the Chinese Army the Real Winner in PLA Reforms?," *Joint Force Quarterly*, no. 83 (Fourth Quarter 2016): 44–48.

122. Wuthnow, "A Brave New World," 186.

123. There is evidence that China has made some progress in this area. See David C. Logan, "Making Sense of China's Missile Forces," in *Chairman Xi Remakes the PLA: Assessing Chinese Military Reforms*, ed. Phillip C. Saunders et al., 393–435 (Washington, DC: National Defense University Press, 2019).

124. Cozad, "PLA Joint Training," 11.

125. Thomas J. Christensen, "The Meaning of the Nuclear Evolution: China's Strategic Modernization and U.S.-China Security Relations," *Journal of Strategic Studies* 35, no. 4 (2012): 447–87; David C. Logan, "Drawing a Line Between Conventional and Nuclear Weapons in China," *Bulletin of the Atomic Scientists*, May 5, 2015; Caitlin Talmadge, "Would China Go Nuclear?: Assessing the Risk of Chinese Nuclear Escalation in a Conventional War with the United States," *International Security*

41, no. 4 (Spring 2017): 50–92; and David C. Logan, "Are They Reading Schelling in Beijing?: The Dimensions, Drivers, and Risks of Nuclear-Conventional Entanglement in China," *Journal of Strategic Studies*, online publication November 12, 2020, https://doi.org/10.1080/01402390.2020.1844671.

126. Michael Glosny, Christopher Twomey, and Ryan Jacobs, "U.S.-China Strategic Dialogue, Phase VIII Report" (Monterey, CA: Naval Postgraduate School Center on Contemporary Conflict, 2014), 10.

127. Thomas C. Schelling, *The Strategy of Conflict* (Cambridge, MA: Harvard University Press, 1960), 187–203.

128. Zhao Tong and Li Bin, "The Underappreciated Risks of Entanglement: A Chinese Perspective," in *Entanglement: Russian and Chinese Perspectives on Non-Nuclear Weapons and Nuclear Risks*, ed. James Acton, 47–75 (Washington, DC: Carnegie Endowment for International Peace, 2017).

129. Liu Chong, "The Relationship Between Nuclear Weapons and Conventional Military Conflicts," in *Understanding Chinese Nuclear Thinking*, ed. Li Bin and Tong Zhao, 149–69 (Washington, DC: Carnegie Endowment for International Peace, 2016).

130. Sun Kuaiji, "Fangyan shijie kan huojian jun jianshe" (The world looks upon the construction of the Rocket Force), *Jiefangjun bao*, May 3, 2016, http://www.81.cn /depb/2016–05/03/content_7032475.htm.

131. Wang and Fang, "Why We Had to Develop."

132. Wang and Fang, "Why We Had to Develop."

133. "Neibu renshi pilu shouci liangxiang de dongfeng 26 weihe ling mei ruci jinzhang" (Insiders disclose why the debut of the Dongfeng-26 makes America so nervous), *Xina junshi*, September 7, 2015, http://mil.news.sina.com.cn/2015–09 –07/0928838594.html?cre=tagspc&mod=g&r=user&pos=1_5.

134. For some discussion of the role of perceptions in driving these escalatory dynamics, see Talmadge, "Would China Go Nuclear?," 50–92.

135. See, for instance, Yu Xijun, ed., *Di er paobing zhanyi xue* (The science of second artillery campaigns) (Beijing: Jiefangjun chubanshe, 2004), 282–96; and Cao Zhengrong, Wu Runbo, and Sun Jianjun, *Xinxihua lianhe zuozhan* (Informationized joint operations) (Beijing: Jiefangjun chubanshe, 2008), 260 (hereafter *Informationized Joint Operations*). For English-language discussions of the risks of certain forms of Chinese signaling, see Michael S. Chase, "China's Transition to a More Credible Nuclear Deterrent: Implications and Challenges for the United States," *Asia Policy*, no. 16 (July 2013): 98–101; Christopher T. Yeaw, Andrew S. Erickson, and Michael S. Chase, "The Future of Chinese Nuclear Policy and Strategy," in *Strategy in the Second Nuclear Age: Power, Ambition, and the Ultimate Weapon*, ed. Toshi Yoshihara and James R. Holmes, 72–75 (Georgetown University Press, 2012); and Cunningham and Fravel, "Assuring Assured Retaliation," 37–38.

136. Cao, Wu, and Sun, *Informationized Joint Operations*, 259–60.

137. See David C. Gompert and Phillip C. Saunders, *The Paradox of Power: Sino-American Strategic Restraint in an Era of Vulnerability* (Washington, DC: National Defense University Press, 2011).

138. See M. Taylor Fravel, "Shifts in Warfare and Party Unity: Explaining China's Changes in Military Strategy," *International Security* 42, no. 3 (Winter 2017–18): 37–83.

139. See Mark E. Redden and Michael P. Hughes, "Global Commons and Domain Inter-relationships: Time for a New Conceptual Framework?," *INSS Strategic Forum* 259 (Washington, DC: National Defense University Press, 2010).

140. "China's Military Strategy."

141. Donald Trump Administration, "National Security Strategy of the United States of America" (Washington, DC: The White House, December 2017); US Department of Defense, *Summary of the 2018 National Defense Strategy of the United States of America* (Washington, DC: Office of the Secretary of Defense, 2018).

142. Phillip C. Saunders, "Managing Strategic Competition with China," *INSS Strategic Forum* 242 (Washington, DC: National Defense University Press, 2009); Gompert and Saunders, *The Paradox of Power*; James Steinberg and Michael O`Hanlon, *Strategic Reassurance and Resolve: U.S.-China Relations in the Twenty-First Century* (Princeton, NJ: Princeton University Press, 2014); and Lyle J. Goldstein, *Meeting China Halfway: How to Defuse the Emerging US-China Rivalry* (Washington, DC: Georgetown University Press, 2015).

SEVEN

Organization of China's Strategic Forces

Bates Gill

As the chapters in this volume make clear, critical developments by the People's Republic of China (PRC) since the late 1990s—involving the strategic environment, deterrence concepts, and technological advancements—have profoundly shaped the country's current and future role as a strategic actor. However, in comparison to the changes across those strategic drivers, the *organization* of China's strategic forces has not, until relatively recently, transformed as rapidly. Even in light of the ambitious and sweeping reorganization of the People's Liberation Army (PLA) announced at the end of 2015, the hoped-for impact on China's strategic posture appears to be still a work in progress and faces a number of challenges.

To shed further light on China's role as a strategic actor in the twenty-first century, this chapter focuses on the organizational underpinnings of the PRC's strategic forces.[1] In doing so I ask and seek answers to the following key questions:

- How does the current organization of China's strategic force compare to the past?
- What are the most important changes affecting the organization of China's strategic force in wake of the PLA reforms set in motion at the end of 2015?
- What does the resulting strategic force structure look like, and why?
- What are the key strategic components—in the nuclear, advanced aerospace (missiles), outerspace, and cyberspace realms—and how do they relate with one another?
- What does the organization of China's strategic forces tell us about the country's doctrinal ambitions, operational capabilities, and ongoing challenges facing those forces?

To address these questions, the chapter first provides a brief background on the organizational evolution of the PRC's strategic forces, from the country's founding in 1949 to 2015. Next is a description of the organizational changes put in place since 2016 that have affected China's principal strategic forces, with a particular focus on the PLA Rocket Force (PLARF) and the PLA Strategic Support Force (PLASSF). The chapter concludes with a discussion of some of the key organizational challenges that continue to face the PRC's strategic forces.

ORGANIZATIONAL EVOLUTION, 1949–2015

Over most of the PRC's history, Chinese political and military leaders have understood their strategic forces not as offensively configured instruments of power projection. Rather, the country's strategic forces have been understood as those that serve to dissuade and deter adversaries from taking strategically threatening actions against it, principally under a posture of "active defense."[2] Hence, the PRC's traditional understanding of what constitutes a strategic force and how it is organized has depended on two key elements: Chinese leaders' perceptions of the strategic threats they must deter and the available military-technical capabilities they could bring to bear to achieve that deterrence.

According to authoritative PLA writings, China's strategic thinking about military aspects of deterrence has evolved across three distinct phases.[3] During the first phase, from the founding of the PRC in 1949 until the mid-1980s, deterrence was intended to prevent large-scale attacks against China, with initial concern focusing on the United States and possibly Kuomintang forces on Taiwan, and then later shifting to the Soviet Union. In the midst of this period, beginning in the 1960s, China's nascent nuclear arsenal aimed to gain just enough credibility to deter a nuclear attack by other nuclear powers, especially the United States and the Soviet Union. However, little in the way of sophisticated conceptual and operational thinking about nuclear deterrence and warfighting was in evidence.[4]

In the second phase, from the early 1990s to the beginning of the twenty-first century, Chinese strategists gave greater priority to the conceptual and operational development of deterrence; their theories and capabilities began to gel into a more cohesive strategy, especially with regard to nuclear weapons.[5] According to Chinese military writings this included an understanding that "limited and effective" nuclear weapons should serve as the "core" of military deterrence while at the same time the gradual development of modern combat systems suited to high-tech warfare would contribute to multilayered and coordinated deterrence capabilities across both conventional and nuclear realms.[6] The development of "assassin's mace" or "trump card" (*shashoujian*) capabilities—unexpected and overpowering asymmetrical weaponry—was seen as an important element of this new and emerging deterrent capacity.[7] Interestingly, it was during this period that the concept of "integrated deterrence" (combining nuclear weapons with other capabilities) began to appear in PLA writings.[8] Nevertheless, PLA writing on deterrence during this second phase primarily focused on nuclear deterrence.

In the third phase, beginning in the early 2000s and continuing into the present, Chinese deterrence has intended to protect China's "strategic window of opportunity" by ensuring a stable external environment that is conducive to the country's expansive economic growth and national development. This stable environment is to be created by "preparation for military struggle" through improvements in mechanization, firepower, mobility, defensive capabilities, and informationization. As explained in *The Science of Military Strategy* in 2001:

> China currently has possessed a limited but effective nuclear deterrence and a relatively powerful capability of conventional deterrence and a massive capability of deterrence of people's war. By combining these means of deterrence, an *integrated strategic deterrence* is formed, with comprehensive national power as the basis, conventional force as the mainstay, nuclear force as the backup power and reserve force as the support. . . . Only by combining nuclear deterrence, conventional force deterrence, space force deterrence, information deterrence, and deterrence of people's war, and concurrently coordinating with the struggle in the fields of diplomacy, economy, science and technology to enable deterrent means to complement each other, can the strategic deterrence be exerted to the utmost extent.[9]

Taken together, the collective application of these capabilities will enhance China's deterrent capabilities by demonstrating that the PLA will "win local wars under informationized conditions" while also introducing "flexible use of different means of deterrence" into its nuclear arsenal.[10] Early on in this phase the PLA had clearly recognized information technology's importance to modern deterrence and warfighting but acknowledged it would take until at least 2020 to "make major progress in informationization."[11] Over the course of this phase the deterrent role of a traditional "people's war" was diminished and eventually recast to apply to civil-military integration in an effort to leverage and absorb the technological advances of the civilian sector for the purposes of military modernization.

As Michael Chase, Daniel Yoon, and Mark Stokes found in their study on the PLA Second Artillery Force, written just prior to the sweeping 2015 PLA reorganization, though the PLA strategic rocket forces had remained largely unchanged organizationally through this third phase there were nevertheless critically important developments between 2000 and 2015.[12] These include the dramatic expansion in the size and diversity of China's conventional missile force; the emergence of those forces—particularly conventional precision strike capabilities—as a critical component of China's approach to deterrence, coercion and warfighting; and the steady development of an effective and credible nuclear deterrent that is based on an assured retaliatory capability.

In an important study by Eric Heginbotham et al., published in 2017, the authors similarly found that China's evolving nuclear deterrent was apparently "moving away from an approach to deterrence that deems the ability to impose some risk of a second strike sufficient" and "toward a more calculated strategy of assured retaliation."[13] They also found that with improved nuclear and conventional capabilities, regional perceptions of Chinese strategic intentions would likely be affected, raising questions about the "credibility of U.S. commitments [and] complicating the U.S. task of assuring allies and partners."

As these works suggest, over the course of the seventy years since 1949 the foundation of China's deterrent posture has shifted significantly as a result of technological breakthroughs, theoretical and conceptual advances, and changing threat assessments. In the first phase, preparing and deploying a people's war had pride of place, and China's early nuclear weapons capability played only a limited deterrent role. In the second phase, nuclear weapons emerged as the core component of China's strategic deterrent in conjunction with an aspiration to deploy more sophisticated, high-tech conventional capabilities for deterrence and warfighting purposes. In the third phase, deterrence theory and practice grew more sophisticated and called for the "informationized" application of other deterrent and warfighting capabilities alongside nuclear deterrence—especially in the outerspace and cyber spheres—to better deter and fight against powerful adversaries in regional contingencies.

Looking ahead, the PLA now appears poised to move toward a new fourth phase in its thinking about deterrence and warfighting wherein nuclear weapons are part of an expanded and diversified portfolio of conventional and other emerging strategic capabilities—such as in aerospace, outer space, and cyberspace—that deliver an "integrated strategic deterrent." In essence, during this nascent fourth phase Chinese strategic deterrence capabilities have begun to align more closely with strategic deterrence concepts and requirements.[14] In the pages that follow I will examine the critical organizational choices China's leaders have made as they pursue these goals.

STRATEGIC REORGANIZATION

Formally launched at the end of December 2015, the ongoing reorganization of the PLA has been the most sweeping and potentially transformative change in its history. These changes have had a profound effect on the politics, structure, and command authorities of the PLA. But, even more important, as far as China's top political and military leaders are concerned, these changes are intended to transform the PLA from a bloated, untested, and corrupt military into a force that is increasingly capable of supporting the country's strategic ambitions: being able to effectively use deterrent and coercive capabilities to conduct joint operations and fight short, intensive, and technologically sophisticated conflicts far from Chinese shores.

Structural Changes

Several important structural changes have been put in place that will shape the PLA's future strategic capabilities. First, the PLA's command structure has been entirely revamped. Prior to the 2015–16 reforms, the PLA command structure was highly complicated with unclear lines of authority. Under the old system, operational units effectively had two chains of command: one that connected operational units to military regions up to the PLA General Staff Department (GSD) and ultimately to China's top military body, the Central Military Commission (CMC); the other went from the operational units to their service headquarters, which also generally acted as functional commands. This dual structure meant that a naval or air force unit could be subject to the commands of both a military region commander and to the service to which it belonged. Further complicating matters, the PLA Army did not have a service headquarters; this role was instead played by the army-dominated General Staff Department. This structure was deemed far too complex and unworkable under the conditions and demands of modern warfare, with its focus on coordination and joint operations.

The new command structure, formally introduced in late 2015, has been simplified and flattened, with clearly delineated areas of responsibility. The four general departments under the old system (General Staff Department, General Political Department, General Logistics Department, and General Armaments Department) were dismantled and their functions have mostly been concentrated under the Central Military Commission (CMC). This change removed an entire bureaucratic layer that was dominated by the PLA Army and had become too independent from the CMC.

Post-reform, the new PLA command system is described as "CMC takes overall charge, theater commands direct operations, [and] service headquarters direct force development" (*junwei guan zong, zhanqu zhu zhan, junzhong zhu jian*). Under this new organizing principle the role of the CMC and its immediate subordinate organs is to provide strategic oversight and command over the activities of the PLA. Day-to-day and wartime operations of the PLA are led by joint theater commanders, who control subordinate units from

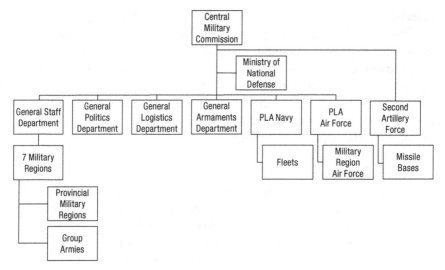

FIGURE 7.1. PLA Organizational Structure Prior to 2016 Reforms

different services and branches that operate together. Generally the individual service headquarters no longer act as functional commands and are instead responsible for force development—including providing troops and equipment, training, and administrative management of units —to prepare for what the United States military would term "organize, train, and equip" missions.

Second, the PLA's organizational structure has been transformed. Under the pre-2016 structure the PLA hierarchy consisted of the CMC, four general departments, seven military regions, and the headquarters of the PLA Navy, the PLA Air Force, and the Second Artillery Force (see figure 7.1). The restructuring resulted in a new Army headquarters command and the elevation of the Second Artillery Force, renamed the PLA Rocket Force, to a full service command equal to the Army, the Navy, and the Air Force. A new service branch, the Strategic Support Force (PLASSF), was established as part of the restructuring[15] (see figure 7.2).

In addition, as part of the reforms the seven military regions were dismantled and replaced with five joint theater commands:

- Eastern Theater Command, headquartered in Nanjing
- Western Theater Command, headquartered in Chengdu
- Northern Theater Command, headquartered in Shenyang
- Southern Theater Command, headquartered in Guangzhou
- Central Theater Command, headquartered in Beijing

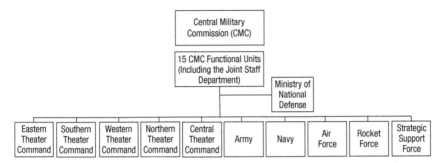

FIGURE 7.2. PLA Organizational Structure Post-2016 Reforms

Strategic Objectives

Underlying the structural reorganization is the strategic operational aim of having the PLA become more effective at "winning local wars under conditions of informationization."[16] This has been a long-standing aim of the PLA, at least since the early 2000s. However, Xi Jinping has brought to bear far more pressure on the PLA to live up to this expectation operationally and not just rhetorically.

In his work report to the Nineteenth National Congress of the CCP in October 2017, Xi candidly presented his strategic expectations for the PLA: "We will upgrade our military capabilities, and see that, by the year 2020, mechanization is basically achieved, IT application has come a long way, and strategic capabilities have seen a big improvement. . . . We will make it our mission to see that by 2035, the modernization of our national defense and our forces is basically completed; and that by the mid-21st century our people's armed forces have been fully transformed into world-class forces."[17] In the same speech Xi emphasized combat capabilities, enhanced military training and preparedness, and improved joint operations utilizing networked information systems.

With these strategic goals in mind, the reorganization set in motion in late 2015 aims to achieve several critical operational outcomes. First, the PLA is to be restructured in ways more suited to the types of combat it will likely encounter in the future. Transforming the PLA from an army-centric force and placing priority on the other services is a key step in this direction. Reorganizing the military regions—each of which traditionally had a stand-alone, largely defensive mission to perform—into five theater commands that are increasingly capable of wartime joint operations and cross-theater coordination is another important structural outcome. The creation of the joint theater commands ostensibly allows for control and coordination across the services in theater in a way the PLA has not operated before. Clarifying the fundamental

FIGURE 7.3. PLA Joint Theater Commands since 2016

Note: All locations are approximate and boundary representations are not authoritative.

Source: Office of the Secretary of Defense, *Military and Security Developments Involving the People's Republic of China 2016*, 2.

responsibilities of the PLA hierarchy—with the CMC in overall command, theater commands directing all warfighting, and the service headquarters handling force development—streamlines command-and-control and smooths any necessary transition from a peacetime to a wartime footing. The ultimate goal is a strategic posture that effectively integrates various military means for maximizing deterrence and warfighting capabilities, including nuclear, conventional, (counter)space, information, and other new and emerging capabilities.[18]

CHINA'S "NEW" STRATEGIC FORCES: THE PLARF

Among the most important changes of the 2015 PLA reorganization is the establishment of two "new" strategic forces: the PLARF and PLASSF. While the basic elements of the PLARF and PLASSF are not new—both being built on the foundations of previously existing capabilities within the PLA—they are nevertheless "new" in terms of how they are organized and how their activities and objectives have been consolidated and prioritized.

At the formal establishment ceremony for the PLARF on December 31, 2015, Chinese leader Xi Jinping stated his expectations for the newly created organization. He declared that the PLARF, as the successor to the PLA's Second

Artillery Force, is at the "core" of China's strategic power: it strengthens China's credible nuclear deterrence and second-strike capability, it intensifies the development of China's medium- and long-range precision-strike capabilities, and it reinforces strategic stability for Chinese interests.[19]

Unlike the Second Artillery Force, which was designated as a *budui* (force), the PLARF is now considered a full-fledged service of the PLA, along with the Army, the Navy, and the Air Force, all having the common designation of *jun* (service). In addition, the PLARF acquired its unique uniform design and flag shortly after it was elevated to a service, indicating its new status, distinct from the former Second Artillery Force, which used PLA Army uniforms and a generic PLA flag.[20]

The rise of China's missile force's prestige, however, does not denote a rise in the bureaucratic status (grade) of the organization within the PLA hierarchy. In fact, the former Second Artillery Force was already on the same grade level as the three traditional services before it was made into a full service. At present the PLARF is a military theater leader–grade organization, the highest grade in the PLA organization hierarchy beneath the CMC.[21] The elevation of China's missile force to a full service signals both to domestic and foreign audiences the increasing importance of conventional and nuclear missile capabilities and their expected contribution to Chinese military strategy.

The PLARF will clearly form a critical component in the PLA's official mandate, as stated in the most recent Chinese defense white paper which is: "Winning informationized local wars" in which "integrated combat forces will be employed to prevail in system-vs-system operations featuring information dominance, precision strikes and joint operations."[22] Boosting the standing of the PLARF within the PLA, investing in its nuclear arsenal, and integrating its growing and diverse conventional ballistic and cruise missile force within joint theater operations are all aimed at strengthening the PLA's range of offensive and deterrent options on the twenty-first-century battlefield. As such it deserves special attention in a volume of this kind; the following pages focus on the organization of the PLARF.

Organization of Nuclear and Missile Forces

The PLARF has largely inherited the organizational structure of the Second Artillery Force, including its top-tier leadership bodies, missile bases, direct subordinate organizations, and military academies and research institutions.[23]

Leadership

An analysis of the background of PLARF's top leaders suggests they generally come from within the missile forces, bringing decades of experience in commanding missile operations. Interestingly, one of the initial deputy commanders of the PLARF had a strong background in information operations while another had extensive experience in missile and satellite testing and launch. These perhaps indicate the increasing importance of information systems and space platforms for missile operations. In addition, one analysis of promotion patterns within the Second Artillery Force and the PLARF indicates that officers with experience and service predominantly in conventionally oriented bases—and especially those who have served at Base 61 (formerly Base 52)—appear likely to be promoted and have a stronger representation at the upper reaches of the PLARF. According to the study, this "suggests a current and future strengthening of the Rocket Force's conventional units and missions, potentially at the expense of its nuclear ones."[24] At a minimum it is reflective of the growing importance of the PLARF's conventional role over the past two decades.

Also significant is that the first commander of the PLARF was Wei Fenghe, who was appointed to the position in December 2015 upon the establishment of the PLARF.[25] Born in 1954 in Shandong province, Wei enlisted in the PLA at the age of sixteen and joined the Communist Party in 1972.[26] By the time of his appointment he had more than forty years of experience serving in China's missile forces. Starting as a private in 1970, he rose to become the commander of the former Second Artillery Force in October 2012. He was also promoted to full general and made a junior (the last, eleventh-ranking) member of the CMC that year. Later he was moved to be the fourth-ranking member on the (smaller) seven-member CMC, behind the chairman (Xi Jinping) and the two vice-chairs (Qu Qiliang and Zhang Youxia). In addition to CMC membership, he was also China's defense minister.[27] According to his official biography, Wei spent nearly all of his career associated with Base 54 (now Base 62), Brigade 813 (which operates nuclear-armed Chinese ICBMs).[28]

It is worth noting that Wei, by virtue of his senior position on the CMC, was the highest-ranking missile force officer in the PLA's history. In addition he was the first non-army general to assume the defense minister role. This suggests the increasing prestige and importance of the missile force within the PLA and fits the broader effort by China's top leaders to change the PLA's army-centric culture.

PLARF Headquarters

The PLARF's headquarter element includes the Staff Department, the Political Work Department, the Logistics Department, the Equipment Department, and the Discipline Inspection Committee.[29] The PLARF Staff Department is responsible for operational planning, command and control, training, force management, personnel management, and oversight of the numerous subordinate organizations. The department consists of the Operations Bureau, the Training

Bureau, the Force Management Bureau, the Planning and Organizational Structure Bureau, and the Direct Subordinate Work Bureau.[30]

Bases and Brigades

The PLARF has six confirmed operational missile bases with a total of around twenty-eight to thirty missile brigades.[31] These missile bases are corps-level organizations that have different deterrence and warfighting missions, some divided along geographic lines. They oversee subordinate missile brigades and supporting facilities and units. The organizational structure of the PLARF missile bases is believed to follow lines similar to the PLARF headquarters element, with key departments for general staff, political work, logistics, and equipment.[32] It is important to note that open-source information available about the types of missiles at these bases is sometimes unclear. Overall the PLARF is continuing the work of its predecessor by introducing new missile types and variants to the bases, including the steady replacement of most of the remaining silo-based, liquid-fueled DF-4 and DF-5 intercontinental-range ballistic missiles (ICBMs). The PLARF's bases and missile brigades are summarized in table 7.1.

Chinese state media officially announced in April 2018 the establishment of a new missile brigade equipped with DF-26 IRBMs. Some reporting, which cited video footage of the newly established brigade, suggests this brigade consists of up to 22 launchers.[33]

Other PLARF Organizations

The PLARF also fields a dedicated engineering force, which is responsible for the construction of facilities infrastructure for the PLARF.[34] Additional identified PLARF functions include tactics and training, and some research suggests that the PLARF has now consolidated and integrated all its testing and training facilities, possibly under a new Base 69, with headquarters in northwest China near Baishan City.[35]

Also subordinate to the PLARF is the Jinlun Engineering Command Department (also known as the Jinlun Engineering Company), which reportedly serves as the entity through which China exports missile technology and trains foreign militaries in operating Chinese missile systems. For example, Chinese-language reporting identifies this unit as being involved in the support services and training aspect of Chinese missile exports to Saudi Arabia in the mid-2000s.[36] The PLARF also has a number of military education and research institutes, including the Command College in Wuhan; the Engineering University in Xi'an; the Noncommissioned Officer (NCO) School in Qingzhou, Shandong province;[37] and the Research Academy in Beijing,

TABLE 7.1. PLARF Bases and Brigades

Base Number	Headquarters	Brigades	Missile Types
Base 61	Huangshan, Anhui province	611	DF-21 MRBMs
		612	DF-21 MRBMs
		613	DF-15 SRBMs
		614	DF-11 SRBMs
		615	DF-11 SRBMs
		616	DF-15 SRBMs
		617	DF-11 SRBMs
Base 62	Kunming, Yunnan province	621	DF-21 MRBMs
		622	DF-21 MRBMs; possibly DF-31 ICBMs
		623	D-10 LACM variants
		624	DF-21 MRBMs
		625	DF-21 MRBMs
		626	DF-21 MRBMs; possibly DF-26 IRBMs
Base 63	Huaihua, Hunan province	631	DF-5A ICBMs
		632	DF-4 ICBMs; transitioning to DF-31 ICBMs
		633	DF-5A ICBMs
		635	DH-10 LACMs
Base 64	Lanzhou, Gansu province	641	DF-31 ICBMs
		642	DF-31 ICBMs
		643	DF-31 ICBMs
		646	DF-21 MRBM variants
Base 65	Shenyang, Liaoning province	651	DF-21 MRBM variants
		652	DF-21 MRBM variants
		653	DF-21 MRBM variants
		654	Possibly DF-21 MRBM variants
Base 66	Luoyang, Henan province	661	DF-5 ICBMs
		662	DF-5 ICBMs; possibly some DF-4 ICBMs
		663	DF-31 ICBMs
		666	DF-26 IRBMs
Base 67	Baoji, Shaanxi province	Responsible for management, storage, and handling of nuclear warheads	

which conducts scientific, technical, and weapons research in support of the PLARF's mission.[38]

Command and Control Mechanisms

Within two months of the establishment of the PLARF a new operational command structure was announced for the PLA.[39] Under the new command arrangement the four service branches are responsible for force development and the five new joint theaters are charged with conducting operations. Under the previous system the commanders of China's seven former military regions did not have peacetime command and control over non-army units. In wartime, these commanders are assigned to naval and air forces.[40] Unlike the three traditional services, the command and control of the Second Artillery Force is highly centralized under the CMC, in both peacetime and wartime.

The reformed PLA command structure has changed the command and control of the PLARF in some important respects. These changes are still unfolding and there is only limited information in the public domain on the nature of the relationships between theater commanders and missile force organizations at different levels. However, some important points stand out.

First and foremost, there is no evidence that the command and control arrangements for the PLARF's *nuclear* forces have changed. Chinese experts strongly assert that the creation of the PLARF and the broader PLA reforms of recent years have not affected the command and control over China's nuclear forces: command authority remains highly centralized under the CMC.[41] Under this "skip echelon" system the country's supreme command authority skips over intermediate commanders and directly gives orders to commanders of missile brigades in the field. Arguably, with the streamlining of the PLA command hierarchy and overall strengthening of the CMC's authority under the latest reforms, this centralized command authority over nuclear weapons may be further reinforced.

There are compelling reasons to believe this command structure over nuclear weapons remains in place. It is important to note that China has consistently emphasized the strategic rationale for its nuclear force.[42] Granting command authorities over PLARF nuclear forces to theater commanders would send strategically ambiguous signals that are inconsistent with officially articulated Chinese nuclear strategic thinking. Moreover, the joint command theaters are still in the process of coming together: transferring control of nuclear forces to an untested command system would be unnecessarily risky, given the high cost of any potential mishaps.

While the command-and-control arrangements for the PLARF nuclear missile forces appear to remain unchanged, there is some evidence that such stasis may not hold for the PLARF's conventional missile forces. First, at the

PLARF missile base level it would appear that early efforts are underway to integrate the missile base command-and-control systems with those of the theater commanders. For example, one PLA article describes the training experience of a particular PLARF missile base and states that this base has entered the "joint operational command information system" and has been integrating into the "joint operations command structure" of a theater command. According to a staff officer from the missile base Training Office, "[the missile base] will participate in multiple joint exercises at the theater level in 2018." The article notes this will serve as a "theater-level pilot to assist other forces entering into the command information system," it will solve issues of joint operations, and it will improve "joint effects" through "leading the setup of operational clusters in [joint] command exercises." This effort seems to have begun in fall 2017 when, for the first time, a missile base staffed an operational cluster command post under the theater joint command structure and led multiple missile brigades in a joint attack exercise.[43]

In another example, during an interview shortly after the establishment of the joint theater command system the commander of the Eastern Theater Command, Gen. Liu Yuejun, stated that "[the Eastern Theater Command] is responsible for commanding theater Army, Navy, Air Force, PLARF and other armed forces in joint operations and military operations other than war." While he did not differentiate between the PLARF's nuclear and conventional forces, presumably he meant command over the latter.[44]

These accounts suggest that the PLARF has started experimenting with integrating its missile bases into the joint command structure of the theater commands with the aim of improving joint operations. One practical obstacle to joint theater command over missile bases is that some missile bases have geographic boundaries that overlap more than one theater command. The logical next step would be to reorganize the missile bases to match geographic boundaries of proximate command theaters.

Other Strategic Systems

In addition to the modernization of China's land-based nuclear forces, the People's Liberation Army Navy (PLAN) is also developing China's first credible sea-based nuclear deterrent capability in the form of four Jin-class (Type 094) SSBNs, each capable of carrying 12 JL-2 submarine-launched ballistic missiles (SLBMs). The JL-2 missiles are MIRV-capable and have a range of about 4,500 mi. China's next-generation SSBN, the Type 096, is currently being developed and construction was set to begin in early 2020.[45] Media reports indicate that China will arm the Type 096 with JL-3 SLBMs that are under development.[46]

There are also indications that China is making progress in acquiring an air-based nuclear deterrent in the form of an effective strategic bomber coupled with nuclear-capable air-launched ballistic missiles (ALBM). Recent reports suggest that China may have conducted up to five tests of a new ALBM that is possibly a variant of the DF-21 MRBM.[47]

In September 2016 the PLAAF confirmed that it is working on the next-generation long-range stealth bomber, designated as the H-20, when the then-commander of the PLAAF, Ma Xiaotian, stated: "China's current long range strike capabilities have increased significantly compared to the past. In the future it will be even greater as you will see; we are currently developing a new-generation long range bomber."[48] Some analysts estimate that the first H-20 prototype could fly as early as 2020.[49] China is also actively pursuing hypersonic glide vehicles (HGV) that are maneuverable, extremely fast, and capable of penetrating existing missile defense systems. China has conducted at least seven successful test flights of its HGV, designated the WU-14 (also known as the DF-ZF).[50] Media reports indicate that China has also conducted two tests of a new kind of HGV-capable ballistic missile (dubbed DF-17) in November 2017.

In addition, the PLARF probably has a counterspace role that involves the operations of anti-satellite missiles. While much of the PLA's military space mission was consolidated under the new PLASSF as part of the reforms at the end of 2015, the PLARF is the logical arm of the PLA to operate China's anti-satellite missiles because of its expertise as well as the missile logistics and supporting capabilities that already existed within the Second Artillery Force. Some PLA sources have argued for the continued involvement of China's missile forces in space warfare of the future. For example, one source asserts that China's missile forces will need to develop "new operational means in response to the changing nature of warfare, especially the intensification of military competition in non-traditional domains, such as outer space."[51]

Therefore, for the PLARF "an important direction in its development" is to "extend its operational capabilities to new areas, such as space."[52] In fact, according to current PLA missile strategy, under special circumstances the PLARF's missiles can be used to strike key nodes in an enemy's space and information network, such as military satellites. It is envisaged that this would create wider effects on the enemy's operational systems, with potential for shock and awe effect, thereby creating the conditions for the PLA to "seize strategic initiative."[53]

Going forward, the scope of the PLARF's strategic role and operational activities will evolve to allow it to undertake a wider range of strategic deterrence and warfighting activities enabled by technological and organizational transformation. At the same time, the PLARF must adjust to increased involvement of other services and branches of the PLA in strategic deterrence and warfighting operations, which raises important questions about coordination, command-and control mechanisms, and bureaucratic competition.

CHINA'S "NEW" STRATEGIC FORCES: THE PLASSF

Established on December 31, 2015, the Strategic Support Force (PLASSF) is one of the newest units within the PLA. Given the organization's relatively recent establishment, combined with the general opacity that characterizes much of the PLA's activities, there is very limited official information on the PLASSF, including its doctrines and concepts, mission, organizational structure, and ongoing growing pains. Moreover, good evidence suggests that the PLASSF at this point remains a work in progress as the PLA and its leadership sort through the establishment and integration of this very new and different kind of organization.[54]

At the establishment ceremony for the PLASSF Xi Jinping declared that the organization will be a "new-type of combat force" to support the nation's security and improve the PLA's overall combat capabilities.[55] Several months later, during an inspection visit to the newly established headquarters, he reminded the organization of its importance to joint operations and stressed the need for innovation, civil-military integration, and enhancement of both its deterrence and its warfighting capabilities.[56] The PLASSF commander has stated that the organization will provide an "information umbrella" for the PLA and support the integration and protection of effective information technology systems for military operations.[57]

In short, it appears the PLASSF, like the PLARF, is set to become a critical element in the PLA's official mandate of winning informationized local wars.[58] Hence, the creation of the PLASSF and the consolidation of most of the PLA's space, cyber, and electronic warfare capabilities within this new body aims to address the PLA's long-standing aspiration to fight jointly and more effectively on the information battlefield.

Organizational Structure of the PLASSF

Open sources probably do not paint a full picture of the PLASSF organizational structure. However, there is good evidence that the top tier administrative bodies of the organization consist of the Staff Department, the Political Work Department, the Discipline and Inspection Commission, and, presumably, logistics and equipment departments.[59] On the operational side of the organization, the two major departments are the Aerospace Systems Department and the Network Systems Department.

The PLASSF's Staff Department is responsible for operational planning, training, command and control, project oversight, and personnel management. At least three bureaus have been confirmed under the Staff Department: the Operational Planning Bureau, the Training Bureau, and the Direct Subordinate Works Bureau.[60] Also under the Staff Department is the PLASSF

Xingcheng Sanatorium, a medical rehabilitation facility located in Xingcheng, Liaoning province. Before the establishment of the PLASSF, this facility was subordinate to the former Shenyang Military Region.[61] The PLASSF's Political Works Department is responsible for political education, propaganda, legal affairs, and other political matters, including overseeing the political work of subordinate organizations.

Leadership

The backgrounds of PLASSF's top leaders provide additional insights into the mission, organization, and aspirations of the PLASSF. The PLASSF is led by officers with substantial past exposure to advanced military technology and theories, including in the fields of missile operations, space and information warfare, joint operations, and military research.

The first commander of the PLASSF is Gao Jin, who was appointed to the position in December 2015 upon the creation of the PLASSF.[62] Gao was promoted to full general on June 28, 2017, and is a member of the Nineteenth Central Committee of the Communist Party of China.[63] Born in 1959 in Jiangsu province, Gao joined the PLA in 1978 and became a member of the CCP in 1980. He spent most of his military career as an officer in the Second Artillery Force, steadily moving up the ranks of operational and later senior command levels. Gao graduated with an engineering degree from the Second Artillery Force Command College in the late 1980s. On the operational side, he has spent considerable time in leadership roles overseeing conventional missile brigades and bases.

Of particular interest is the fact that Gao served as the commander of a missile brigade (1997–2001) stationed at then-Second Artillery Force Missile Base 52 (now Base 61), which launched missiles bracketing the north and south of Taiwan during the cross-strait standoff of 1995–96.[64] Gao also briefly served as assistant to the chief of staff of the former GSD (in 2014) and later as the president of the PLA Academy of Military Science (2014–15). These two roles would have offered opportunities to follow and understand the PLA's efforts to develop and implement greater coordination across the forces. Gao's past appointments also include chief of staff of the Second Artillery Force (2011–14) and a variety of leadership positions at missile Base 52 (now Base 61), such as deputy chief of staff, chief of staff, and deputy commander.

Aerospace Systems Department

On the operational side of the PLASSF, the Aerospace Systems Department (ASD) is responsible for executing the organization's space-related missions. The ASD has consolidated nearly every aspect of the PLA's space operations, including space launch and support, telemetry, tracking, and control (TT&C);

communication; and intelligence, surveillance, and reconnaissance (ISR). Before the establishment of the PLASSF, the PLA's space elements largely resided within the former PLA General Armaments Department and, to a lesser extent, within the former General Staff Department.

The ASD also oversees a large network of organizations involved in China's military and civilian space operations. These organizations mostly have their own civilian organizational identities even though they are controlled by the PLASSF ASD and led by PLASSF military officers.

For example, the ASD oversees the activities of China's four principal space launch and missile testing facilities. The Jiuquan Satellite Launch Center is China's largest and longest-serving launch facility for low earth orbit military reconnaissance and civilian satellites, missile testing, and manned space missions.[65] The Taiyuan Satellite Launch Center's responsibilities include the launching of reconnaissance and meteorological satellites and microsatellites, and the testing of ballistic missiles and carrier rockets.[66] Xichang Satellite Launch Center is responsible for the testing, command and control, measurement and surveying, safety assurance, data processing, information transmission, meteorological support, debris recovery, and technology research with respect to the launch of broadcast, communications, and meteorological satellites in geosynchronous transfer orbit.[67] Wenchang Spacecraft Launch Site is the newest of the four major space launch facilities created within the PLASSF ASD. It is officially subordinate to the Xichang Satellite Launch Center.[68] The facility's mission includes the launch of geostationary orbit satellites, polar orbiting satellites, cargo spacecraft, and deep space probes. The facility consists of five subsystems: test launches, measurement and control, communication, meteorological services, and technical service support.[69]

In addition to launch facilities, the ASD oversees space TT&C sites that are critical to China's space program and the PLA's military space operations. The Xi'an Satellite Control Center, also known as the PLA 26th Testing and Training Base (Unit 63750), is China's primary satellite control facility. It is the administrator of China's land-based TT&C network for space operations and has responsibility for command and control, information exchange, data processing, communication, and the recovery of reentry modules.[70]

The Xi'an Center exercises command and control over land-based space TT&C stations throughout China.[71] Its staff has also signed agreements with partner governments to operate TT&C stations in Chile (Santiago), in Namibia (Swakopmund), and in Pakistan (Karachi).[72] The center may also be involved in joint space research and TT&C activities in other countries, including Argentina (Neuquén), Australia (Dongara), Brazil (Alcântara, Maranhão), and Kenya (Malindi).[73] The center also runs a Communications Main Station and the State Key Laboratory of Astronautics Dynamics, whose main research fields include precise orbit determination, orbit and altitude control, and spaceflight environment monitoring.[74] The ASD further controls China's ocean-based space TT&C network via the China Satellite Maritime Tracking and Control Department, known variously as the PLA 23rd Testing and Training Base (Unit 63680) or the Aerospace Oceanic Tracking Ship Base.[75] Another organization under the ASD, the Beijing Aerospace Flight Control Center, is the flight command-and-control center for China's manned space and deep space exploration programs.[76]

In addition to these space organizations, which carried over from the former GAD, the PLASSF ASD has also taken control over space units from the former GSD, including the Aerospace Reconnaissance Bureau (Unit 61646), which is responsible for aerospace intelligence, surveillance, and reconnaissance;[77] and the Satellite Communications Main Station (Unit 61096), which is responsible for managing the PLA's military satellite communication network.[78]

Both the Aerospace Reconnaissance Bureau and the Satellite Communications Main Station have been split off from the former GSD Intelligence Department and the GSD Informationization Department, respectively. Under the GSD's successor, the CMC Joint Staff Department (JSD), these two departments have become new bureaus: the new JSD Intelligence Bureau and JSD Information Communications Bureau (ICB). Dividing and reallocating these GSD units in this way is another clear indication of the PLASSF's responsibility for space-related activities.

Further, the ASD has also taken over a number of aerospace research organizations under the former GAD, including:

- Aerospace Engineering University;[79]
- Aerospace Research Development Center;[80]
- Engineering Design Research Institute;
- China Aerodynamics Research Development (Base 29); and
- Beijing Institute of Tracking and Communication Technology.

The PLASSF ASD also has oversight of the China Astronauts Group, which appears to be an administrative and personnel organization for China's astronaut corps, who are believed to be PLASSF officers.[81] However, the overall responsibility for China's human spaceflight program rests with a different organization outside the PLASSF: the CMC Equipment Development Department.[82]

Network Systems Department

The Network Systems Department (NSD) is responsible for PLASSF signal-and-network intelligence, cyber reconnaissance, espionage, and probably network attack-and-defense operations. The NSD is built around the former GSD Technical Reconnaissance Department (Unit 61195), which is China's top cyber espionage organization (and is analogous to the National Security Agency in the United States).[83] There is strong evidence that the NSD has taken over nearly all elements of the former GSD Technical Reconnaissance Department and the organizations affiliated with it. For example, GSD 56th and 58th Research Institutes under the GSD Technical Reconnaissance Department have moved across to the NSD.[84] Prior to their transfer, these two institutes reported directly to the Technical Reconnaissance Department's headquarters and were tasked with research and development, testing, and acquisition in support of its missions. It is important to note that the headquarters address of the former Technical Reconnaissance Department has been linked to the NSD, indicating that the NSD is the likely successor organization.[85]

Prior to the reorganization, computer network attack was handled by the GSD Electronic Countermeasures and Radar Department and computer network defense was handled by the GSD Informationization Department. Some evidence suggests these capabilities have been transferred to the NSD, including the transfer of an electronic countermeasures brigade that was previously part of the GSD Electronic Countermeasures and Radar Department.[86] One possibility is that these elements will gradually move to the PLASSF over the next few years. Given the PLA's aspirational strategy of integrated network reconnaissance and attack and defense, it is likely that both offensive and defensive cyber capabilities will fall entirely or at least primarily under the PLASSF's remit.[87]

Electronic Warfare Units

Traditionally the GSD's Electronic Countermeasures and Radar Department was responsible for the PLA's strategic-level electronic warfare. Unlike in the space and cyber domains, where responsibilities and capabilities had been scattered across several PLA organizations, the PLA's electronic warfare mission fell under the sole responsibility of the Electronic Countermeasures and Radar Department. If electronic warfare is now under the PLASSF's remit, then the Electronic Countermeasures and Radar Department and its affiliated organizations should be eventually transferred to the PLASSF.

Some former Electronic Countermeasures and Radar Department units, such as its 54th Research Institute, have been transferred to the PLASSF. The 54th's transfer from the Technical Reconnaissance Department to the NSD, similar to the transfer of the 56th and 58th Research Institutes, indicates that the Electronic Countermeasures and Radar Department's core functions may have already moved to the PLASSF NSD. However, there is far less evidence in the public domain to suggest that operational elements of the Electronic

Countermeasures and Radar Department have been reassigned to the PLASSF, as is the case with the Technical Reconnaissance Department.

Information Support Units

As already mentioned, there is evidence that PLASSF units serve to provide information support within larger, ostensibly joint, units (such as a division).[88] However, on an all-PLA and national strategic level, it appears the successor to the former GSD Informationization Department—which was responsible for providing strategic information support to the PLA—is the Information Communications Bureau under the CMC's JSD and not the PLASSF NSD. This suggests that tactical PLASSF NSD units probably operate at theater-level and below and that non-PLASSF units oversee and control national and PLA-wide information infrastructure.

Command-and-Control Mechanisms

The PLASSF's command structure appears to be a work in progress, with little open-source evidence available to provide a clear picture of the organization's lines of authority. Initial evidence suggests three possible command relationships. None of the models described here are necessarily mutually exclusive and all require further examination and research.

The first would suggest that the CMC JSD issues commands and the PLASSF executes. Under this model the JSD would have command over PLASSF operational units and bypass PLASSF headquarters when issuing orders. For example, the JSD ICB would exercise functional command and order PLASSF units to execute the allocation of satellite communication resources.[89] In this scenario satellite resource allocation decisions are made by JSD ICB and then communicated to the PLASSF Satellite Communication Main Station for completion.[90] Under this model the operational units responsible for satellite communication have been transferred to the PLASSF but the command and decision-making functions remain with the JSD.

The strongest explanation for this model is the need for integration and coordination. Because military satellite communication resources are in high demand across the PLA, the JSD—rather than any one of the services—would want to retain authority over their allocation. It would be illogical and not conducive to cooperation and efficiency for the PLASSF headquarters to make these decisions, especially when it does not have the mandate for joint operations. This model may hold true for other assets, resources, and capabilities that are operated by the PLASSF as well, especially those that are considered to have PLA-wide application or are strategic in nature.

A second command model would give PLASSF headquarters functional command, at least with respect to some of its missions. For example, because the PLASSF NSD is built around the former GSD Technical Reconnaissance Department, the PLASSF headquarters would exercise functional command over the day-to-day activities of the PLA's cyber intelligence–gathering mission. There are no indications that the JSD has a cyber capability that would exercise this functional command and bypass PLASSF headquarters.

A third model would see theater-level or lower-level commanders exercising command authority over some PLASSF units. For example, the PLA ninetieth anniversary battlefield parade in 2017 showed that force elements (such as the divisions) may contain supporting PLASSF units.[91] This means that the operational commanders at the theater level or lower would have some operational command authority over PLASSF units in the field.

Some researchers have speculated on a possible fourth hybrid model whereby "the PLASSF reports to the CMC JSD during peacetime, while its units would be attached to a theater command during wartime."[92]

Interestingly, some important aspects of China's space-based information network remain under the command of the JSD, with no evidence that the responsibility for these systems has been transferred to the PLASSF. One example of this is China's global navigation satellite system, known as Beidou (a counterpart to the US Global Positioning System [GPS]). There are no indications that the PLASSF deploys any units with operational control over the Beidou system. The JSD (not the PLASSF) is apparently seen as a more appropriate unit to control this national strategic asset.[93]

LOOKING AHEAD: ORGANIZATIONAL CHALLENGES

The sweeping organizational changes within China's strategic forces send a powerful signal about China's ambitions as a strategic actor in the twenty-first century. Militarily speaking, these changes are intended to enable Chinese leaders to pursue national interests in part through stronger deterrent, coercive, and joint warfighting capabilities. In particular the reorganization aims to bring about a more effective integration of these capabilities, with a particular emphasis on traditional and emergent strategic realms such as the nuclear, advanced aerospace, outerspace, and cyberspace domains. By moving in this direction it appears the PLA is poised to enter a new phase in its thinking about deterrence and warfighting in an effort to achieve "integrated strategic deterrence."

At the same time, however, the reorganization and reform of China's strategic forces present their own sets of difficult challenges. China's near-term success as a strategic actor—particularly in the military realm—will depend on how well the PLA can address these challenges, three of which deserve particular scrutiny.

First, the PLA is still working through the organizational changes that were launched in late 2015 and organizational "growing pains" continue to present problems. The PLASSF, in particular, is still in the midst of reorganization: clarifying lines of authority, defining roles and operational concepts, reconstituting new units, and learning how to most effectively pursue its mission. PLA sources openly explain that the PLASSF is still in the early stages of strengthening institutional arrangements, introducing new leadership and managerial capabilities, and standing up effective structures and standards for administrative oversight, work regulations, finances, accountability, supervision, and human resources development; these come first.[94] Second is integration and training. Third is command and control.

There is evidence that the reorganization has resulted in some disgruntlement within the PLASSF ranks. To begin with, the creation of the PLASSF came about in part through the dismantling of two former PLA powerhouses: the GSD and the GAD. Units transferred from those organizations to the PLASSF have in essence been relegated to a lower status within the PLA. Additional institutional growing pains have resulted as diverse units from disparate parts of the uniformed services are forced to work together for the first time.[95]

Second, China's strategic forces continue to grapple with their mandate to develop greater joint capabilities. Ostensibly the PLASSF is operationally based on a core guiding principle of being a "new combat power" (*xinxing zuozhan liliang*). Commitment to this principle necessitates the integration of different types of forces across the multiple domains of space, cyber, and electromagnetic spectra. However, as the PLA and PLASSF are finding out, this is far easier said than done: according to Chinese sources, the PLASSF is still in some of the early stages of research into operational theories relating to its areas of responsibility in cyber, space, electronic warfare, and the enhancement of joint operations.[96]

At a practical level this directive necessitates ongoing efforts by the PLA to introduce new technologies and improve training in order to meet the mandate of enabling greater coordination and force integration. For example, Chinese sources claim the PLASSF is working to strengthen and expand more modern communication systems into the disparate force elements; to fuse its activities with that of ground, sea, air and missile forces; and to be involved in every step of the combat process. But the reporting suggests these efforts are a work in progress.[97]

Likewise, realistic combat training is often cited as a crucial element in building the PLARF into a world-leading missile force. There is certainly evidence that the PLARF leadership, like many other parts of the PLA, is pushing for the training culture to change by making its training exercises more realistic.[98] This effort also includes the use of military training supervision and inspection teams to ensure training quality and the regularization of confrontational exercises that use realistic and competent opposing forces to improve training outcomes.[99] Parts of the PLARF have begun training in joint operations under the new joint theater command structure.[100] That said, it will be many more years before the PLARF could be effectively integrated into the new theater command structure and lead to a high level of coordination for joint operations.

Third, China's strategic forces are facing a number of challenges in developing and refining new command-and-control structures. In the case of the PLASSF, it appears lines of command authority are still being sorted out and the PLASSF's core mission is not fully settled. The command relationships among and between the PLASSF (and its operational units), the CMC, the theater commands, and other service branches remain unclear. Evidence suggests that owing to the multiple missions of the PLASSF, different command relationships affect the different functions that fall under the PLASSF's remit.

Command-and-control mechanisms are an ongoing challenge for the PLARF in at least two critical aspects. On the conventional weapons side of the PLARF mission, new relationships and communications infrastructures will need to be tested and established among the CMC, the joint theater commands, and the PLARF. These challenges will likely increase as the PLARF continues to expand, diversify, and disperse its conventional missile arsenal. The role of the PLASSF in supporting the PLARF's conventional missile communications systems could add a layer of complexity and deserves closer scrutiny.

Other larger command-and-control puzzles have emerged, owing to the rapid modernization and expansion of China's nuclear forces. The introduction of new communications technologies and missile systems (such as the DF-26 and the DF-41), the increasing dispersal of land-mobile missiles, and the steady increase in the number of deployable nuclear weapons all add new complications to the command-and-control system of China's land-based systems.

Even more challenging is China's intention to develop a bona fide nuclear triad; it adds new—and, for China, unprecedented—layers of complexity to its nuclear command-and-control system. Authoritative Chinese-language open-source literature is silent on how or whether the PLARF will be involved with the PLA Navy or the PLA Air Force as those services take up nuclear missions. At a minimum the Navy and the Air Force will need to develop the capacity to manage, store, and transfer nuclear weapons, to introduce appropriate communications systems, and to train nuclear weapons systems technicians and operators. As far as nuclear-armed submarine patrols are concerned, it is possible that the Chinese leadership and the PLA introduce predelegation authority; doing so would be a major change in China's traditional command, control, and readiness posture. It seems likely that the PLARF would play some role in advising and providing direct support to the Navy and the Air Force as they take on their nuclear missions, but this has not been made clear in open sources.

In reflecting on the emergence of these new nuclear roles for the PLA Navy and the PLA Air Force, Chinese interlocutors insist the command-and-control structure will be similar, with the supreme command authority having direct command over navy and air force nuclear weapons. While this may be true, China's nuclear command-and-control system is entering a vastly more complex arena, especially with the nascent ability to deploy nuclear weapons at sea.[101]

Yet despite these and other challenges, the ambitions and expectations of China's strategic forces seem clear. The sweeping reorganization of those forces launched in late 2015 are part of a transformation of the PLA that is intended to result in a military force that is increasingly capable of supporting the country's strategic ambitions, including through its use of more powerful deterrent and integrated joint warfighting capabilities. The PLA appears to be entering a new fourth phase in its thinking about strategic deterrence and warfighting. We can expect to see China's expanding nuclear arsenal become increasingly integrated conceptually and operationally, with a growing and diversifying portfolio of conventional and other emerging strategic capabilities—such as in aerospace, outer space, and cyberspace—to deliver an "integrated strategic deterrent." It is likely that the gap between China's strategic requirements on the one hand and its strategic capabilities on the other will continue to narrow.

NOTES

The author wishes to thank Adam Ni for his excellent research assistance; and acknowledges the support of the US Defense Threat Reduction Agency (DTRA) Project on Advanced Systems and Concepts for Countering WMD (PASCC) for the research contributing to this chapter.

1. In this chapter "organization of strategic forces" refers principally to the bureaucratic structures within the Chinese military hierarchy as well as the interaction among those structures, as related to China's strategic military capabilities.

2. M. Taylor Fravel, *Active Defense: China's Military Strategy since 1949* (Princeton, NJ: Princeton University Press, 2019).

3. These phases are described in Junshi Zhanlue Yanjiubu, Jiefangjun Junshi Kexueyuan (Military Strategy Research Department, PLA Academy of Military Science), *Zhanlue xue* (Science of military strategy) (Beijing: Military Science Press, 2013), 141–45 (hereafter referred to as Military Strategy Research Department, *Science of Military Strategy*).

4. John Wilson Lewis and Hua Di found "no evidence that any overarching strategic doctrine informed Chairman Mao Zedong's decision to proceed with the strategic missile program in the mid-1950s. . . . [U]ntil the early 1980s, there were no scenarios, no detailed linkage of the weapons to foreign policy objectives, and no serious strategic research." See Lewis and Hua, "China's Ballistic Missile Programs: Technologies, Strategies, Goals," *International Security* 17, no. 2 (Fall 1992): 5–6.

5. For an excellent review of Chinese strategic thinking on the role of nuclear weapons in deterrence and warfighting in the early stages of this phase, see Alastair Iain Johnston, "China's New 'Old Thinking': The Concept of Limited Deterrence," *International Security* 20, no. 3 (Winter 1995–96): 5–42, especially 10–23.

6. Military Strategy Research Department, *Science of Military Strategy*, 142–43.

7. Military Strategy Research Department, *Science of Military Strategy*, 142.

8. See Wang Wenrong et al., eds., *Zhanlue xue* (Science of military strategy) (Beijing: National Defense University Press, 1999), 363.

9. Peng Guangqian and Yao Youzhi, eds., *The Science of Military Strategy* (official English translation of the 2001 Chinese-language edition) (Beijing: Military Science Press, 2005), 222, 226 (emphasis added).

10. This point is made in the official defense white paper *China's National Defense in 2008* (Beijing: Information Office of the State Council of the People's Republic of China, 2009), sec. 2.

11. *China's National Defense in 2008*, sec. 2.

12. Michael S. Chase, Daniel Yoon, and Mark Stokes, "The People's Liberation Army Second Artillery Force (PLASAF) as an Organization," in *The PLA as Organization v2.0*, ed. Kevin Pollpeter and Kenneth W. Allen, 388–435 (Vienna, VA: Defense Group, 2015).

13. Eric Heginbotham et al., *China's Evolving Nuclear Deterrent: Major Drivers and Issues for the United States* (Santa Monica, CA: RAND Corporation, 2017), xi, xiii. See also Fiona S. Cunningham and M. Taylor Fravel, "Assuring Assured Retaliation: China's Nuclear Posture and U.S.-China Strategic Stability," *International Security* 40, no. 2 (Fall 2015): 7–50; and M. Taylor Fravel and Evan S. Medeiros, "China's Search for Assured Retaliation," *International Security* 35, no. 2 (Fall 2010): 48–87.

14. A similar conclusion is found in Michael S. Chase and Arthur Chan, *China's Evolving Approach to "Integrated Strategic Deterrence"* (Santa Monica, CA: RAND Corporation, 2016), 54–55.

15. "Lujun lingdao jigou huojian jun zhanlue zhiyuan budui chengli dahui zaijing juxing" (Army leadership organ, Rocket Force, and Strategic Support Force inauguration ceremony occurs in Beijing), *Xinhua*, January 1, 2016, http://www.xinhuanet.com/mil/2016–01/01/c_128588494.htm.

16. State Council Information Office, *China's Military Strategy* (Beijing, May 2015), sec. 3, http://english.gov.cn/archive/white_paper/2015/05/27/content_281475115610833.htm.

17. Xi Jinping, "Secure a Decisive Victory in Building a Moderately Prosperous Society in All Respects and Strive for the Great Success of Socialism with Chinese Characteristics for a New Era," report delivered at the Nineteenth National Congress of the Communist Party of China, October 18, 2017, http://www.xinhuanet.com/english/download/Xi_Jinping's_report_at_19th_CPC_National_Congress.pdf.

18. Xiao Tianliang et al., eds., *Zhanlue xue* (Science of military strategy) (Beijing: National Defense University Press, 2015), 119–35.

19. See China's Ministry of Defense website, "China Establishes Rocket Force and Strategic Support Force," January 1, 2016, http://eng.mod.gov.cn/ArmedForces/ssf.htm.

20. "Jintian huan shang xin rong yi mingri qingying ti rui lu" (Today new uniform, tomorrow the mentioning of top brigades), Ministry of National Defense of the People's Republic of China, June 30, 2016, http://www.mod.gov.cn/reports/2016/hz

/2016–06/30/content_4685072.htm; and "Zhong bang xinwen! Huojian jun junqi puguang!" (Heavyweight news! Rocket Force flag revealed!), *Zhongguo jun wang*, August 18, 2016, http://www.81.cn/depb/2016–08/18/content_7213931.htm.

21. "Jungai hou zhanqu jibie danwei" (Postmilitary reform of military theater grade organizations), *Weibo*, June 15, 2017, https://weibo.com/6100158923/F7UkckZ4J ?type=comment#_rnd1524447567859.

22. State Council Information Office, *China's Military Strategy* (Beijing, May 2015).

23. For more information on the organizational structure of the Second Artillery Force, see Chase, Yoon, and Stokes, "People's Liberation Army Second Artillery Force," 388–435; and Bates Gill, James Mulvenon, and Mark Stokes, "The Chinese Second Artillery Corps: Transition to Credible Deterrence," in *The PLA as Organization v1.0.*, ed. James C. Mulvenon and Andrew N. D. Yang, 510–86 (Santa Monica, CA: RAND Corporation, 2002), https://www.rand.org/pubs/conf_proceedings/CF182 .html.

24. David C. Logan, "Career Paths in the PLA Rocket Force: What They Tell Us," *Asian Security*, January 25, 2018, https://doi.org/10.1080/14799855.2017.1422089.

25. "Huojian jun: Wei Fenghe ren siling yuan, Wang Jiasheng ren zhengzhi weiyuan, xiong pai puguang" (Rocket Force: Wei Fenghe appointed commander, Wang Jiasheng as political commissar, chest emblem revealed), *Pengpai xinwen*, January 1, 2016, https://www.thepaper.cn/newsDetail_forward_1415845.

26. Biographical details on Wei's life are drawn from Adam Ni, "Who Will Be China's Next Defense Minister?," *Asia Times*, February 13, 2018, http://www.atimes .com/will-chinas-next-defense-minister; and "Wei Fenghe Jianli" (Wei Fenghe's resume), *Xinhua*, March 19, 2018, http://www.xinhuanet.com/politics/2018lh /2018–03/19/c_1122560874.htm.

27. Hou Lei, "Wei Fenghe bei renming wei guowu weiyuan, guofang bu buzhang" (Wei Fenghe appointed as state councillor and minister of defense), *Zhongguo jun wang*, March 19, 2018, http://www.81.cn/2018zt/2018–03/19/content_7977140.htm.

28. "Wei Fenghe's Resume."

29. Nanchang Gongcheng Xueyuan (Nanchang Institute of Technology), "Huojian jun canmou bu budui guanli ju lingdao shiha xuexiao dingxiang peiyang zhi zhao shiguan gongzuo" (Leaders from the PLARF Staff Department's Force Management Bureau inspect the school's work orientation on the cultivation and direct recruitment of noncommissioned officers), September 22, 2017, http://www.nit .edu.cn/info/1057/16412.htm; "Wang Dingfang shaojiang churen huojian jun zhengzhi gongzuo bu fu zhuren" (Maj. Gen. Wang Dingfang is appointed as the PLARF Political Works Department's deputy director), *Pengpai xinwen*, June 20, 2017, https://www.thepaper.cn/newsDetail_forward_1713042; "Jun gai hou da dongzuo: 1 ge yue nei jin 50 ren jinsheng jiangjun (mingdan)" (Big move post military reform: Nearly fifty promoted to general within a month [name list]), *Fenghuang wang*, June 19, 2016, http://news.ifeng.com/a/20160619/49193801_0.shtml; "Zhongguo renmin jiefangjun huojian jun 21 wan yuan zhizhu Zhenfeng 421 ming xiaoxuesheng" (PLARF donates 210,000 yuan to 421 primary school students in Zhenfeng County), *People's Daily Online*, July 6, 2016, http://qxn.people.com.cn /n2/2016/0706/c362415-28620685.html; and Yue Huairang, "Yuan er pao zhuangbei bu buzhang Mo Junpeng shaojiang gai ren huojian jun zhuangbei bu buzhang" (Director of the former Second Artillery Force Equipment Department Maj. Gen. Mo Junpeng reappointed as the director of the PLARF Equipment Department),

Pengpai xinwen, March 7, 2016, https://www.thepaper.cn/newsDetail_forward_1440426.

30. Guangxi Zhuangzu zizhiqu fazhan he gaige weiyuanwei (Guangxi Zhuang Autonomous Region Development and Reform Commission), "Wo shi youguan lingdao fu huojian jun canmou bu zuozhan ju huibao xianjie Hezhou zhixian jichang xiangmu xuan zhi gongzuo" (Relevant leaders of our city report to the PLARF Staff Department's Operations Bureau on the site selection work for the Hezhou regional airport project), June 23, 2017, http://www.gxdrc.gov.cn/xsjg/gsfgw/hzs/gzdt_39008/201706/t20170623_736170.html; Cai Ruijin and Yang Yonggang, "Congci, yiyan ren hu huojian jun" (From now, recognize the Rocket Force with one glance), *Zhongguo jun wang*, June 30, 2016, http://www.81.cn/jmywyl/2016–06/30/content_7128279.htm; Nanchang Institute of Technology, "Leaders from the PLARF Staff Department's Force Management Bureau inspect"; Beijing shi Haidian qu renmin zhangfu (People's government of Beijing Haidian district), "Bayi weiwen song wennuan jun di gong jian qingyi shen zhen lingdao zoufang weiwen zhu zhen budui" (August 1 greeting and send warmth, the military and local authorities built friendship with township leaders visiting stationed units), July 27, 2017, http://www.bjhd.gov.cn/jiezhen/zzfnew/wqznew/jzxw1/201707/t20170727_1399772.htm.

31. Based on the author's estimate. Also see "China's Military Modernization in 2017," in *2017 Annual Report of the U.S.-China Economic and Security Review Commission*, 219–20, https://www.uscc.gov/Annual_Reports/2017-annual-report.

32. See Chase, Yoon, and Stokes, "People's Liberation Army Second Artillery Force," 408.

33. See "China's Rocket Force Embraces New Medium–Long Range Ballistic Missile," *China Military Online*, April 16, 2018, http://eng.mod.gov.cn/news/2018–04/16/content_4809589.htm; and Ankit Panda, "China Announces Commissioning of DF-26 Intermediate-Range Ballistic Missile Brigade," *The Diplomat*, April 18, 2018.

34. Lengshuijiang shi renmin zhangfu (People's government of Lengshujiang city), "Lengshuijiang shi renwu bu wubu kaizhan xinbing huifang 'san ge yi' huodong" (Lengshuijiang city department of the People's Armed Force launches new recruit return visit "Three Ones" campaign), September 30, 2017, http://www.lsj.gov.cn/Item/51970.aspx.

35. Mark Stokes, *PLA Rocket Force Leadership and Unit Reference*, Project 2049 Institute, working reference updated April 9, 2018.

36. "Er pao chang zhu Shate? Jiemi shenmi de jinlun gongcheng" (Second Artillery has long been in Saudi Arabia? Exposing the mysterious Jinlun engineering), *Sohu*, March 10, 2017, http://www.sohu.com/a/128409403_557768.

37. "Guofang bu tiaozheng gaige hou jundui yuan xiao mingcheng" (Ministry of National Defense announces the names of military academies and universities after adjusting to reforms), *Xinhua*, June 29, 2017, http://www.xinhuanet.com/politics/2017–06/29/c_1121235216.htm.

38. "Kaizhan zhuanti jiaoyu jifa chuangye jiqing" (Carry out special topics education, inspire entrepreneurial passion), *Fenghuang wang*, August 30, 2017, http://news.ifeng.com/a/20170830/51803114_0.shtml.

39. "China's Military Regrouped into Five PLA Theater Commands," *Xinhua*, February 1, 2016, http://www.xinhuanet.com/english/2016–02/01/c_135065429.htm.

40. See Gill, Mulvenon, and Stokes, "Chinese Second Artillery Corps," 521.

41. Author discussions with Chinese strategists and retired PLA officers, Beijing, April 2018.

42. See, for example, State Council Information Office, *China's Military Strategy* (2015), sec. 4; and State Council Information Office, *The Diversified Employment of China's Armed Forces*, 2013, sec. 3.

43. Statements in this paragraph are drawn from Zhang Weidong and Song Haijun, "Xi zhuxi shichaguo de budui: qianxin lijian, zhanlue tieguan yue lian yue ying" (Force inspected by chairman Xi: Focus on grinding sword, strategic iron fist becomes harder), *Jiefang jun bao*, February 6, 2018, http://www.mod.gov.cn/power /2018–02/06/content_4804300.htm.

44. Dai Yi, Wang Yugen, and Luo Guangyi, "Dongbu zhanqu siling yuan Liu Yuejun tan lianhe zuozhan zhihui nengli jianshe" (Eastern Theater Command commander Liu Yuejun discusses building joint operations command capability), *Bayi dianshi*, March 4, 2016, http://jz.chinamil.com.cn/zhuanti/content/2016–03/04 /content_6940918.htm.

45. Office of the Secretary of Defense, *Military and Security Developments Involving the People's Republic of China 2017* (Washington, DC, 2017), 24.

46. See Joseph Dempsey and Henry Boyd, "Beyond JL-2: China's Development of a Successor SLBM Continues," *Military Balance Blog* (International Institute for Strategic Studies), August 7, 2017, https://www.iiss.org/en/militarybalanceblog/blogsections /2017-edcc/august-b660/chinese-nuclear-powered-submarines-041d.

47. Ankit Panda, "Revealed: China's Nuclear-Capable Air-Launched Ballistic Missile," *The Diplomat*, April 10, 2018, https://thediplomat.com/2018/04/revealed-chinas -nuclear-capable-air-launched-ballistic-missile/.

48. Daguo zhi yi (Wings of a major nation), "Kongjun siling zhengshi: Zhongguo zheng yanfa xin yidai yuancheng hongzhaji" (Air force commander verifies: China is currently developing a new-generation long distance bomber), *Weibo*, September 2, 2016, https://weibo.com/ttarticle/p/show?id=2309404015218966530141.

49. Andreas Rupprecht, "The PLA Air Force's 'Silver-Bullet' Bomber Force," *China Brief* 17, no. 10 (July 21, 2017), https://jamestown.org/program/the-pla-air-forces -silver-bullet-bomber-force/.

50. Stephen Chen, "China Builds World's Fastest Wind Tunnel to Test Weapons that Could Strike US within 14 Minutes," *South China Morning Post*, November 15, 2017, http://www.scmp.com/news/china/policies-politics/article/2120072/china -builds-worlds-fastest-wind-tunnel-test-*weapons*.

51. Military Strategy Research Department, *Science of Military Strategy*, 232–33.

52. Military Strategy Research Department, *Science of Military Strategy*, 233.

53. Military Strategy Research Department, *Science of Military Strategy*, 236.

54. Several studies provide additional information about the PLASSF and its organization: John Costello, "China's Strategic Support Force: A Force for a New Era," testimony presented before the U.S.-China Economic and Security Review Commission, Washington, DC, February 15, 2018; John Costello and Joe McReynolds, *China's Strategic Support Force: A Force for a New Era*, China Strategic Perspectives 13 (Washington, DC: National Defense University Press, 2018).

55. See China's Ministry of Defense website, "China Establishes Rocket Force and Strategic Support Force," January 1, 2016, http://eng.mod.gov.cn/ArmedForces/ssf.htm.

56. "Strive to Build a Strong, Modern Strategic Support Force: Xi," *Xinhua*, August 29, 2016, http://eng.chinamil.com.cn/view/2016–08/29/content_7231309.htm.

57. PLASSF Commander Gao Jin, as quoted in Ni Guanghui, "Jiemi wo jun shou zhi zhanlue zhiyuan budui" (Revealing our army's first strategic support force), *People's Daily*, January 24, 2016, http://military.people.com.cn/n1/2016/0124/c1011 -28079245.html.

58. From State Council Information Office, *China's Military Strategy* (2015).

59. On the Staff Department, see "Yuan zong zhuangbei bu fu buzhang Li Shangfu ren zhanlue zhiyuan budui fu siling yuan jian canmou zhang" (Former General Armaments Department deputy director Li Shangfu appointed deputy commander and chief of staff of the Strategic Support Force), *Pengpai xinwen*, February 29, 2016, https://www.thepaper.cn/newsDetail_forward_1417430; on the Political Work Department, see "Xi'an Jiaoda tui rencai peiyang zhongda gaige chengli Qian Xuesen xueyuan" (Xi'an Jiaotong University promotes major reform in talent development, establishes Qian Xuesen Institute), *Guangming wang*, December 26, 2016, http://edu.gmw.cn/2016–12/26/content_23334912.htm.

60. On the Operational Planning Bureau, see "Guanyu juban 2016 nian 'fuwu baixing jiankang xingdong' quanguo daxing yizhen huodong zhou de tongzhi" (Notice in relation to the holding of the 2016 "health service for the people" national campaign's large-scale discussion week), Zhongguo Renmin Gongheguo guojia weisheng jiankang weiyuanwei (National Health Commission of the People's Republic of China), August 19, 2016, http://www.nhfpc.gov.cn/yzygj/s3593 /201608/b0432dc9a8084f769bfca1760c7b273d.shtml; on the Training Bureau, see "Xi'an Jiaotong University." On the Direct Subordinate Works Bureau, see "Zhong zhanlue zhiyuan budui jiguan zhishu danwei shou pi xinbing shunli ru ying" (First batch of recruits successfully march in for a direct subordinate organization of an organ of the Strategic Support Force), *Dongfang toutiao*, September 22, 2016, http://mini.eastday.com/a/160922125452887.html.

61. "Jun gai jiushi yao xunzhao 'tongdian' bing 'zhitong'" (Military reform must find "pain points" and "stop pain"), *Jiefang jun bao*, October 10, 2016, http://www.81.cn /jmywyl/2016–10/10/content_7293065.htm.

62. Biographical information on Gao is drawn from: "Gao Jin," *Baidu Encyclopedia*, https://baike.baidu.com/item/%E9%AB%98%E6%B4%A5; and Yue Huairang, "Zhanlue zhiyuan budui: Gao Jin ren siling yuan, Liu Fulian ren zhengzhi weiyuan, xiong pai puguang" (Strategic Support Force: Gao Jin appointed as commander, Liu Fulian as political commissar, chest emblem revealed), *Pengpai xinwen*, January 1, 2016, https://www.thepaper.cn/newsDetail_forward_1415847.

63. "5 ming junguan jinsheng shang jiang junxian, Xi Jinping banfa mingling zhuang" (Five officers promoted to full general, Xi Jinping issues certificates), *Pengpai xinwen*, July 28, 2017, http://m.thepaper.cn/newsDetail_forward_1745639; and "Shijiu da shouguan fabu: Zhongguo gongchangdang di shijiu jie zhongyang weiyuanhui weiyuan mingdan" (Nineteenth Party Congress authorized to issue: List of the members of the Nineteenth Central Committee of the Communist Party of China), *Xinhua*, October 24, 2017, http://www.xinhuanet.com/politics/19cpcnc /2017–10/24/c_1121848878.htm.

64. The missile base is the largest operational force element in China's missile force and each base is assigned to a geographic area of responsibility. Base 52, headquartered in Huangshan, Anhui province, is responsible for areas to the southeast of China, especially Taiwan.

65. Jiuquan Satellite Launch Centre, *China Space Report*, https://chinaspacereport .wordpress.com/facilities/jiuquan/.

66. Mark A. Stokes and Dean Cheng, "China's Evolving Space Capabilities: Implications for US Interests," Project 2049 Institute, April 26, 2012, https://www.uscc.gov/Research/chinas-evolving-space-capabilities-implications-us-interests.

67. Liangshan yizu zizhizhou renmin zhengfu (The people's government of Liangshan Yi autonomous prefecture), "Xichang weixing fashe zhongxin" (Xichang Satellite Launch Center), April 24, 2015, https://web.archive.org/web/20161002071536/http://www.lsz.gov.cn/lszrmzf/xcs48/1942898/index.html.

68. Zhongguo renmin gongheguo guofang bu (Ministry of national defense of the People's Republic of China), "Rang qingchun zai zhuizhu qiang jun mengxiang zhong zhanfang" (Let youth bloom in the dream of pursuing a strong military), May 8, 2016, http://www.mod.gov.cn/power/2016-05/08/content_4654402.htm; and "'Yanjing keyi shiming, dan zhui mengde jiaobu buneng mishi fangxiang'—ji Hainan Wenchang hangtian fashe chang gongheng jianshe zhihui bu gongcheng-shi Zhou Xianghu" ("The eyes can be blinded, but the footsteps chasing a dream cannot lose direction"—remembering Hainan Wenchang spacecraft launch site's engineering construction headquarters engineer Zhou Xianghu), *Xinhua*, November 1, 2016, http://news.xinhuanet.com/2016-11/01/c_1119830374.htm.

69. "'Zhongguo Wenchang hangtian fashe chang' huo mingming, jiben manzu weixing fashe ge zhong yaoqiu" ("China Wenchang Spacecraft Launch Site" is named, fundamentally meets various requirements for satellite launches), *Pengpai xinwen*, November 3, 2016, https://www.thepaper.cn/newsDetail_forward_1554751.

70. Li Gaochao, "Xi'an weixing cekong zhongxin zai Nanning zhaokai zhenggui hua xunlian xianchang jingyan jiaoliu hui" (Xi'an Satellite Control Center convenes conference in Nanjing on exchanging experience on formalized training), *Jixu jiaoyu* 1, no. 64 (1993); Weinan shi renmin zhangfu (People's government of Weinan city), "63750 budui zoufang weiwen Linwei qu Yangguo zhen pinkun qunzhong" (Unit 63750 visits and greets poor people of Linwei district Yang Guo township), October 21, 2014, http://www.weinan.gov.cn/news/bmdt/mzj/417905.htm; Zhang Yunzhi, "Xi'an Satellite Control Center and Orbit Dynamics Technology," http://aero.tamu.edu/sites/default/files/faculty/alfriend/S1.1%20Zhang.pdf; and Shaanxi sheng difanzhi bianzuan weiyuanhui (Shaanxi Provincial Records Committee), "Di er pian junshi zuzhi di er zhang zhujun di san jie 63750 budui" (vol. 2, chap. 2, sec. 3: Military Organizations, Military Garrison, Unit 63750), Shaanxi shengzhi: junshi zhi (Shaanxi Provincial Records: Military Records) (Shaanxi, Xi'an: Sanqin, 2015).

71. Zhang, "Xi'an Satellite Control Center"; and "Yinxiang Shaanxi: Xi'an weixing cekong zhongxin" (Shaanxi impression: Xi'an Satellite Control Center), *Xibu wang*, January 8, 2007, http://shaanxi.cnwest.com/content/2007-01/08/content_396633.htm.

72. On Chile, see Ma Jing, "Xi'an weixing cekong zhongxin ji cekong zhan 'ying-zhan' chang'e er hao renwu" (Xi'an Satellite Control Center and telemetry stations are "ready for combat" for the Chang'e II mission), *People's Daily Online*, October 2, 2010, http://scitech.people.com.cn/GB/12872418.html; on Namibia: Ministry of Education, Arts and Culture of the Republic of Namibia, "Namibia and China Sign an Employment Agreement," March 29, 2012, http://www.moe.gov.na/news_article.php?id=60&title=Namibia%20and%20China%20sign%20an%20employment%20agreement; on Pakistan: "Ji Tai 'jianjiao' jingshi Zhongguo haiwai hangtian cekong zhan anquan" (Kiribati and Taiwan "establishing relations" is a warning to the security of China's overseas telemetry, tracking, and control station), *Guoji xianqu daobao*, November 19, 2003, http://www.china.com.cn/chinese/2003/Nov/445211.htm.

73. On Argentina, see "Zhongguo zai Agenting jianshe de kongjianzhan jiang yu 2017 nian 3 yue touru yunxing" (China's [ground-based] space station built in Argentina will enter operation by March 2017), *Agenting Huaren zaixian*, April 28, 2016, http://www.argentong.com/article-49074–1.html; on Australia: "Zhongguo hangtian cekong wang fugai quanqiu, zai Aozhou she zhan Meiguo wei zulan" (China's space tracking, telemetry, and control web covers the world, station in Australia not blocked by United States), *Fenghuang wang*, December 9, 2013, http://news.ifeng.com/mil/4/detail_2013_12/09/31938311_1.shtml; on Brazil: "Zhongguo weixing shu jin ci yu Mei, dan zai zhege zhongyao lingyu hai bi Mei chai hen yuan" (The number of Chinese satellites is second only to the United States, but it trails far behind the United States in this important area), *Tengxun wang*, February 13, 2018, https://new.qq.com/omn/20180213/20180213A01QDD.html; on Kenya: "Kiribati and Taiwan."

74. Regarding the Main Station, see "Shen liu jin tou zhao san qin ernu xinxue" (Shenzhou VI mission is saturated with the heart and blood of the sons and daughters of Sanqin), *Tengxun wang*, October 25, 2005, https://news.qq.com/a/20051025/000722.htm; and "Zhanglue Zhiyuan Budui mou bu nu bing ban canyu Chun Lei jihua xian aixin (Female soldier class from a department of the Strategic Support Force participates in charity activities with Chun Lei), *Zhongguo xinwen wang*, September 26, 2016, http://military.china.com/news/568/20160926/23645676.html. Regarding the State Key Laboratory, see "State Key Laboratory of Astronautic Dynamics, Xi'an Satellite Control Center," *natureINDEX*, https://www.natureindex.com/institution-outputs/china/state-key-laboratory-of-astronautic-dynamics-xi-an-satellite-control-center/568b819d140ba009068b4569; and Zhang, "Xi'An Satellite Control Center."

75. Wu Fei, "Sheng lingdao zoufang weiwen zhu cheng 63680 budui" (Provincial leaders visit and greet Unit 63680 stationed at Cheng), *Jiangyang wang*, July 29, 2014, http://www.cnjsjy.cn/content/2014–07/29/content_240835.htm.

76. Zou Weirong and Zong Zhaodun, "Beijing hangtian feixing kongzhi zhongxin: shixing xinghao tuandui jizhi yingzhan gao midu hangtian renwu" (Beijing Aerospace Flight Control Center: Implementing model-based team mechanism to meet the high frequency of space missions), *Jiefang jun bao*, April 10, 2016, http://chuansong.me/n/518219552684; "Mengxiang zhanfang jiutian shang—Beijing hangtian feixing kongzhi zhongxin chuangxin fazhan jishi" (The dream blooms in the heavens—A chronicle of the innovation and development of the Beijing Aerospace Flight Control Center), *Xinhua*, April 11, 2016, http://www.xinhuanet.com/mil/2016–04/11/c_128883524_3.htm; and Chen Jie and Liu Qiuli, "Beijing hangtian feixing kongzhi zhongxin zhuren Chen Hongmin tan fei kong zhongxin fazhan licheng" (Chen Hongmin, director of the Beijing Aerospace Flight Control Center, discusses the flight control center's historical development), *Zhongguo jun wang*, June 23, 2016, http://www.81.cn/2016cz7h/2016–06/23/content_7115830.htm.

77. "Jundui 15 wei 'da ka' changtan ruhe tisheng junshi huangxin nengli" (Fifteen "big shots" in the military talk about how to improve military innovation), *Jiefang jun bao*, April 9, 2016, http://www.81.cn/jwgz/2016–04/09/content_6998103_2.htm; and Liu Wei and He Bo, "Zhanlue zhiyuan budui mou zongzhan dangwei zai zhuan tiaozheng zhong fahui ning xin ju li zuoyong jishi" (Documenting the leadership role played by the party committee of a main station of the Strategic Support Force

during the resubordination and adjustment process), *Jiefang jun bao*, February 29, 2016, http://www.81.cn/jfjbmap/content/2016–02/29/content_2686.htm.

78. "Zongcan weixing tongxin zongzhan 61096 budui qianshen fanhao shi shenme" (What is the true unit designator of the General Staff Department satellite communications main station, unit 61096), *Baidu zhidao*, March 17, 2016, https://zhidao.baidu.com/question/1447797369760696940.html; "Zongcan mou tongxin zongzhan jinji zeng kai weixing zhongduan" (A General Staff Department communications main station urgently opens new satellite terminals), *Sohu*, May 28, 2008, http://news.sohu.com/20080528/n257122553.shtml.

79. "Ministry of National Defense announces the names of military academies and universities."

80. Zou and Zong, "Beijing Aerospace Flight Control Center."

81. Lai Jinhong, "Jing Haipeng bizhang tou xuanji hangtian yuan gai li zhanlue zhiyuan budui" (Jing Haipeng's shoulder emblem reveals a secret, astronauts resubordinated under the Strategic Support Force), *Shijie ribao*, October 19, 2017, https://udn.com/news/story/11556/2766096; and "Liu Yang he yi qun hangtian yuan lai Xia'an le" (Liu Yang and a group of astronauts came to Xi'an), *Xinlang*, http://k.sina.com.cn/article_2162541102_p80e5c22e0270085en.html?cre=tianyi&mod=pcpager_fintoutiao&loc=23&r=9&doct=0&rfunc=100&tj=none&tr=9.

82. Other organizations related to China's human spaceflight program that are not part of the PLASSF ASD include the Manned Spaceflight Office (921 Office) and the Beijing Institute of Space Medicine and Engineering (507 Institute, also known as the Astronaut Center of China), which in the past managed the China Astronaut Group. On the 507 Institute, see "Shenzhou Program (Project 921)," Sinodefence .com, August 25, 2017, http://sinodefence.com/shenzhou-project-921/.

83. "Zongcan moubu buzhang Meng Xuecheng jieti Zheng Junjie, ren jiefang jun xinxi gongcheng daxue xiaozhang (Department head of the General Staff Department, Meng Xuezheng, appointed as the president of the People's Liberation Army Information Engineering University, succeeds Zheng Junjie), *Pengpai xinwen*, May 6, 2015, https://www.thepaper.cn/newsDetail_forward_1328391.

84. Jiaoyu bu gaoxiao xuesheng si (Department of Education, Higher Education Student Branch), "2018 nian kaoyan chushi chengji chaxun" (2018 initial exam results inquiry), http://yz.chsi.com.cn/yzzt/kyfs2018; and "2017 Zhongguo renmin jiefang jun zhanlue zhiyuan budui wangluo xitong bu di wushiliu yanjiu suo kaoyan chengli chaxun shijian" (2017 Chinese PLASSF Network Systems Department Fifty-Sixth Research Institute examination results inquiry time), *Kaosheng kaoshi wang*, http://www.edu-hb.com/Html/201612/30/20161230202131.htm.

85. "Zhanlue zhiyuan budui mou bu shuang lu fuwuqi jingzheng xing caigou jieguo gongshi" (SSF Department two-way server competitive tender results announcement), *Quan jun wuqi zhuangbei caigou xinxi wang*, December 6, 2016, http://www.weain.mil.cn/cggg/zbgg1/539568.html.

86. See "Zongcan dianzi duikang lu xinbing ying: wei mengxiang chuan shang rongzhuang" (General Staff Department electronic countermeasures brigade's new recruits barrack: putting on armor for the dream), *Zhongguo wang*, December 19, 2014, http://military.china.com.cn/2014–12/19/content_34360144.htm; and Zeng Shijing, Huang Qiyuan, and Li Wen, "Wei jun fuwu zuotan hui dou you sha kan dian?" (What are the highlights for the military service forum?), *Zhongguo jun wang*, May 16, 2017, http://www.81.cn/zghjy/2017–05/16/content_7603928.htm

87. Military Strategy Research Department, *Science of Military Strategy*, 192–94.

88. "Xinxi zhiyuan fangdui: weihu guojia anquan de xinxing zuozhan liliang" (Information Support Team: New combat power to maintain national security), *Xinhua*, 30 July 2017, http://news.xinhuanet.com/mil/2017–07/30/c_129667488.htm.

89. Yu Shi, Pei Changqian, and Xiang Chungang, "Wo jun weixing tongxin yingyong xianzhuang fenxi yu yanjiu (The current situation, analysis and research of our military's satellite communications applications), *Xinxi tongxin*, no. 7 (2017): 108–9, http://cms.emat.com.cn/a/xingyeyanjiu/2017/0824/18794.html.

90. Song Jihe, "Chang hao jieng budui xinwen baodao zhe tai xi—zongcan mou tongxin zongzhan zhua xinwen baodao gongzuo de ji dian zuofa" (Singing grassroot unit news—A few methods for pushing news reporting from a communications headquarters), *Junshi jizhe*, no. 4 (1995): 18–19, http://www.cqvip.com/QK/81377A/199504/4001280373.html.

91. "Jian jun 90 zhounian yuebing: ting dang zhihui, neng da shengzhang, zuofeng youliang (PLA's ninetieth anniversary parade: Listen to the command of the Party, can win battles, have a fine style of work), *Zhongguo ribao*, July 30, 2017, http://www.chinadaily.com.cn/interface/flipboard/1142846/2017–07–30/cd_30295614.html.

92. Kevin L. Pollpeter, Michael S. Chase, and Eric Heginbotham, *The Creation of the PLA Strategic Support Force and its Implications for Chinese Military Space Operations* (Santa Monica, CA: RAND Corporation, 2017), ix–x.

93. "Xue Guijiang shaojiang ren junwei lianhe canmoubu zhanbaoju juzhang" (Maj. Gen. Xue Guijiang serves as head of the Central Military Commission Joint Staff Department Battlefield Support Bureau), *Sohu*, February 19, 2016, http://news.sohu.com/20160219/n437891766.shtml; "Yuan zongcan cehui daohangju juzhang Xue Guijiang shaojiang ren junwei lianhe canmoubu zhanbaoju juzhang" (Maj. Gen. Xue Guijiang, former director of the General Staff Department's Survey, Mapping, and Navigation Bureau, serves as head of the Central Military Commission Joint Staff Department Battlefield Support Bureau), *Pengpai xinwen*, February 19, 2016, http://www.thepaper.cn/newsDetail_forward_1433620; and "Junwei lianhe canmoubu nei she jigou liangxiang han zuozhan daohang deng ju" (Central Military Commission Joint Staff Department internal structure revealed, contains operations, navigation and other bureaus), *Wangyi*, April 11, 2016, http://news.163.com/16/0411/07/BKBSQQ5700014AED.html.

94. Zou Weirong and Zong Zhaodun, "Zujian yi nian duo, zhanlue zhiyuan budui zheyang beizhan dazhang" (One year since establishment, this is how the Strategic Support Force prepares for battle), *Zhongguo jun wang*, June 5, 2017, http://www.81.cn/jmywyl/2017–06/05/content_7627841_4.htm.

95. Author's discussions with PLA and defense community scholars, Beijing, April 2018.

96. "Pojie jiakuai xinxing zuozhan liliang jianshe nanti" (Solve the problem of accelerating new combat power construction), *Jiefang jun bao*, December 20, 2017, http://www.81.cn/jfjbmap/content/2017–12/20/content_194944.htm; Gao Jin and Liu Fulian, "Pulu dianji chuangxin chaoyue nuli jianshe yi zhi qiangda de xiandaihua zhanlue zhiyuan budui" (Paving the way and laying the foundation, innovate and surpass, strive to build a strong and modern Strategic Support Force), *Qiushi*, January 13, 2017, http://www.qstheory.cn/dukan/qs/2017–01/13/c_1120305336.htm; and Zou Weirong, "Yi xue cu jian duanzao xinxing zuozhan liliang" (Using

learning to promote construction and forge new combat power), *Jiefang jun bao*, August 18, 2016, http://zlzy.81.cn/ll/2016–08/18/content_7231996.htm.

97. "Zhuanjia: zhanlue zhiyuan budui jiang guanchuan zuozhan quan guocheng shi zhisheng guanjian" (Expert: Strategic support force will penetrate the whole combat process, is key to victory), *People's Daily Online*, January 5, 2016, http://military.people.com.cn/n1/2016/0105/c1011-28011251.html.

98. Wang Weidong and Yang Yonggang, "Huojian jun 'shizhan hua junshi xunlian de wenhua sikao' xilie baodao zhi er (Rocket Force's "Thinking on the realistic combat training culture" series, report number 2), *Jiefang jun bao*, March 8, 2018, http://www.mod.gov.cn/power/2018–03/08/content_4806251.htm.

99. Liu Xintu and Yi Yongfei, "Huojian jun changtai kaizhan junshi xunlian jiancha 'wenti gui ling' tisheng xunlian zhiliang" (Rocket Force normalizes military training supervision, "reduces problems to zero" and raises training quality), *Jiefang jun bao*, February 23, 2018, http://www.mod.gov.cn/power/2018–02/23/content_4805236.htm; and Liu Chaofan and Gao Yang, "Huojian jun mou lu changtaihua zuzhi quan yuan quan zhuang duikang yanlian" (A Rocket Force brigade normalizes all-member all-equipment confrontational drills), *Jiefang jun bao*, May 14, 2018, http://www.mod.gov.cn/power/2018–05/14/content_4813484.htm.

100. Zhang and Song, "Force Inspected by Chairman Xi."

101. For a detailed discussion of the motivations and challenges of China's nuclear-armed submarine program, see Tong Zhao, *China's Sea-Based Nuclear Deterrent* (Washington, DC: Carnegie Endowment for International Peace, 2016), https://carnegietsinghua.org/2016/06/30/china-s-sea-based-nuclear-deterrent-pub-63909.

EIGHT

China on Arms Control, Nonproliferation, and Strategic Stability

Nancy W. Gallagher

China and the United States view each other as potential adversaries with mixed motives and divergent value systems, yet both can benefit from cooperation to reduce the risk of war, avert arms races, and prevent proliferation or terrorist access to weapons of mass destruction. The two countries have more common interests, fewer ideological differences, and greater economic interdependence than the United States and the Soviet Union had during the Cold War. In principle, arms control broadly defined (i.e., as cooperation to reduce the likelihood of war, the level of destruction should war occur, the cost of military preparations, and the role of threats and use of force in international relations), could be at least as important in this century as it was in the last. In practice, though, China's rise as a strategic power has not been matched by a corresponding increase in the kinds of cooperative agreements that in the past helped keep the costs and risks of superpower competition from spiraling out of control. Why not?

American experts often assert that China sees no value in agreeing to cooperative constraints that would limit its own military capabilities and behavior. Elbridge Colby, the deputy assistant secretary of defense for strategy and force development early in the Donald Trump administration, opined that the Chinese were "uninterested in meaningful steps toward the kind of nuclear risk-reduction measures" that were developed by Washington and Moscow.[1] Lt. Gen. Frank Klotz (Ret.), a top nuclear policy official in the Obama administration, concurred that "China does not appear the least bit interested . . . in formal discussions on ways to limit or reduce its own nuclear weapons."[2] The Hudson Institute's Richard Weitz went further, denouncing China's arms control and nonproliferation policies as a prime example of its "free-riding at the world's expense."[3]

It is true that as China's strategic capabilities have advanced and narrowed the gaps with US and Russian capabilities, China has remained reluctant to join their agreements limiting long-range nuclear forces and banning intermediate-range missiles. It has resisted some US requests for more transparency about its nuclear, space, and cyber programs, while responding positively to other queries. It would be wrong, though, to conclude that China wants the political, economic, and military benefits of being a superpower without any responsibility for cooperative risk reduction. China has long championed forms of arms control that enjoy broad international support but are unacceptable to the United States. It has been constructively engaged in cooperative nonproliferation efforts even as it has remained critical of coercive counterproliferation. It has also advocated for and consistently exercised more strategic restraint than it often gets credit for, even in recent years.

This chapter argues that because China's strategy rests on different assumptions about security and nuclear deterrence than US strategy does, its ideas about arms control are different too. China has historically put more value on broad declarations of intent, behavioral rules, and self-control, while the United States has prioritized specific quantitative limits on capabilities, detailed verification and compliance mechanisms, and operational transparency. When progress on various forms of arms control has occurred, it has not been because China finally matched the United States in some military capability or because Chinese officials and experts "learned" to think about arms control like their American counterparts do. Rather, it has happened when Chinese leaders believed that the United States and other countries with nuclear weapons were moving closer toward its ideas about security cooperation—hopes that have repeatedly been disappointed.

This chapter draws on a range of sources, including official Chinese government statements and actions, authoritative Chinese publications, and writings by influential Chinese arms control experts and American analysts who interact regularly with their Chinese counterparts. Before assessing Chinese positions on specific arms control issues, this chapter begins by surveying different US and Chinese assumptions about international relations that shape each's approach to security cooperation. The second section reviews key points of continuity and change in China's approach to arms control during and immediately after the Cold War and focuses on three issues: nonproliferation, confidence-building measures (CBMs), and the Comprehensive Test Ban Treaty (CTBT) as it affected China's own nuclear capabilities. The third section considers how security policies pursued by the United States under George W. Bush and Barack Obama influenced Chinese attitudes toward arms control. It also explores how advances in space, cyber, and other nonnuclear strategic capabilities have compounded the challenges for US-Chinese security cooperation that are caused by different conceptions of nuclear deterrence. Contrary to claims that China is "just not interested" in arms control, some progress was made during the Obama years but differences in US and Chinese approaches to arms control precluded the achievement of any major breakthroughs.

Understanding Chinese attitudes toward security cooperation has gained added importance under the Trump administration for two reasons. Trump's national security strategy depicts China and Russia as equally capable antagonists facing the United States in a new era of great-power competition, so the feasibility and desirability of mutually beneficial cooperation with China have become more urgent questions. Trump officials have also linked the continuation of US-Russian strategic arms control negotiations to China's willingness to join agreements similar to the Intermediate-range Nuclear Forces (INF) Treaty and the New Strategic Arms Reduction Treaty (START) accord. Regardless of whether or not these officials are genuinely interested in negotiating nuclear accords with China, their ability to do so has been greatly complicated by the Trump administration's trade war with China and its antipathy toward arms control agreements negotiated by previous US administrations, most of which include or impact China.

The costs and risks of coercive competition will keep growing until both sides accept that they outweigh whatever benefits might accrue from trying to maximize power and freedom of action in a tightly interconnected world. Therefore, the chapter conclusion summarizes lessons about Chinese arms control attitudes and actions over time that could be used to improve the prospects for cooperation when US-Chinese relations improve. It argues that instead of resuming unproductive efforts to convince the other side to change how it thinks about security cooperation, the United States and China should seek out small steps that each can accept as beneficial according to its own strategic logic. If they build confidence by honoring those commitments over time, they may gradually be able to cooperate in more ambitious ways despite continued differences in interests and ideas about international security.

ASSUMPTIONS UNDERLYING US AND CHINESE APPROACHES TO ARMS CONTROL

Americans often assume that China's historically small nuclear arsenal is due to its economic and technological underdevelopment compared with the Cold War superpowers, and that as China becomes a stronger global power, its nuclear forces and other strategic capabilities will rival those of the United States and Russia. If so, the key question is whether China will use those capabilities in ways that threaten its neighbors and challenge the global status quo or be a "responsible" great power that cooperates with other countries to reduce nuclear risks and manage other global problems. Early in the Obama administration Deputy Secretary of State James Steinberg posed this very question. He put the onus on China to provide "strategic reassurance" by being more transparent about how it intends to develop and use its nuclear, space, and cyber capabilities—or leave other countries to assume the worst and plan accordingly.[4]

Those who assert that China should be more receptive to US proposals for increased transparency, for other types of CBMs, and for legally bind-ing arms control agreements often assume that such actions reflect widely accepted principles and decades of successful practice. Such confidence that US proposals represent the right way to cooperate ignores the history of heated debates among US policymakers and experts about nuclear arms control. It discounts dissatisfaction among arms control supporters over what Washing-ton and Moscow accomplished during the Cold War, and what they have done together since then, compared with the residual and (re)emerging problems in their security relationship. It also overlooks some fundamental differences in US and Chinese thinking about international relations, strategic stability, and nuclear deterrence that lead to two internally consistent but different ways of viewing security cooperation, which can exacerbate mistrust and frustration even during time periods when US and Chinese officials have both been genu-inely interested in working together.

Li Bin, a Tsinghua University professor and leading Chinese arms con-trol expert, attributes the problem to underlying assumptions about interna-tional relations. He argues that Americans see security in terms of "threats" that can be kept at bay by convincing potential adversaries that the costs of attack outweigh the gains. Chinese officials and experts, however, think in terms of security "challenges." They seek to mitigate vulnerabilities and mini-mize risky situations that arise due to internal or external causes. For example, if China's understanding of some technology lags behind another country's, the more advanced country could use that capability in a way that deliberately exploits a Chinese vulnerability or has unintended negative consequences for China.[5] Thus one motivation for many of China's nuclear, space, cyber, and missile defense projects is to avoid "technological surprise" by learning about advanced technologies that the United States has mastered or is trying to develop. Another is to gain a seat at the table in future international discus-sions about how the capabilities should be used.[6]

US and Chinese conceptions of power also differ even among "realists" who see maximizing relative power as the key to advancing national interests. American realists think in terms of a hierarchy of power tools, with military capabilities at the top; economic resources in the middle; and various types of "soft power"—political, social, and normative—near the bottom. China's concept of Comprehensive National Power is more like a pie chart, with military, economic, and sociopolitical wedges of different sizes. American realists assume that national leaders will spend whatever economic resources are required to acquire more military power than potential rivals, and that leaders will violate social norms and political principles to increase wealth or keep a valuable ally. Chinese decision-makers give more equal weight to military, economic, and political considerations. This explains why they have kept military spending at about 2 percent of a rapidly rising GDP for the past three decades even though the country could afford a larger nuclear arsenal and faster conventional military modernization. It also explains why the Chinese care much more about declaratory policies and normative principles regarding the use of nuclear weapons than they do about relative capabilities.

Since Chinese strategists do not see nuclear weapons as the apex of a power pyramid, they have a much narrower conception of the utility of those weapons than many American strategists hold, and thus correspondingly smaller nuclear requirements. The 2018 US Nuclear Posture Review (NPR) argues that the United States needs a large and diverse arsenal to deter nuclear and nonnuclear attacks, to assure allies and partners, to achieve US objectives and limit damage if deterrence fails, and to hedge against an uncertain future.[7] Chinese leaders have consistently maintained that China has a purely defensive nuclear posture and only needs "the minimum means of retaliation" to deter nuclear coercion and attack.[8] They have been equally insistent that China will never make nuclear threats to deter nonnuclear attacks, nor use nuclear weapons first, nor try to gain a military advantage by retaliating rapidly or reciprocally to any sized nuclear attack.[9] This self-imposed restraint is central to China's self-perception as the most responsible of the major nuclear powers, even without legally binding constraints on its nuclear forces.

This limited role for nuclear weapons in Chinese policy does not reflect the belief held by many Americans, that nuclear weapons render great-power war obsolete. Chinese military planners have consistently prioritized having conventional capabilities to prevent or defeat a large-scale conventional invasion (e.g., during a bid for independence by Taiwan) rather than assuming that a small nuclear arsenal could deter any type of attack. Mao Zedong believed that the outcome of war is determined by the people's level of commitment, not just the quality or quantity of weapons. Therefore, Chinese political leaders have always expressed confidence that their country could successfully defend itself against conventional aggression by being a more capable country and without resorting to using nuclear weapons first.[10]

Chinese writings about "limited deterrence" and its pursuit of some counterforce capabilities do not indicate movement from a concept of deterrence based on assured retaliation to one based on damage limitation like the one that underpins current US thinking about arms control and strategic stability.[11] Authoritative Chinese military publications include writings about retaliatory use of nuclear weapons against military targets, but the objective of such "key point counterstrikes" is to demonstrate resolve in an effort to deter further nuclear attacks on China, not to gain a war-fighting advantage.[12] Chinese strategists assert that if another country uses a few nuclear weapons against China, it will retaliate in a limited way and without uncontrolled escalation that leads to mutual annihilation.[13] This assumption rests on philosophical convictions rather than on practical experience. Acquiring nuclear weapons has not changed the traditional Chinese belief that top military commanders can skillfully manage the course of a war to achieve their political objectives at an acceptable cost. Since Chinese leaders have not historically made nuclear threats to obtain bargaining leverage, they have less experience with misperceptions, miscommunications, and near-misses during nuclear crises than the superpowers gained during the Cold War.[14]

American and Chinese ideas about strategic stability also reflect different conceptions of power and political relationships. Americans typically analyze different forms of strategic stability and the likelihood of deterrence failure, crisis escalation, or arms racing in techno-military terms.[15] They focus on the distribution of military capabilities; the characteristics of weapons systems; the quality of command, control, communication, and intelligence capabilities; the detection probabilities of verification arrangements; and so on. The impact of economic factors are secondary; realists and mercantilists see them in zero-sum terms as contributing to the overall power balance while liberals hope that positive-sum interactions in the economic sphere can reduce the likelihood of war by increasing shared interests that would be damaged in a conflict.[16]

Chinese leaders care deeply about maintaining stability, broadly defined as harmonious relations at home and abroad, for the sake of continued economic growth and Communist Party control rather than for urgent concerns about nuclear war. So long as Chinese security experts remain confident that the United States cannot neutralize China's nuclear retaliatory capability through some combination of offense and defense, they assume a low risk of nuclear attack despite US military superiority. This helps explain why China has not (yet) undertaken a major quantitative nuclear buildup in response to US advances in long-range precision conventional weapons and missile defense.

Chinese assessments of strategic stability assume that the overall context of US-Chinese political relations matters more than the specific details of the military balance.[17] Chinese authors often prefer terms like "strategic reassurance" or "strategic trust" over "strategic stability" because of the latter's mechanical connotations. Chinese policymakers and security experts often complain that they cannot figure out what type of relationship the United States wants to have with it or how the US political system and decision-making processes produce specific policy outcomes that will affect China. They want strategic reassurance from the more powerful United States even more than the United States wants it from China.

Some Chinese strategic analysts have used the concept of Comprehensive National Power to argue that increasing complex interdependence—a web of cross-cutting political, economic, and security interests—is more important for strategic stability than how many weapons each side has. This fits with its depictions of harmonious international relations, where China's "peaceful rise" is mutually beneficial rather than threatening to other countries.[18] Of course, combining strategic and economic issues in stability dialogues between senior US and Chinese officials also fits the idea of comprehensive national power and lets China use its economic advantages for leverage on security issues. This view of strategic stability also suggests that Trump's efforts to get better terms of economic engagement with China by imposing sanctions risks further destabilizing US-China political and military relations, perhaps more than someone who thinks about economic deals in purely transactional terms might realize.

American and Chinese experts see transparency connected to strategic stability in different ways. Americans typically assert that transparency about capabilities and behavior enhance strategic stability by increasing predictability, reducing uncertainty about a potential adversary's current or planned military forces, and providing reassurance or early warning of a surprise attack. This is in keeping with Western political ideas about citizens using information to hold their elected officials accountable and private entities needing information to ensure that contractual obligations are fulfilled. A willingness to provide sensitive information is often used to judge whether a political candidate, company, or country has honest intentions. When American officials make extensive transparency a prerequisite for security cooperation with a potential adversary, they typically depict this demand as necessary for confidence that the other side will comply with its commitments. Yet there is a long history of Americans calling for greater transparency because they want to "open up" a closed country like the Soviet Union or gain intelligence about the number and location of weapons, troops, or other assets.[19]

Americans often declare that Chinese officials seem categorically opposed to US requests for greater transparency due to a cultural bias toward secrecy or to a strategic assessment that "transparency is a tool of the strong to be used against the weak."[20] Yet, David Shambaugh notes that the People's Liberation Army (PLA) is "actually quite transparent about a wide range of subjects in Chinese-language publications," but these sources are rarely used by American scholars or translated into English.[21] This reflects a lack of interest in trying to understand the Chinese on their own terms, rather than through the words and concepts that are more familiar to Americans.

In an effort to increase transparency and confidence by lowering language barriers, China initiated a joint project involving representatives from the five countries that are allowed to have nuclear weapons under the Treaty on the Non-Proliferation of Nuclear Weapons (NPT). This group translated information related to arms control, nonproliferation, disarmament, and nuclear energy into English, Russian, Chinese, and French.[22] The glossary they produced will have practical utility but does not get at deeper philosophical differences.

To explore the deeper differences, the Union of Concerned Scientists assembled a group of US and Chinese arms control experts to discuss how each side thought about transparency and how China might satisfy Western desires for greater transparency in ways that fit its own culture and interests. They observed that Chinese culture values a different form of transparency because it holds that obligations to behave in particular ways reflect the general nature of relationships more than the details of specific contracts. The Chinese are less interested in knowing how many weapons with what characteristics are based in which locations than they are in figuring out whether the United States sees China more as a potential adversary or as a partner in global trade and problem-solving. The priority placed by Chinese officials and security experts on transparency of intentions makes the no first use (NFU) stance and other declarations of peaceful intent much more meaningful to them than such declarations are to US officials and experts. A key finding is that Western "refusal to at least acknowledge" the legitimacy of Chinese views on transparency and the great weight the Chinese attach to declarations of intent "may be responsible for many of the difficulties in the bilateral relationship."[23]

There is a consensus among Chinese security experts that verification is an "integral part" of designing and implementing arms control treaties, but what is acceptable in the context of a legally binding agreement may not be acceptable as a stand-alone "transparency" measure.[24] During negotiations on the CTBT in the 1990s China did not question the importance of including both an international monitoring system (IMS) based on various forms of remote sensing and on-site inspections (OSIs). When China took a position on verification that differed from the one taken by the United States, it generally reflected Chinese concerns about the asymmetry between a small number of countries, including the United States, with extensive and technologically advanced national intelligence capabilities versus the vast majority of other countries, including China, that would be highly dependent on the international verification system. China argued unsuccessfully that the IMS should include imagery satellites; the United States saw this as unnecessarily expensive because it already had its own reconnaissance satellites. China also advocated for more restrictive rules for initiating an OSI out of concern that powerful countries might misuse verification arrangements for espionage purposes.

In short, whether or not China agrees to a particular form of security cooperation is not a reliable indicator of whether it values peaceful relations, supports arms control, or is a "responsible" great power rather than a dangerous expansionist state. China's attitude toward a given measure depends on whether it seems to be in China's interest given how its decision-makers think about security, power, nuclear weapons, and strategic stability, as well as the type of domestic and international environment they are operating in at that particular point in time. Some forms of security cooperation that American policymakers and experts consider mutually beneficial, given their own ideas about international security and their own country's domestic and international environment, may not appear that way to their Chinese counterparts, and vice versa.

This suggests that academic debates about whether China's security policies are designed to advance national interests and increase relative power like any other country in its position would do, or if they are different in important ways because of China's unique strategic culture, rest on a false dichotomy. China is no more nor less inherently peaceful than the United States; instead, both make choices about competition or cooperation based on the strategic logic that informs policymakers' thinking about their objectives and how they can best advance those objectives. Of course, this does not mean that everything Chinese officials and experts say about arms control should be taken at face value, any more than one should believe everything that American officials say. The more consistency there is between words and actions across issues and over time and as adapted for changing contexts, though, the more valid the explanations are likely to be.

CONTINUITY AND CHANGE IN CHINESE VIEWS ON NUCLEAR ARMS CONTROL

Interpreting China's positions on arms control in light of these different assumptions about security, power, stability, and nuclear weapons makes it easier to understand why some Chinese positions have changed and some have stayed the same as China has opened up more to the outside world, has integrated into global markets and institutions, and has become a strategic power. This section looks first at changing Chinese attitudes toward nonproliferation, because one of the earliest objectives of US-Soviet arms control was to prevent China from acquiring nuclear weapons. Major changes in China's domestic context, particularly the reform and opening-up policy adopted in the late 1970s, and changes in the international environment, especially the ending of the Cold War, gradually convinced China to engage constructively in a wide range of arms control initiatives, including some forms of nonproliferation. This section also examines various voluntary arms control efforts that were aimed to relax tensions, reduce suspicion, correct misperceptions, and avoid or manage crises so that they did not spiral out of control. Both Beijing and Washington aspired to transform the overall security relationship by doing relatively simple things, like getting top officials from their two militaries together on a regular basis. Each had hoped that they could change the other's behavior more quickly and extensively than they were willing and able to change their own, which caused frustration on both sides. The final part focuses on China's decision to make the major concessions needed for successful negotiation of the CTBT and on why China decided to accept negotiated constraints on its own nuclear weapons at the time but has not done so since.

Nonproliferation

China's ambivalence about arms control and nonproliferation as practiced by the United States dates back to the 1950s, when the superpowers were just starting to think seriously about how they might both benefit from limited cooperation to reduce the costs and risks of nuclear deterrence. Until that time the superpowers had been competing for favorable international opinion by advocating mutually incompatible approaches to what was then called General and Comprehensive Disarmament. Each justified the necessity of its own nuclear and conventional military buildup because the other side refused to accept their requirements for disarmament. Most of the world was relieved when the three countries that already had nuclear weapons—the United States, Soviet Union, and the United Kingdom—stopped this cynical game and started negotiating a ban on nuclear tests in 1958. The People's Republic of China (PRC) disliked the shift in focus from comprehensive nuclear disarmament to limited arms control because it assumed that the main motivation for prohibiting nuclear tests, but not nuclear weapons, was to preserve the Big Three's nuclear monopoly in the face of Chinese and French efforts to join the nuclear club.[25] Yet the PRC lacked the diplomatic standing to object because Taiwan represented China in the United Nations at that time.

Mao had authorized a full-scale effort to get nuclear weapons in 1955, during a confrontation with Taiwan over two small offshore islands that the United States had pledged to defend with nuclear weapons. He decided that his country needed its own nuclear weapons to fend off coercion by the United States and subordination by the USSR. He also asserted that by demonstrating that a developing country could acquire nuclear weapons, China might persuade the superpowers to abolish nuclear weapons as the only alternative to global proliferation. China took great national pride in overcoming numerous obstacles in order to master the technology, including the lack of indigenous expertise, Western export controls, and the loss of Soviet nuclear assistance in 1959. Mao's revolutionary rhetoric and his nonchalant references to nuclear weapons as "paper tigers" worried the John F. Kennedy administration enough that it considered preventive military action. Nikita Khrushchev was not interested in cooperating with the United States against China at the time, partly because the United States was not equally concerned about France's nuclear ambitions and partly because he accurately anticipated that Mao would become "more restrained" once he had nuclear weapons.[26]

When China conducted its first nuclear test in 1964, it tried to reconcile its advocacy for comprehensive nuclear disarmament with its development of nuclear weapons by insisting that the superpowers' refusal to give up their nuclear weapons left China no choice but to have them too and promising to be more "responsible" than the other countries were. To underscore that it only wanted a few nuclear weapons for purely defensive purposes, China made an unconditional NFU declaration that "at no time and under no circumstances would China be the first to use nuclear weapons." [27] Even though it qualified as a nuclear weapon state it refused to sign the 1968 NPT because the pact contained a two-tiered structure that discriminated against other developing countries. China offered peaceful nuclear cooperation to some developing countries but not help in acquiring nuclear weapons. Although China had split with the USSR by then and was trying to "build a coalition of radical forces in the Third World against the 'U.S. imperialism' and the 'Soviet revisionism,'" it recognized that further proliferation would complicate its long-term objective of global nuclear disarmament.[28]

China became more active in multilateral arms control as its diplomatic isolation ended. Involvement in organizations like the Conference on Disarmament required more people in China to develop nuclear expertise and interact with foreign scientists, diplomats, and military representatives.[29] The PRC delivered its first speech on disarmament to the UN General Assembly in 1971, the year it took back UN representation of China from Taiwan. China reiterated its call for complete nuclear disarmament and insisted that the two countries with the most nuclear weapons should take the lead, starting with their own unconditional NFU pledge. After China reestablished normal diplomatic relations with the United States (in 1979) and the USSR (in 1982), it toned down its objections to the NPT and publicly pronounced its "three no's policy"—no advocating, no encouraging, and no engaging in nuclear proliferation.[30]

China continued to criticize the superpowers for taking only small steps toward slowing their arms race rather than renouncing nuclear threats and committing to nuclear disarmament. When the Cold War arms race was near its peak in 1982, China said that if the superpowers reduced their nuclear arsenals by half and permanently stopped nuclear weapons testing, improvement, and production, then China also would end these activities and join subsequent negotiations for further reductions in nuclear arms. This "three stops and one reduction" proposal followed another step China wanted all nuclear states to take: an unconditional multilateral NFU pledge.[31] The Soviet Union did make an NFU declaration that year but did not make corresponding changes to its operational plans or training to match China's level of consistency. The United States put no more faith in the Soviet pledge than it did in the Chinese one, and maintained that it needed the nuclear option to deter the Soviets from using their superior conventional military force to overrun Europe.

China's improving relations with the superpowers led Chinese leader Deng Xiaoping to shift the focus of national attention from security to economic growth because involvement in a large war seemed unlikely in the forthcoming twenty years. China's 1978 Reform and Opening Up policy changed the emphasis of fissile material production from military to civilian uses and the motivation for civilian nuclear cooperation from geopolitics to economics.[32] Chinese military expenditures fell from 4.6 to 2.1 percent of gross national product between 1978 and 1984, reflecting the new assessment that large-scale war was not likely to occur in the near term.[33] The leadership authorized numerous internal government ministries, including the one responsible for China's nuclear program, to establish foreign trade companies and become more self-supporting. As a new entrant into the global nuclear energy market, China approved some deals that more established suppliers had rejected, including the export of nuclear power plants to Pakistan and small research reactors to Iran. It also sold heavy water to India in the 1980s despite the tense state of Sino-Indian relations after their 1962 border conflict.

In the early years of economic restructuring the Chinese government lacked the motivation, the knowledge, and the legal authority to control dual-use nuclear exports by its foreign trade companies. That slowly changed, for a mix of cooperative and coercive reasons. To attract foreign capital, apply for financial aid, or participate in global markets, China had to adopt standard practices, including regular and reliable reporting of data that had previously been withheld from the Chinese public and kept secret from the rest of the world.[34] It began bilateral negotiations with the United States on a nuclear cooperation agreement in 1981, which necessitated disclosure of some Chinese nuclear information. This led to China joining the International Atomic Energy Agency (IAEA) in 1984, which required gathering and providing sensitive information about nuclear exports to international authorities. Participation by Chinese nuclear industry leaders in IAEA meetings socialized them about accepted practices related to export controls.

Opening its economy to foreign trade made China more vulnerable to sanctions. This increased US leverage to dissuade China from nuclear trade outside of IAEA safeguards. China gradually became more cautious about nuclear commerce and avoided controversial deals, especially when it calculated that the potential cost of US sanctions for allegedly violating nonproliferation norms would outweigh whatever economic benefits it might get from a transaction.[35] Thus China's own experience with international efforts to change its proliferation-related behavior is consistent with its position that, over time, constructive engagement with countries like Iran and North Korea (DPRK) is more likely to have a positive impact compared to sanctions alone.

After lengthy debate, Chinese leaders finally decided that changed security circumstances warranted joining the NPT in 1992. The United States had made NPT membership a condition for full implementation of the nuclear cooperation agreement it signed with China in 1985. China's nuclear industry was eager for the government to take this step. Economic benefits from increased access to US nuclear technology, though, were not enough to convince China's government leaders to join the NPT before the superpowers made major changes to their own nuclear weapons policies.

By 1992 Washington and Moscow had taken a number of steps that gave China good reasons to believe that the superpowers were moving toward its assumptions and preferences regarding nuclear weapons and arms control. They issued a joint declaration in 1985 recognizing that a "nuclear war cannot be won and must never be fought" and renouncing efforts to gain military superiority. To China this sounded like an endorsement of its position that nuclear weapons should be used for a retaliatory form of deterrence only. The superpowers committed in 1987 to eliminate all of their intermediate-range nuclear missiles. They agreed to large cuts in long-range nuclear weapons in the 1991 START accord and started working on START II. Finally, US and Russian leaders made parallel unilateral commitments in 1991 to return all land- and sea-based nonstrategic nuclear weapons to their own territories, including removing nuclear artillery and bombs from South Korea (ROK) and tactical warheads from ships and submarines in the Pacific.

China had also come to see proliferation, particularly by India, as a global security problem more than a form of resistance by developing countries toward great-power hegemony. Egypt, Vietnam, North Korea, Saudi Arabia, and a number of other developing countries had signed the NPT in the 1980s. Their endorsements, despite the NPT's two-tiered structure, increased the pact's legitimacy in China's eyes. The upsurge of support for the NPT also made membership increasingly important for China's image as a responsible nuclear power.[36]

China took other arms control and nonproliferation steps in the 1990s that fit its strategy of focusing on economic growth in a more peaceful regional and global security environment. It joined the Biological Weapons Convention (BWC) in 1984, twelve years after that treaty opened for signature. China signed the 1993 Chemical Weapons Convention (CWC) on the first day possible. China joined the Zangger Committee, the coordinating body for nuclear export controls, in 1997. In 1994 it pledged not to export ballistic missiles that could carry weapons of mass destruction, and not to help any country develop missiles covered by the Missile Technology Control Regime (MTCR) in 2000, although major questions remained about Chinese compliance with these commitments.

Confidence-Building Measures

As the primary driver of arms control efforts during the Cold War, the United States was mainly interested in reducing nuclear risks through legally binding constraints on capabilities—ceilings, then reductions, for existing nuclear arsenals and prohibitions on new countries acquiring nuclear weapons. It also engaged in various forms of "behavioral" arms control measures with the Soviet Union—agreed-upon rules that proscribed some operational practices, like provocative naval maneuvers that could cause a collision (the 1972 Incidents at Sea Agreement) and prescribed others, like establishing a dedicated hotline that the presidents could use to facilitate crisis communication. It likened such CBMs to "arms control junk food"—satisfying in the short term but in the long term much less substantial than capabilities-based arms control because intentions and behaviors could change much more quickly than capabilities could.[37] It considered other types of behavioral arms control, particularly NFU pledges, to be pure propaganda: popular for public opinion, perhaps, but completely unreliable.

This began to change in the late 1980s, in part due to the sequence of CBMs that began with the 1975 Helsinki accord, gained momentum with the 1986 Stockholm accord, led to the Organization for Cooperation and Security in Europe (OSCE), and were credited with alleviating suspicions and helping to transform security relations at the end of the Cold War. Although there was much less history of cooperative security in Asia, China began to apply some of these lessons to its own security challenges in the 1990s. It resolved a number of long-standing territorial disputes and developed mechanisms to more cooperatively manage the remaining ones. It reached border demarcation agreements with twelve neighboring countries, making concessions to countries that seemed comfortable with the status quo but taking a more hardline approach with countries like India, which China saw as too revisionist.[38] China ratified the UN Law of the Sea Convention in 1996. It used this and other diplomatic mechanisms to dampen disputes with Japan and several Southeast Asian countries over ownership of islands by facilitating joint economic development agreements while not conceding sovereignty claims.

In addition to settling border disputes with Russia and other former Soviet republics, China negotiated several CBMs, some of which mirrored agreements previously developed by the superpowers (e.g., the 1963 hotline agreement and the 1994 agreement not to target nuclear weapons at each other) or by the OSCE (e.g., notification and observation of large military exercises in border areas). Others went beyond precedents set in those contexts, at least in symbolic ways. China and Russia paired their 1994 nontargeting pledge with a reciprocal NFU commitment. Their Agreement on Prevention of Dangerous Military Activities included proscriptions already adopted by the US and Soviet militaries, such as prohibitions of the use of eye-damaging lasers and electronic jamming that interfered with command-and-control networks during peacetime. It also added some positive prescriptions, such as safeguards against accidental missile launches and use of early warning systems to prevent each other's ships, planes, and helicopters from inadvertently straying too close to the other side's territory.[39]

China's willingness to negotiate CBMs with Russia encouraged the United States to reinitiate military-to-military discussions after a series of dangerous interactions between US and Chinese naval forces, the 1995–96 Taiwan Strait crisis, and recurrent complaints about US military aircraft encroaching on Chinese airspace. Military-to-military contacts and US arms sales to China had been occurring intermittently since 1980, sometimes being pursued (when the United States wanted to improve its relationship with China for various reasons) and sometimes suspended (when one side wanted to protest an action by the other). Examples include the 1989 killings of pro-democracy protestors in Tiananmen Square and the 1995 speech by Taiwan's president at Cornell University that precipitated the Taiwan Strait crisis.

Resumption of military-to-military exchanges with China was part of a broader effort by some top officials in the Clinton administration, including Defense Secretary William Perry, to develop a new type of relationship with former Communist adversaries that was based on principles of cooperative security.[40] Whereas the most urgent objective with Russia was to help it reorient the huge nuclear, biological, and conventional military program it had inherited from the Soviet Union to a much smaller, more purely defensive capability—without creating new security risks in the process—the main objective with China and other countries in the Asia-Pacific region was to prevent an incipient arms race.[41] As part of this larger effort the Clinton administration began a new US-China lab-to-lab program that brought together scientists to discuss technical issues and do demonstration projects related to shared arms control and nonproliferation objectives.[42] It also created a Joint Defense Conversion Commission to help Chinese military plants redirect productive capacity to civilian products, like electric cars and air traffic control.

Kurt Campbell and Richard Weitz argue that US-Chinese military-to-military cooperation in the 1990s was disappointing because both sides had tried to use a narrow form of engagement to change the other's behavior more broadly. The Clinton administration hoped to convince China "of the correctness of the U.S. worldview on such issues as military transparency, international law, and China's need to participate more actively in multilateral security institutions."[43] China not only sought changes to US policies on Taiwan, export controls, and military sales, it also wanted a more equal political relationship overall.

Different assumptions about the confidence-building process also generated misunderstandings that left both sides dissatisfied. The American side assumed that confidence and trust could develop through successful cooperation on specific functional issues. The Chinese side believed that improving mutual understanding through dialogue that clarified strategic intentions and mutual commitment to general principles for a peaceful relationship would create the confidence needed for specific cooperative undertakings.[44]

The two militaries did agree in 1998 to start holding annual consultations between naval and air forces operating in close proximity, to stop routinely targeting strategic nuclear weapons at each other, and to set up a presidential hotline. The following year, though, China suspended military-to-military interactions to protest the US bombing of the Chinese embassy in Belgrade during a NATO military operation undertaken after China and Russia blocked the UN Security Council from authorizing an intervention into the Kosovo conflict.[45] The United States had become much less optimistic about what it could accomplish through military-to-military interactions. It made little effort to convince China to resume consultations and other activities.

One problem involved lack of reciprocity on actions that fit the US agenda but not the Chinese one. Since the US side believed that greater transparency about capabilities and operations would reduce misunderstandings, misperceptions, and uncertainty, US military officers gave detailed briefings, shared publications, and offered visits to sensitive sites in the hope of getting the same in return. The Chinese did take a number of steps that were unprecedented for them, even though other countries were already much more transparent, including publishing the first official white papers on security (1995), on arms control (1996), and on defense (1998). They also allowed high-ranking US military personnel to visit a number of installations that had never been visited by an American. Americans thought such steps were "minimal and marginal," though, in comparison to what the United States wanted to see and was willing to show China.[46]

The PLA mistrusted US motives for military-to-military exchanges, which it assumed were to collect intelligence, intimidate China with shows of US strength, and improve Chinese attitudes toward US policies and practices. Chinese officials deemed it too dangerous and embarrassing for a much weaker country to reveal equally sensitive information about its own capabilities. They also wanted the United States to be more understanding of cultural differences regarding transparency and not expect quick changes by China. Some American experts acknowledged a degree of truth to the reasons China gave but thought they "mask[ed] a fundamental reluctance to open up the Chinese military establishment to foreign scrutiny . . . [which] breeds suspicion."[47]

True believers in cooperative security like Perry were frustrated. In a 1997 speech at China's National Defense University, Joint Chiefs of Staff chairman John Shalikashvili told the PLA that unless it provided information on a fair and equitable basis, efforts to improve relations would fail.[48] Without rapid and dramatic transparency gains to show from cooperative military-to-military engagement, the Clinton administration shifted to a containment-oriented approach. It used military-to-military dialogues to underscore what US "red lines" were and what could happen if the Chinese crossed them. It also took actions in the region that it considered "unrelated" to confidence-building with the PLA, but these actions—such as maintaining Cold War troop levels in Asia, selling advanced missiles and an early warning radar system to Taiwan, and intensifying military cooperation with Japan, including on theater missile defense—only deepened Chinese suspicions about US strategic intentions.[49]

Campbell and Weitz argue that this tougher approach worked to "disabuse Chinese military and political leaders of any belief that the United States was in invariable decline or lacked the will or capacity to counter adventurism." They credit it and the "decisive U.S. victory, under NATO auspices, in the 1999 Kosovo campaign with deterring China from directly challenging the United States over Taiwan, nonproliferation, or other issues."[50] The unintended effect, though, may have been to reinforce Chinese suspicions that the United States' true objective was not mutual confidence-building but rather intimidation through shows of US strength. This may have decreased Chinese willingness to share sensitive security information.

Some US conservatives wanted to terminate any and all exchanges that could provide useful information about US technologies and operational practices to the Chinese military.[51] In the 1999 Cox Committee report and elsewhere, critics charged China with using every means at its disposal, including espionage, to learn how the United States was using information technology to spur its "revolution in military affairs." They assumed that China was, and always would be, dependent on outsiders for defense technology innovations. They hoped that were the United States to end all forms of cooperation that could help the PLA improve its nuclear weapons, ballistic missiles, or other military capabilities, the United States would always be able to advance its high-tech weapons systems faster than China could close the technological gap on its own.[52]

In 1998 Congress began to impose legislative limits and oversight requirements on US-Chinese military-to-military interactions and other forms of cooperation that could give the PLA militarily useful information. The National Defense Authorization Act for 1999 tightened export control processes in ways that essentially ended US companies' ability to launch commercial satellites at much lower cost by using Chinese rockets; US experts had participated in several launch failure investigations and had provided information that could be relevant to Chinese ballistic missiles.[53] The National Defense Authorization Act for 2000 contained a lengthy list of military operations, information, capabilities, and facilities to which no PLA personnel could be exposed, including all nuclear and military space operations, Defense Department laboratories, and all arms sales or military-related technology transfers (Sec 1201). The United States continued to press China to be more transparent about its defense expenditures, military operations, and other sensitive subjects while severely curtailing joint activities intended to increase mutual understanding, develop professional relationships, prevent crises and arms races, and provide economic benefits to both sides.

Strategic Arms Control

The process that led to China's acceptance of the first legally binding constraint on its own nuclear deterrent followed a similar arc. The 1996 CTBT prohibited nuclear explosions, including those used to develop new weapons designs and ensure the safety and reliability of existing weapons. China moved from being opposed to a stand-alone ban on nuclear tests to a stance of gradual engagement in multilateral negotiations to cautious optimism about the declining salience of nuclear weapons in the post–Cold War world, but eventually to disappointment caused by a backlash in the United States against security cooperation with China and arms control writ large. This history is worth remembering when people complain that China is "free-riding" on global nonproliferation efforts or declare that "Asia is a region that has no history of arms control agreement, [and] there aren't incentives for arms control agreement."[54]

China's initial opposition to a stand-alone test ban treaty softened after Mikhail Gorbachev announced a moratorium on Soviet nuclear testing in 1985 as one of his early moves to end the nuclear arms race. In 1986 China voluntarily ended atmospheric testing and joined ad hoc discussions among scientific experts of technologies for test ban verification. The United States neither reciprocated the Soviet moratorium nor supported a negotiating mandate for the Conference on Disarmament (CD) during the Ronald Reagan and George H.W. Bush administrations. This meant that China could burnish its peace-loving image by saying that it was willing to participate in multilateral test ban treaty negotiations because it didn't expect them to start anytime soon.

That changed in 1992, when Congress mandated a US testing moratorium and directed the next administration to seek a multilateral agreement ending nuclear tests by 1996. The timing caught China in the middle of a series of underground tests needed to maintain confidence that it still had a secure retaliatory capability, despite improvements made to the superpowers' counterforce capabilities in the 1970s and 1980s. China wanted to improve the survivability of its small nuclear force by shifting from liquid-propellant missiles stationed in silos to solid-propellant missiles for mobile delivery vehicles, which required miniaturized warheads with a higher yield-weight ratio than those China already possessed. It needed to add modern safety features to prevent accidental warhead detonation. It was also considering whether the resurgence of US interest in missile defense sparked by Reagan's Strategic Defense Initiative and Republican efforts to end the 1972 U.S.-Soviet Antiballistic Missile (ABM) treaty would eventually lead China to join the other four NPT nuclear weapons states (NWS) by deploying missiles that carried multiple warheads.[55]

Because the CD works by consensus, it made sense for China to participate actively in the test ban treaty negotiations from the start, rather than joining near the end as it had done with the 1992 Chemical Weapons Convention. It proposed provisions that suited its beliefs about nuclear security, such as commitments by all nuclear weapons states not to threaten or to use them against nonnuclear countries and not to use them first against each other. It also opposed proposals that would hurt China's national interests, such as the prohibition against "peaceful" nuclear explosions (PNEs) for economic development or the permissive criteria for OSIs.

The harder decision for China was whether to drag out negotiations until it had completed its planned test series or participate "constructively," that is, make compromises and drop unpopular positions quickly enough to meet a target completion deadline that would preclude some important developmental tests. Alastair Ian Johnston uses this question to assess whether Chinese officials had fundamentally changed their worldview and embraced cooperative security or if they were merely making tactical adaptations to advance their national interests and increase their relative power in the aftermath of the Cold War. Although he found that China had developed an arms control community with transnational links to the same nongovernmental groups that had influenced Gorbachev's "new thinking," Johnston expected that Chinese officials would still "free-ride" on superpower arms control for realpolitik reasons.

Based on evidence through the fall of 1995, he predicted that China would cooperate in negotiations enough to improve its image and foster a peaceful international environment conducive to economic growth but would not commit to a comprehensive test ban in 1996 if that would constrain its ability to develop a more flexible deterrent.[56]

China defied Johnston's prediction about free-riding by making several major concessions during the final year so negotiators could meet their deadline. It dropped its initial linkage to a multilateral NFU agreement and its call for an exemption for peaceful nuclear explosions. It compromised on the criteria for authorizing OSIs. It also agreed to let states use "national technical means" (NTM) of verification (which is a euphemism for reconnaissance satellites, remote seismic monitoring systems, and other nonhuman ways of gathering information about treaty compliance) in addition to data from the International Monitoring System for OSI requests, even though only a few countries had sophisticated NTM. China held firm, along with many other states, on stringent requirements for entry-into-force, including ratification by India, Pakistan, Israel, and the five nuclear weapons states recognized by the NPT. It did, however, commit to a nuclear testing moratorium beginning on the day it signed the CTBT rather than reserve the right to keep testing until the treaty entered into force—reflecting the political cost China paid to continue testing while the negotiations were underway.

According to experts from China's nuclear weapons laboratory and the PLA, cutting short the planned sequence of tests had a more negative impact on China than it did on the other NPT nuclear weapon states (NWS). China had only conducted 46 nuclear tests by 1996, compared with 1,030 conducted by the United States, 715 by the USSR/Russia, 210 by France, and 45 by Britain (which also received test data from the United States). The smaller amount of historical test data a country has, the harder it is to make small modifications in the core of a nuclear weapon and have confidence that it will work properly without explosive testing. If China could not test again, it "would halt or at least slow the development of essentially new nuclear weapons," such as warheads with higher volume and yield-to-weight ratios that were compatible with multiple independently targetable reentry vehicles (MIRVs) for long-range missiles, a technology the other four NPT NWS had already mastered.[57]

Ending nuclear tests also raised concerns about China's relative ability to maintain the safety and reliability of its existing nuclear stockpile. In addition to having fewer experienced weapons designers and less test data than the other NWS, China also had less money for routine stockpile surveillance (the main methods used by other countries to confirm reliability), less sophisticated scientific equipment, and less powerful computer simulations.

China's decision to sign the Test Ban Treaty in 1996 was not evidence of "learning" to value arms control and cooperative security in the same way that the United States and Russia understood them. Instead, it reflected Chinese officials' assessment that the end of the Cold War created both an opportunity and an imperative to "make greater efforts to promote world peace and development" because the superpowers were beginning to agree with China's ideas about minimal deterrence.[58] They had essentially met the "three stops and one reduction" criteria, so China decided that it, too, needed to take a major step to advance the nuclear disarmament agenda, even though the United States still refused to make an NFU pledge and Russia had revoked its promise in 1993. Ending nuclear testing had always been a top priority for nonnuclear weapons states, so China needed to advance that objective to be a "responsible major power" in the eyes of other developing countries. Most important, Chinese officials concluded that further testing was not necessary for maintaining an arsenal that could deter either threats or the use of nuclear weapons in a post–Cold War world, particularly where arms control and cooperative security are playing a bigger role than before.[59]

Many expectations that informed China's decision to sign the CTBT soon proved to be unfounded. It wanted to do cooperative stockpile stewardship projects with the United States but congressional opposition to nuclear weapons–related cooperation with China ruled that out.[60] It had hoped that international pressure would compel India to sign the Test Ban Treaty despite its dissatisfaction with the treaty text and the process that was used to open it for signatures over India's objections, but India and Pakistan each conducted a series of nuclear tests in 1998. The May 1999 bombing of the Chinese embassy in Belgrade precipitated a reevaluation of China's nuclear-deterrent needs. The United States began to look like a global hegemon that was prepared to intervene militarily without UN Security Council approval or use force in ways that directly hurt China's interests.[61] Shortly thereafter the US Senate voted against Test Ban Treaty ratification.

The one major consideration that remained true through the end of the Clinton administration was US support for the ABM treaty despite pressure from Republicans for rapid deployment of a national missile defense system. In September 2000 Clinton decided against authorizing a missile defense system that would exceed what the ABM Treaty allowed. He assessed that the technology was not ready and that deploying a few interceptors of unknown capability could have a net negative effect on national security were Russia and China to respond by deploying more offensive missiles.[62] Soon after taking office, though, George W. Bush announced the US withdrawal from the ABM treaty and ramped up efforts to integrate national and theater missile defense into a comprehensive global system of "layered defenses" capable of intercepting "missiles of any range at every stage of flight."[63] Despite these negative developments, China has remained committed to the CTBT, it has maintained its moratorium on nuclear testing, it has contributed to building a verification system, and it has promised to ratify the Test Ban Treaty as soon as the United States does.[64] In other words, although it took a long time and a series of small steps before China's political and military leaders were ready to sign the CTBT, they have upheld that cooperative commitment even though incentives to test again quickly increased after China signed the accord. The same pattern holds for China's decisions to join the NPT and tighten nuclear export controls and to become somewhat more transparent about its military doctrine, defense budget, and conventional force operations. Part of what China learned from these experiences was that the United States' democratic system of government made it a much less reliable cooperative partner. Congress could prevent the president from ratifying a major multilateral accord and a new leader could quickly repudiate a foundational treaty on which all other strategic arms control agreements rested.

CHINA AND ARMS CONTROL IN THE TWENTY-FIRST CENTURY

China's current positions are more understandable in the light of its own security concepts and its historical experiences with nonproliferation, CBMs, and arms control. Chinese positions should also be evaluated in the context of recent US policies, many of which have shown a lack of interest in, and sometimes an outright aversion to the kinds of cooperative actions, processes, and agreements with which China is most comfortable. During the George W. Bush years, China largely reverted to arms control positions it had taken during the Cold War because the United States seemed primarily interested in being the world's sole superpower rather than in cooperative security. The Obama era was more confusing for China because parts of his inner team enthusiastically endorsed the president's Prague agenda for eventual nuclear disarmament while a broader cross-section of officials in the administration and in Congress favored making a military, political, and economic "pivot" to Asia in a comprehensive strategy to counter China's growing power. During that period neither China nor the United States showed the level of interest in arms control that they had exhibited during the 1990s, but they did make some progress together, not only on nuclear issues but also on cybersecurity and space.

George W. Bush Administration

China's evaluation of its security environment deteriorated after George W. Bush took office because of the new US administration's more unilateralist approach to security. Its NPR made coercive prevention, not stable mutual deterrence, the central principle for US nuclear policy. It called for the development of new, more "usable" nuclear weapons and redefined the strategic triad so the offensive leg included both nuclear and precision-guided conventional capabilities that were sized for use in various immediate- and near-term contingencies, including scenarios involving China.[65] This stoked Chinese fears that as the sole superpower the United States would rely more heavily on nuclear threats and unilateral military action than it had when it was being counterbalanced by the USSR.

Numerous Bush administration actions revived Chinese suspicions that the United States did not really see arms control as a means to "enhance the security of all countries . . . [but as] a tool for stronger nations to control weaker ones . . . [so they could] optimize their own armament in order to seek unilateral security superiority."[66] The administration rejected US-Russian arms control as an outmoded relic of the Cold War, it withdrew from the ABM treaty in 2002, and it replaced the START process with easily reversed self-restraint.[67] Secretary of State Colin Powell tried to reassure China that the United States only planned to build a limited missile defense against a potential proliferator like North Korea or Iran. Yet the expansive US plans for missile defense presented in other contexts seemed sized to neutralize many more strategic weapons than China currently possessed or planned to develop.[68] The United States also began explicitly pursuing a highly ambitious form of unilateral space dominance that contradicted the principles of peaceful cooperation and reciprocal strategic restraint stated in the 1967 Outer Space Treaty and other international agreements. The goals of the new US space policy amounted to securing the ability to use space assets to find, track, target, and help destroy any potential threat on earth and to prevent other countries from using space in ways that potentially threatened US interests.[69]

The Bush administration preferred coercive counterproliferation to cooperative nonproliferation agreements (like the NPT) that included arms control obligations for countries with nuclear weapons. Coercive counterproliferation eschews nondiscriminatory rules in favor of applying different standards to friendly countries that the United States considers "responsible" nuclear states than those used for so-called rogue states. The Bush administration was undecided about China in this regard: the deputy secretary of state gave a major speech asserting that it was time for China to become a "responsible stakeholder" in global governance, which he defined in ways that went beyond being more transparent about its military capabilities to include adopting more market-oriented economic policies and more democratic practices.[70] Coercive prevention also relies on secrecy, export controls, sanctions, and other denial strategies to thwart the assumed desires of a "hostile" state or terrorist group in its bid to obtain weapons of mass destruction and associated technologies. The 2003 Iraq War—initiated by the United States over the objections of close allies and without Security Council approval—demonstrated what the United States was willing to do if it suspected (rightly or wrongly) that a hostile state might be secretly trying to acquire dangerous dual-use technology or material.

China took on its first nonproliferation leadership role in early 2003 when the Bush administration requested its help with North Korea. As the United States was preparing for war with Iraq, it was also ratcheting up pressure on North Korea. North Korea responded by announcing plans to withdraw from the NPT. China wanted to avoid both North Korean proliferation and US military action on the Korean Peninsula, so it organized a trilateral meeting in hopes of preventing disruptive actions by either side while inching toward a diplomatic resolution. Those talks deadlocked before they formally began: North Korea wanted to resume bilateral negotiations with the United States but Bush prohibited anyone on the US delegation from any type of bilateral meeting with their North Korean counterparts.[71]

China eventually convinced the United States and North Korea to accept a six-party format, with Russia, Japan, and South Korea joining them around a hexagonal table. The meetings in Beijing went nowhere because the United States insisted that North Korea had to completely, verifiably, and irreversibly destroy all of its dual-use nuclear capabilities before discussing any other issues. In frustration, North Korea declared in 2005 that it had nuclear weapons. Despite strong Chinese efforts at dissuasion, North Korea corroborated that claim with its first nuclear test the following year, giving China only twenty minutes' advanced notice. This led Beijing to work more closely with Washington. It also convinced the Bush administration to adopt a more flexible position, including the beginning of bilateral talks with North Korea and replacing its demand for complete capitulation with a phased sequence of steps that paired nuclear restraint with political reassurance and energy assistance. The new diplomatic approach was only partly successful but it did slow North Korea's nuclear progress without having to engage military action.[72]

The United States did not reciprocate the help it had received from China on North Korea's nuclear program when China tried to keep constraints on India's nuclear program in place. India wanted the Bush administration to drop sanctions imposed after India's nuclear tests and change US law and Nuclear Suppliers Group practice so that India could purchase dual-use nuclear material and technology for civilian programs that could also help India produce enough fissile material for 50 weapons a year.[73] The 2006 US-Indian civilian nuclear deal demonstrated use of US power to exempt India from restrictions on nuclear trade with countries that had not signed the NPT, which weakened the global nonproliferation regime in a way that was particularly problematic for China.[74] That deal reinforced the view among many Chinese analysts that sanctions might sometimes play a role in arms control but were often imposed or lifted by "hegemonic powers like the United States in a discriminatory, self-serving, and ultimately fruitless fashion."[75]

China did not react to the Bush administration's unilateralism by leaving any of the arms control agreements or organizations it had joined when the United States was an enthusiastic supporter. Yet it no longer felt the need to do more than reiterate its NFU policy and negative assurances to nonnuclear weapons states in order to be seen as a more responsible nuclear power than the United States. With the United States actively blocking rather than leading multilateral efforts to negotiate the types of arms control agreements that China favored, China also had little incentive to invest much diplomatic energy or technical expertise in the effort.

China did vote for UN Security Council Resolution 1540, which directed all member states to take steps to prevent nonstate actors from acquiring weapons of mass destruction. First, though, it insisted on the removal of language that the United States or other countries acting on their own could invoke to justify the preventive use of force. China did not join the Bush administration's main multilateral counterproliferation mechanism, the Proliferation Security Initiative (PSI). It maintained that the interdiction of ships suspected of illicitly carrying weapons of mass destruction or related materials required Security Council approval or some other formal international legal authority.[76] This was a sensitive subject for China. In 1993, before the CWC entered into force, the United States stopped and searched a Chinese ship suspected of taking chemical weapons to Iran, based on faulty evidence.[77]

When China showed initiative on arms control, the United States assumed it had ulterior motives. China and Russia tried to start negotiations in the CD on the Prevention of an Arms Race in Outer Space (PAROS) treaty, but Bush officials insisted that there was no arms race in space and thus no need for negotiations.[78] They believed the popular PAROS resolution calling for negotiations was meant to make the United States look aggressive and to preclude space-based missile defense, the one mode that in theory might eventually work against missiles launched from deep inside these two large countries. Bush officials also presumed that China was trying to get public relations benefits by professing support for the Fissile Material Cut-off Treaty (FMCT) negotiations while preventing them from starting by insisting that PAROS negotiations begin at the same time. When China agreed in 2003 to a program of work for the CD that included FMCT negotiations and ad hoc discussions of topics related to PAROS, the Bush administration announced that it could no longer support the existing mandate for FMCT negotiations.[79]

From China's perspective, cooperative constraints on military space activities and fissile material production are logically linked. Chinese leaders saw their country's space program as increasingly important to China's comprehensive development strategy, so US export controls and political restrictions that essentially ended all US space cooperation with China were a major problem. More broadly, Bush administration aspirations for "full-spectrum" US military space dominance, including space-based missile defense, force projection, and control over which players could use it for which purposes threatened China's economic, technological, political, and security objectives.[80]

China had stopped producing highly enriched uranium and plutonium in 1987, when the superpowers reached agreement on their first nuclear arms reduction treaty. China never officially announced a moratorium on fissile material production for weapons as the other NPT NWS did, however. Its relatively small stock of fissile material was more than enough for the nuclear modernization program underway during the Clinton administration. It would be inadequate, though, for the ten-fold increase in nuclear weapons that some Chinese experts thought would be necessary to preserve a limited retaliatory deterrent were the Bush administration to fulfill its ambitious plans for a multilayered missile defense system.[81] Because the United States was refusing to negotiate some constraints on its military space and missile defense programs to help address China's "legitimate security concerns," China also wanted to keep its options open until it could assess the magnitude of the "challenge" it faced and the best way to address it.

By 2006 some American strategists claimed that the United States was on the cusp of regaining "nuclear primacy" because of its dramatic technological advances, Russia's nuclear decline, and China's "glacial pace" of nuclear modernization.[82] Computer modelling done by academic analysts Keir A. Lieber and Daryl Press suggested that the United States could use its nuclear and precision conventional weapons in a disarming first strike against China's or Russia's long-range nuclear weapons, with missile defenses "mopping up" whatever small number of nuclear warheads survived an initial attack. Lieber and Press maintained that the United States had achieved "immense strategic benefits" from its nuclear primacy in the early years of the Cold War, in the form of both bargaining leverage and confidence in war plans. They noted that nuclear primacy could embolden the United States to take more risks and behave more aggressively and that nuclear vulnerability could incentivize China and Russia to take steps that increased crisis instability. Nevertheless, they argued that if the objectives of US security policy were to maintain global preeminence, to preclude the rise of a peer competitor, and to prevent lesser powers from challenging the United States in critical regions, then the "benefits of nuclear primacy might outweigh the risks."[83]

Li Bin and Nie Hongyi have assessed how Chinese-US strategic stability was affected by US efforts to design more "usable" nuclear weapons, to move nuclear-armed submarines from the Atlantic to the Pacific, to deploy layered missile defense, and to develop space-based radars for continuous tracking and targeting of mobile missiles. They argue that these efforts were not needed to dissuade China from trying to become a peer competitor; Chinese leaders had already prioritized economic development over military spending, to avoid what they blamed for the Soviet Union's downfall. To the extent that US military advances made Chinese missiles more vulnerable, Li and Nie doubt this would incentivize China to deploy a much larger long-range arsenal. Instead, it would discourage China from being more transparent about the number of nuclear weapons it had, where they were located, and what their alert status was. The authors conclude that China could take relatively easy and inexpensive steps in order to maintain its limited retaliatory capability but that arms control would be preferable, for several reasons.[84]

Li and Nie do not believe that the United States would deliberately attack in the mistaken belief that it could neutralize China's deterrent. They warn, though, that "blind confidence" might cause US leaders to take more risks and make more nuclear threats, thus increasing the chance of an inadvertent nuclear war. They expect China to experiment with various military capabilities being developed by the United States in order to avoid "technological lagging" and they worry that US reactions to Chinese experimentation could trigger an asymmetrical arms race.

Li and Nie also warn about a negative form of nuclear learning. Whenever US officials and nuclear experts engage in strategic dialogues with Chinese counterparts, the Americans justify the United States' unwillingness to make an NFU pledge by arguing that it would be rational for any nuclear-armed state to escalate rather than lose a conventional war. Li and Nie worry that these Track II interactions erode some Chinese strategists' support for NFU, writing that this "academic propagandizing objectively weakens the confidence of Chinese scholars in the nuclear taboo."[85]

China's January 11, 2007, test of a kinetic energy weapon against one of its own defunct satellites spurred the destabilizing dynamics that concern Li and Nie. It also amplified the effects of increased mistrust on both sides due to the lack of cooperative mechanisms to reduce misunderstandings. The Bush administration interpreted the test as evidence that China intended to neutralize US military superiority by attacking vulnerable satellites used for imagery, targeting, missile defense, and many other purposes. But the test used technology that China had started exploring in response to Reagan's Strategic Defense Initiative; it was the next logical step in a lengthy process of technology development rather than a deliberate challenge to the United States in space.[86]

China's 2007 test of an anti-satellite (ASAT) weapon similar to ASAT tests conducted decades earlier by the superpowers did parallel its 1964 test of a nuclear weapon after years of nuclear arms racing and nuclear threats from the superpowers: it symbolized a deep commitment not to let technological inferiority leave China vulnerable to coercion or attack in space. The Bush administration's ambitions for US military space dominance, and Congress's ban on space-related cooperation with China, together threatened all aspects of China's power because its space program had become a major driver for technological development and economic growth as well as a source of political prestige. Eric Hagt argues that China went ahead with its own ASAT test after years of pressing for PAROS negotiations not because it was a hypocrite but because it wanted to deter US attacks on China's growing number of space assets.[87] The Bush administration's argument that new restrictions on space weapons were not needed because the United States was not in a space arms race with its peer competitors may have also convinced China to try a "peace through strength" strategy in this domain.

Even if neither side had aggressive motives in space, both relied on worst-case assumptions because the PLA's large role in China's space program was not transparent, key parts of US space doctrine and spending were classified, and US-Chinese military-to-military interactions rarely occurred. American proponents of space dominance used the Chinese ASAT test as a rationale for redoubling US efforts. A year later the United States demonstrated how easily it could convert a missile defense interceptor into an anti-satellite weapon when it used an interceptor aboard an Aegis cruiser to shoot down a failed American spacecraft that posed an extremely small risk of becoming a public health problem when it fell back to earth.[88]

Two proposals for enhancing space security cooperation also failed in 2008. The United States and its allies ridiculed the draft treaty on the Prevention of Placement of Weapons in Outer Space that Russia and China circulated at the CD because the pact would have prohibited space-based missile defense but not the ground-based direct-ascent ASAT weapon that China had just tested.[89] The code of conduct drafted by the European Union (EU) looked equally one-sided because it defined responsible behavior in space as ruling out debris-generating actions unless undertaken to address urgent health and safety concerns.[90]

The Obama Administration

The newly elected Obama administration responded to this deteriorating security environment by calling for a "reset" of US-Russian relations, including a renewed commitment to nuclear arms control and disarmament. It also reoriented US proliferation policy, from coercive counterproliferation to "strategic patience" with North Korea and negotiations based on NPT principles with Iran. Regarding China, the United States lacked an arms control legacy to return to, which led to more concern about the military, economic, and political advances that China had made during the Bush years.

Obama administration officials disagreed among themselves and with influential members of Congress about how much and what type of security cooperation the United States should pursue with China, and what to offer in return. Key US players wanted China to join future strategic arms reduction talks and accede to the US-Russian treaty that banned all intermediate-range missiles and also to follow international norms for maritime behavior, to be more transparent about its intentions in space, and to stop engaging in various types of cyber attacks. At the same time they were reluctant to weigh seriously the merits of making a mutual NFU pledge with China or to explicitly acknowledge mutual nuclear vulnerability. They were unwilling to negotiate legally binding limits on missile defense, military space activities, or cyber operations. They were also unable to ratify the Comprehensive Test Ban Treaty or the Law of the Sea Convention.

Any of these steps would have reassured China that the Bush administration years had been an aberration that delayed but did not derail progress toward a new global security context in which nuclear weapons played a less important role in great-power relations than they had during the Cold War. This perspective could have made China more receptive to US arms control proposals. Despite the mutual frustration, though, more progress was made on nuclear, space, and cyber cooperation than is recognized by Americans who insist that China is "just not interested" in arms control. Rather than proposing any such concrete measures, the Obama administration's China policy offered an amorphous tacit bargain: the United States would not try to thwart China's rise if China provided credible reassurance that its "growing global role will not come at the expense and security of others."[91] Unfortunately, the United States and China had very different conceptions of credible reassurance.

The Obama administration tried to use an elevated and broadened strategic and economic dialogue between the two countries to reduce misunderstandings, increase transparency, build confidence, promote responsible behavior, and foster reciprocal restraint. To indicate openness to Chinese perspectives and concerns it offered to discuss strategic stability "without any content on what that would require."[92] Yet each side had such different starting assumptions about security that their high-level dialogue was like "chickens talking with ducks."[93]

Discussions about nuclear deterrence, strategy, and arms control never got past basic issues of declaratory policy. The 2010 NPR tried to provide reassurance to China and the world that the United States was returning to a more restrained nuclear doctrine than its predecessor had enunciated.[94] Yet inter-agency debates, fueled in part by congressional opposition and allied concerns about major nuclear policy changes, limited how far the NPR went on questions of greatest interest to China. The NPR said that the "fundamental purpose" of US nuclear weapons was to deter nuclear attack (which left open other possible uses) and promised to work toward a world in which that would be their "sole purpose." It also added an important negative security assurance: the United States would not use nuclear weapons first against NPT NWS in good standing (without also ruling out first use against China, Russia, North Korea, and Iran).[95]

China received much more attention in the 2010 NPR than it had in pre-vious versions. Chinese experts were sensitive to implications in US writings on strategic stability and arms control, that their country was a "little Russia" rather than a major power whose nuclear and security policies rested on very different premises from Russia's. One such US concern involved classical arms race instability, that is, whether a wealthier China would race to catch up with the United States militarily. Yet China had a long-standing policy of not trying to match or outpace US nuclear capabilities, not only because Chinese strat-egists believed that having the "minimum means of reprisal" would deter a nuclear attack but also because they blamed arms racing for the Soviet Union's collapse. Chinese experts worried more about other sources of instability, par-ticularly that US advances in missile defense and precision-guided conven-tional weapons would accelerate Chinese research on underlying technologies like guidance systems and on asymmetrical countermeasures such as anti-ship ballistic missiles; and that China's efforts to prevent a "science surprise" would provoke a US counterreaction.[96]

Chinese experts agreed with language in the NPR about the importance of taking cooperative steps to avoid crisis instability. They assumed, however, that China's "peaceful rise" would preclude the frequent, intense crises of the Cold War, and thought that adopting mutual NFU policies would obviate pressure for nuclear escalation.[97] At the same time, Chinese experts began to openly debate whether China should threaten to retaliate with nuclear weapons in the event of a US precision conventional attack that compromised its nuclear deterrent or spread radioactive contamination, even though doing so would violate China's categorical NFU pledge. Fiona Cunningham and Taylor Fravel argue that the Chinese government is using ambiguity to deter a type of attack that Chinese experts already consider highly unlikely because they do not want to waste money building more nuclear weapons to assure a survivable deter-rent, and that this strategy reinforces American doubts about whether China's NFU pledge really applies in other circumstances too.[98]

Chinese arms control experts were intrigued by Obama's vision of a nuclear-free world but skeptical for many reasons. Some questioned his main motive: was it truly to end shared nuclear risk, or was it meant to enshrine US hegemony by reducing nuclear arms and demanding greater transparency but also refusing to limit vastly superior US conventional military power and missile defense? They noted that the modest reductions in New START would not decrease the threat to China because the United States was reassigning more nuclear submarines to the Asia-Pacific region. Given how hard it was to get US Senate approval for a treaty whose biggest effect was simply to restore verification of the limit of 1,550 deployed strategic warheads, Chinese experts doubted that the president could push through ratification of more significant reductions. They also saw a sharp contradiction between Obama's pledges to work toward a nuclear weapons–free world and his plan to spend $180 billion over the forthcoming ten years rejuvenating the entire US nuclear triad and supporting infrastructure to ensure that the US nuclear deterrent could last for many more decades.

Chinese officials wanted to begin a nuclear-focused Track 1 dialogue by getting the United States to acknowledge mutual vulnerability and discuss the stabilizing effects of a reciprocal NFU pledge. Their consistent emphasis on the NFU pledge caused their American counterparts to doubt that they would get the real story about China's nuclear doctrine from its diplomats and Ministry of Defense personnel. The Americans wanted senior Chinese officers from the Second Artillery, which operated China's land-based missiles, to participate in the dialogue because US experts often misinterpreted references to "limited deterrence" in Second Artillery training materials as evidence of a Chinese shift from a purely retaliatory nuclear posture to a "damage limitation" form of deterrence. Chinese political leaders, who establish doctrine and make key decisions for the military, were reluctant to send military officers who had little experience interacting with foreigners to an official governmental dialogue. They also objected strenuously to US suggestions that it had to reveal the exact number of current and planned nuclear weapons in its arsenal during the opening round of the dialogue. Frustrated, the Obama administration decided in March 2011 not to participate in nuclear talks led by the Chinese Foreign Ministry and to let US officials continue attending an annual Track 1.5 dialogue on strategic nuclear relations but only in a private capacity.[99] By the end of the Obama administration the Track 1.5 hosted by the Pacific Forum yielded some interesting ideas, such as equitable but asymmetric pledges by the United States to maintain the credibility of China's deterrent and by China to keep its nuclear arsenal small. But the two sides never managed to agree on the participants or agenda for a Track 1 nuclear dialogue.[100]

The Obama administration did seriously consider officially acknowledging mutual nuclear vulnerability with China. Senior members knew this would mean a lot to their Chinese counterparts and did not expect to incur big political costs at home or with allies by talking openly about something these officials accepted as a fact of life. Such a statement would also make the United States' reassurance that missile defense was not meant to weaken China's deterrent more credible. Neither the uniformed military nor the civilian leaders at the Department of Defense objected. The main concern, as discussed in interagency meetings, was that the Chinese government would be able to pocket the concession and provide nothing in return. Therefore the Obama administration decided to use the prospect of eventually getting such an acknowledgment as an inducement for China to include in strategic stability talks the senior military officials with nuclear responsibilities, something that had never occurred.[101] The military-to-military interactions that did occur during the Obama administration were focused primarily on conventional CBMs, such as maritime rules of the road and advanced notification of major military exercises.[102]

Near the end of Obama's second term his security team discussed making an NFU pledge as one of many options for advancing his Prague agenda. The president and vice president thought that the United States could safely take this step because they had high confidence that the US military could deter and defend the United States and its allies against nonnuclear threats without resorting to using nuclear weapons, but the DoD voiced objections about alliance politics. The NFU option was dropped after a leak to the *Washington Post* prompted Japanese objections that China might misinterpret such a policy shift as evidence of decreased commitment to Japan's defense.[103] It is much more likely that Chinese officials would have welcomed an American NFU declaration as evidence that the United States finally agreed with them about the limited utility of nuclear threats, which would have made strategic stability talks more productive.

China did play a constructive role on several other nuclear risk reduction initiatives during the Obama years. It continued trying, without much success, to convince both North Korea and the United States to make reciprocal concessions. The Six-Party Talks broke down shortly after Obama took office, possibly because South Korea had elected a hardline president just before the Bush administration left office. China eventually persuaded North Korea to return to the table, but Kim Jong-il died before the Six-Party Talks could resume. A tit-for-tat cycle ensued, with North Korea conducting increasingly provocative satellite launches and nuclear weapon and missile tests, which spurred UN sanctions and US-ROK military exercises, which led to more defiant actions by the DPRK and more missile defenses by the United States and Japan.

The United States criticized China for not using enough economic and political leverage to stop these North Korean activities, while China complained that the Obama administration's "strategic patience" policy refused to address North Korea's legitimate security concerns because it believed that sustained pressure would eventually cause regime collapse.[104] Secretary of State John Kerry tried to incentivize China to "crack down hard enough" to make North Korea's new leader give up his nuclear ambitions by suggesting that such an outcome would reduce the United States' need for a "robust forward leaning posture of defense."[105] Chinese experts worried not only that a phased deployment of missile defense would eventually impact China's deterrent, but also that the same sensor network being developed to track and target incoming missiles could also be used to facilitate conventional offensive strikes, including the type of disarming first strike discussed by Lieber and Press.[106] Nearly three years passed without North Korea conducting another nuclear test but also with no resulting effect on US plans to increase the number of ground-based interceptors it had based in Alaska or to send another forward-based X-band radar to Japan (both announced in early 2013). North Korea's January 2016 nuclear test, however, prompted South Korea to announce that it would finally agree to host a US theater-range missile defense system, including a radar that China feared could track its ICBMs and undermine its deterrent.[107]

China participated in the Nuclear Security Summit process orchestrated by the Obama administration, gradually doing more to protect nuclear and radiological materials and prevent nuclear terrorism. It completed several joint projects with the United States, including the establishment of a nuclear security center of excellence in Beijing and the conversion of a miniature neutron source research reactor that could convert highly enriched uranium (HEU) fuel to low enriched uranium (LEU). After being one of the more passive participants in the earlier summits, China had a "burst of activity" at the final summit in 2016, joining other countries that had already pledged to undertake various sets of steps known as "gift baskets" and making a number of other commitments.[108] This led to China playing an "outsized role" in a multinational project to replace HEU with LEU in a reactor in Nigeria in order to ensure that a terrorist organization like Boko Haram could not steal weapons-grade material from a poorly guarded site.[109]

Other forms of US-Chinese cooperation to reduce nuclear risks were constrained by congressional concerns that China might gain some type of military benefit or transfer US-origin technology or material to a country like North Korea. The defense laboratories and facilities that control most of China's weapons-usable fissile material and all of its nuclear weapons remained unable to formally participate in any nuclear security activities with their US counterparts. Some members of Congress also opposed the 2015 renewal of a Reagan-era agreement that provided the legal basis for peaceful nuclear cooperation with China, including completion of a sale in 2007 by Westinghouse of four advanced AP1000 reactors worth $8 billion. They were concerned not only that China could use some of the technology transferred as a condition of that sale to improve its naval nuclear reactors but also that China planned to build its own version of this design for export, taking market share away from the United States and potentially selling dual-use goods to North Korea or other proliferators.[110] These concerns led to policy changes by the Trump administration in October 2018 that significantly reduced US nuclear trade with China, including a new presumption of denial for requests related to small modular reactors, new technology transfers, and entities competing for sales with US firms.[111]

China also agreed to some modest transparency and confidence-building measures to provide reassurance about how it would use its rapidly advancing capabilities in two other strategic domains that Steinberg mentioned in his 2009 speech: the cybersphere and outer space. China, like Russia and a number of other non-Western countries, would prefer that international cooperation related to information and communication technologies (ICT) enhance "information security," that is, greater government control over both content and infrastructure in their territories.[112] This has led to many heated debates in multilateral fora between China and the United States and other countries that supported cooperation based on the free flow of ideas across borders, protections for privacy and intellectual property, and a multistakeholder approach to internet governance. China participated in the process that produced agreement in the United Nations on some very high-level principles for ICTs, including that sovereignty applies to ICT activities and infrastructure inside a state, that international law is applicable in cyberspace, and that human rights should be respected everywhere. Not surprisingly, though, China is much more likely to invoke the first principle while the United States is much more supportive of the last two.[113]

The most significant bilateral cybersecurity agreement was reached during President Xi Jinping's state visit to the United States in September 2015. The two leaders agreed that neither country would conduct or condone cyberenabled theft of intellectual property, including trade secrets and other confidential business information, for the purpose of providing a competitive advantage to companies or commercial sectors in their own countries.[114] This commitment led to a notable decrease in economic cyber espionage by Chinese entities against US firms that lasted at least through mid-2018, although those types of activity did not stop completely.[115] The agreement did not, however, cover cyber espionage for intelligence or military purposes, something that both sides often do to get a better understanding of the other's capabilities.[116]

China responded to international opprobrium about its 2007 debris-generating ASAT test in several ways during the Obama years. Efforts to restore its reputation as a "responsible" space power began with self-restraint, including a promise not to conduct that type of test again.[117] Subsequent tests of the same interceptor used in the 2007 ASAT test were announced in advance and characterized as missile defense tests done against suborbital targets in ways that did not generate long-lasting space debris.[118] China declined to support the EU's efforts to get international agreement on a code of conduct for outer space activities because it was not included in the EU's drafting process. It did participate constructively, though, in the UN Group of Governmental Experts on transparency and confidence-building measures in space as well as the UN Committee on Peaceful Uses of Outer Space's Working Group on the Long-Term Sustainability (LTS) of Outer Space Activities—reportedly even taking Russia to task for blocking consensus on a report recommending that all space-faring countries follow additional best practice guidelines that members of the LTS working group had agreed on in 2018.[119]

The members of the Obama administration and Congress who were most concerned about China becoming a near-peer competitor placed no stock in Chinese space diplomacy. They assessed that China's so-called missile defense tests were really intended to advance its ASAT capabilities (the same accusa-tion that the Chinese and Russians had made about US missile defense tests for decades). They also asserted that the Obama administration's efforts to induce reciprocal restraint from China and Russia regarding the development of offensive military space capabilities had been an abject failure, necessitating a return by the United States to the more offensive orientation toward space security pursued by the Bush administration. A top-level strategic space port-folio in the summer of 2014 review led to a partial reorientation of the Obama administration's space security strategy and increased funding for capabilities to defend US satellites and attack space assets used by adversaries to gain a military advantage. The Trump administration has taken this reorientation much further, including by establishing a Space Force as a first step toward a new military service and reviving efforts to deploy missile defense interceptors in space, which (if it ever became economically and technologically feasible) might enable boost-phase defense weapons against ICBMs launched from the interior of China.

Viewing China's advances in space in the context of the choices it has made about nuclear weapons suggests that the United States may be overreacting primarily because it does not understand China's motives or intentions. One oft-cited example of threatening Chinese advances in space is the work on maneuvering satellites and other technologies that could be used for legitimate purposes, like servicing a satellite on orbit or removing space debris, though these also have potential ASAT applications. Another involves a 2013 launch of a high-altitude rocket for what China called a "scientific mission," which US officials consider a test of technology that could someday be used to destroy extremely important and expensive satellites that were previously considered beyond the reach of potential adversaries. Given that the United States already has or is actively working on comparable technologies, though, both programs could be intended primarily to explore what is possible, avoid "technological surprise," and enhance China's status as an advanced space power rather than being dedicated weapons-development programs. To the extent that US military mission statements about being able to control who can use space for what purpose have convinced Chinese leaders that they need to be able to hold US space assets at risk in order to deter US attacks on Chinese satellites, the nuclear example suggests that China could be satisfied with a relatively limited ASAT capability that is used for retaliatory purposes only.[120]

There are some tantalizing hints that the space component of the Obama administration's strategic stability dialogue with China made some progress along these lines before being cut short by the 2016 election. The first meeting of the official US-China Civil Space Dialogue occurred in June 2015, followed by a Space Security Exchange in May 2016. That timing indicates that the Obama administration decided to move away from its original policy of reciprocal restraint in space before discussing in any detail with China what reciprocal restraint meant.

The US official responsible for space security had had some earlier informal conversations with his Chinese counterpart on the margins of multilateral meetings, trying to interest him in the types of space transparency and confidence-building measures (TCBMs) favored by the Obama administration. In late 2014 the Chinese finally implemented one such measure by providing the telephone number for a point of contact at the Beijing Institute for Telecommunications and Tracking to the US military unit that provides warnings when its space situational awareness system indicates an elevated risk of collision between two space objects.[121] The Joint Space Operations Center (JSPOC) still does not provide China with the same level of detailed analytical information it gives to US and allied satellite operators so they can make informed decisions about whether the risk of a satellite collision (which could destroy the satellites and generate long-lasting debris) outweighs the cost of moving their satellite into a safer position. But at least the JSPOC no longer must transmit notifications through the State Department and the Chinese Ministry of Foreign Affairs to reach the Chinese space agency.

This small step has led to conversations about other ways the two countries might cooperate to minimize space debris. The United States proposed the release of a joint statement that the two countries would refrain from kinetic-energy ASAT tests and other military activities likely to create long-lived space debris. The PLA was reportedly interested in reducing space debris because it is increasingly reliant on satellites. It was uncertain, though, about pledging not to conduct debris-generating ASAT activities because the US military is better prepared to disable or destroy a satellite without smashing it into thousands of pieces and because the United States is not willing to also rule out using satellites for purposes like comprehensive missile defense, which China finds particularly threatening. The most that could be done in the remaining months of the Obama administration was a vague commitment that came out of the September 2016 presidential visit, that space debris is a serious problem and the two sides will intensify cooperation to address the challenge. The PLA eventually decided to support a joint declaration about refraining from debris-generating military activities in space, despite the disadvantages to them. The Chinese government reached out to the Trump administration in the spring of 2017 but top Trump officials were not interested in making such a pledge with the Chinese.[122]

CONCLUSION

This review should put to rest claims that China is categorically uninterested in arms control or other forms of cooperation to reduce nuclear risks. Some American officials and experts who make that assertion are opposed to arms control themselves but want to blame China and Russia for the absence of agreements. Others are familiar with and supportive of US-Russian arms control agreements like INF and New START but know little about what China has done in a wide range of multilateral arms control forums. Both groups also overlook or discount the many ways in which China has consistently demonstrated more nuclear self-control than either the United States or Russia.

It would be more accurate to say that China, like other countries, is interested in arms control when its leaders think that the political, military, and economic benefits of a particular measure outweigh the costs and risks *and* that they make those calculations based on assumptions about international relations, nuclear deterrence, and arms control that are very different than the assumptions of their American or Russian counterparts. In other words, the debate about whether China is becoming more like other great powers or will always be different for cultural reasons is a false dichotomy; all countries make decisions about what mix of competition and cooperation will best advance their interests by using whatever strategic logic or logics have greatest sway over policymakers' calculations at that time.

The assumptions that have informed Chinese views on arms control, nonproliferation, and strategic stability have been much more consistent over time than the strategic logics that have shaped US policies on these same issues. Chinese positions on specific issues, like the NPT and the CTBT, have changed when the context has shifted in ways that make cooperation more attractive from their point of view. Engagement and positive inducements have historically increased Chinese interest in cooperation more than threats and sanctions have, which explains why the Chinese think that the former will also be more effective than the latter when considering how to address countries like Iran and North Korea. The most important impetus for Chinese shifts toward greater cooperation, though, have been arms control advances made by Washington and Moscow that seem consistent with Chinese assumptions about nuclear weapons and international relations and that make Chinese leaders feel that they need to do more to burnish their image as the most responsible nuclear weapons state.

The Trump administration has taken a number of actions that make the context much less conducive to constructive engagement with China on arms control, nonproliferation, and strategic stability. Its repudiation of the nuclear deal with Iran, of the Paris climate agreement, and of the INF treaty make the United States seem like an unreliable negotiating partner that cannot be trusted to honor its commitments. Its depiction of China as a strategic adversary and great-power competition as the central problem for US national security strategy frames all interactions between these two countries in zero-sum terms. And Trump's decision to launch a trade war with China greatly reduces whatever moderating effects economic interdependence may have had on the US-Chinese security relationship. The two countries may still engage in transactional cooperation on issues like North Korea's nuclear program, when their interests are aligned, but even that will become more difficult if the United States refuses to provide any sanctions relief in return for North Korea's suspension of nuclear and long-range missile tests until it acquiesces to the United States' definition of complete denuclearization.

Over time the economic costs and security risks of unconstrained competition are likely to become increasingly obvious to leaders on both sides. When the context becomes more conducive to cooperation again, progress will be much more likely if Americans have used the intervening time to learn about the underlying assumptions that shape Chinese preferences and policy choices. US policymakers do not need to embrace these ideas themselves but they do need to take them seriously as the starting point for Chinese thinking about what forms of cooperation will reduce nuclear risks and enhance strategic stability. And, if US officials want their Chinese counterparts to provide more reassurance about how China intends to use its nuclear, space, and cyber capabilities, then they need to provide more meaningful reassurances on the issues of greatest concern to China. Chinese interest in arms control would increase if US officials were willing to accept mutual vulnerability as an enduring fact of life, if they clarified what if any circumstances would be extreme enough for the United States to use nuclear weapons first, and if they took concrete actions to increase Chinese confidence that the evolution of US missile defense will neither erode China's nuclear deterrent capability nor delude American leaders into taking big risks in Asia because they no longer care about minimizing the risk of inadvertent nuclear war. The United States and China should seek out small steps that each views as beneficial according to its own strategic logic. If they build confidence by honoring their commitments over time, they may gradually be able to cooperate in more ambitious ways despite continued differences in interests and ideas about international security.

NOTES

The author thanks Jonas Siegel, Li Bin, Gregory Kulacki, Lora Saalman, and Tong Zhao for comments on earlier versions of this chapter, and the MacArthur Foundation for support of the underlying research.

1. Elbridge Colby, quoted in "China's Nuclear Submarine Plans Raise Concerns over Bilateral Dialogue," *Congressional Quarterly News*, November 3, 2014.

2. Lt. Gen. Frank G. Klotz and Oliver Bloom, "China's Nuclear Weapons and the Prospects for Multilateral Arms Control," *Strategic Studies Quarterly* (Winter 2013): 7, https://www.airuniversity.af.edu/Portals/10/SSQ/documents/Volume-07_Issue-4/2013winter-Klotz.pdf.

3. Richard Weitz, "When It Comes to Nonproliferation, China Has Been a 'Free Rider,'" *World Politics Review*, August 19, 2014, https://www.worldpoliticsreview.com/articles/14010/when-it-comes-to-nonproliferation-china-has-been-a-free-rider.

4. James B. Steinberg, "Administration's Vision of the U.S.-China Relationship," keynote address at the Center for a New American Security, Washington, DC, September 24, 2009, https://2009-2017.state.gov/s/d/former/steinberg/remarks/2009/169332.htm.

5. Li Bin, "Differences between Chinese and U.S. Nuclear Thinking and Their Origins," in *Understanding Chinese Nuclear Thinking*, ed. Li Bin and Tong Zhao, 3–18 (Washington, DC: Carnegie Endowment for International Peace, 2016).

6. Gregory Kulacki and Jeffrey G. Lewis, "A Place for One's Mat: China's Space Program, 1956–2003," American Academy of Arts and Sciences, 2009, amacad.org/publication/place-ones-mat-chinas-space-program-1956-2003.

7. US Department of Defense, Office of the Secretary of Defense, *Nuclear Posture Review*, February 2018, vii.

8. Jeffrey G. Lewis, *The Minimum Means of Reprisal: China's Search for Security in the Nuclear Age* (Cambridge, MA: MIT Press, 2007).

9. Xu Weidi, "China's Security Environment and the Role of Nuclear Weapons," in *Understanding Chinese Nuclear Thinking*, ed. Li Bin and Tong Zhao, 19–43 (Washington, DC: Carnegie Endowment for International Peace, 2016).

10. Li Bin, "An Analysis of China's Nuclear Strategy," *World Economics and Politics* 9 (2006): 16–22.

11. Nancy W. Gallagher, "Rethinking U.S.-China Security Cooperation," CISSM working paper, August 2014, http://www.cissm.umd.edu/publications/classifying-cyber-events-proposed-taxonomy. For the contrary view regarding damage limitation, see Alastair Iain Johnson, "China's New 'Old Thinking': The Concept of Limited Deterrence," *International Security* 20, no. 3 (Winter 1995–96): 5–42.

12. M. Taylor Fravel and Evan S. Medeiros, "China's Search for Assured Retaliation," *International Security* 35, no. 2 (Fall 2010): 76–77.

13. Fiona S. Cunningham and M. Taylor Fravel, "Assuring Assured Retaliation," *International Security* 40, no. 2 (Fall 2015): 13–14.

14. Tong Zhao and Li Bin, "The Underappreciated Risks of Entanglement: A Chinese Perspective," in *Entanglement*, ed. James A. Acton, 47–75 (Washington, DC: Carnegie Endowment for International Peace, 2017).

15. Elbridge A. Colby and Michael S. Gerson, eds., *Strategic Stability: Contending Interpretations* (Carlisle, PA: Strategic Studies Institute, 2013).

16. Thomas J. Christensen, "Fostering Stability or Creating a Monster?: The Rise of China and U.S. Policy toward East Asia," *International Security* 31, no. 1 (Summer 2006): 81–126.

17. Lu Yin, "Reflections on Strategic Stability," in *Understanding Chinese Nuclear Thinking*, ed. Li Bin and Tong Zhao, 127–42 (Washington, DC: Carnegie Endowment for International Peace, 2016).

18. Lora Saalman, "Placing a Renminbi Sign on Strategic Stability and Nuclear Reductions," in *Strategic Stability: Contending Interpretations*, ed. Elbridge A. Colby and Michael S. Gerson, 350–55 (Carlisle, PA: Strategic Studies Institute, 2013).

19. For an early critique of the "peculiarly American ideology" that an open world is a safe world and that US efforts to make Soviet military activities more transparent are not threatening to the USSR but are in both countries' interests, see Hedley Bull, *The Control of the Arms Race*, 2nd ed. (New York: Praeger, 1965), 191.

20. Kevin Pollpeter, *U.S.-China Security Management: Assessing the Military-to-Military Relationship* (Santa Monica, CA: RAND Corporation, 2004), xiv.

21. David Shambaugh, *Modernizing China's Military: Progress, Problems, and Prospects* (Berkeley: University of California Press, 2002), 347.

22. The glossary is available at http://pircenter.org/media/content/files/13/1431398 9580.pdf.

23. Gregory Kulacki, "Chinese Perspectives on Transparency and Security," Union of Concerned Scientists, January 13, 2003, ucsusa.org/resources/Chinese-perspectives-transparency-and-security.

24. Lora Saalman, "How Chinese Analysts View Arms Control, Disarmament, and Nuclear Deterrence after the Cold War," in *Engaging China and Russia on Nuclear Disarmament*, ed. Cristina Hansell and William C. Potter, 47–72 (Monterey, CA: Monterey Institute of International Studies, April 2009), 58.

25. Fan Jishe, "Nuclear Nonproliferation: China's Thinking and Practices," in *Understanding Chinese Nuclear Thinking*, ed. Li Bin and Tong Zhao, 193–218 (Washington, DC: Carnegie Endowment for International Peace, 2016), 197.

26. William Burr and Jeffrey Richelson, "Whether to 'Strangle the Baby in the Cradle': The United States and the Chinese Nuclear Program, 1960–64," *International Security* 25, no. 3 (Winter 2000–2001): 71.

27. Statement by the Government of the People's Republic of China," *People's Daily*, October 17, 1964.

28. Joseph Tse-Hei Lee, "China's Third World Policy from the Maoist Era to the Present," *Global Asia Journal*, paper 3 (2008), 5, http://digitalcommons.pace.edu/global _asia_journal. On Soviet revisionism, see Fan Jishe, "Nuclear Nonproliferation," 198–200; and Guo Xiaobing, "China's Understanding of the Threat of Proliferation," in *Understanding Chinese Nuclear Thinking*, ed. Li Bin and Tong Zhao, 171–92 (Washington, DC: Carnegie Endowment for International Peace, 2016), 172.

29. Fravel and Medeiros, "China's Search," 72; and Alastair Iain Johnston, "Learning Versus Adaptation: Explaining Change in Chinese Arms Control Policy in the 1980s and 1990s," *China Journal* 35 (January 1996): 38–43.
30. Wang Jia, "China's Views on the Road Map to Nuclear Disarmament," in *Understanding Chinese Nuclear Thinking*, ed. Li Bin and Tong Zhao, 103–26 (Washington, DC: Carnegie Endowment for International Peace, 2016), 106.
31. Zhenqiang Pan, "A Study of China's No-First-Use Policy on Nuclear Weapons," *Journal for Peace and Nuclear Disarmament* 1, no. 1 (2018): 126.
32. Hui Zhang, "Why China Stopped Making Fissile Material for Nukes," *Bulletin of Atomic Scientists*, March 15, 2018, thebulletin.org/2018/03/why-china-stopped -making-fissile-material-for-nukes.
33. Deng Xiaoping speech to Central Military Commission in 1985, quoted in Fan, "Nuclear Nonproliferation," 201.
34. Kulacki, "Chinese Perspectives on Transparency and Security."
35. Fan, "Nuclear Nonproliferation," 200–204.
36. Evan S. Medeiros, *Reluctant Restraint* (Palo Alto, CA: Stanford University Press, 2007), 71–73.
37. Strobe Talbott, *Deadly Gambits* (New York: Vintage, 1985), 323.
38. Nie Hongyi, "Explaining Chinese Solutions to Territorial Disputes," *Journal of International Politics* 4, no. 2 (December 2009): 487–523.
39. Ming-Yen Tsai, *From Adversaries to Partners?: Chinese and Russian Military Cooperation after the Cold War* (Westport, CT: Praeger, 2003), 98.
40. Ashton B. Carter, William J. Perry, and John D. Steinbruner, *A New Concept of Cooperative Security* (Washington, DC: Brookings Institution, 1992).
41. Harry Harding, "Cooperative Security in the Asia-Pacific Region," in *Global Engagement*, ed. Janne E. Nolan, 419–46 (Washington, DC: Brookings Institution, 1994), 443.
42. Nancy Prindle, "The U.S.-China Lab-to-Lab Technical Exchange Program," *Nonproliferation Review* (Spring–Summer 1998): 111–18.
43. Kurt Campbell and Richard Weitz, "The Limits of U.S.-China Military Cooperation: Lessons from 1995–1999," *Washington Quarterly* 29, no. 1 (Winter 2005–6): 170.
44. David Finkelstein and Jonathan Unangst, "Engaging DoD: Chinese Perspectives on Military Relations with the United States," CRM99-0046.90 (Arlington, VA: CNA Corporation, 1999); Pollpeter, *U.S.-China Security Management.*
45. The United States insisted the bombing was an accident, but China believed, with good reason, that it was not. See John Sweeney, Jens Holsoe, and Ed Vulliamy, "NATO Bombed Chinese Deliberately," *Guardian*, October 16, 1999, https://www .theguardian.com/world/1999/oct/17/balkans.
46. Shambaugh, *Modernizing China's Military*, 343.
47. Shambaugh, 345.
48. Gen. John M. Shalikashvili, "U.S.-China Engagement: The Role of Military-to-Military Contacts," speech at PLA National Defense University, May 14, 1997, archive.defense.gov/news/newsarticle.aspx?id=41002.
49. Jane Perlez, "Mindful of China, U.S. Agrees to Weapons Deal for Taiwan," *New York Times*, April 18, 2000, https://www.nytimes.com/2000/04/18/world/mindful -of-china-us-agrees-to-weapons-deal-for-taiwan.html.
50. Campbell and Weitz, "The Limits," 182–83.
51. Bill Gertz, "Military Exchange with Beijing Raises Security Concerns," *Washington Times,* February 19, 1999.

52. Thomas J. Christensen, "Posing Problems without Catching Up: China's Rise and Challenges for U.S. Security," *International Security* 25, no. 4 (Spring 2001): 8.

53. Robert D. Lamb, "Satellites, Security, and Scandal: Understanding the Politics of Export Control," CISSM working paper, January 2005, cissm.umd.edu/research -impact/publications/satellites-security-and-scandal-understanding-politics -export-control.

54. Madelyn Creedon, remarks at Brookings Institution Panel "Falling Apart: The Politics of New START and Strategic Modernization," January 7, 2019, 38, transcript at https://www.brookings.edu/wp-content/uploads/2019/01/fp_20190107_new _start_transcript.pdf.

55. Xiangli Sun, "Implication of a Comprehensive Test Ban Treaty for China's Security Policy," Stanford University Center for International Security and Arms Control, June 1997, cisacfsi.stanford.edu/publications/implications_of_a_comprehensive _test_ban_for_Chinas_security_policy.

56. Johnston, "Learning versus Adaptation."

57. Xiangli Sun, "Implications of a Comprehensive Test Ban Treaty," 3–4.

58. Zao Yunhua, "China and the CTBT Negotiations," Stanford University Center for International Security and Arms Control, December 1998, 6, cisacfsi.stanford.edu /publications/china_and_the_ctbt_negotiations.

59. Xiangli Sun, "Implications of a Comprehensive Test Ban Treaty," 11.

60. Zou Yunhua, "China and the CTBT Negotiations," 26–30.

61. Wu Riqiang, remarks on panel entitled "Why Is China Modernizing Its Nuclear Arsenal?," Carnegie International Nuclear Policy Conference, March 24, 2015.

62. Charles Glaser and Steve Fetter, "National Missile Defense and the Future of U.S. Nuclear Weapons Policy," *International Security* 26, no. 1 (Summer 2001): 40–92.

63. Missile Defense Agency director General Kadish, quoted in Steven A. Hildreth, "Missile Defense: The Current Debate," CRS report RL311 (updated July 19, 2005), 4.

64. This is credible because China ratified the CWC immediately after the United States did on April 25, 1997.

65. Excerpts from classified Nuclear Posture Review provided to Congress on December 31, 2001, https://fas.org/wp-content/uploads/media/Excerpts-of-Classified -Nuclear-Posture-Review.pdf.

66. Chinese government official quoted in Hui Zhang, "China and a Fissile Material Cutoff Treaty," *Journal of Nuclear Material Management* 30, no. 4 (Summer 2002): 54.

67. Steven Miller, "Skepticism Triumphant: The Bush Administration and the Waning of Arms Control," *La Revue Internationale et Strategique* (May 2003), https://www .belfercenter.org/publication/skepticism-triumphant-bush-administration-and -waning-arms-control.

68. Michael O'Hanlon, "Double Talk on Missile Defense," Brookings Op Ed, July 31, 2001, https://brookings.edu/opinion/double-talk-on-missile-defense/.

69. Nancy W. Gallagher and John D. Steinbruner, *Reconsidering the Rules for Space Security* (Cambridge, MA: American Academy of Arts and Sciences, 2008), https:// www.amacad.org/sites/default/files/publication/downloads/space_security.pdf.

70. Robert B. Zoellick, "Whither China: From Membership to Responsibility?," remarks to National Committee on U.S.-China Relations, New York City, September 21, 2005.

71. Fu Ying, "The Korean Nuclear Issue: Past, Present, and Future," Strategy Paper 3, John L. Thornton China Center at Brookings, May 2017.

72. Jonathan D. Pollack, *No Exit: North Korea, Nuclear Weapons, and International Security* (London: International Institute for Strategic Studies, 2011), 133–56.

73. Jim VandeHei and Dafna Linzer, "U.S., India Reach Deal on Nuclear Cooperation," *Washington Post*, March 3, 2006, http://www.washingtonpost.com/wp-dyn/content/article/2006/03/02/AR2006030200183.html.

74. Jagannath P. Panda, "China's Posture on the Indo-US Nuclear Deal," Institute for Defence Analyses and Studies, October 10, 2007, https://idsa.in/idsastrategic comments/ChinasPostureontheIndoUSnuclearDeal_JPPanda_101007.

75. Saalman, "How Chinese Analysts View Arms Control," 60.

76. Mark J. Valencia, "The Proliferation Security Initiative: A Glass Half Full," *Arms Control Today*, June 2007, https://www.armscontrol.org/act/2007_06/Valencia.

77. Patrick E. Tyler, "No Chemical Weapons Aboard China Ship," *New York Times*, September 7, 1993, 4.

78. Statement by Ambassador Robert T. Grey Jr. to the Conference on Disarmament, Geneva, Switzerland, February 15, 2001, fas.org/programs/ssp/nukes/armscontrol/grey01cd.htm.

79. "Fissile Material Negotiations in the Conference on Disarmament," UNIDIR Briefing Paper, version 2, updated February 2011, unidir.org/files/publications/pdfs/fissile-material-negotiations-in-the-conference-on-disarmament-version-2-updated-february-2011-357.pdf.

80. Joan Johnson-Freese, *Space as a Strategic Asset* (New York: Columbia University Press, 2007), 197–232.

81. Zhang, "China and a Fissile Material Cutoff Treaty," 51.

82. Keir A. Lieber and Daryl Press, "The Rise of U.S. Nuclear Primacy," *Foreign Affairs* (March–April 2006): 42–54.

83. Lieber and Press, "The Rise of U.S. Nuclear Primacy," 54.

84. Li Bin and Nie Hongyi, "An Investigation of China-U.S. Strategic Stability," trans. Gregory Kulacki, originally published in Chinese in *World Economics and Politics*, no. 2 (2008), https://www.ucsusa.org/sites/default/files/legacy/assets/documents/nwgs/Li-and-Nie-translation-final-5-22-09.pdf.

85. Li Bin and Nie Hongyi, "An Investigation of China-U.S. Strategic Stability," 9.

86. Kulacki and Lewis, "A Place for One's Mat."

87. Eric Hagt, "China's ASAT Test: Strategic Response," *China Security* (Winter 2007): 31–51.

88. Noah Shachtman, "Experts Scoff at Sat Shootdown Rationale," Wired.com, February 15, 2008, https://www.wired.com/2008/02/fishy-rationale/.

89. Find the document at https://documents-dds-ny.un.org/doc/UNDOC/GEN/G06/615/91/pdf/G0661591.pdf?OpenElement.

90. Council of the European Union, "Council Conclusions and Draft Code of Conduct for Outer Space Activities," Brussels, Belgium, December 3, 2008, 16560/08, http://register.consilium.europa.eu/pdf/en/08/st17/st17175.en08.pdf.

91. Steinberg, "Administration's Vision of the U.S.-China Relationship."

92. Brad Roberts, former deputy assistant secretary of defense for nuclear and missile defense policy, presentation at the Stimson Center on August 26, 2013, quoted in Gregory Kulacki, "U.S. Shares Responsibility for Lack of Dialog with China on Nuclear Weapons," October 16, 2013, allthingsnuclear.org/gkulacki/u-s-shares-responsibility-for-lack-of-dialog-with-china-on-nuclear-weapons.

93. Gregory Kulacki, "Chickens Talking with Ducks: The U.S.-Chinese Nuclear Dialogue," *Arms Control Today*, October 2011, 15–20.

94. Department of Defense, "Nuclear Posture Review Report," April 2010, https://dod.defense.gov/Portals/1/features/defenseReviews/NPR/2010_Nuclear_Posture_Review_Report.pdf.

95. DoD, "Nuclear Posture Review Report," 15–16.

96. Quoted in Lora Saalman, *China and the U.S. Nuclear Posture Review*, Carnegie-Tsinghua Center for Global Policy, February 2011, 25, carnegieendowment.org/2011/02/28/china-and-u.s.-nuclear-posture-review-pub-42705.

97. Saalman, *China and the U.S. Nuclear Posture Review*, 6–7.

98. Cunningham and Fravel, "Assuring Assured Retaliation," 21.

99. Gregory Kulacki, "Chickens Talking with Ducks"; and Ralph A. Cossa et al., "US-China Strategic Nuclear Relations: Time to Move to Track 1 Dialogue," *Pacific Forum Issues & Insights* 15, no. 7 (2015).

100. Christopher Twomey et al., "The U.S.-China Strategic Dialogue Phase IX report," Naval Postgraduate School and Center for International and Strategic Studies, December 2016, alhoun.nps.edu/handles/10945/51030.

101. Private communication with senior Obama administration official, October 17, 2014.

102. US Fact Sheet for President Obama's Bilateral Meeting with President Xi Jinping, September 3, 2016, obama.whitehouse.archives.gov/the-press-office/2016/09/03/us-fact-sheet-president-obamas-bilateral-meeting-president-xi-jinping.

103. Tomoko Kurokawa, "Determinants of the Nuclear Policy Options in the Obama Administration: An Interview with Jon Wolfsthal," *Journal for Peace and Nuclear Disarmament* 1, no. 2 (2018): 500–503.

104. Fu Ying, "The Korean Nuclear Issue," 20.

105. Michael R. Gordon, "Kerry in China to Seek Help in Korea Crisis," *New York Times*, April 13, 2013, 1.

106. Christopher P. Twomey and Michael S. Chase, "Chinese Attitudes towards Missile Defense," in *Regional Missile Defense from a Global Perspective*, ed. Catherine M. Kelleher and Peter Dombrowski, 197–216 (Palo Alto, CA: Stanford University Press, 2015), 202–4.

107. Jaganath Sankaran and Bryan L. Fearey, "Missile Defense and Strategic Stability: Terminal High-Altitude Area Defense (THAAD) in South Korea," *Contemporary Security Policy* 38, no. 3 (2017): 321–44.

108. Hui Zhang, "China's Nuclear Security: Progress, Challenges, and Next Steps," Report of Project on Managing the Atom, March 2016, https://www.belfercenter.org/sites/default/files/files/publication/Chinas%20Nuclear%20Security-Web.pdf; and "China Makes Significant Nuclear Security Pledges at 2016 Summit," *Nuclear Security Matters blog*, April 8, 2016, https://www.belfercenter.org/publication/china-makes-significant-nuclear-security-pledges-2016-summit.

109. Aaron Mehta, "How the U.S. and China Cooperated to Get Nuclear Material Out of Nigeria—and Away from Terrorist Groups," *Defense News*, January 14, 2019, https://www.defensenews.com/news/pentagon-congress/2019/01/14/how-the-us-and-china-collaborated-to-get-nuclear-material-out-of-nigeria-and-away-from-terrorist-groups/.

110. Mark Holt and Mary Beth D. Nitikin, "U.S.-China Nuclear Cooperation Agreement," Congressional Research Service, May 6, 2015.

111. Kelsey Davenport, "U.S. Restricts Nuclear Trade with China," *Arms Control Today*, November 2018, https://www.armscontrol.org/act/2018-11/news/us-restricts-nuclear-trade-china.

112. See, for example, the informal translation of the April 30, 2015, agreement between Russia and China titled "Cooperation in the Field of International Information Security," in Theresa Hitchens and Nilsu Goren, "International Cyber Information Sharing Agreements," CISSM Report, October 2017, annex 2, cissm.umd.edu /research-impact/publications/international-cybersecurity-information-sharing -agreements.

113. For a more extensive analysis of agreements reached and controversies unresolved by the UN Group of Governmental Experts in the Field of Information and Tele-communications, see Theresa Hitchens and Nancy Gallagher, "Building Confidence in the Cybersphere: A Path to Multilateral Progress," *Journal of Cyber Policy* 4, no. 1 (April 2019): 4–21.

114. FACT SHEET: President Xi Jinping's State Visit to the United States, September 25, 2015, obamawhitehouse.archives.gov/the-press-office/2015/09/25/fact-sheet -president-xi-jinpings-state-visit-united-states.

115. "Redline Drawn: China Recalculates Its Use of Cyber Espionage," Fireeye Special Report, June 2016, fireeye.com.blog/threat-research/2016/06/red-line-drawn -china-espionage.html; and National Counterintelligence and Security Center, "Foreign Economic Espionage in Cyberspace," https://www.dni.gov/files/NCSC /documents/news/20180724-economic-espionage-pub.pdf.

116. Herb Lin, "What the National Counterintelligence and Security Center Really Said about Chinese Economic Espionage," *Lawfare*, July 31, 2018, https://www .lawfareblog.com/what-national-counterintelligence-and-security-center-really -said-about-chinese-economic-espionage.

117. Dingli Shen, "A Chinese Perspective on China-United States Cooperation in Space," *Space and Defense* (Winter 2009): 72.

118. Brian Weeden, "Through a Glass Darkly: Chinese, American, and Russian Anti-Satellite Testing in Space," Secure World Foundation, March 17, 2014, swfound.org /media/167224/through-a-glas-darkly-march2014.pdf.

119. Theresa Hitchens, "Forwarding Multilateral Space Governance," CISSM Working Paper, August 2018, cissm.umd.edu/research-impact/publications/forwarding -multilateral-space-governance-next-steps-international.

120. For a critique of alarmist US interpretations of Chinese views on military uses of space that is based on an analysis of the textbook used to train soldiers and officers responsible for China's nuclear and conventional missile forces, see Gregory Kulacki, "An Authoritative Source on China's Military Space Strategy," Union of Concerned Scientists, March 2014, ucsusa.org/sites/default/files/2019-10/china-s -military-space-strategy.pdf.

121. Frank Rose, "Safeguarding the Heavens: The United States and the Future of Norms of Behavior in Outer Space," Brookings Foreign Policy Brief, June 2018, brookings.edu/research/safeguarding-the-heavens-the-united-states-and-the -future-of-norms-of-behavior-in-outer-space/.

122. Personal communication with former senior Obama administration official, October 16, 2018.

NINE

China's Strategic Future

Brad Roberts

Having surveyed in the preceding chapters the multiple factors bearing on China's strategic future, what have we learned? What can we confidently predict about China's strategic future? What are the major uncertainties? What factors will drive alternative possible futures and how might choices by the United States shape China's future? This closing chapter sets out answers to these questions, drawing on others' work included in this volume. More precisely, it sets out some hypotheses with the hope that these will become the basis for further analysis and debate in the United States, China, and elsewhere.

DEFINING "STRATEGIC"

As a point of departure, it is appropriate and necessary to acknowledge the fuzziness that attaches to the word "strategic." It is an elastic term, usable in multiple ways. Contributors to this volume have used it as a modifier to characterize:

- Basic high-level choices about a country's world role and grand strategy (as in "fundamental strategic principles" of the Chinese Communist Party [CCP])
- A set of security and defense concepts related to geography, history, and culture that are enduring in character (as in a "strategic worldview" of the People's Liberation Army [PLA])
- A form of deterrence, operating at the highest level, on the intentions of foreign leaders to jeopardize Chinese interests (as in "strategic deterrence")
- Weaponry promising effects of a potentially immediate and decisive kind (as in "strategic weapons" and "strategic forces")—especially but not exclusively nuclear weapons

China's experts and officials also use the term with these varied meanings.[1] I will not overly simplify the matter by opting for a single definition because, in fact, the diversity of usages correctly conveys the complexity of the topic. The term strategic encompasses a variety of meanings and they must all be captured if we are to have a plausible notion of China's strategic future.

Let's also be clear about "the future." The contributors generally have not taken the long view, preferring instead either a near-term view that is shaped by the dynamics of contemporary political factors or a medium-term view shaped by factors that can be projected over two to three decades. This summary chapter works within the latter framework, albeit with one important exception.

SOME PREDICTIONS

Based on the analyses contained in this volume, we can with confidence make at least three predictions about China's future.

China will be more capable from a military and technical perspective. As Hans Kristensen argues, China's nuclear forces will increase quantitatively and qualitatively over the decade or two ahead. As Sugio Takahashi argues, this increase will bring with it qualitative developments in nuclear strategy as China gains an invulnerable retaliatory capability and the capability to credibly threaten nuclear counterforce strikes. China also will gain significant new regional nuclear strike capabilities. The expectation of continued improvements in the nuclear force has been clearly established by the Chinese approach to the development of next-generation capabilities: it embeds steps for next-generation development in current-generation acquisition in a process that is very much like the spiral development practices of the United States.

In addition, China's strategic military toolkit will become increasingly diverse and robust with the addition of more, and more diverse, nonnuclear precision-strike capabilities, nonkinetic capabilities with potential strategic consequences, and space and counterspace capabilities. As Phillip Saunders and David Logan argue, these advances will offer China significant new forms of leverage in time of military crisis or war because of the new costs and risks they will impose on others considering military action against China.

These diverse tools of strategic influence will also be more effectively integrated in order to reinforce each other and to support military operational and political objectives. Recent PLA organizational reforms, as analyzed by Bates Gill, promise that such integration will become a reality rather than simply an aspiration. An open question remains, however, about the degree to which nuclear capabilities will be integrated in the manner in which other countries, and especially Russia, have integrated them (deeply and comprehensively).[2]

In addition to becoming more capable, China will be more technically competitive with the United States (and Japan, India, the European Union, etc.). China's science and technology base will continue to grow and in a decade or two it can be expected to lead globally in many areas. Whether its capacity for innovation will also continue to improve is, however, an open question, given the social, economic, and cultural barriers to sustained innovation.

This last point has a particular consequence in the strategic military domain, given the potential for a future remaking of China's strategic military forces in a sudden and substantial way. In the arms control arena this is referred to as "breakout potential." It describes the latent capacity of a party to an arms control agreement to abandon the obligation for restraint to gain some decisive strategic advantage with a sudden surge of new and/or additional military capabilities. In the future China will have a robust capability to create a new strategic military force of a technically advanced kind and to do so quickly. This introduces a new element of uncertainty and unpredictability into thinking about the future of China's strategic forces and, from a US policy perspective, a new question about how best to hedge against surprises emanating from China.

China will also be more confident in its ability to accept military risk. These capability improvements will enable military action in a much wider array of contingencies against modern military adversaries than would otherwise be the case. Such contingencies involve multiple risks of escalation, especially if they involve a peer adversary for which China historically has been unprepared.

THE MAIN UNCERTAINTIES

The uncertainties are numerous and in some cases profound. They call into question our ability to anticipate the consequences of the predictions noted already.

First and foremost, we cannot now know whether a more capable, competitive, and confident China will also be a more assertive China, either militarily or politically. China's leaders regularly reassure their neighbors that China's rise will be peaceful and that it has ambitions for a harmonious and peaceful world. With a fully modern military China's leaders may feel less vulnerable and also more satisfied with the regional and global order. A more satisfied China might also be willing to cooperate for mutual benefit. It may also be willing to accept some burdens of international leadership. A more confident China may be more willing to accept the nuclear transparency practices of other states and join in arms control of a kind that could improve the political relationship with the United States and enhance predictability in the strategic relationship. As Nancy Gallagher argues, the foundations for some progress in this direction may already be in place.

But these outcomes are not what the bulk of the evidence so far suggests. A more capable, competitive, and confident China is also a China whose leaders have articulated a deep sense of historical grievance, a revisionist agenda for the regional order, and a frustration with a global order they see as hostile to their efforts to restore China to its proper place "at the center of the world stage." China has become much more forceful in pressing its maritime claims, some of which have been rejected in international arbitration. Some non-Chinese experts argue that the sense of insecurity that grips China's leaders is deeply engrained in their historical and cultural experience; it is reinforced by the inherent illegitimacy of an authoritarian regime and cannot be washed away by increased military strength.[3] As Takahashi argues, China has proved itself to be a difficult neighbor in the region, and expectations that a more capable, competitive, and confident China will also be a better neighbor are low. Instead, Takahashi argues that China's increasing confidence at the strategic level of war will encourage risk-taking at the regional-conventional level of war (in what scholars refer to as the stability-instability paradox).[4]

This line of argument suggests that the consequences of China's strategic military modernization are intimately connected with the fate of political reform in China. The apparent failure to liberalize as it modernizes has sharply lowered the expectations of those Chinese who had hoped that embracing economic reform would generate political change of a kind valued by democratic states.[5] But China's leaders have gone beyond a mere rejection of liberalization. Rather, they have framed the competition with the United States as significantly ideological in character, with the aspiration to provide a competing model for the correct ordering of political life and to see that model flourish elsewhere. They have embraced an agenda that seeks to diminish the legitimacy of the institutions and norms of the US-led global order, to create competing institutions and norms, and to otherwise remake the international political system in ways that are congenial to Chinese ideological requirements.[6] These choices fuel the expectations of Graham Allison and others that the United States and China are seemingly destined for war.[7]

Second, we cannot know at this time whether improved Chinese strategic capabilities will result in a significant shift in the strategic military balance with the United States or if it will lead to meaningful gain in strategic influence. China's capabilities are only half of this equation. The other half are the capabilities of the United States. These too can be expected to evolve over the next two to three decades, but whether and how that development comes is a matter of debate and future choice (discussed later). This is a reminder that any assessment of the consequences of China's military developments requires a net assessment encompassing the actions of others, whether in response to China's developments or driven by other factors.

One possibility is that the net benefit to China will be marginal or nonexistent if the United States and its allies and perhaps others respond in a manner that seeks to preserve strategic balance as they define it. Another possibility is that China's sense of security might actually decline as the responses of others reinforce its sense of vulnerability, disadvantage, and grievance (the so-called security dilemma). Another possibility is that China will see an opportunity to seize some gain and hold it. This possibility is of course most evident regarding the effort to settle once and for all the dispute over Taiwan.

Third, we cannot know at this time whether China's nuclear policy traditions will fade away with time and capability improvements. The origins of China's commitment to no first use, to minimum deterrence, and to a "lean but effective" nuclear force are deeply rooted in the leadership culture of the 1940s and 1950s and thus also in the security environment as then perceived from Beijing. Will those rationales look and sound appropriate to China's leaders a century later?

A strong case can be made for continued Chinese nuclear minimalism. It has served China well. Any movement away from minimalism would attract significant attention, harsh criticism, and military responses from among China's neighbors, and perhaps domestically as well, which the CCP might well find unhelpful. It could, for example, deeply unsettle the anti-nuclear consensus within Japan. Moreover, China's traditions appear deeply engrained in both the Party and the PLA and China's leaders seem strongly convinced of their virtue.

But a strong case can also be made that the future will hold something different. Signs of change are already evident, as China's improving capabilities to detect incoming attacks, to operate on alert, and to conduct counterforce attacks drive new thinking about the ends of China's nuclear strategy, as Takahashi and Chris Twomey have argued. The reorganization of the PLA's strategic capabilities in 2015 can be expected to have an impact on PLA thinking on these matters, as Bates Gill argues.

Fourth, we cannot know at this time whether China's approach to military competition in the new strategic domains of cyberspace and outer space will be guided by a notion of strategic stability analogous to that which has so far guided its approach to nuclear deterrence. This notion builds on the idea that deterrence is well served by a minimalist approach and that a stable situation exists when no actor contests the core relationship of mutual vulnerability and mutual deterrence. Will China accept similar concepts in these new domains or will it seek dominance and superiority? If it seeks stability, will it be prepared to exercise restraint in the development and application of advancing new technologies to military purposes?

There is reason to be pessimistic on this score: the expert and official communities in China have been reluctant to embrace strategic stability as an organizing concept even in the nuclear domain. They have generally seen it as a Western concept rooted in Cold War experiences and view US efforts to introduce it as an organizing principle in the US-PRC strategic relationship as a trick to draw China into a Cold War–style arms race. In the period from approximately 2014 to 2018, China's expert community on nuclear policy by and large came to embrace the concept. But the government has been reluctant to do so, repeatedly rejecting strategic dialogue with the US government while also criticizing the United States for actions it deems detrimental to strategic stability. This bodes ill for a future Chinese embrace of strategic stability as an organizing concept in the new domains.

Fifth, and finally, we cannot know what impact the year 2049 will have on China's strategic future. That year China will celebrate the centennial of the founding of the People's Republic. China's leaders and experts are much clearer about the means and ends of China's grand strategy and of China's military modernization in the period before 2049 than in the period after it. It will clearly be a watershed moment, marking China's intended full re-emergence onto the world stage as a modern state and society. It may well be more consequential for China's role in the world than the end of the Cold War was for the US international role.

Xi Jinping's "China dream" reflects the long-standing ambition of China's leaders to return China to what they see as its rightful place in the world. As Andrew Scobell observes, they envision China in 2049 as living harmoniously in the world: strong and making new and greater contributions in the centers of world power. The period between now and then is conceived as an interim period of strategic opportunity, when China can and should focus on growing stronger and on remaking the world in ways that make future harmony possible. In fact, China's leaders clearly expect that China will have a dominant position in the international political system of 2049 and beyond. China's return to such a position brings with it a legacy of thinking about China's proper place in the international system—and of the attributes of the international system that China requires. China's leaders anticipate a restoration of a hierarchical regional order in which states pay respect to China's status, seek its permission, and pay tribute. They may also seek a global order that is more congenial to their autocratic ways and influence. This is a world that will seem both uncongenial and inharmonious to many of China's neighbors and to other powers disinclined to show the deference expected of them.

KEY DRIVERS OF ALTERNATIVE OUTCOMES

The authors in this volume point to many different factors that will influence further technical, military, and political developments. Some of these are structural. Others are wildcards or black swan events that might generate severe shocks. And some relate to basic choices made by political leaders.

Among the structural factors, technological change will be a cross-cutting factor that brings opportunities for new military advantages but also potentially significant disruptive effects on the security environment. China has an ambitious agenda to develop world-class science and technology and has invested considerable resources toward that end. But innovation is far easier said than done and it is by no means clear that China's political and social structures will readily enable the kind of sustained innovation that can be turned into military advantage over time. So far, however, China appears to be having some success in imitating and emulating many high-end capabilities pioneered by others.

Military experience—or the continued lack of it—will also have a potentially significant impact on China's confidence in its emerging military toolkit and on the willingness of China's leaders to take military risks. Especially consequential would be a Chinese miscalculation that the strategic window of opportunity is open to military action to accelerate the remaking of the regional security order. A decisive defeat for China could jeopardize the continued rule of the CCP, as it would suggest severe misjudgment. A military "draw" could also be politically toxic, because the Party would come under criticism for paying costs with no gain. But even a win could be costly, if the price paid is too high. Put differently, a more capable and competitive China could also be an overconfident China whose leaders believe that risks are manageable when in fact they remain static even if they are also somewhat reduced.

An important related military question is whether Russia will emerge as a factor in China's strategic policy development, in contrast to its present and past marginal role. The driver here will be China's assessment of Russia's response to the strategic problem presented by the United States. Both countries face the challenge of "deterring and defeating a conventionally superior nuclear-armed major power and its allies."[8] They both see an urgent need to ensure the effectiveness of their strategic deterrents in the face of the changing character of the US strategic posture, especially as the United States integrates missile defense and nonnuclear strike capabilities. Both countries have tailored their nuclear modernization programs toward that end. But the similarities end there. Russia has gone much further than China in responding. China has modestly increased the number and diversity of the forces assigned to its nuclear deterrent while also taking steps to ensure their ability to penetrate US missile defenses (i.e., countermeasures). In contrast, Russia has developed a new generation of novel strategic nuclear systems while also fully integrating nonstrategic nuclear systems into its concepts and capabilities for regional war. It has prepared for the absolute worst case and in so doing has generated major new threats to its neighbors. Whether China will come to see Russia's response as either a model to be emulated or a threat in its own right is now an open question.

The political context could well be the most consequential of the structural factors, as China's domestic institutions struggle to adapt and survive within a very dynamic situation, including the many significant economic, social, and environmental challenges. Demographic factors will aggravate all of these challenges, potentially crippling the most ambitious plans of the CCP. This points to a potential black swan event: the collapse of Communist Party rule in China and the transition to a more open and competitive political process. This seems quite unlikely in the next two to three decades. But such dramatic changes have rarely been expected before abruptly taking place. The Party has placed a bet that the Chinese people are in fact illiberal and will be content to trade their freedom for prosperity. Authoritarian regimes have often placed such bets and then found themselves cast on the dustbins of history.

Absolutely fundamental as a driver of future outcomes will be China's own vision of its strategic future. As noted previously, Chinese leaders' stated aspiration is to emerge as a nation-state of a certain kind by 2049—modern, powerful, socialist, and living in harmony in an international political system that does not undermine its ideology or deny it the status it seeks. But its behaviors send troubling messages. It rejected the vision of "responsible stakeholder" offered up by the United States a decade ago. Instead, Xi Jinping has aligned himself with Vladimir Putin's aggressive pushback against what Putin perceives to be an unjust world dominated by a unipolar power driven by dangerous values and pursuing a strategy of encirclement and containment intended to keep Russia weak, while also seeking absolute security at the expense of all and plotting to bring regime change to Russia. Xi pursues a selectively revisionist agenda in East Asia as well, through policies driven by a sense of grievance and humiliation, including with the use of military means to signal resolve. China's compliance with the rules-based international order might best be described as "a la carte," that is, episodic when it suits its interests and otherwise when it doesn't.

China's vision will also be informed by its leaders' assessment of the evolving international environment. Will they perceive it as receptive to China and increasingly harmonious in character? Or will they perceive it as hostile to China's interests and organized with the aim of preventing China's return to what the CCP sees as China's proper place under the sun? Such an assessment will be shaped most fundamentally by Chinese leaders' view of the United States. Will they believe that the United States is hostile, and increasingly so, to China's ambitions or that the United States has acquiesced to a declining global role? Will China's leaders perceive American leaders to be strong and resolved to defend American and allied interests or will they indulge in the wishful thinking common to dictators, that democracies are led by weak and indecisive people and are thus easily bullied and divided? This line of argument points to one obvious conclusion: one of the most important factors that will drive alternative future outcomes is the United States.

THE UNITED STATES AND CHINA'S STRATEGIC FUTURE

What answers will America provide to the questions above? Will it become increasingly hostile to China's ambitions? Might it acquiesce? Will its leaders be strong and resolved? Regarding such questions we do not start with a clean sheet of paper. And although past decisions do not bind future decision-makers, there have been significant elements of continuity in US policy with which China must contend. But it must also contend with potential disconti-nuities ahead.

On the fundamental political question about the orientation of the United States to China's rise, there has been a great deal of continuity in US policy. For decades American leaders have welcomed China's recovery and reengage-ment with the world. At times American leaders have even praised the virtues of a strong China, as a strong China holds out the promise of a China that feels secure and able to join the United States as a "responsible stakeholder" in the protection of the international rules-based order. But, as suggested earlier, there is a rising American debate about whether cooperation with China in the economic realm will ultimately generate the desired political liberalization of China and its emergence as a more "normal" power that doesn't contest the rules-based order. Moreover, there is a rising American appreciation of the extent to which China has set competition with the United States as a primary state objective.

This fundamental question has taken on an important new dimension during the Trump presidency and the pursuit of a national security strategy and foreign policy that "puts America first" and often treats allies and alliances as encumbrances from the past. These tendencies have helped to reignite the debate in East Asia about whether decline will bring retreat—that is, whether the United States will remain a long-term presence in the region, militarily, politically, and economically. This has greatly increased anxiety among US allies in the region about the durability and credibility of US security guaran-tees. In China it has fueled a broader discussion of how to effectively challenge the US position in the region.

Each new US presidential administration has debated the balance needed between cooperation and competition in the bilateral US-PRC relationship; the dial usually has been set increasingly toward competition. This competi-tion has clearly emerged as a central theme in the national security strategy of the Trump administration, especially in the economic realm. While leaders in Washington and Beijing appear to have a clear vision of an increasingly competitive relationship, their vision of the cooperative aspects of the relationship appear less well developed. China's leaders offered up a "new type of great power relations," which was understood outside China as an invitation to a bilateral condominium over East Asia and thus unacceptable to the United States.[9] Since the failure of the responsible stakeholder vision, US leaders haven't set out a clear and compelling vision of a more cooperative bilateral relationship. On the contrary, in the Trump era the focus has been on a vision of intensifying competition.

These factors have their analogues in the strategic military dimension of the relationship. Regarding the modernization of China's nuclear forces, the United States was for a long time largely untroubled; this is now changing. On the balance between cooperation and competition in the strategic military domain, the dial is being set toward the more competitive end of the spectrum. On the needed vision of the desired future strategic military relationship, none has been offered.

Even if US policymakers do not particularly welcome China's nuclear modernization, they generally understand the logic of China's efforts to adapt its deterrent so that it remains credible in the face of changes the United States has been making to its deterrent effectiveness vis-à-vis rogue states. As the United States has introduced missile defenses and prompt nonnuclear strike capabilities, some Chinese responses to secure its small and vulnerable nuclear force made sense to US policymakers. Thus the United States adopted a generally laissez-faire attitude toward such developments even while it expressed concerns about the lack of transparency and the uncertainty about how many weapons China might ultimately deploy for attack on the United States. But this laissez-faire attitude is giving way to a different view: that China's growing strategic potential is generating significant new threats to US power projection capabilities and to US allies and thereby encourages China to play a more assertive regional military role. For example, regional missile defenses deployed by the United States in East Asia are now in part about the China missile threat and hypersonic developmental programs are being designed in part for the strategic balance with China.

On the balance between cooperation and competition in the strategic military domain, for the last thirty or so years the United States has put the emphasis on cooperation. Each presidential administration has called upon China's leaders to join in a dialogue about the nuclear relationship between the two countries, with the aim of enhancing strategic stability, predictability, and transparency in a manner that would serve the interests of both countries. And each administration has been rebuffed by China.[10] Until recently, U.S. policymakers have been concerned that too competitive a strategic military relationship with China could result in an arms race that neither side seeks and which would have a corrosive impact on the ability to cooperate politically and economically. More recently there has been a rising US concern that the desire to cooperate and messages of strategic restraint are received in Beijing as messages of appeasement, reinforcing the spirit of opportunism in China. Symptomatic of this shift is the commitment to "overmatching" military capabilities in an effort to gain "strategic dominance," the plan articulated by Trump administration strategy documents.[11]

In the development of US strategic policy China has not been the primary factor—nor even the secondary one. Russia and "rogue states" (especially North Korea) have been central (although this is not, of course, how China perceives it). US strategic policy has accepted mutual nuclear deterrence with Russia and rejected it with North Korea (and other potential nuclear-armed rogue states). Thus China has repeatedly posed a simple question to the United States: Does it accept or reject mutual vulnerability as the basis of the strategic military relationship? No US administration has provided a direct answer. The Clinton, George W. Bush, Obama, and Trump administrations have all said, in one way or another, that missile defense protection of the American homeland is not intended to negate China's deterrent. But that is a somewhat indirect answer. The United States has de facto tolerated, without compensatory developments in its own posture, China's efforts to ensure the credibility of its deterrent. But its failure to directly address Beijing's fundamental question of US intentions is problematic. It leaves many in Beijing to conclude that the United States will, sooner or later, commit to negating China's deterrent—or that the United States has already done so but hides its ambition in order to gain advantage without prompting a reaction from China.

In the years ahead the United States will face a number of decisions about the design of its strategic forces with major implications for China. Will it continue to grow its missile defenses with advanced technologies (such as space-based interceptors) and significant sea-based systems capable of anti-ICBM protection? Will it acquire prompt nonnuclear strike capabilities in numbers and with ranges that put at risk large numbers of targets across China? Will it develop new nuclear weapons because of particular targeting requirements in China? Will it acquire kinetic means to put China's space assets at risk? Will its cyber capabilities take on a more explicit counter-China dimension? Decisions about such matters will be interpreted in Beijing for what they seem to imply about American pursuit of new means to regain the strategic leverage over China it enjoyed before China developed the atomic bomb.[12]

Whether the United States continues to push for a more cooperative strategic military relationship will also be a critical factor. It has not gotten far with developing a positive vision; abandonment of the project could potentially tip the balance of debate in Beijing in a direction the United States and its allies would consider unwelcome. Some experts in both the United States and China are optimistic that the foundations exist for renewed progress in developing a more cooperative relationship.[13] The informal bilateral Track 1.5 processes clearly demonstrate China's rising interest in strategic stability and rising capacity to engage productively in substantive dialogue on such matters.[14] Continued US engagement and patience may yet pay useful dividends. But this depends on the United States becoming more effective at creating a vision of a future strategic military relationship that meets the interests of both countries because it is inclusive and "win-win."[15]

CONCLUSIONS

With confidence, we can predict that China's modernization of its strategic military capabilities brings with it a China that is more capable, more competitive, and more confident. But its confidence should not get the better of us. The landscape ahead is also littered with uncertainties, many of them deeply consequential for China's future international role and military orientation. Whether capability, competitiveness, or confidence will turn into a more assertive and indeed aggressive China is an open question, given the profound economic, political, and military challenges that still lie ahead.

Although China's strategic future will be determined primarily by choices made by China's leaders, the United States won't be irrelevant to those choices. From a US policy perspective, the central question must be what difference the United States can make to achieve best-case outcomes and avoid worst-case ones. The United States cannot simply avoid military competition with China unless it is willing to give up its role as a security guarantor in the region. The manner in which it chooses to compete will shape China's reactions. Here the question of goals is critical. If the United States chooses to compete for strategic dominance of China, the negative repercussions could be substantial. A better objective would be "second to none" (to borrow a phrase from the nuclear context), that is, compete to ensure that China does not gain strategic dominance.

But we should acknowledge that the trajectory may already be set. China's strategic military modernization is well-launched and well-funded and its leaders seem largely unconcerned about the risks and costs of intensifying competition. It may be that there is little that can be done now to shape China's future choices in ways that serve the strategic stability the United States and its allies might prefer. In this case, the best approach is to do whatever is necessary to safeguard the interests that China might attempt to challenge by military means and set aside for now the project of building a more positive strategic military relationship. This would mean not just competing militarily but also identifying the instabilities introduced by competition into the strategic military balance and proposing joint measures that can insulate it from the worst consequences.

But this is too a pessimistic reading of the current situation. As the authors in this volume argue, there are opportunities to avoid worst-case outcomes and to work toward best-case or at least better-case outcomes. Strategic competition is constrained by economic interdependence and by a mutual desire to avoid an arms race. Success in avoiding undesirable outcomes requires a vision of the bilateral strategic military relationship that is more positive than competition-in-perpetuity, punctuated by the occasional test of political resolve and flashpoints to military conflict. Success requires a vision of the regional security environment that is win-win. The onus to formulate and advocate for such a vision falls on the United States and its allies. China's political class has not demonstrated the will or capacity to generate such a vision. Instead, it appears wedded to a vision of continued economic and military competition and political and ideological confrontation, with 2049 as a gateway to major uncertainty. The realization of a positive vision will not be possible in the near term and may prove elusive in the long term but it can be helpful in dampening some of the worst instabilities in the unfolding strategic military relationship.

NOTES

The views expressed here are those of the author and should not be attributed to any institution with which he is affiliated. The author benefited from comments on initial outlines and drafts by other contributors to this volume as well as by Ben Bahney, Fiona Cunningham, Doug Kean, Rod Lyon, Mike Markey, Jonathan Pearl, Wu Riqiang, Caitlin Talmadge, and Mike Urena. The author alone is responsible for the arguments contained here.

1. By way of illustration, see Li Bin and Tong Zhao, eds., *Understanding Chinese Nuclear Thinking* (Washington, DC: Carnegie Endowment for International Peace, 2016).
2. See Michael Chase and Arthur Chan, *China's Evolving Approach to "Integrated Strategic Deterrence"* (Santa Monica, CA: RAND, 2016).
3. Sulmaan Wasif Khan, *Haunted by Chaos: China's Grand Strategy from Mao Zedong to Xi Jinping* (Cambridge, MA: Harvard University Press, 2018).
4. See also Thomas J. Christensen, "The Meaning of the Nuclear Evolution: China's Strategic Modernization and US-China Security Relations," *Journal of Strategic Studies* 35, no. 4 (2012): 447–87.
5. Aaron Friedberg, "The Debate Over US China Strategy," *Survival* 57, no. 3 (2015): 89–110.
6. Bradley A. Thayer and John M. Friend, *How China Sees the World: Han Centrism and the Balance of Power in International Politics* (Lincoln, NE: Potomac, 2018).
7. Graham Allison, *Destined for War?: Can China and America Escape the Thucydides Trap?* (Boston: Houghton Mifflin Harcourt, 2017).

8. For fuller elaboration, see Brad Roberts, *Theories of Victory, Red and Blue*, Livermore Paper no. 7 (Livermore, CA: Center for Global Security Research, 2020), 7–25.

9. Phillip C. Saunders and Julia G. Bowen, "U.S.-China Military Relations: Competition and Cooperation," *Journal of Strategic Studies* 39, no. 5–6 (2016): 662–84.

10. This story is told in the chapter on China in Brad Roberts, *The Case for U.S. Nuclear Weapons in the 21st Century* (Stanford, CA: Stanford University Press, 2015).

11. See *Summary of the National Security Strategy, 2017,* and the August 2018 memorandum on technologies for strategic dominance by Assistant Secretary of Defense for Research and Engineering Michael Griffin. See also Rebecca L. Heinrichs, "Regaining the Strategic Advantage in an Age of Great Power Competition: A Conversation with Michael Griffin," Hudson Institute, April 13, 2018, https://www .hudson.org/research/14284-full-transcript-regaining-the-strategic-advantage-in -an-age-of-great-power-competition-a-conversation-with-michael-griffin.

12. For a survey of key issues in the US-PRC bilateral strategic military relationship and their US policy implications, see Eric Jacobson and Phil Goldstein, "Emerging Challenges in the China-US Strategic Military Relationship, Workshop Report," March 28–29, 2017, https://e-reports-ext.llnl.gov/pdf/881654.pdf.

13. See, for example, Nancy Gallagher in this volume; Lewis Dunn, "Exploring the Role of U.S.-China Mutual and Cooperative Strategic Restraint," in *Building Toward a Stable and Cooperative Long-Term U.S.-China Strategic Relationship*, ed. Brad Glosserman and David Santoro, 73–79 (Honolulu, HI: Pacific Forum CSIS, 2012); Tong Zhao, "What the United States Can Do to Stabilize Its Relationship with China," *Bulletin of Atomic Scientists* 75, no. 1 (2019): 19–24; and Lu Yin, "Reflections on Strategic Stability," in *Understanding Chinese Nuclear Thinking*, ed. Li Bin and Tong Zhao, 127–47 (Washington, DC: Carnegie Endowment for International Peace, 2016).

14. Dialogue summaries are available at https://www.pacforum.org/analysis/issues -insights-vol-16-no-20-reaching-inflection-point-tenth-china-us-dialogue -strategic. See, particularly, Ralph Cossa, Brad Glosserman, and David Santoro, "Reaching an Inflection Point?: The 10th China-US Dialogue on Strategic Nuclear Dynamics," *Pacific Forum* (2016).

15. For more on inclusiveness and win-win, see Ashley Tellis, *Balancing Without Containment* (Washington, DC: Carnegie Endowment for International Peace, 2014); Tom Fingar, *The United States and China: Same Bed, Different Dreams, Shared Destiny* (Washington, DC: Wilson Center, 2015); and Ash Carter, *Reflections on American Grand Strategy in Asia* (Cambridge, MA: Harvard Kennedy School Belfer Center, 2018).

CONTRIBUTORS

PAUL J. BOLT is a professor of political science and department head at the United States Air Force Academy. He received his BA from Hope College and his MA and PhD from the University of Illinois at Urbana-Champaign. Bolt has taught at Zhejiang University and Baicheng Normal College in the People's Republic of China as well as the University of Illinois. In 2009–10 he served as a Fulbright Scholar at Nanyang Technological University in Singapore. His most recent book is the coauthored *China, Russia, and Twenty-First Century Global Geopolitics* (Oxford, 2018).

NANCY W. GALLAGHER is the director of the Center for International and Security Studies at Maryland (CISSM) and a research professor at the University of Maryland's School of Public Policy. Her research interests include a book project on strategic logics for arms control; public opinion surveys about security policy in the United States and Iran; cybersecurity risk reduction; and space security. Gallagher was previously the executive director of the Clinton administration's Comprehensive Test Ban Treaty Task Force, an arms control specialist in the US State Department and the Arms Control and Disarmament Agency, and a faculty member at Wesleyan University.

BATES GILL is professor of Asia-Pacific security studies at Macquarie University, Sydney, Australia, and a senior associate fellow with the Royal United Services Institute, London. The author or editor of eight books and over 150 other publications, his thirty-year career as a researcher, educator, and advisor on Asian security matters has focused on China in particular. He was previously director of the Stockholm International Peace Research Institute, the Freeman Chair in China Studies at the Center for Strategic and International Studies, and Senior Fellow in Foreign Policy Studies and inaugural director of the Center for Northeast Asian Policy Studies at the Brookings Institution.

HANS M. KRISTENSEN is director of the Nuclear Information Project at the Federation of American Scientists in Washington, DC, where he is responsible for researching and documenting the status and operations of nuclear forces of the nine nuclear armed global states. He is a frequent advisor to the news media on the status of nuclear forces and policy. Kristensen is coauthor of the bimonthly FAS Nuclear Notebook column in the *Bulletin of the Atomic Scientists* and the annual "World Nuclear Forces" overview in the *SIPRI Yearbook*.

DAVID C. LOGAN is a PhD candidate in security studies at the Princeton School of Public and International Affairs, where he also serves as a Fellow in Princeton's Center for International Security Studies (CISS). His research interests lie in nuclear strategy, arms control and nonproliferation, strategic stability, and the US-Chinese security relationship. His writings have appeared in *Asian Security, Nonproliferation Review, Foreign Affairs, Joint Force Quarterly, Bulletin of the Atomic Scientists,* and *National Interest.* He speaks and reads Chinese, Russian, and Italian.

BRAD ROBERTS is director of the Center for Global Security Research at Lawrence Livermore National Laboratory in California. From April 2009 to March 2013 he served as deputy assistant secretary of defense for nuclear and missile defense policy. Prior to joining the Obama administration, Roberts was a member of the research staff at the Institute for Defense Analyses, an adjunct professor at George Washington University, and editor of the *Washington Quarterly.* He has a BA from Stanford University, an MSc from the London School of Economics and Political Science, and a doctorate from Erasmus University, Rotterdam.

PHILLIP C. SAUNDERS is director of the National Defense University's Center for the Study of Chinese Military Affairs. He is also a Distinguished Research Fellow at the Institute for National Strategic Studies since January 2004. Saunders has written and edited eight books, most recently *Chairman Xi Remakes the PLA: Assessing Chinese Military Reforms* (Washington, DC: NDU Press, 2019). He previously worked at the Monterey Institute of International Studies, where he served as director of the East Asia Nonproliferation Program from 1999–2003, and served as an officer in the US Air Force.

ANDREW SCOBELL is senior political scientist at the RAND Corporation's Washington, DC, office and adjunct professor of Asian Studies at Georgetown University's Edmund A. Walsh School of Foreign Service. During 2020 he served as the Bren Chair in Non-Western Strategic Thought in the Krulak Center at Marine Corps University. Scobell earned a doctorate in political science from Columbia University. His publications include: *PLA Influence on China's National Security Policymaking* (Stanford University Press, 2015), *China's Search for Security* (Columbia University Press, 2012), and *China's Use of Military Force* (Cambridge University Press, 2003).

JAMES M. "JIM" SMITH is director of the Air Force Institute for National Security Studies housed within the Department of Political Science at the US Air Force Academy. On active duty he served as an air force pilot and operational planner. He also served academic assignments at the Air Force Special Operations School, the Air Command and Staff College, and West Point's Department of Social Sciences, where he was also associate dean for academic research. Smith holds a BS from USAFA, an MS from the University of Southern California, and a doctorate from the University of Alabama.

SUGIO TAKAHASHI is director of the Policy Simulation Office, NIDS, in Tokyo, Japan. He was a deputy director of the Office of Strategic Planning of the Ministry of Defense from 2008 to 2016. In that capacity he was part of a team that drafted the National Defense Program Guidelines of 2010 and 2013 and Guidelines for US-Japanese Defense Cooperation. He received an MA and BA from the Waseda University and an MA from George Washington University. Takahashi has published extensively in the areas of nuclear strategy, the Japanese-US alliance, and East Asian regional security, including *The End of Nuclear Forgetting: Nuclear Weapons Coming Back* (Keiso Shobo, 2019) (in Japanese, coedited with Nobumasa Akiyama).

CHRISTOPHER P. TWOMEY is an associate professor in the Department of National Security Affairs at the Naval Postgraduate School, where he focuses on Chinese foreign policy and East Asian security issues. He authored *The Military Lens: Doctrinal Differences and Deterrence Failure in Sino-American Relations* (Cornell University Press, 2010) and articles in journals such as *Security Studies, Journal of Contemporary China,* and *Asian Survey.* He has led a Track 2 diplomatic engagement with China centering on strategic issues since its inception in 2005. Twomey earned his PhD in political science from the Massachusetts Institute of Technology and has conducted postdoctoral research at Harvard University.

INDEX

A page number followed by a *f* in italics indicates a figure.
A page number followed by a *t* in italics indicates a table.

CPSIA information can be obtained
at www.ICGtesting.com
Printed in the USA
JSHW020546130123
36216JS00001B/61